Lecture Notes
in Business Information Processing

197

Series Editors

Wil van der Aalst
Eindhoven Technical University, The Netherlands
John Mylopoulos
University of Trento, Italy
Michael Rosemann
Queensland University of Technology, Brisbane, Qld, Australia
Michael J. Shaw
University of Illinois, Urbana-Champaign, IL, USA
Clemens Szyperski
Microsoft Research, Redmond, WA, USA

Ulrich Frank
Pericles Loucopoulos
Óscar Pastor
Ilias Petrounias (Eds.)

The Practice of Enterprise Modeling

7th IFIP WG 8.1 Working Conference, PoEM 2014
Manchester, UK, November 12-13, 2014
Proceedings

 Springer

Volume Editors

Ulrich Frank
University of Duisburg-Essen, Germany
E-mail: ulrich.frank@uni-due.de

Pericles Loucopoulos
University of Manchester, UK
E-mail: pericles.loucopoulos@manchester.ac.uk

Óscar Pastor
Universitat Politècnica de València, Spain
E-mail: opastor@dsic.upv.es

Ilias Petrounias
University of Manchester, UK
E-mail: ilias.petrounias@manchester.ac.uk

ISSN 1865-1348   e-ISSN 1865-1356
ISBN 978-3-662-45500-5   e-ISBN 978-3-662-45501-2
DOI 10.1007/978-3-662-45501-2
Springer Heidelberg New York Dordrecht London

Library of Congress Control Number: 2014953261

Typesetting: Camera-ready by author, data conversion by Scientific Publishing Services, Chennai, India

Printed on acid-free paper

Springer is part of Springer Science+Business Media (www.springer.com)

Preface

The ever-growing penetration of organizations with IT demands for approaches that support the design and implementation of information systems that are aligned to an organization's operations and its strategy. Enterprise modeling (EM) is addressing this demand. It refers to the explicit representation of knowledge according to some structured framework that facilitates different perspectives on an enterprise. An enterprise model integrates models of the organizational action system such as goal models or business process models with models of the corresponding information system such as object models or component models. It does not only contribute to reducing complexity, but also fosters communication and collaboration between various groups of stakeholders. By providing an integrated representation of the business and the information system, an enterprise model can serve as a laboratory for elaborate investigations of complex phenomena such as the alignment between enterprise strategy and technology strategy as well as between enterprise operations and respective application systems. At the same time, an enterprise model facilitates creating or generating code. As a research field, EM builds on contributions from computer science and information systems. Over the past 20 years a number of different languages, methods, and tools have emerged both in academia and in industry. Consequently, there is substantial empirical evidence on various aspects of EM.

The PoEM (Practice of Enterprise Modeling) series of conferences aims to provide a forum where such evidence is critically evaluated and new needs of industry and commerce are examined with a view to identifying challenges for researchers and developers. PoEM 2014, supported by the IFIP WG8.1, was the seventh conference in this series. This year's conference was held in Manchester, UK, hosted by the Manchester Business School of the University of Manchester.

The proceedings comprise 16 full papers and four short papers. The majority of contributions are focused on various aspects of business process modeling. Sepideh Ghanavaty, Silvia Ingolfo, and Alberto Siena present an approach to explore legal business process paths. Merethe Heggset, John Krogstie, and Harald Wesenberg report on experiences from a case study that involves large-scale collections of industrial processes. Anis Boubaker, Dhouha Cherif, Abderrahmane Leshob, and Hafedh Mili investigate how to discover value chains from business process models. Richard Braun and Werner Esswein present a classification of domain-specific extensions of BPMN. Thomas Baier, Andreas Rogge-Solti, Jan Mendling, and Mathias Weske analyze business process models with respect to the matching of events and activities. Finally, Isel Moreno-Montes de Oca, Monique Snoeck, and Gladys Casas-Cardoso use the technology acceptance model to investigate business process modeling guidelines.

Four papers deal with aspects of enterprise architecture. Sarah Boone, Maxime

Bernaert, Ben Roelens, Steven Mertens, and Geert Poels analyze the visualization of an enterprise architecture approach for SMEs. Mika Cohen presents a simulation approach for enterprise architecture. Wanda Opprecht, Jolita Ralyté, and Michel Léonard outline a framework for steering the evolution of enterprise information systems. Georgios Plataniotis, Sybren De Kinderen, and Henderik Proper present a case study on capturing design rationales in enterprise architecture.

A further topic is the investigation of EM methods. Alexander Bock, Monika Kaczmarek, Sietse Overbeek, and Michael Heß present an elaborate comparison of four selected approaches to enterprise modeling. Kurt Sandkuhl and Hasan Koç report on experiences with a component-based approach to method development. Anne Persson and Janis Stirna propose recommendations for the organizational adoption of enterprise modeling methods.

Two papers focus on requirements engineering issues. Jelena Zdravkovic, Janis Stirna, Jan-Christian Kuhr, and Hasan Koç present an approach to requirements engineering for capability-driven development. Tong Li, Jennifer Horkoff, and John Mylopoulos use goal models to integrate security patterns with security requirements analysis.

Further contributions deal with more specific aspects of EM. Frank Wolff proposes an approach to partition enterprise modeling governance by stressing a usage perspective. Alimohammad Shahri, Mahmood Hosseini, Keith Phalp, Jacqui Taylor, and Raian Ali look at gamification as an approach to interact with enterprise models and propose creating a respective code of ethics. Soroosh Nalchigar, Eric Yu, and Steve Easterbrook link system dynamics and the business intelligence model to present a novel approach to business intelligence. Wen Chen, Alan Wassyng, and Tom Maibaum focus on the analysis of large enterprise systems presenting an approach to analyze the impact of software changes. Constantinos Giannoulis and Jelena Zdravkovic present an empirical study on model-driven alignment of business and IT.

Finally, we would like to thank the authors and the members of the Program Committee, whose work resulted in a program that we regard as very attractive. The reviewing process and the creation of the proceedings were supported by EasyChair.

November 2014   Ulrich Frank
                                                              Oscar Pastor
                                                       Pericles Loucopoulos
                                                          Ilias Petrounias

Organization

Program Committee

Dimosthenis Anagnostopoulos	Harokopio University of Athens, Greece
Marko Bajec	University of Ljubljana, Slovenia
Giuseppe Berio	Université de Bretagne Sud, France
Robert Andrei Buchmann	University of Vienna, Austria
Rimantas Butleris	Kaunas University of Technology, Lithuania
Artur Caetano	IST, Technical University of Lisbon, Portugal
Albertas Caplinskas	Institute of Mathematics and Informatics, Lithuania
Jaelson Castro	Universidade Federal de Pernambuco, Brazil
Panagiotis Chountas	Westminter University, UK
Tony Clark	Middlesex University, UK
Rolland Colette	Université Paris 1 Pantheon Sorbonne, France
Wolfgang Deiters	Fraunhofer Institute for Software and Systems Engineering, Germany
Sergio España	Universitat Politècnica de València, Spain
Xavier Franch	Universitat Politècnica de Catalunya, Spain
Ulrich Frank	Universität of Duisburg-Essen, Germany
Janis Grabis	Riga Technical University, Latvia
Stijn Hoppenbrouwers	HAN University of Applied Sciences, The Netherlands
Marta Indulska	The University of Queensland, Australia
Paul Johannesson	Royal Institute of Technology, Sweden
Juergen Jung	DHL Global Forwarding, Germany
Håvard Jørgensen	Commitment AS, Norway
Monika Kaczmarek	University of Duisburg-Essen, Germany
Ron Kenett	KPA Ltd. and Univ. of Torino, Italy
Lutz Kirchner	BOC GmbH, Germany
Marite Kirikova	Riga Technical University, Latvia
Vassilis Kodogiannis	University of Westminster, UK
John Krogstie	IDI, NTNU, Trondheim, Norway
Birger Lantow	University of Rostock, Germany
Ulrike Lechner	Universität der Bundeswehr München, Germany
Pericles Loucopulos	Manchester University, UK
Florian Matthes	Technische Universität München, Germany
Raimundas Matulevicius	University of Tartu, Estonia
Graham Mcleod	Promis Solutions AG, Switzerland
Jan Mendling	Wirtschaftsuniversität Wien, Austria

Andreas Opdahl	University of Bergen, Norway
Sietse Overbeek	University of Duisburg-Essen, Germany
Oscar Pastor Lopez	Universitat Politècnica de Valencia, Spain
Anne Persson	University of Skövde, Sweden
Michael Petit	University of Namur, Belgium
Ilias Petrounias	University of Manchester, UK
Henderik Proper	Public Research Centre Henri Tudor, Luxembourg
Jolita Ralyté	University of Geneva, Switzerland
Irina Rychkova	Université Paris 1 Pantheon-Sorbonne, France
Kurt Sandkuhl	University of Rostock, Germany
Ulf Seigerroth	Jönköping University, School of Engineering, Sweden
Khurram Shahzad	Royal Institute of Technology, Sweden
Nikolay Shilov	SPIIRAS, Russia
Pnina Soffer	University of Haifa, Israel
Janis Stirna	Stockholm University, Sweden
Darijus Strasunskas	NTNU, Norway
Stefan Strecker	University of Hagen, Germany
Stefan Sturm	IREB GmbH, Germany
Victoria Torres	Universitat Politècnica de Valencia, Spain
Francisco Valverde	Universitat Politècnica de Valencia, Spain
Barbara Weber	University of Innsbruck, Austria
Frank Wolff	DHBW Mannheim, Germany
Eric Yu	University of Toronto, Canada
Jelena Zdravkovic	Stockholm University, Sweden

Additional Reviewers

Danesh, Mohammad Hossein
Hauder, Matheus
Lienert, Uwe
Oldenhave, Danny

Rosenthal, Kristina
Ruiz, Marcela
Waltl, Bernhard

Table of Contents

Exploring Legal Business Process Paths

Sepideh Ghanavati[1], Silvia Ingolfo[2], and Alberto Siena[3]

[1] CRP Henri Tudor, Luxembourg City, Luxembourg
[2] University of Trento, Trento Italy
[3] FBK, Trento, Italy
sepideh.ghanavati@tudor.lu, silvia.ingolfo@disi.unitn.it, siena@fbk.eu

Abstract. Nowadays, enterprises are very complex systems, often comprised of a large number of business processes run by actors working together to achieve business objectives. Ensuring compliance with applicable laws is mandatory to avoid heavy penalties or even business failure. To this purpose, an increasingly important challenge consists of finding and resolving discrepancies between strategic goals, business processes and laws. In this paper, we envisage a formal approach that uses two modeling languages, User Requirements Notation (URN) and Nòmos, to represent enterprise goals, processes and applicable laws. Automated reasoning techniques allow us to analyze models for compliance checking and detecting conditions of unwanted concurrent executions.

1 Introduction

Modern enterprises are complex systems comprised of actors, as well as software and hardware components working together in interleaved processes to support high-level enterprise objectives. Well-designed processes are essential to ensure efficiency and effectiveness in the production of goods and services. Enterprises are also subject to laws and regulations which can be costly to comply with. Being non-compliant may introduce more cost to the enterprise, such as heavy fines, bad reputation or business disruption. Since business processes can be very large and articulated, they generate a potentially large number of alternative execution paths. Similarly, laws are generally comprised of a large set of conditional elements, such as conditions, exceptions and so on, which create an even potentially larger number of admissible paths to comply. This raises the need to ensure that (i) every possible process or process path respect complies with applicable laws; and (ii) for every law or law fragment, one (or more) process or process branch exists, which fulfills the necessary legal accomplishments. While doing (i) and (ii), the achievement of strategic objectives must also be ensured.

Several work has been done to analyze the compliance of business processes with laws and regulations. LEGAL-URN [1], [2], based on User Requirements Notation (URN) [3], is one of the main frameworks which aims to model regulations, organizational goals and business processes in the same notation and provides analysis for compliance. However, this approach does not explore the alternatives for compliance in detail. In [4] obligations are decomposed into operational

U. Frank et al. (Eds.): PoEM 2014, LNBIP 197, pp. 1–10, 2014.

level rules, and Key Performance Indicators are used to measure compliance objectives and balance them with business objectives.

Although few approaches exist for business process compliance, in a recent systematic literature review [5], the authors identify the needs for having a concrete framework with guidelines on how to map legal prescriptions to business processes and how to analyze the compliance.

In [6] a modeling approach is presented, which focuses on modeling the organizational regulatory space (ORS), comprised by both, the internals of the enterprise, such as business processes and goals, and applicable regulations. In [7] a new approach is proposed for assessing compliance of business processes using the compliance checker REGOROUS. The used language defines a more fine-grained concept of obligation and compliance. Using FCL, a rule-based logic which combines defeasible and deontic logic, the authors formalize regulations and validate the business process model.

In this position paper we envision an approach for the exploration of business process paths to detect potential violations of the law. We define an *legal business process path* a path in the process such that the supported requirements are satisfied, while the applicable norms are not violated. We model the process in Use Case Maps (UCM), which is the scenario notation part of URN, and the requirements in Goal-oriented Requirements Language (GRL), which is the goal modeling notation of URN. Other business process modeling such as BPMN or UML activity diagrams can be used instead of UCM, however, the advantage of UCM over these approaches is that it has links to GRL for goal models and includes capabilities for analyzing scenarios, conflict detection and propagating the result of the analysis from UCM to GRL and vice-versa.

The applicable norms are represented in Nòmos [8], a modeling language for representing laws and regulations. The novelty of our approach stays in the capability to model *alternatives* in the combination of processes, law prescriptions and goals. Also in our approach, we support automated reasoning to explore *exhaustively* the models, ensuring compliance with laws and allowing at the same time, to achieve enterprise goals that the processes have to support.

The paper is structured as follows: Section 2 introduces the underlying modeling techniques; Section 3 presents the envisioned modeling approach and shows how reasoning is supported; finally, Section 4 concludes the paper and outlines some future work.

2   Baseline

2.1   User Requirements Notation (URN)

The User Requirements Notation (URN) [3] is an International Telecommunications Union (ITU-T) standard which helps requirements engineers and business analysts documenting requirements and/or analyzing these requirements for correctness and completeness. URN combines two modeling notations, *Goaloriented Requirement Language* (GRL) and the *Use Case Maps* (UCM) [9]. GRL is used to model goals and Non-Functional Requirements (NFR) with goals and softgoals, and provides means to reason about alternatives. UCM aims at modeling scenario concepts of operational and functional requirements, and help reasoning about performance and architectural decisions [10].

Goal-oriented Requirements Language (GRL) – The Goal-oriented Requirement Language (GRL) is a goal modeling notation based on i^* language and the NFR Framework's concepts and syntax. High-level business goals, NFRs and the alternatives are modeled with intentional elements in GRL. GRL also models beliefs to capture the rationales behinds stakeholders' decisions, as well as stakeholder dependencies.

GRL intentional elements are: softgoals ($\bigcirc$), goals ($\bigcirc$), tasks ($\bigcirc$), beliefs or resources ($\square$). Softgoals are abstract and have no clear measure of satisfaction while goals are quantifiable and can be fully satisfied. Softgoals usually model NFRs and quality requirements, whereas goals deal with and model functional requirements. Tasks capture solutions or alternative means to achive goals or softgoals. Resources are sometimes utilized to achieve tasks, goals and softgoals. Actors ($\bigcirc$), represent stakeholders of the system who can have certain goals to achieves and set of tasks to perform.

GRL includes a set of link to connect intentional elements to each other. These links are: decomposition links (+—), contribution links (→), correlation links (⋯→) or dependency links (—▶—). Decomposition links are used to decompose an intentional element into sub-elements and can be a type of AND, IOR, or XOR. XOR and IOR decomposition links. Contribution links which can have qualitative or quantitative values illustrate the impact of one intentional element's satisfaction on another intentional element's satisfaction value. Correlation links are similar to contribution links, but indicate side-effects of one intentional element on the other. Dependency links model relationships and the dependencies between actors.

To analyze the satisfaction value of each intentional element as well as the overall satisfaction of actors in the system, GRL provides both bottom-up and top-down evaluation mechanisms. These evaluation mechanisms can also be quantitative, qualitative, hybrid or constraint-based. The detail of these evaluations mechanism are explained in [11].

Use Case Maps (UCM) – UCM aims at modeling scenarios and use cases. It depicts the causal sequences of tasks and activities allocated to *components* ($\square$). Components can be actors, agents, roles, software modules, sub-systems, etc. and they can be decomposed into sub-components. Scenario paths connect *start points* (●) to *end points* (▮). Paths contain *responsibilities* (✗) which are the actions and activities that need to be done. They can be performed in sequence, concurrently (┼), or as alternatives (⌐).

UCM has the capability to decompose complex scenario maps into several sub-maps (i.e. plug-in maps) via *stubs* (◇). Stubs can be static or dynamic. Input and output of the stubs are connected to the start points and end points in the plug-in to ensure scenario continuity across various levels of details. Dynamic stubs are used to specify alternative maps in the same location.

To define *scenarios* in UCM, preconditions and postconditions are captured. Scenarios are triggered and started when a set of preconditions are satisfied. Based on the set of the preconditions, one alternative path is taken at any point in time. Resposibilities which are usually linked to tasks or other intentional elements in GRL can get the satisfaction value of the tasks or intentional elements linked to them. When the preconditions, postconditions and other values in a scenario are defined, a a *path traversal mechanism* helps simulating different scenarios and the traversed paths. *Path traversal mechanism* can be used in regression testing and it provides operational semantics to UCM models.

2.2   Nòmos 2

Nòmos 2 is a modeling language that aims at capturing the variability of compliance alternatives for norms [8]. Nòmos 2 models allow us to represent fragments of laws or regulations by representing the different conditions and rules described by a law or regulation, and the alternative ways to comply with it. The conditions on a norm's applicability and satisfiability are represented through the concept of situations denoting states-of-affairs (partial states of the world), such as "Christmas season" or "Driving on the highway". Situations are partial states of the world that we may know to hold (meaning the situation is satisfied), not hold, or neither (when we can't conclude satisfaction or denial). If some situations are satisfied, the norm will apply, and when other situations are satisfied, the norm will be satisfied. In our model, situations are linked to norms in terms of four basic relations acting as a label-propagation mechanism to identify when situations make a norm applicable/not-applicable (activate, block), or satisfied/not-satisfied (satisfy, break). When a norm (duty or right) is applicable, it is *complied with* when it is satisfied and *violated* if it is not satisfied. If the norm is not applicable or it is unknown whether the norm applies or not, it is either *tolerated* or *undefined* (see [8] for more details). Relations between norms are used to represent exceptions and special other cases where norms may make other norms applicable, not applicable, or complied with.

Figure 1 represents an example of a Nòmos 2 of a hypothetical tax law. When a product is bought from a seller the duty to pay taxes applies ($S_1 \xrightarrow{\text{activate}} D_1$). In order to satisfy the norm — and therefore comply with it — it is possible to either pay the taxes ($S_2 \xrightarrow{\text{satisfy}} D_1$), or by filling in the VAT-claim tax form ($S_3 \xrightarrow{\text{satisfy}} D_1$). For example, since VAT-free product are untaxed by definition, if the product is VAT-free (and S_4 holds), the duty is no longer applicable ($S_4 \xrightarrow{\text{block}} D_1$). For the purpose of this example, we consider that the stores allow a return policy when a valid receipt of the purchase is shown. The two situations — of 1) having bought a product and 2) having a valid receipt — activate the right to return the product to the store, which in turn is complied with when the product is indeed returned ($S_6 \xrightarrow{\text{satisfy}} R_1$). However, if the product is damaged, then the right is no longer applicable ($S_7 \xrightarrow{\text{break}} R_1$). The main idea behind Nòmos 2 is that leveraging on the applicability and satisfiability of different norms and

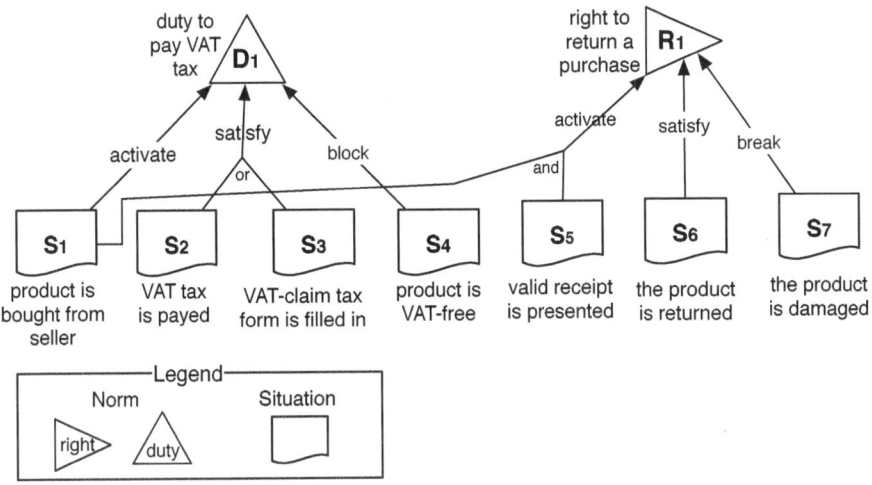

Fig. 1. An example of a Nòmos 2 model

situations holding, it is possible to identify how to comply with a law in different ways (e.g., by paying the VAT tax, by buying a VAT-free product, ...).

3   Legal Business Process Paths

A business process consists of a set of activities to be executed in sequence. Gateways, such as decision points and parallelisms, split the activity sequence into different possible flows, potentially executed in parallel by multiple actors (lanes). The presence of parallelism, in particular, generates a sort of indeterminism in process execution, which in turn causes multiple execution instances to be possible, depending on the concurrency conditions. For example, given two activities, a and b, a parallelism between them implies that three executions exist: a is executed before b, b is executed before a, and a and b simultaneously. If there is a legal constraint on the output of a, b, or both, it becomes necessary to identify these alternative executions and explore them to detect potential violation conditions of a business process, in order to change the process structure.

3.1   Modeling

To design a process that satisfies strategic goals while complying with applicable laws, we need a modeling language capable to model business processes, goals and laws. There are mature, standardized languages to model business processes, such as BPMN; also, there are modeling languages to model goals and some to model legal prescriptions. However, to model the three aspect of the problem and be able to support automated reasoning, we need to combine two or more existing languages. In this paper, we evaluate the combination of URN and

Nòmos since the integration of goals and business process models has already been made in URN standard.

Figure 2 depicts an example of our approach. The picture represents an electronic commerce scenario, in which tax laws have to be taken into account. Two actors are represented, the Buyer and the Seller, and two business processes are shown: one process involves both the Buyer and the Seller, while the other concerns only the Buyer. Different activities have been introduced in both processes to comply with the legal provisions already depicted in Figure 1. The processes run in parallel, so there is no way to ensure that a certain flow of activities is executed. While we can ensure that when each activity is performed, its corresponding legal requirement is satisfied, it is possible that performing a combination of activities results in a violation.

To represent a satisfiability conditions between the business process and the law, we use traceability links from the path branch of the business process to the corresponding situation in Nòmos model. For example, in the business process related to the tax law, two conditional verifications must happen. First, it is necessary to check if the product is tax free. If it is, situation S4 is satisfied. Next, if the product is not tax-free, the second check has to be done to verify whether the buyer filled up the tax exemption form or not. The two paths created from this satisfy S2 and S3 in Nòmos.

In the process of 'returning the product', the seller only accepts the product as returned if three conditions (i.e. having bought the product, having valid receipt, and returning the purchased product with no damage) are satisfied. These three conditions satisfy the situations, S5, S6 and S7 in Nòmos respectively. If the buyer does not satisfy all of the three conditions, then the main goal, return product will not be satisfied, as shown with red X in Figure 2.

In previous works [8], we have used Nòmos to model pieces of real laws and studied the scalability of this modeling approach for legal document. Therefore — despite using a preliminary small example for this paper — we are confident in the ability of this approach in capturing all of the possible combinations that may emerge from very complex processes.The combinations emerge in particular from the design of the business processes and law, and their execution. This is achieved by using formal reasoning on the models, as described in the following.

3.2   Formal Reasoning

Once a process starts, at any given time t_k, a set of activities, from 0 to n, are executed. The trace of the process at time t_k consists of all the activities that have been executed from time t_0 to time t_k. Figure 3 illustrates the exhaustive generation of multiple paths within a given business process. In the left part, the figure depicts a simple business process with 5 activities and two branches executed in parallel. Due to the parallelism, many different execution traces can be defined: in the right part, 9 different partial traces defined by the process are shown. In the first trace, the process has been started (activity 's' executed); in the second, 'x1' has been executed; and so on. At a certain point, when the activities can be executed in parallel, the number of possible traces grows rapidly

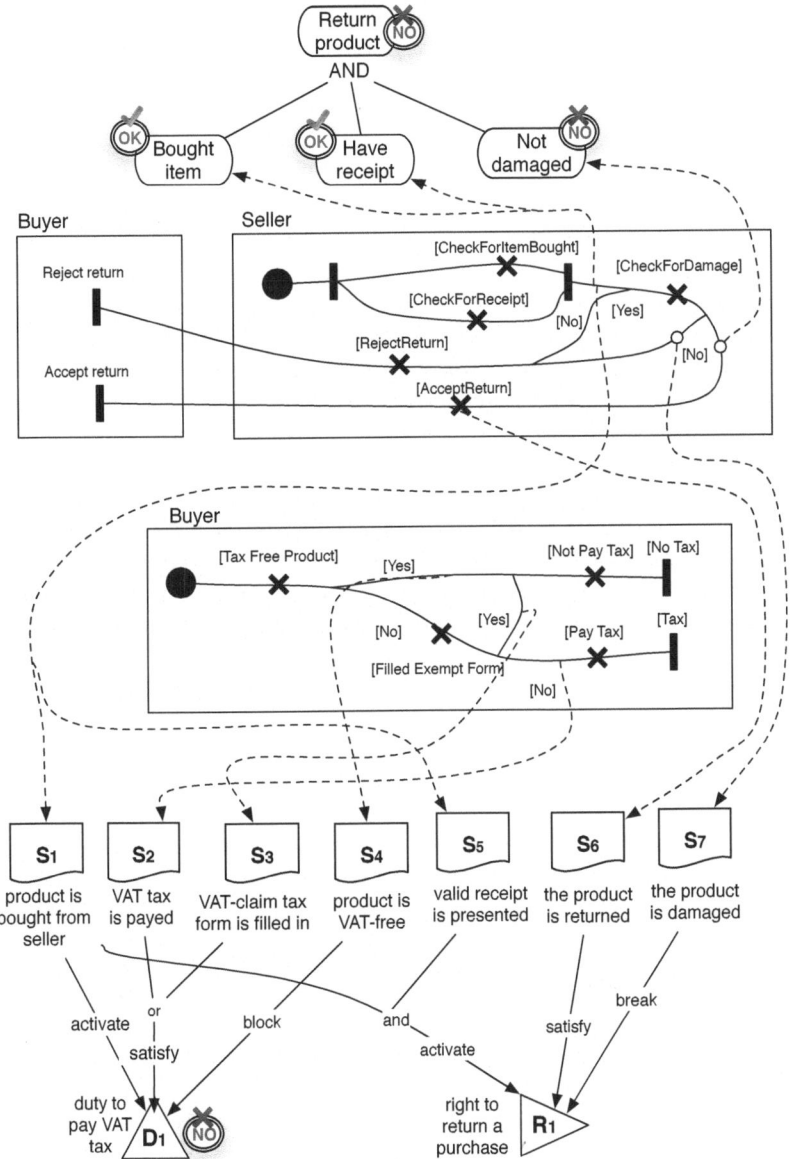

Fig. 2. Example of URN-Nòmos Reasoning

because of the concurrency conditions described above. We hypothesize that, given a process and a law, each activity of the process can bring about an arbitrary number of conditions defined in the law to be compliant with, that are the legal prescriptions. The set of activities in a trace form an execution assignment to that prescriptions: the activities that belong to the trace are considered to actually fulfill the legal prescriptions; while the activities that do not belong to the trace leave the corresponding prescriptions not fulfilled. Depending on how the law is structured, failing in fulfilling one or more prescriptions can generate a violation to that law. To generalize, given a process P and a set of norms L, we define a *legal business process path* as a path in the process, such that for each possible trace in the path L is not violated. The intuition behind the present work is that we can use URN and Nómos to enforce modeling business processes that satisfy stakeholder requirements and at the same time comply with applicable laws. In particular, URN offers basics to model requirements with GRL, and business processes with UCM, and to establish *traceability links* between them. Nòmos allows modeling of the legal prescriptions and provides support for automated reasoning. Specifically, Nòmos enables for *exhaustive* exploration of legal alternatives within a given model of law. Adopting similar traceability links between business processes and laws, we can perform exhaustive search in the space of traces generated by a given business process.

Table 1 illustrates how our approach can be formalized using Disjunctive Logic Programming (DLP) [12]. DLP is a declarative, first-order logic language and a deductive system, where facts and deduction rules are expressed as predicates of the logic language. Disjunctions may appear in the rule heads to allow multiple alternative consequences to be drawn from a rule. Solvers, such as DLV [13]

Table 1. An excerpt of the formalisation in DLP

```
done(s,p) :- start(p).

done(x1,p) v pending(x1,p) :- done(s,p).

%parallelism
done(x21,p) v pending(x21,p) :- done(x1).
done(x22,p) v pending(x22,p) :- done(x1).

done(x23,p) v pending(x23,p) :- done(x22).

done(x3,p) v pending(x3) :- done(x21,p), done(x23,p).

done(e,p) v pending(e,p) :- done(x3,p).

end(p) :- done(e,p).

% link to situations
st(s1) :- done(x1,p).
sf(s1) :- not done(x1,p).

start(p) v not_start(p).
```

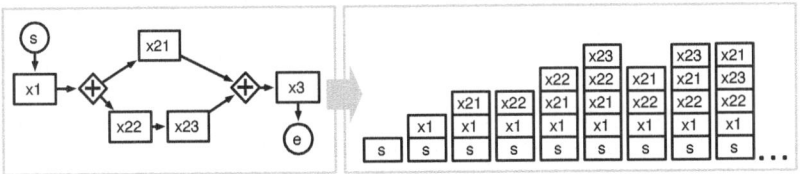

Fig. 3. Set of possible traces defined on a given process

allows *exhaustively* exploring the alternative models defined on a set of predicates, searching for desired properties.

We use DLP to introduce alternative traces, as in [14]. Each activity in a given process is represented as a variable. If an activity x is executed in a process p, the predicate done(x,p) is triggered. If the activity that precedes x has been executed, but x still has not been executed, the predicate pending(x,p) is triggered. After x has been executed, it is possible that either the next one, say y is executed, or that the transition has not accomplished, so we have that done(y,p) v pending(y,p) :- done(x,p). If an activity is far from being executed, nothing is deducted. In both cases, whether the activity is pending or discarded, not done(y,p) holds. This mechanism allows us to provide a Nòmos model with the true values coming from the process trace. In the table, a certain situation s1 is considered satisfied (i.e., id *holds*) when the activity x1 is executed in the process p.

4   Discussion and Conclusion

In this position paper, we have proposed an approach to support modeling enterprises in their strategic dimension (goals) as well as operational dimension (business processes), while ensuring compliance to applicable laws. Our approach relies on two existing modeling languages, URN and Nòmos, and extends them to allow linking activities of the business processes to the situations belonging to the legal model. Models are translated into disjunctive logic programs and exhaustively checked by means of an automated reasoning tool. Our approach allows exhaustively generating all possible execution traces on a given process, and contrast them to the linked situations to check for compliance.

While aligning business processes to the goals is a consolidated method in both research and practice, to the best of our knowledge there is a lack in analysis capabilities to what concerns the alignment of the internal structure of the enterprise to the legal environment, where the enterprise operates in. The main drawback of this approach is the need to explicitly model the links between business process and law models. However, supporting this kind of analysis through automated reasoning, is of particular importance when considering large enterprises, with many processes distributed over several legislations.

In our current work in progress, we are planning to apply our approach to a larger example for a more thorough evaluation of our proposal. This will allow us to evaluate its feasibility in a real-size case study, and to evaluate the scalability of the approach in this larger settings by means of artificial models (see for example [14]). An important limitation that we plan to investigate in our future work is for sure the creations of our models (currently done manually), where we envision a systematic process to help the analyst in the compliance evaluation of the model, as well as in the amendment of such model to reach compliance.

Acknowledgments. This work has been partially funded by AFR - PDR grant #5810263 and by the ERC advanced grant 267856 "Lucretius: Foundations for Software Evolution".

References

1. Ghanavati, S.: Legal-URN framework for legal compliance of business processes, Ph.D. thesis, University of Ottawa, Canada (2013), http://hdl.handle.net/10393/24028
2. Sepideh Ghanavati, D.A., Rifaut, A.: Legal goal-oriented requirement language (Legal-GRL) for modeling regulations. In: MiSE @ICSE, India(to be appeared, 2014)
3. ITU-T, Recommendation Z.151 (10/12), User Requirements Notation (URN) - Language definition (2012), http://www.itu.int/rec/T-REC-Z.151/en
4. Shamsaei, A.: Indicator-based policy compliance of business processes, PhD Thesis, University of Ottawa, Canada (2012)
5. Ghanavati, S., Amyot, D., Peyton, L.: A systematic review of goal-oriented requirements management frameworks for business process compliance. In: RELAW, pp. 25–34 (2011)
6. Grabis, J., Kirikova, M., Zdravkovic, J., Stirna, J. (eds.): PoEM 2013. LNBIP, vol. 165. Springer, Heidelberg (2013)
7. Governatori, G.: Ict support for regulatory compliance of business processes. CoRR, vol. abs/1403.6865 (2014)
8. Siena, A., Jureta, I., Ingolfo, S., Susi, A., Perini, A., Mylopoulos, J.: Capturing variability of law with Nòmos 2. In: ER 2012 (2012)
9. Weiss, M., Amyot, D.: Designing and evolving business models with URN. In: MCETECH 2005, pp. 149–162 (2005)
10. Amyot, D., Mussbacher, G.: User Requirements Notation: The first ten years, the next ten years (invited paper). Journal of Software (JSW) 6(5), 747–768 (2011)
11. Amyot, D., Ghanavati, S., Horkoff, J., Mussbacher, G., Peyton, L., Yu, E.S.K.: Evaluating goal models within the goal-oriented requirement language. Int. J. Intell. Syst. 25, 841–877 (2010)
12. Minker, J.: Overview of disjunctive logic programming. Ann. Math. Artif. Intell. 12(1-2), 1–24 (1994)
13. Alviano, M., Faber, W., Leone, N., Perri, S., Pfeifer, G., Terracina, G.: The disjunctive datalog system DLV. In: de Moor, O., Gottlob, G., Furche, T., Sellers, A. (eds.) Datalog 2010. LNCS, vol. 6702, pp. 282–301. Springer, Heidelberg (2011)
14. Siena, A., Ingolfo, S., Perini, A., Susi, A., Mylopoulos, J.: Automated reasoning for regulatory compliance. In: Ng, W., Storey, V.C., Trujillo, J.C. (eds.) ER 2013. LNCS, vol. 8217, pp. 47–60. Springer, Heidelberg (2013)

Ensuring Quality of Large Scale Industrial Process Collections: Experiences from a Case Study

Merethe Heggset[1], John Krogstie[1], and Harald Wesenberg[2]

[1]Norwegian University of Science & Technology - NTNU, Norway
merethhe@gmail.com, krogstie@idi.ntnu.no
[2] Statoil ASA, Norway
hwes@statoil.com

Abstract. As approaches and tools for process and enterprise modelling are maturing, these techniques are in an increasing number of organizations being taken into use on a large scale. In this paper we report on the use over many years of process-modelling in connection to the quality system of Statoil, a large Norwegian oil-company, in particular on the aspects found necessary to emphasis to achieve the right quality of the models in this organisation. The Statoil-guidelines for enterprise structure and use of standard notation are mapped to the levels of SEQUAL, a generic framework for understanding the quality of models. Guidelines for modelling are found on most levels. More detailed guidelines than in general work on quality of business process models are found in particular on the physical, empirical, and syntactic level, where the number of detailed guidelines in Statoil has increased over the years due to needs identified.

Keywords: Enterprise process modelling, case study, experience paper.

1 Introduction

Statoil is a global oil company headquartered in Norway. It has more than 20.000 employees in more than 30 countries worldwide, and has spent significant resources for enterprise modelling over the years. They report to have achieved a fair success with enterprise modelling in its corporate management system [29] where workflow models are used extensively to communicate requirements and best practices throughout the enterprise. The current management system contains more than 2000 business process and workflow models with associated requirements and best practices, all available through a corporate web portal from anywhere in the company. The models are used daily in large parts of the organization, and are a significant contributor in reducing operational, environmental and safety risks. As an example, the important SIF-index (Serious Injury Frequency) which counts the number of incidents per million work hours has been reduced from 6 to around 0.8 in the period since the models where introduced. Every week Statoil employees perform approximately 2 million work hours. That said the process model is only one approach to risk mitigation. One also experience that the process models could be utilized even better.

U. Frank et al. (Eds.): PoEM 2014, LNBIP 197, pp. 11–25, 2014.

From the start, Statoil has been aware of the need to balance different levels of quality of the models. According to [26, 30] Statoil have found that it makes sense to talk about three dimensions of model quality: Syntactic quality (how well the model uses the modelling language), semantic quality (how well the model reflects the real world) and pragmatic quality (how well the model is understood by the target audience), building upon distinctions first described in [12], which is a predecessor to the current SEQUAL framework on quality of models and modelling languages [6]. In enterprise models the balance between these dimensions becomes very important based on the goal of modelling; else the model will not be used by its intended target audience in the right way.

Enterprise models being part of a quality system exists over a longer period of time, and is distributed widely throughout the enterprise [30]. Enterprise models thus must be managed properly. They need to be subject to strict versioning routines, configuration management practices and release plans. In many ways enterprise models used in this manner are similar to source code, and should be subject to similar professional practices. If the models are not managed properly they will not be trusted and they will subsequently fail to achieve their full potential as enterprise models.

To manage the development and evolution of their enterprise process models, Statoil has developed detailed requirements for modelling. We have in this case study looked upon these requirements in the light of the SEQUAL-framework for understanding quality of models. Other frameworks for evaluating quality of process models exist including Guidelines of Modeling (GoM) and Quality of Modeling (QoMo). GoM is focused on managing the subjectivism involved when building models. The framework consists of two dimensions; one for the range of model use, and one for the degree of precision or concretion [22]. QoMo is focused on knowledge state transitions, cost management, and goal structure [2]. Our choice of SEQUAL rests on that Statoil has already used a subset of SEQUAL. Quite detailed overviews of quality of process models in the light of SEQUAL exist [7] and the aim of this experience paper is to illustrate the additional level of detail on such guidelines that is needed to gain value from these kinds of models in professional practice. The case study has taken as outset different version of official modelling guidelines/requirements in Statoil, and mapped this to SEQUAL by an expert of the framework, partly by document study, and partly in interaction with the developers of requirements in Statoil. General background on modelling and SEQUAL is provided in section 2. In section 3 we describe the Statoil quality system in more detail, before we in section 4 describe the mapping of the Statoil modelling guidelines to SEQUAL. Ideas on further work on understanding the trade-off on different quality aspect are found in section 5.

2   Background on Modeling and Quality of Models

According to general model theory [24] there are three common characteristics of models: *Representation, Simplification* and *Pragmatic orientation*.
- *Representation*: Models represents something else.
- *Simplification*: Models possess a reductive trait in that they map only a subset of attributes of the phenomenon being modelled.

- *Pragmatic orientation*: Models have a substitutive function in that they substitute a certain phenomenon as being conceptualized by a certain subject in a given temporal space with a certain *incentive* or operation in mind

Thus a model is not just a representation of something else, it is a conscious construction. Enterprise process modelling is always done in some organizational setting. One can look upon an organization and its information system abstractly to be in a state (the current state, often represented as a descriptive 'as-is' model) that are often to be evolved to some future wanted state (represented as a prescriptive 'to be' model).

The state includes the existing processes, organization and computer systems. These states are often modelled, and the state of the organization is perceived (differently) by different persons through these models. Different usage areas of conceptual models as described in [6, 19] are:

1. Human sense-making: The descriptive model of the current state can be useful for people to make sense of and learn about the current perceived situation.
2. Communication between people in the organization: Models can have an important role in human communication. Thus, in addition to support the sense-making process for the individual, a model can act as a common framework supporting communication both relative to descriptive and prescriptive models.
3. Computer-assisted analysis: This is used to gain knowledge about the organization through simulation or deduction, often by comparing a model of the current state and a model of a future, potentially better state.
4. Quality assurance, ensuring compliance e.g. that the organization acts according to a certified process developed for instance as part of an ISO-certification process.
5. Model deployment and activation: To integrate the model of the future state in a new information system directly. Models can be activated in three ways:
    a. Through people, (manual activation) with no active tool-support.
    b. Automatically, where the system plays an active role, as in most automated workflow systems.
    c. Interactively, where the computer and the users co-operate in bringing the process forward.
6. To be a prescriptive model to be used in a traditional system development project, without being directly activated.

SEQUAL [6] is a framework for assessing and understanding the quality of models and modelling languages. It builds on early work on quality of model [12, 15], but has been extended based on theoretical results [16, 17, 20] and practical experiences [6, 10] with the original framework. It has earlier been used for evaluation of modelling and modelling languages of a large number of perspectives, including data [8], ontologies [3], process [7, 11], enterprise [9], topological [18] and goal-oriented modelling [4, 5]. Quality has been defined referring to the correspondence between statements belonging to the following sets:

- *G,* the set of goals of the modelling task.
- *D,* the domain, i.e., the set of all statements that can be stated about the situation. The goal of modelling typically restricts the domain to only those things relevant to achieve this goal

- *L*, the language extension, i.e. what can be expressed by the modelling language used.
- *M*, the externalized model itself.
- *K*, the explicit knowledge that the audience (both modelers and model interpreters) have of the domain.
- *I*, the social actor (human) interpretation of the model
- *T*, the technical actor (tool) interpretation of the model

The main quality types are:

- Physical quality: The basic quality goal is that the externalized model *M* is available to the relevant actors (and not others) for interpretation (*I* and *T*).
- Empirical quality deals with comprehensibility of the model *M*.
- Syntactic quality is the correspondence between the model *M* and the language extension *L*. Is the language used correctly in the model?
- Semantic quality is the correspondence between the model *M* and the domain *D*.
- Perceived semantic quality is the similar correspondence between the social actor interpretation *I* of a model *M* and his or hers current knowledge *K* of domain *D*.
- Pragmatic quality is the correspondence between the model *M* and the actor interpretation (*I* and *T*) of it. Thus whereas empirical quality focus on if the model is understandable according to some objective measure that has been discovered empirically in e.g., cognitive science, we at this level look on to what extend the model has actually been understood.
- The goal defined for social quality is agreement among social actor's interpretations of the models.
- The deontic quality of the model relates to that all statements in the model *M* contribute to fulfilling the goals of modelling *G*, and that all the goals of modelling *G* are addressed through the model *M*.

When we structure different quality aspects according to these levels, one will find that there might be conflicts between the levels (e.g. what is good for semantic quality might be bad for pragmatic quality), thus to make a trade-off between achieving the different quality levels is important for achieving the main goals of modelling.

3   Case-environment - Statoil Quality Management System

The Statoil Management System is "the set of principles, policies, processes and requirement which support our organization in fulfilling the tasks required to achieve our goals" [27]. It defines how work is done within the company, and all employees are required to act according to relevant governing documentation.

The Management System consists of three main parts:

- ARIS, the modelling solution from which all governing documentation is accessed by the end users.
- Docmap, used for handling and publishing textual governing documentation

- Disp, a tool which supports the process of handling applications for deviation permits in cases where compliance with a requirement is difficult or impossible to achieve.

The three main objectives of the Statoil Management System are

1. Contributing to safe, reliable and efficient operations and enabling compliance with external and internal requirements
2. Helping the company incorporating their values, people and leadership principles into everything they do
3. Supporting business performance through high-quality decision-making, fast and precise execution and continuous learning

Governing documentation describes what is to be achieved, how to execute tasks, and ensures standardization. Each process area has governing documentation in the form of documents and/or process models, accessible from the Management System start page on the Statoil intranet. This is kept up to date by the management system function [28]. The main purpose of the management system function is to ensure that:

- The management system is developed and improved based on learning and business needs.
- Governing documentation is understood and implemented.
- Compliance with requirements is monitored.

This is done in close collaboration with line management and owners of governing documentation. The governing documentation is managed in a systematic five step cycle: Assess and plan, design, implement, use, and monitor and control.

The enterprise process model is created according to a set of rules for structuring and use of notation, and can be used for a variety of purposes, such as compliance management, competence management, portfolio management, decision making and performance analysis. There are three levels of abstraction in the enterprise model: The contextual level, the conceptual level and the logical level, including the following interrelated diagrams:

- The top-level diagram as a mandatory navigational diagram visualizing core value chain processes, management processes, and support processes, capturing what they in Statoil term the contextual level. This is similar to what others have termed a process map [13].
- The navigation diagram(s) are optional diagrams to support more tailored access to the processes than the top-level diagram.
- Model diagram: Is a mandatory diagram that visualizes the model of one process area in the organization.
- Process navigation diagram is an optional model for navigational support on the conceptual level.
- Workflow diagram - BPMN models [23] on the logical levels.

When designing diagrams in the enterprise model, requirements in TR0002 - Enterprise structure and standard notation [25] shall be met. We will look at these in more detail in the next section as they map to the levels of SEQUAL, with focus on the guidelines for development of workflow models on the logical level.

4   Development of the Understanding of Quality of Models in Statoil

As indicated in the introduction, modelling has been used for a number of years in Statoil. The requirements for modelling to achieve a balance of syntactic, semantic and pragmatic quality has through this period evolved based on concrete needs identified through the quality cycle described above. Thus, although we here in particular look upon the current requirements (Version 3, valid from Dec. 5 2013) [25] we also look on the development, in particular relative to version 1 of the requirements, that was made available Feb. 12 2009[26]. Although the levels of syntactic, semantic, and pragmatic quality are emphasized, the existing requirements are not structured according to these levels. As we will see, also other levels of SEQUAL are relevant, partly since the original SEQUAL-categories have been divided in sub-areas in the later versions of the framework (e.g. splitting pragmatic quality into empirical quality (for aspects that at least in theory can be fully evaluated objectively by a tool) and pragmatic quality for aspects of understanding that has to take the human interpreter into account). Looking first at the sets of SEQUAL in the light of the case of the Statoil management system, we have the following:

- *M:* The models we look upon here are in particular the workflow-model part of the overall model-framework. Relative to the description of purpose of modelling in Section 2 the models are meant to be as-is models, to support communication on the current process, manual activation (i.e. supporting human action in the organization according to the models), and checking of compliance (area 4: quality assurance).
- *G:* Whereas the general requirements for the quality system was described in Section 3, five main more concrete usage areas are listed as:

1. Compliance management: To monitor and control that the way of working is compliant with the standards set for the way to work. This enables producing predictable output from work.
2. Competence management: Document the competency profiles needed to perform tasks, compare required competency profiles with competence represented in the organization, and therefore manage the competency gap.
3. Portfolio management: Gain an overview of the current portfolio of e.g. processes, information systems, and technologies. This gives opportunities for analyzing whether the existing portfolio will meet future needs, and to plan the roadmap to get from the current to the future portfolio.
4. Analysis and decision making: The model and its subsets enables analysis of the relationships between different objects in the models and how changes to one object (e.g. a process) will impact other objects (e.g. the information systems used by that process or relations between different work processes)
5. Performance analysis: Monitoring of these results to get experience and data on the quality. This information can be used to analyze if the way of working produce the best possible result.

Even if several possible purposes are listed, one model always has one primary purpose, with potentially a (set of) secondary purpose. The current primary purpose of the enterprise model is compliance management therefore the priority is given on achieving the right quality of governing documentation models with corresponding governing elements, roles and responsibilities. We notice that two of these goals were not in version 1 of the requirements (competency management and performance analysis). Rather than being an example of 'goal creep' (that models used for one purpose over time is used also for other things not originally envisioned [10]) it is because the models have to be current as-is models (due to focus on compliance). First recently the underlying infrastructure to support competency management and performance analysis has been put in production.

- D: Domain: The work processes in Statoil.
- L: The language for workflow modelling is a subset of BPMN2.0. In the original version of the requirements [26] it was a similar sub-set of BPMN 1.
- A: The target audience comes from the whole company. It is therefore necessary to do a stakeholder analyses to ensure that models have the right abstraction level, complexity, terminology suitable for the target audience.
- K: The relevant explicit knowledge of the actors (A) .
- T: The tool currently used is ARIS. We note that two other tools (APOS and QLM/BPM) were used in version 1 of the requirements, since ARIS was introduced at a later stage.
- I: Relates to how easy it is for the different actors to interpret the data as it can be presented in ARIS.

4.1   Physical Quality

Physical quality relates to if the model is:
- Available to the right people in a physical form (through the ARIS-tool) when needed for interpretation.
- People are able to find the right model (e.g. through navigation and search), knowing if all relevant parts of the model is found.
- Availability of both the current and previous versions of the model.
- Possibility to store relevant meta-data e.g., on purpose and validity (what part of the organization the model is valid for).
- Only available for those that should have access in case of there being security aspects.

Each governing documentation model and governing element shall have only one documented, published, and valid version that is properly numbered. Old versions must be kept available though. There are two types of updates of governing documentation models and other governing elements: regular and minor.

To support the storage and presentation of models, ARIS is used. Some guidelines for how to use ARIS are described (the usage of the different aspects are described under other quality levels as appropriate).

In ARIS, before publishing you shall select the relevant increase option. Only regular update increases trigger the publication workflow mechanism. Once the update is approved the system automatically increases the value and publishes the model or an element with the new version number.

In ARIS the information regarding the deviation handling process shall be given in the field *"Deviation Permit"*. The following options are available:

- Level 1: Owner acceptance and line manager approval required
- Level 2: Line manager approval required

The descriptive field *„Validity"* is used to provide information about who the model applies to, using a validity register. The validity register is used to store and maintain a list of locations and organizational entities.

The purpose of the governing documentation model shall be represented by the *"Purpose"* attribute in work process model and basic document model

4.2   Empirical Quality

We here focus on naming and language conventions described in [25]. Few concrete guidelines for graph layout are provided in the Statoil requirements.

General Naming Conventions: To ensure a common naming practice across the management system, one shall use names according to the following set of rules:

- Names on symbols and expressions shall be formulated in singular form.
- Avoid names with more than four words if possible.
- A name shall not be a detailed description.
- The first letter in the first word of a symbol name shall be in upper case. All other letters shall be in lower case.
- Proper names shall start with upper case letters.
- If the same concept has several alternative names, the Statoil official name shall be used in the models. The other names are synonyms and can be presented as such if suitable for the business.
- Abbreviations should be avoided.
- Avoid names starting with: 'receive', 'send', 'manage', and 'process', as they do not reflect value added.

In documents with additional information there are also guidelines on the language. Whereas one in [6] mainly mention the use of readability indexes as a technique here, the Statoil guidelines mention a broader set of guidelines.

- Address the reader - write rather 'When you submit...' than 'When someone submits...'.
- Use words and phrasings familiar to all users - e.g. 'present' rather than 'prevailing'.
- Ensure that content is sufficiently explained.
- Mindfully use the word "focus" - rather than write 'The purpose of this information is to focus on safety' write 'The purpose of this information is to highlight safety'.

- Apply negative confirmation. When the reader expect to find content in the text, but no content exist, apply negative conformation by using 'not applicable' or 'none'.
- Use active sentences - write 'The process owner representatives handle improvement suggestions' rather than 'Improvement suggestions are handled in the Process Owner dimension'.
- Use verbs (do not use heavy nouns) - write' when the role actor complied with the specific requirement....' rather than' When there has not been a deviation to the specific requirement by the role actor...'.
- Organize your message content. Extract information by using verbs and pronouns. Divide information into suitably sized pieces and use periods wherever possible (cf. readability index). Postpone restrictions and additions to the next sentence.
- Use lists where possible.

Process role name shall consist of following elements:

- Use process role name that is qualified against the RACI-principle (Responsible, Accountable, Consulted, Informed).
- Write competence or focus area as a free text.

The name of a work process role must be a noun in the singular form or an expression in the singular form starting with a noun or an adjective. The process role name shall be written in full, no abbreviations shall be used. The process role name shall contain no organization units or terms indicating organization of tasks or services. The process role can exist only once within one work process.

In addition to its name, a process role is characterized through its role description and competence requirements, which represent more detailed description of the competency profile. Process roles are represented in the workflow diagram through a lane. The lane shall have as minimum the identifier attribute. The identifier is necessary when linking the role to one or more actors.

The role description and competence requirements of specific process role are described and visualized through an attribute in a form of descriptive text connected to the lane. From earlier work, we know that the lane-concept in BPMN is overloaded [21], thus having detailed guidelines for how to use this is very important.

Responsibilities represented by specific process role are carried out by an actor.

An actor is an object in the organizational structure. It is used to group positions in order to ease assignment of process roles to persons. One process role can be linked to one or more actors. Assignment of two or more process roles to the same actor in the same work process has to be carefully evaluated. Actor name indicates organizational assignment, operated asset type and type of operation.

Some additional naming conventions are

- Task: You shall define the title of a task as 'verb imperative noun', where the verb reflects the activity performed in order to add value to an asset. The noun shall reflect the asset.
- Start event: The title is a noun reflecting the asset and a verb past particle that reflect the activity performed in order to add value to the asset.
- End event: The label follows the same structure as a start event.

- Diverging exclusive gateway: The title consists of 2 parts. A term 'control' (or a similar term e.g. check, verify, evaluate, clarify) and a noun that reflects the object submitted to control.
- Converging exclusive gateway. No label .
- A sequence flow can be given a title that describes the flow between a source and a target. It is mandatory to add a title after a diverging exclusive gateway, which should be the adjective reflecting the result of the control. If possible the text shall be placed over the flow close to the arrow exit.
- Data: The title is a noun/noun expression in singular.

4.3   Syntactic Quality

Diagrams (used for work process model and document model) shall be designed in accordance with the requirements and symbols table available in the requirements. A subset of BPMN is used, following mostly the BPMN visual notation. This is similar to the analytical subset of BPMN [23], although not having support of intermediate events (this was supported in earlier versions of the standard, also we see that the use of the different concepts is supported with more detailed guidelines in the current version of the requirements). In addition some extensions to standard BPMN are included, and a number of specific requirements are introduced.

- Task: A task symbol represents what actors do as "individuals" in their process roles and thus shall be limited to a specific lane only. Tasks can be optional (dotted border). You shall not connect any governing elements classified as requirement to an optional task. A task can be collapsed, i.e. a decomposition as a separate workflow diagram can exist with the same title as the collapsed task. One should not introduce new roles in a decomposition. The sequence flow inputs to and outputs from the collapsed sub-process workflow diagram shall match start events and end events of the sub-process workflow diagram.
- Call task, to be able to reuse sub-tasks between different process models can be defined indicating this with a special border.
- A collaborative activity is a group of activities executed across lanes. These activities should not be sequenced in time or have other dependencies. Note that this is a particular extension to BPMN which is arguably poor at depicting (multiparty) collaborations [1]. The name of the collaboration activity symbol shall be unique and you shall not name the collaboration activity with names that have been used in the tasks framed by the collaboration activity symbol. Each of the tasks framed by a collaboration activity symbol must have a unique title clarifying different type of activities performed by different roles. You shall not place an optional task, a call task or a sub-process within a collaboration activity.
- Start event: Describe the state of the asset that triggers work. You shall not connect any governing elements to an event as no assigned person will be accountable for complying with them. An event shall be placed inside a lane.
- End event describe the state when terminating the workflow.
- Parallel gateway. Visualize the parallel divergence and convergence. It can split the flow into two or more parallel flows. "Event", "Exclusive gateway" or an activity

related symbol can be used as preceding or resulting symbols of the parallel gateway symbol. It is not allowed to leave split parallel flows not merged again in the same work process.

- Diverging exclusive gateway. Indicate a choice of path in the workflow. Event, any type of gateway or an activity related symbol can be used before resulting symbols of the exclusive gateway symbol. Each exclusive flow may have different end events.
- Converging exclusive gateway. Match a diverging exclusive gateway.
- Sequence flow: Sequence flows to and from collaboration activities are connected to and from the same task within that collaboration activity. The flow is connected to and from the task performed by the role that is responsible for the output of the collaboration activity. You shall not use more than one sequence flow arrow from an activity. You shall not connect sequence flows to an optional task.
- Data: Used to describe a physical collection of information. Data association: To link data to the rest of the model.
- Association: To link text annotations together with other symbols.
- Lane: Represent a process role.
- Presence of requirement: A Statoil-specific symbol being a triangle with an exclamation mark to show the presence of one or more governing elements classified as requirements. Symbols representing presence of requirements or information shall be placed at the lower right corner of an activity related symbol. Any activity symbol and gateway symbol except a collapsed activity can have requirements linked to them.
- Presence of information: Use to show presence of one or more governing elements classified as information.

4.4   Semantic Quality

How the model represents the real world, it is a model of. Any model is an abstraction of the real world for a given purpose [24] and can never be a complete representation of the world. The semantic quality of the model is based on how well the model reflects the real world in light of the goal of the model.

The content of a governing element shall explain scope, adhere to the purpose and be described with necessary level of details. Special rules apply for describing the content of a key control. This description shall include:

- Control activity
- Actions in case of deviations
- Audit trail
- Key control characteristics

Process role represents a method of grouping of activities and decision gates according to responsibility and competence within a work process. The purpose of process role is to:

- Secure necessary segregation of duties
- Achieve efficient recognition and allocation of the competence in the work process

It is important that the end-users easily recognize the process role names. Process role is organization and location independent and helps different process users to better relate to their work processes and it is indicating which activities are performed by the role itself. The categorization of process roles have been established to secure necessary segregation of duties. Categorization is based on the RACI (Responsible-Accountable-Consulted- Informed) principle as described above.

4.5   Pragmatic Quality

A number of the guidelines listed under empirical and syntactic quality above are made to support the development of understandable models. In addition it is important to be clear on the intention of the model. Each governing documentation model shall as a minimum have a defined purpose that includes:

- Risk – a description of the risk that the model mitigates.
- Objective – a description of the intended result (output).
- Target group – the main end-users of the process and the main users of the result.

4.6   Social Quality

Each governing documentation model and governing element shall have a documented validity (i.e. organizational area where it applies). There are 2 validity dimensions: location and organization. The location validity is based on geography. The organizational validity is based on business area. The following rules apply when defining validity:

- If validity is set for a specific organizational entity then location validity is by default unspecified (covers all locations)
- If validity is set for specific location then organizational validity by default remains unspecified (covers all organizational entities)

Note that validity indicates who needs to agree on the model. The deviation attribute is used to document the deviation approval method of the governing documentation model, its workflows or governing element categorized as requirement.

Each governing documentation model and governing element shall have documented one single owner and minimum one owner representative. The ownership attribute is used to identify who is responsible for the right quality of a model or element attributes, references, links as well as to enable deviations and improvement proposals handling process, and thus who has the last say when not all agree.

4.7   Deontic Quality

As discussed in Section 3, the main goal of the models is to fulfil the goals of the quality systems which are:

1. Contributing to safe, reliable and efficient operations and enabling compliance with external and internal requirements.

2. Helping the company incorporating their values, people and leadership principles into everything they do.
3. Supporting business performance through high-quality decision-making, fast and precise execution and continuous learning.

A straightforward relation between the different goals of modelling, different quality aspects and the goals of the quality systems above are not explicitly written in the requirements. Neither are the cost/benefit tradeoffs between effort used and sufficient quality achieved. As for quality trade-off, it is clearly stated already in [26] that pragmatic quality is the most important whereas syntactic and semantic quality is primarily a mean to achieve pragmatic quality.

5   Final Discussion and Further Work

The quality system of Statoil is developed supporting in particular compliance to reduce risk, an area where large improvements have been observed over the last decade. Quality maturity can be claimed to be high, with a balanced concern of syntactic, semantic and pragmatic (including empirical) quality. When mapping the guidelines for modelling to the current SEQUAL framework, we find relevant aspects on all areas, not only on the core syntactic, semantic and pragmatic levels. Most of the aspects related to in the Statoil-guidelines as pragmatic are in current SEQUAL-terms rather to be classified as empirical, supporting the achievement of understanding of the model in general. The paper illustrates that much more detailed guidelines are devised on especially the physical (linked to the particular modelling environment used), empirical and syntactic level than what is found in generic overviews of quality of business process models [7, 14]. On the other hand, we observe that links of the quality features to the main goal of the models and trade-off as for resource usage vs. model quality (deontic quality) is discussed in less detail.

A recent evaluation of the models also points to potentials for improvements: During the end of 2013 and the beginning of 2014, a large-scale user survey was conducted in Statoil in order to identify the most prominent challenges related to the management system and governing documentation. 4828 employees took part in the survey, which was about half of those invited. The survey indicated opportunities for improvements on the physical level (related to finding all relevant models), empirical level (relative to the use of abbreviations), semantic level (supporting efficient feedback and learning from users of the model for model evolution), pragmatic level (lack of clarity and being aware of the intention of the model), social level (through leadership support for using the model), and deontic level (by supporting the full range of goals of the organization, not only safety and reliability).

As this is a case study, there are challenges relative to threat to validity of the results. Since there is one main informant (co-writer of the paper) one can claim some limitations relative to internal validity, as representatives of all involved roles have not been interviewed thoroughly. As for descriptive validity (what happened in specific situations) the close day to day interaction with the development of the quality system by one of the researchers gives us confidence on the accuracy here. As for the interpretive validity (what it means to the people involved) we have again in-depth, accounts from central people in main roles. The same can be said on evaluative validity (judgements of the worth and value of actions and meaning). That we find many results that fit the categories of existing theoretical frameworks (SEQUAL) gives us confidence on the theoretical validity of the results. A main issue as with all case studies is the external validity i.e. the generalizability of the results.

In future work, we will follow how the results from the assessment can be addressed by updating the requirements and models, and in particular

- Do changes to the Management System have a measurable effect on efficient model use, e.g. as for higher achievement of the overall goals such as less incidents due to non-compliance?
- How to balance the different types of model quality to get the best support of the organizational goals of modelling as defined in section 3.

Also doing similar case studies in other organization would be very interesting.

References

1. Aagesen, G., Krogstie, J.: Analysis and design of business processes using BPMN. In: vom Brocke, J., Rosemann, M. (eds.) Handbook on Business Process Management. Springer (2010)
2. van Bommel, P., Hoppenbrouwers, S.J.B.A., Proper, H.A., van der Weide, T.: QOMO: A modeling process quality framework based on SEQUAL. In: Proceedings of EMMSAD (2007)
3. Hella, L., Krogstie, J.: A Structured Evaluation to Assess the Reusability of Models of User Profiles. Paper presented at the EMMSAD Hammamet, Tunis, 7-8/6 (2010)
4. Krogstie, J.: Using Quality Function Deployment in Software Requirements Specification. Paper presented at the Fifth International Workshop on Requirements Engineering: Foundations for Software Quality (REFSQ 1999), Heidelberg, Germany, June 14-15 (1999)
5. Krogstie, J.: Integrated Goal, Data and Process Modeling: From TEMPORA to Model-Generated Work-Places. In: Johannesson, P., Søderstrøm, E. (eds.) Information Systems Engineering From Data Analysis to Process Networks, pp. 43–65. IGI (2008)
6. Krogstie, J.: Model-based development and evolution of information systems: A quality approach. Springer, London (2012)
7. Krogstie, J.: Quality of business process models. In: Sandkuhl, K., Seigerroth, U., Stirna, J. (eds.) PoEM 2012. LNBIP, vol. 134, pp. 76–90. Springer, Heidelberg (2012)
8. Krogstie, J.: Quality of Conceptual Data Models. In: Proceedings 14th ICISO, Stockholm, Sweden (2013)
9. Krogstie, J., Arnesen, S.: Assessing Enterprise Modeling Languages using a Generic Quality Framework. In: Krogstie, J., Siau, K., Halpin, T. (eds.) Information Modeling Methods and Method-ologies. Idea Group Publishing (2004)
10. Krogstie, J., Dalberg, V., Jensen, S.M.: Process modeling value framework. In: Manolopoulos, Y., Filipe, J., Constantopoulos, P., Cordeiro, J. (eds.) Selected papers from 8th International Conference, ICEIS 2006, pp. 309–321. Springer, Paphos (2008)
11. Krogstie, J., Jørgensen, H.D.: Quality of Interactive Models. In: Olivé, À., Yoshikawa, M., Yu, E.S.K. (eds.) ER 2003. LNCS, vol. 2784, pp. 351–363. Springer, Heidelberg (2003)

12. Lindland, O.I., Sindre, G., Sølvberg, A.: Understanding Quality in Conceptual Modelling. IEEE Software 11(2), 42–49 (1994)
13. Malinova, M., Leopold, H., Mendling, J.: A Meta-Model for Process Map Design. In: CAiSE Forum 2014, Thessaloniki, Greece, June 16-20 (2014)
14. Mendling, J., Reijers, H.A., van der Aalst, W.M.P.: Seven Process Modeling Guidelines (7PMG). Information and Software Technology (IST) 52(2), 127–136 (2010)
15. Moody, D.L., Shanks, G.G.: What Makes a Good Data Model? Evaluating the Quality of Entity Relationship Models. In: Loucopoulos, P. (ed.) ER 1994. LNCS, vol. 881, pp. 94–111. Springer, Heidelberg (1994)
16. Moody, D.L.: Theorethical and practical issues in evaluating the quality of concep tual models: Current state and future directions. Data and Knowledge Engineering 55, 243–276 (2005)
17. Nelson, H.J., Poels, G., Genero, M., Piattini, M.: A conceptual modeling quality framework. Software Quality Journal 20, 201–228 (2012)
18. Nossum, A., Krogstie, J.: Integrated Quality of Models and Quality of Maps. In: Halpin, T., Krogstie, J., Nurcan, S., Proper, E., Schmidt, R., Soffer, P., Ukor, R. (eds.) Enterprise, Business-Process and Information Systems Modeling. LNBIP, vol. 29, pp. 264–276. Springer, Heidelberg (2009)
19. Nysetvold, A.G., Krogstie, J.: Assessing Business Process Modeling Languages Using a Generic Quality Framework. In: Siau, K. (ed.) Advanced Topics in Database Research, vol. 5, pp. 79–93. Idea Group, Hershey (2006)
20. Price, R., Shanks, G.: A semiotic information quality framework: Development and comparative analysis. Journal of Information Technology 20(2), 88–102 (2005)
21. Recker, J., Rosemann, M., Krogstie, J.: Ontology- versus pattern-based evaluation of process modeling language: A comparison. Communications of the Association for Information Systems 20, 774–799 (2007)
22. Schuette, R., Rotthowe, T.: The guidelines of modeling - an approach to enhance the quality in information models. In: Ling, T.-W., Ram, S., Li Lee, M. (eds.) ER 1998. LNCS, vol. 1507, pp. 240–254. Springer, Heidelberg (1998)
23. Silver, B.: BPMN Method and Style. Cody-Cassidy Press (2012)
24. Stachowiak, H.: Allgemeine Modelltheorie. Springer, Wien (1973)
25. Statoil: TR0002 Enterprise Structure and Standard Notation. version 3 (2013)
26. Statoil: TR0002 Enterprise Structure and Standard Notation. version 1 (2009)
27. Statoil: Statoilboken (2014),
    http://www.statoil.com/no/About/TheStatoilBook/Downloads/Sta
    toil-Boken.pdf
28. Statoil FR20 Management System (2014)
29. Wesenberg, H., Landre, E.: Using the corporate Management System to communicate architecture, Presentation SATURN 2011, San Francisco, California (May 2011),
    http://www.sei.cmu.edu/saturn/2011/abstracts-
    presentations.cfm#25
30. Wesenberg, H.: Enterprise modeling in an agile world. In: Johannesson, P., Krogstie, J., Opdahl, A.L. (eds.) PoEM 2011. LNBIP, vol. 92, pp. 126–130. Springer, Heidelberg (2011)

Value-Chain Discovery from Business Process Models

Anis Boubaker, Dhouha Cherif, Abderrahmane Leshob, and Hafedh Mili

University of Quebec at Montreal - LATECE Laboratory

Abstract. Companies model their business processes either for documentation, analysis, re-engineering or automation purposes; usually using normalized *business process modeling* languages such as EPC or BPMN. Although these models explain *how* the processes should be performed and by *whom*, they abstract away their business rationale *(i.e. what* is offered and *why). Business modeling* aims to answer the latter and different frameworks have been proposed to express the process in terms of value-chains. Ensuring alignment between both of these views manually is error prone and labor intensive. In this paper, we present a novel approach to derive a value-chain - expressed in REA - from a business process model expressed in BPMN. At the heart of our approach and our main contribution lies a set of nine general business patterns we have defined and classified as structural and behavioral patterns.

1 Introduction

The ubiquity of business processes (BPs) in nowadays corporations raises them as first class citizens by being considered corporate assets and their need for ongoing management has been recognized. BPs are captured by business process models (BPMs) to depict the set of actions that should be carried out by a given BP, in what order they should be performed and by whom. Languages such as EPC[21] or BPMN[17] define both a set of concepts and a graphical representation convention to model business processes. Therefore the focus of a BPM is on the operational and dynamic aspects of the process (i.e. *How* are we doing it? and *Who* is doing it?). However, the business intent - expressing the *why*'s of the activities we perform - is not explicitly modeled and that is where *business modeling* comes in handy.

A business model (BM) is a conceptualization of the BP using pure business terms such as economic resources, economic agents and value adding activities and their relationships. It may take the form of a resource centric view of the process - called a *value-chain* - that exhibits the sequence of economic resource acquisitions and transformations. A value-chain let us answer questions such as (1) how is the company using up its economic resources? and (2) why are these resources consumed or relinquished? There are three main frameworks widely recognized in the literature, namely REA[14], e^3value[9] and BMO[18].

Authors have argued on the necessity of not overlooking the business rationale in BPM projects (e.g. [20,10]). Indeed, business process management is

U. Frank et al. (Eds.): PoEM 2014, LNBIP 197, pp. 26–41, 2014.

an ongoing iterative process[23] and we should ensure that the evolving business processes do not deviate from higher level business objectives. Ensuring the alignment between BMs and BPMs can be achieved in one of three ways: (1) manually, (2) by reducing both views to a common view and comparing them (e.g. see [19]), or (3) by deriving one view from the other. The latter has only been considered going from a BM to generate a BPM ([8,25,1]). The other way around had yet to be explored and this work intends to fill this gap.

Apart from business process re-engineering, business models are useful during the analysis phases of various IT projects. For example, in architectural design, the TOGAF® framework recommends the use of value-chain diagrams in its Phase A (Architecture Vision) to "quickly on-board and align stakeholders for a particular change initiative, so that all participants understand the high-level functional and organizational context of the architecture engagement"[22, pp.382]. Furthermore, in the business activity monitoring field (BAM) or business process mining, knowledge about the business rationale can be used for real-time detection or *a posteriori* diagnosis of deviances from the business strategic goals (e.g. [13]). Business models can also help in automatic BP generation approaches. In particular, our team used a value centric view of the BP in two research projects. In the first project, we used value models to perform a question based BP specialization[16]. In the second project, we focused on the automatic generation of compensation processes of a BP (i.e. reversing the effects of a running process that needs to be aborted) [4,5]. We argued that compensation is a business problem - rather than technical - and therefore must be tackled from a business standpoint[15]. Hence, we used the value-chain of the BP as an input in order to infer compensation processes.

In this work, we propose a four-steps approach that aims to generate a value-chain expressed in REA[14] from a BPM expressed in BPMN. The problem is not trivial considering the large conceptual distance between both views[10]. Hence our purpose is to infer business intensions that are not explicit in the original BPM. We tackle this by relying on a set of structural and behavioral patterns we have identified through the analysis of a sample of BP models.

The remainder of this paper is organized as follows. In Section 2, we briefly present business modeling and the REA ontology. In Section 3 we review some existing related works then we give a high-level overview of our approach in Section 4. Sections 5 and 6 focus on the inference of REA concepts and REA economic processes based on five structural and three behavioral patterns we will introduce. The validation of our approach will be presented and discussed in Section 7, before concluding in Section 8.

2   Business Modeling - The REA Ontology

A business model is an abstraction of the BP focusing on the business rationale, specifically on how the company intends to create added value through it's *value-chain*. Different ontologies have been proposed to perform value-chain modeling ([18,9,14]). In this paper, we chose arbitrarily the Resource-Event-Agent (REA) that was introduced by McCarthy in an early work and has been getting wider attention recently from the community [14]. However, our approach could be applied to any of the above mentioned ontologies as the concepts used in our approach are shared among them [2].

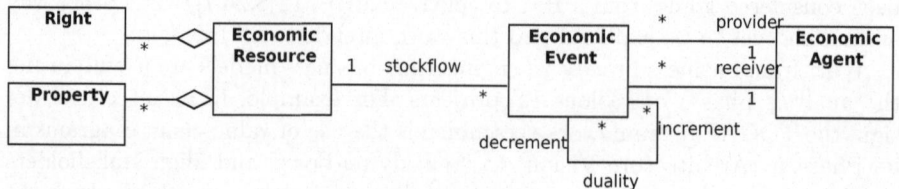

Fig. 1. REA metamodel

McCarthy proposed the REA framework as a way of capturing the economic phenomena that needed to be accounted, from an *accounting* perspective. In REA, an enterprise can increase or decrease the value of its resources through either *exchanges* or *conversions*[11]. An **exchange** is a process in which an enterprise receives economic resources from external economic agents, and provides other resources in return. A **conversion** is a process in which an enterprise uses or consumes resources in order to produce new or modified resources.

Figure 1 shows the basic REA metamodel. **Economic resources** are objects that are scarce, have utility, and are under the control of an enterprise[14]. In an exchange, a resource is perceived as a set of **rights** (e.g.: ownership, usage, etc.) being exchanged whereas, in a conversion, it is defined by the set of **properties** (i.e. features contributing to resource's overall value) being altered. **Economic events** are defined as "a class of phenomena which reflect changes in scarce means resulting from production, exchange, consumption, and distribution"[26]. An *economic event* represents either an *increment* or a *decrement* in the value of economic resources. An **Economic Agent** is an individual or an organization capable of having control over economic resources, and transferring or receiving that control to or from other individuals or organizations [11]. The **duality relationship** links increment events to decrement events. The set of events related by a duality relationship form a so-called **REA process**[1].

In the remainder of this paper, we will use an abbreviated graphical modeling notation of REA processes. Figure 2 shows the legend of our notation.

3   Related Works

Generally speaking, our work lies within the scope of model transformations, and more specifically, in reverse-engineering model transformations[6]. Reverse engineering is defined as "the process of analyzing a subject system to (i) identify the

---

[1] Note that the term "process" here do not necessarily mean the entire business process. In fact, a given business process may be decomposed into several REA processes.

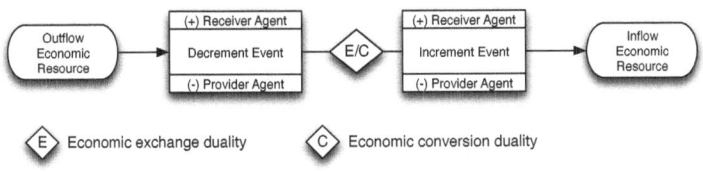

Fig. 2. REA abbreviated notation

system's components and their interrelationships and (ii) create representations of the system in another form or at a higher level of abstraction"[7]. Indeed, our work seeks to transform an operational representation of a BP into a business view of the same BP. Although to the best of our knowledge this particular problem did not draw authors attention yet, some works were interested in BPM and BM transformations that we can classify into two classes.

The first focused on transforming BMs into BPMs. Generally, the proposed approaches followed a common transformation schema by (1) extending the BM with business process operational aspects and (2) inferring concrete business process activities and orchestration relying on a pattern library. They varied on the choice of abstraction to extend the BM and their automation degree. Andersson et al. focused on making explicit in the BM the transfers of resource custodies and evidence documents [1]. Wieringa et al. tackled the same problem by relying on what they call *physical delivery models*[25]. Their claim is that while value models depict value streams between BP actors, the actual delivery of the value objects does not necessarily follow the same path. More recently, Fatemi et al. analyzed the interactions between the business actors to generate a BPMN model from an e³value model[8]. They proposed a taxonomy of interactions that include six classes and involve the analyst to classify the interactions and to specify who initiates each interaction. Our approach globally follows the same schema but varies (1) in the direction of the transformation (i.e. BPM into BM) and thus the information needed to extend the model, (2) in the generality of our patterns and (3) in the degree of automation and analyst involvement required.

The second class is about ensuring the alignment of BMs and BPMs. Pijpers et al. [19] proposed a method based on a reduction of both models to a common metamodel with two main concepts: *business units* and so-called *common value objects*. They model the relationship between these concepts as a set of transfers of common value objects to/from business units. Although this approach can give an approximation of the alignment between both views (as mentioned by the authors, false negatives could be observed), we cannot use this approach to derive a value model from a BPM. Indeed, the reduced model disregards the relationships between value transfers (i.e. dualities in REA) that we believe is the core concept of a value model expressing the intents behind these transfers. Other approaches to ensure view alignment that do not involve model transformation (e.g. [3]) were not reviewed. In the next section, we provide a high level view of our approach.

4   Approach Overview

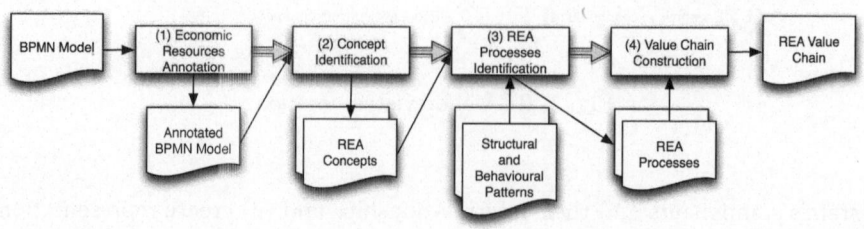

Fig. 3. Global view of our approach

Going from a dynamic view of the BP (i.e. BPMN) to infer a value centric view conforming to the REA ontology raises three main questions: (1) how to identify REA concepts (i.e. Resources, Events, and Agents) from a BPMN process model?, (2) how to determine and/or infer relationships between these identified concepts? and (3) once we have determined a set of *REA Processes*, how to connect them in order to build a global value-chain of the BP? This paper will focus on answering the first two questions.

Answering the first question involves matching between REA concepts and BPMN constructs. This constitutes the first two steps of our approach and will be discussed in Section 5. Once we have identified the concepts, we need to determine and infer the relationships between them to form a set of *REA Economic Processes*. Some of these relations are explicit from the BPM while others, such as dualities, need to be inferred. In Section 6 we explain how we tackle this problem using a set of structural and behavioral patterns we have identified.

In the last step of our approach, we construct the value-chain by connecting the obtained REA processes relying on a partial order over the set of occurrences of each BP resource. We derive this order from the partial order over BPM activities and the traceability links between the activities and REA economic events. Space limitation prevents us from going into further details about this step in this paper. We illustrate the global view of our approach in fig. 3.

In order to perform preliminary validations of our work and prove its feasibility, we implemented the three last steps by defining our patterns as rules in JBoss Drools rule engine. The rules implemented the transformations from the BPMN2.0 metamodel[2] into our REA metamodel[4] defined using the Eclipse Modeling Framework.

Before going into the details of our approach, in the following subsections we present the hypothesis and assumptions on which we will base our approach. We also present a simple sale-and-delivery example of an e-retailer that we will use as a running example to illustrate our approach.

---

[2] http://www.eclipse.org/bpmn2-modeler/. Last accessed: March 3rd 2014.

4.1   Modeling Assumptions and Hypothesis

First, we assume that the BP collaboration is modeled from the perspective of the entity under study (e.g. a company). Therefore, the BPM must include the private process of the so-called entity whereas only public processes of collaborating partners are needed. We also assume that the provided BPMN model is valid both syntactically and semantically. Syntactic validity refers to the conformance to BPMN specifications[17] and observed best practices [24] while semantic validity means that the model makes general operational and business sense for the entity under study.

Under these assumptions we make two hypothesis on our approach. First our approach will discover at least 80% of the REA processes that could be discovered from the input process (H1). Hence, we want to generate REA value-chains at the lowest granularity level. As we will see in the remainder of this paper, our approach will generate REA processes that are syntactically correct by construction. However we want to ensure semantic correctness and make the hypothesis that these generated REA processes are relevant and consistent with the business process under study with a precision rate of 80% or more (H2). A given REA process is relevant if it describes an economic phenomenon involving economic resources and agents that could be observed in the business process. A relevant REA process is also consistent if it describes correctly the type of phenomenon (i.e. exchange vs conversion) and shows all the economic resources that should be involved from what could be gathered from the BP.

4.2   ABCInc Sale-and-Delivery Example

We will use through this paper a simplified sale-and-delivery BP used by an e-retailer (*ABCInc*) that we have depicted in fig. 4 in BPMN notation. The process starts when a *Customer* gets online and orders books. Then *ABCInc* starts preparing the order by enclosing the products in a box and sticking a label with the shipping address. At the same time, ABCInc's *Bank* debits customer's credit account and ABCInc's account is credited the transaction amount.

Once both of these parallel operations are performed, the products are shipped to the customer by a *Shipping company* who provides ABCInc with a tracking number after picking-up the parcel. ABCInc will in turn send the tracking number to his *Customer*. Once the *Shipping company* delivers the parcel to the *Customer*, it sends ABCInc the delivery confirmation (i.e. customer's signature) and the process ends with a successful result.

5   Identification of REA Concepts

We presented in section 2 the REA ontology and explained its three core concepts: *Resources*, *Events* and *Agents*. In this section, we explain how we identify each of these concepts from a BPMN process model.

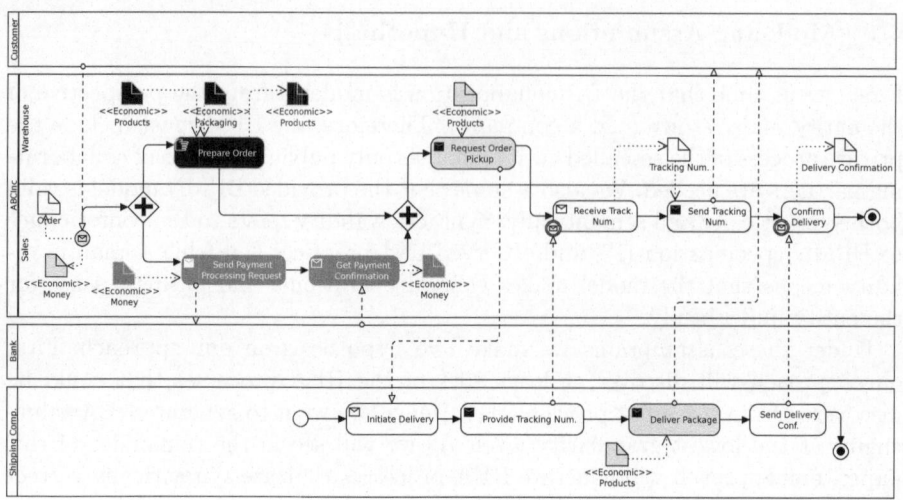

Fig. 4. ABCInc sale-and-delivery simplified (and fictive) example

5.1 Economic Agents

REA Agents are modeled explicitly in a BPMN collaboration as *Participants*. Indeed, BPMN defines participants as "...specific PartnerEntity (e.g., a company) and/or a more general PartnerRole (e.g., a buyer, seller, or manufacturer) that are Participants in a Collaboration..."[17]. External participants are modeled as process *pools* whereas internal participants (e.g. economic units) are represented as *swimlanes* within the pool of the entity under study. In our ABCInc example, ABCInc is the company under study having two internal agents: the *sales department* and the *warehouse*. The *customer*, the *shipping company* and the *bank* are three external agents.

5.2 Economic Resources

Economic resources involved in the BP can be explicitly modeled as objects, called in BPMN terms *Item Aware Elements* and defined as elements that "are subject to store or convey items during process execution"[17]. Item Aware Elements could be either informational or physical and specialize as Data Objects, Data Object Inputs, Data Object Outputs and Data Object References. Hence, this appears to be an appropriate construct to represent economic resources. However, not all Data Objects[3] involved in the BP are economic resources. For example, an order document usually appears in BP models but does not answer the scarcity property of economic resources' definition (see Section 2). Therefore, Data Objects representing economic resources must be clearly distinguished from non economic objects and we propose to stereotype them as "Economic".

---

[3] In the remainder of this paper, we will use the terms DataObject and ItemAwareElement interchangeably.

We do this as the first step of our approach (Step 1, fig. 3). We conjecture that all *Physical Data Objects* should be considered as economic resources and will be stereotyped as such automatically. However, we cannot infer systematically the economic nature of informational *Data Objects*. Therefore, we involve the analyst who is asked to manually stereotype all non-automatically identified economic resources. In fig. 4, we have stereotyped all relevant economic resources.

5.3   Economic Events

As seen in Section 2, economic events are actions producing changes in the economic resources (their rights or properties). Thus, we relate economic events to BPMN activities but we still need to determine, from the set of BPM's activities, which should be considered as economic events. We can intuitively filter out those activities that are not related to an economic resource (i.e. as input or output). However, this is not sufficient as some of the remaining activities may not be economic events. Let's imagine that in our ABCInc BP we wanted to weight the package before shipping. This activity would take the package as an input but will not produce any change neither in package's properties nor rights.

There are two types of economic events: the ones that transfer some resource rights and the ones that alter some resource properties. We infer the first class of events from message sending/receiving activities[4] in the BPMN model (e.g. "Send Process Payment Request" from fig. 4). As BPMN only allows communications between participants through messages, the economic resource sent (resp. received) by a sending (resp. receiving) activity will be it's output (resp. input) economic Data Object (see [17, pp.48]). The second category of events implies activities producing some new resource(s) or a modified version of its input(s). Therefore an economic event will be related to *each* input and *each* output resource of the activity. From our example in fig. 4, we will derive three economic events from the "Prepare order" activity.

6   BPMN to REA Patterns

As seen in the previous section, identifying REA concepts is a straight forward process applying simple rules. However, we cannot determine all concept instances relying solely on these rules. In our example, the "Products" leave ABCInc at some point and end-up being in the possession of the customer. We cannot determine using our rules how the Products' location got changed. There must be an economic event in charge of altering the *location property* but how to determine it? Intuitively we think of the shipping company being responsible of doing the transportation but does it involve any other resource? Another question we might ask is how are these REA concept instances associated? Some associations are explicit in the model as the provider/receiver relationships between agents and economic events or the associations between economic events

---

[4] These activities need to have an input or output economic resource as we ruled out those that do not.

and resources. But what about associations between economic events (i.e. dualities)?

We believe the answer to these question could be inferred as - through the analysis of a set BP collaborations - there seem to be a handful of business collaboration scenarios that we could codify as patterns. In this section we present these patterns classified into two categories: *structural* and *behavioral* patterns. Structural patterns give us a one to one mapping between a portion of the BPMN model and an REA process (or a set thereof). Behavioral patterns, on the other hand, exploit execution semantics of the BPMN model in order to *refine* the inferred REA processes.

Before detecting the patterns, we perform a preliminary step that replaces messages exchanged between *external* participants by two messages: one from the original sender to the company under study, and one from the company to the original receiver. Indeed, as mentioned in 4.1 the BPM should reflect the BP of the company under study and we assume that communications between external participants should be done on behalf of the company.

In the following, we present the structural and behavioral patterns in turn. We illustrate each pattern in its simplest form in fig. 5. However, the reader should note that each pattern may be declined into an infinite set (e.g. involving more resources, different order of activities, etc.).

6.1   Structural Patterns

Conversion Pattern. From our ABCInc example, the "Prepare Order" activity encloses the ordered products in a box on which a shipping label is sticked. Thus we went from a pile of products to a box containing the products that is proper for shipping. This activity along with its input and output economic resources (elements on a black background in fig. 4) constitute what we call a *conversion pattern*. A conversion patterns occurs when an activity creates an added value by consuming and/or using some input economic resources and produces some output resources that are either new resources or an enhanced version of the inputs. In the former the created resource does not appear as an inflow resource whereas in the latter it is part of the input set. A conversion pattern will naturally be translated into an REA conversion process where input economic resources will form the *inflows* of the process and the output resources will form the *outflows*. This pattern is illustrated in fig. 5(a).

Exchange Pattern. ABCInc sends some products to his customer for which it gets a money payment. This "sale" is a typical example of an *exchange pattern*, i.e. one of the participants provides some economic resources in order to gain some other (*different*) economic resources in exchange. An exchange pattern is converted into an REA exchange process having the business events associated to the provided resources as inflows events and the business events related to the economic resources received by the company as outflows. We illustrate this pattern in fig. 5(b).

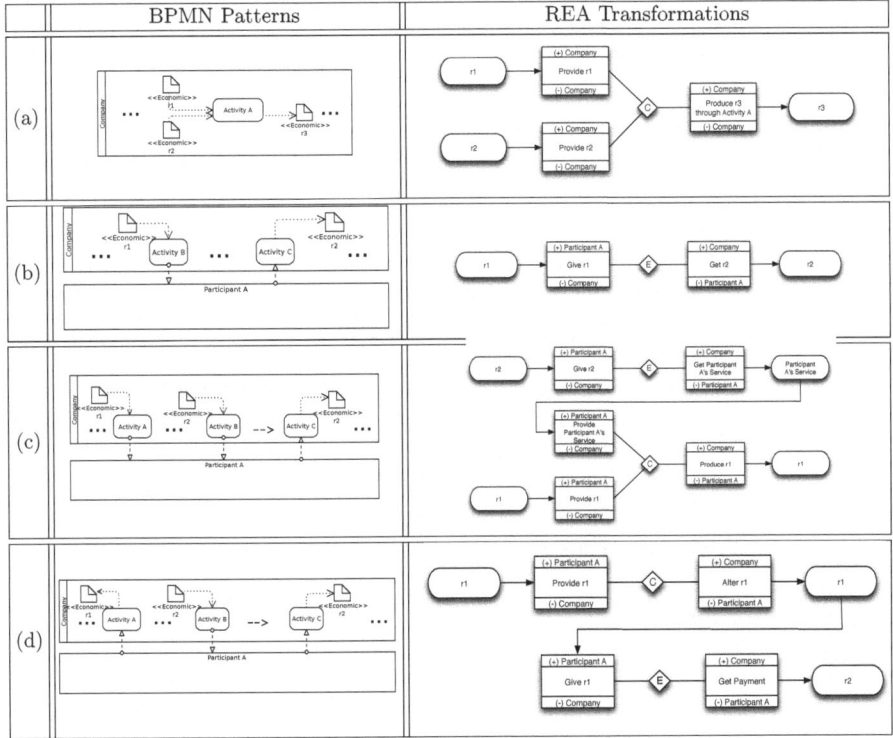

Fig. 5. Four structural patterns: (a) conversion, (b) exchange, (c) outsourcing and (d) renting pattern. (A--→B: A must precede B; A...B: the order is irrelevant).

Outsourcing and Insourcing Patterns. It happens that a company wants to delegate part of its production workflow to an external company. For example, in our ABCInc case, the company relies on a banking institution to transfer the money from customer's bank account into its own. We define an outsourcing as the delegation by a company of part of the value adding process to an external partner. A resource (or a set thereof) is provided to the partner in order to be transformed and received back once done. The partner does the work for a "fee" thus we expect another (different) resource being provided by the company as a payment.

An outsourcing pattern will be transformed into two REA economic processes: an REA conversion process and an REA exchange process [11, pp. 316-318]. In the conversion process the resource is transformed by the partner. The conversion will also consume an intermediate resource we'll call a "Service" resource. This service resource is acquired with the economic resource provided as a payment, thus forming the REA economic exchange. We illustrate the pattern and it's corresponding REA transformation in fig. 5(c).

We call the reciprocal the *insourcing pattern* in which the company alter some resource(s) for the benefit of a partner. However, the corresponding REA transformation will only contain the exchange as, in this case, the private process is known and the resource alteration will be matched as a conversion pattern.

The Renting Pattern. Say we are a car renting company and rent cars to individuals. During the rent period, we lose the *usage* (right) on the rented car and receive a money payment (*ownership*). The payment we receive covers for both our inability to rent the car to someone else as well as the wear-and-tear sustained by the car. Modeling this in REA terms would involve an REA exchange process where the car's usage right is exchanged for the money, and a conversion process expressing the alteration of the car. This is what we call the *renting* pattern (see fig. 5d).

Generally speaking, we assume that when a resource is relinquished and leaves company's control, it will sustain alterations. However, we can envision cases where this is not true, specifically when the lent resource is non-tangible. Consider for example a loan process: the money lent and recovered will not sustain any alteration. In such cases, the REA conversion in the transformation model on fig. 5(d) will have no effect.

6.2   Behavioral Patterns

The patterns presented above showed how to translate portions of a BPMN model into a set of REA processes relying solely on structural aspects. Conversely, behavioral patterns exploit execution semantics in order to *refine* the REA processes obtained from the structural patterns. Therefore, behavioral patterns are not self sufficient and must be combined with a structural pattern.

For example, consider the case where a customer provides the company with the raw material in order to perform some production and the money payment for the service and, once done, the company gives back the finished good. In such a scenario, our *Exchange Pattern* will be matched (money and raw material exchanged for finished goods). However, the raw material should not be part of the exchange as the company do not acquire the ownership on the raw material, but will be consumed by the conversion process that produces the finished good. This is what we call the *resource provisioning pattern*. We have identified three more behavioral patterns: *independent branches, internal responsibility* and *resource dependency*. Due to space limitations, these patterns will be presented more thoroughly in an extended version of this paper.

6.3   Patterns Detection and Transformation

As we mentioned, behavioral patterns are meant to be combined with structural patterns. Therefore structural patterns along with different allowed combinations of structural patterns and behavioral patterns form an extended set of self-sustaining patterns, each with a corresponding REA transformation. This extended set forms a rule base in which each rule have the BPMN pattern as its left-hand side and the corresponding REA transformation as its right-hand side.

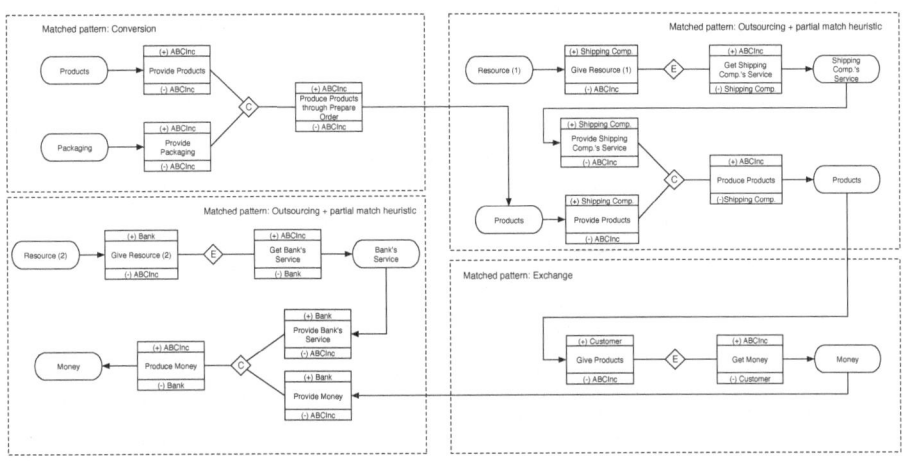

Fig. 6. Final result of our approach applied on the ABCInc example from fig. 4

However, in order to perform the transformation in a rule-based system, we first need to address two problems.

The first problem concerns the non-confluence of our rules[12]. We can easily see that our rules are not confluent if we consider, for example, the exchange and the outsourcing patterns. In a sense, the outsourcing patterns "embeds" an exchange. Thus, both rules could fire, each producing a different transformation. To address this problem, we elected to define the order in which the rules should be fired. We conjecture that more specific rules should have precedence over less specific rules. A rule A is more specific then a rule B if (1) matching A implies matching B (i.e. A embeds B), or if (2) both are the same structural pattern but A has more combined dynamic patterns.

The second issue is the partial matches of the BPMN patterns. The dark greyed portion of fig. 4 concerns the handling of *Money* transfer by the *Bank* and should match an outsourcing pattern, but a resource given by *ABCInc* to the *Bank* is missing in the BP (i.e. the service fees). Indeed, a given BP does not live in isolation and paying *Bank*'s fees could be handled by a separate account-receivable BP. However, we still need to account for the missing resource as it is part of the value-chain that supports the BP. Our solution to this problem is based on an heuristic that extends the original BPMN model by adding an anonymous resource flowing to/from the company to/from each of the partici-pants. Then the rules are fired and the extension that produces the more specific pattern match is selected. If two equally specific rules are matched, we ask the analyst to resolve the conflict.

We present in fig. 6 the resulting REA model generated by our implementation after applying our approach on the *ABCInc* case.

7 Validation

We performed an experiment on a population of eight (8) graduate students from our laboratory with a research focus on electronic commerce. While all of our participants knew how to read and interpret either a BPMN model or an UML activity diagram, none of them knew about business modeling.

The experiment was divided into two phases. The first was a two hours session where the experimenter presented the REA ontology to the participants, it's objectives and modeling syntax. Following the presentation, participants were asked, as an exercise, to model the REA transformation of the *ABCInc* example presented in fig. 4. The session was concluded by presenting to the participants three BPMN models on which the experiment will be performed: a software engineering process (P1), a travel booking process (P2) and a manufacturing process (P3). At the end of the session, we asked each participant to annotate the three models by identifying economic resources from *Data Objects*. In between the two sessions, participants were asked to model the REA transformations of each of the three BPMN models relying on their intuition and understanding of the process. They were given two instructions: (1) to respect the REA modeling syntax, and (2) to model to the lowest granularity level permitted by the provided BPMN model (i.e. including as much REA processes as possible).

The second session took place a week later as one-on-one interviews. They were presented with the automatically generated transformations, with respect to their provided annotations, and were asked to answer the following questions for *each* REA process from the generated value models:

- (Q1) Relevancy: Should the REA process be part of the value-chain?
- (Q2) Consistency: If relevant, does the REA process contains any semantic inconsistencies with respect to the BP?
- (Q3) Global consistency: If relevant, is the REA process' placement within the value-chain and its relationships with other REA processes coherent?

Then they were given the opportunity to modify their annotations (e.g. by adding an economic resource they overlooked in the first session). We generated a new REA transformation according to the new annotated model and the participants were asked, for each REA process from the new generated model, to answer the previous questions, as well as:

- (Q4) Could you match the REA process to an REA process from your manual transformation?

7.1 Results

Table 1 presents the compiled results for each BPMN model of our experiment (P1, P2 and P3). The table is divided into three sections. The first two sections are related to the generated value-chains (1) from the original annotations and (2) after the annotations were revised. In each section, we compiled the average count of the answers to each of the questions presented in the previous subsection.

Table 1. Experimental results

| Process | Automatic Transformation | | | | | | | | Manual Transformation | | P | R |
| | Original annotations | | | | Revised annotations | | | | | | | |
	Gen	Q1	Q2	Q3	Gen	Q1	Q2	Q3	Man	Q4		
P1	12.00	11.87	11.62	10.12	12.62	12.62	12.25	12.62	8.25	7.81	0.97	0.95
P2	3.12	3.00	2.75	2.50	4.50	4.37	4.37	4.37	4.00	3.37	0.97	0.84
P3	5.37	5.37	5.00	4.75	5.87	5.87	5.37	5.87	4.37	4.00	0.91	0.91
All	6.83	6.75	6.46	5.79	7.66	7.62	7.33	7.62	5.54	5.06	0.96	0.91

The third section shows the average number of REA processes obtained from participants' manual transformations (#Man). Column Q4 shows the average REA processes from the manual transformations that were matched to an REA process in the generated model. The last line of the table gives the average values per process and per participant.

From these results we computed the precision (P) and recall (R) of automatic transformations after annotations were revised as $P = \frac{Q2}{Gen}$ and $R = \frac{Q4}{Man}$.

7.2   Validity Threats

The major threat to the validity of our experiment lies in the limited expertise of our subjects that we mitigated by providing a two hours lecture on business modeling and divided the experiment into two sessions, giving them a hands-on experience in-between sessions. We also recognize that the small number of BPs on which we tested our approach threatens its generalizability. While we believe that the results provide a weight of evidence in support to our hypothesis, a more extensive validation involving more business processes has still to be done.

7.3   Discussion

As presented in table 1, our approach permitted to recall 91% of the REA processes identified by our study participants. Furthermore, we generated a total of 183 REA processes deemed relevant out of 133 discovered manually. This supports our hypothesis of discovering all the REA processes that could be detected from the given annotated BPM (H1). Our results also show that 96% of the discovered REA processes were judged by our participants to be relevant and consistent, thus supporting our second hypothesis (H2).

From a pragmatic standpoint, the results and interviews with participants reflected the ways in which our approach could help analysts in designing value models of business processes. First, the experiment showed that we generated 38% more relevant REA processes as compared to manual transformations. Furthermore, comparing results before and after annotations were revised allowed us to see how participants were able to refine their results. Indeed, our approach makes it easy to spot missing or erroneous annotations, enabling iterative refinements until getting a sensible value-chain. Finally, during one-on-one interviews, participants unanimously acknowledged that producing REA processes through our approach much more efficient than the manual approach.

The experiment results also helped to highlight some problems with our approach. Indeed, 7 REA processes out of 184 were deemed inconsistent. The main inconsistency that surfaced through our analysis is related to the outsourcing pattern when the participant involved is the customer of the company under study. Indeed, the customer may be involved in a given conversion process, but our participants advised that the "service" he provides should not be accounted for in the conversion. We believe this is a subjective opinion that is more related to modeling decisions and compromises made by the analyst than to the existence of the consumed service *per se*. We can account for such compromises by relying on a classification of process participants (i.e. customer vs. providers).

8   Conclusion

A business process model (BPM) cannot capture all aspects of the business process it supports as it is only one of the many viewpoints from which the process could be considered. In fact, a BPM depicts *how* the process should be performed and by *whom*. In particular, it abstracts away from questions like *what* is involved and *why*? This is answered by the business model (BM) of the process. Keeping the BPM and the BM in sync is important in order to ensure that business process execution is aligned with strategic decisions and goals.

In this work, we propose a semi-automatic systematic approach to generate a BM from a BPM and, more specifically, to transition from a BPMN model into an REA value-chain. The first step is partly manual and requires an analyst to identify economic resources from data objects in the BPMN model. The next step maps REA concepts to BPMN concepts. The third step relies on a set of structural and dynamic patterns to infer the relationships between the identified REA concept instances and obtain so-called REA processes. Finally, we construct the overall value-chain by linking the REA processes.

We applied our approach on a case study we used as a running example and performed a preliminary validation that showed a precision rate of 96% and a recall of 91%. Our major contribution lies in the definition of the set of generic business patterns that are at the heart of our approach. Our preliminary validation provides a weight of evidence in support of our approach and a thorougher validation has still to be performed.

References

1. Andersson, B., et al.: From Business to Process Models: a Chaining Methodology. In: BUSITAL 2006, Luxembourg (2006)
2. Andersson, B., et al.: Towards a reference ontology for business models. In: Embley, D.W., Olivé, A., Ram, S. (eds.) ER 2006. LNCS, vol. 4215, pp. 482–496. Springer, Heidelberg (2006)
3. Bodenstaff, L., Wombacher, A., Wieringa, R., Reichert, M.: An approach for maintaining models of an ecommerce collaboration. In: CEC/EEE, pp. 239–246 (2008)
4. Boubaker, A., Mili, H., Charif, Y., Leshob, A.: Methodology and Tool for Business Process Compensation Design. In: EDOC 2013 Workshops, Vancouver, Canada (2013)

5. Boubaker, A., Mili, H., Charif, Y., Leshob, A.: Towards a Framework for Modeling Business Compensation Processes. In: Nurcan, S., Proper, H.A., Soffer, P., Krogstie, J., Schmidt, R., Halpin, T., Bider, I. (eds.) BPMDS 2013 and EMMSAD 2013. LNBIP, vol. 147, pp. 139–153. Springer, Heidelberg (2013)
6. Czarnecki, K., Helsen, S.: Classification of model transformation approaches. In: Gen Techniques in the Context of Model-Driven Architecture, pp. 1–17 (2003)
7. Demeyer, S., Ducasse, S., Nierstrasz, O.: Object-oriented reengineering patterns. Elsevier (2002)
8. Fatemi, H., van Sinderen, M., Wieringa, R.: Value-oriented coordination process modeling. In: Hull, R., Mendling, J., Tai, S. (eds.) BPM 2010. LNCS, vol. 6336, pp. 162–177. Springer, Heidelberg (2010)
9. Gordijn, J.: Value-based Requirements Engineering. PhD thesis, Vrije Universiteit Amsterdam (2002)
10. Gordijn, J., Akkermans, H., van Vliet, H.: Business modelling is not process modelling. In: Mayr, H.C., Liddle, S.W., Thalheim, B. (eds.) ER Workshops 2000. LNCS, vol. 1921, p. 40. Springer, Heidelberg (2000)
11. Hruby, P.: Model-Driven Design Using Business Patterns. Springer (2006)
12. Küster, J.M., Abd-El-Razik, M.: Validation of model transformations – first experiences using a white box approach. In: Kühne, T. (ed.) MoDELS 2006. LNCS, vol. 4364, pp. 193–204. Springer, Heidelberg (2007)
13. Maggi, F.M., Di Francescomarino, C., Dumas, M., Ghidini, C.: Predictive Monitoring of Business Processes. arXiv.org (December 2013)
14. McCarthy, W.E.: The REA Accounting Model: A Generalized Framework for Accounting Systems in a Shared Data Environment. The Accounting Review 57(3), 554–578 (1982)
15. Mili, H., Godin, R., Tremblay, G., Dorfeuille, W.: Towards a Methodology for Designing Compensation Processes in Long-Running Business Transactions. In: MCETECH 2006, Montreal, Canada, pp. 137–148 (2006)
16. Mili, H., Leshob, A., Lefebvre, E., Lévesque, G., El-Boussaidi, G.: Towards a Methodology for Representing and Classifying Business Processes. In: Babin, G., Kropf, P., Weiss, M. (eds.) E-Technologies: Innovation in an Open World. LNBIP, vol. 26, pp. 196–211. Springer, Heidelberg (2009)
17. OMG. Business Process Model and Notation (BPMN). OMG (January 2011)
18. Osterwalder, A.: The Business Model Ontology. PhD thesis, Université de Lausanne École des Hautes Études Commerciales (2004)
19. Pijpers, V., Gordijn, J.: Consistency checking between value models and process models: A best-of-breed approach. In: BUSITAL 2008, Montpellier, pp. 58–72 (2008)
20. Pitschke, J.: Integrating Business Process Models and Business Logic: BPMN and The Decision Model. In: Dijkman, R., Hofstetter, J., Koehler, J. (eds.) BPMN 2011. LNBIP, vol. 95, pp. 148–153. Springer, Heidelberg (2011)
21. Scheer, A.-W., Thomas, O., Adam, O.: Process modeling using event-driven process chains. In: Process-Aware Information Systems, pp. 119–146 (2005)
22. The Open Group. TOGAF. The Open Group (2011)
23. Van Der Aalst, W.M.P.: Business Process Management: A Comprehensive Survey. ISRN Software Engineering 2013(1), 1–37 (2013)
24. Weske, M.: Business Process Management: Concepts, Languages, Architectures, 2nd edn. Springer (2012)
25. Wieringa, R., Pijpers, V., Bodenstaff, L., Gordijn, J.: Value-driven coordination proces design using physical delivery model. In: ER, Barcelona, pp. 216–231 (2008)
26. Yu, S.C.: The Structure of Accounting Theory. The Uni. Press of Florida (1976)

Classification of Domain-Specific BPMN Extensions

Richard Braun and Werner Esswein

Technische Universität Dresden
Chair of Wirtschaftsinformatik, esp. Systems Development
01062 Dresden, Germany
{richard.braun,werner.esswein}@tu-dresden.de

Abstract. BPMN is a standard for modeling business processes and provides meta model concepts for the design of extensions. Thus, domain-specific extensions of the BPMN are facilitated. This research article provides an overview of BPMN extension development by the descriptive analysis and classification of 30 BPMN extensions. An extensive literature review was conducted in order to find published extensions. Further, a classification framework was designed to enable a comprehensive analysis of each extension. The analysis showed, that four out of five extensions are not compliant with the BPMN standard. Also, we found several methodological shortcomings that should be tackled in further research.

Keywords: BPMN Extensions, Domain-specific Extension, Modeling Languages, DSML, DSML Repository, Business Process Modeling.

1 Introduction and Motivation

The Business Process Model and Notation (BPMN) is an ISO standard for modeling business processes and a de-facto standard in professional practice [1], [2]. BPMN provides a set of generic business process elements, independent from a specific domain. However, it is often necessary to extend BPMN with individual concepts in order to represent characteristics of a particular domain (e.g., health care or security management). On the one hand, such domain-specific aspects can be integrated within a dedicated domain-specific modeling language (DSML) [3], [4]. On the other hand, BPMN can be extended with domain-specific concepts in order to reuse the modeling language, take advantage of its benefits (e.g., standardization, tool support) and avoid expensive development of a DSML from the scratch. This research article investigates the current state of the art of BPMN extension development. A BPMN extension is understood as the enhancement of functionality of the BPMN, following the extension mechanism defined in specification. In its own, the standard-conform BPMN extension is neither useful nor functional (referring to [5], [6]).

U. Frank et al. (Eds.): PoEM 2014, LNBIP 197, pp. 42–57, 2014.

1.1   BPMN Extensibility

BPMN is one of very few modeling languages that provides generic extension elements within the meta model that enables the definition of domain-specific language extensions [7]. BPMN provides an extension by addition mechanism that ensures the validity of the BPMN core elements ([8], [7], p. 44). The following elements are defined for the specification of valid BPMN extensions: An *Extension Definition* is a named group of new attributes which can be used by BPMN elements. Thus, new elements can be built implicitly. An *Extension Definition* consists of several *Extension Attribute Definitions* that define the particular attributes. Values of these *Extension Attribute Definitions* can be defined by the *Extension Attribute Value* class. Therefore, primitive types from the Meta Object Facility can be used [7]. The element *Extension* binds the entire extension definition and its attributes to a BPMN model definition. By doing so, all extension elements are accessible for existing BPMN elements ([7], p. 58). Further, external relationships can used for the integration of BPMN artifacts and UML elements, for instance (see [7], p. 62). Despite the fact that BPMN provides a well-defined extension interface, a process model for the straightforward development of extensions is missing. To the best of our knowledge, there is only one research article addressing this problem: [8] defines a model-transformation based procedure model for the methodical development of valid BPMN extensions models based on conceptual domain models. However, the approach lacks in terms of a detailed analysis and consideration of the domain since it is a more engineering driven approach that aims to provide clear transformation rules. Therefore, [9] extends the method with regard to the domain analysis and outline several preceded steps in order to conceptualize the domain and identify a reasoned need for extension.

1.2   Research Objective

As stated above, a detailed process model for the application of these extension elements is missing and the development of an extension remains more or less "ad hoc". Especially from a design science perspective, this lack of rigor is insufficient (e.g., [10]). For example, there is neither guidance in terms of the domain conceptualization nor a semantic analysis between a specific domain concept and BPMN elements. The mentioned approaches address this issue, but either lack in terms of domain analysis [8] or level of detail and applicability [9]. We argue, that it is crucial to evolve a holistic process model for BPMN extension development to ensure standard conformity, comprehensibility and falsifiability. Therefore, it is unavoidable to gain a comprehensive overview of the state of the art in the context of BPMN extensions. Thus, this research article aims to provide a systematic, descriptive analysis of BPMN extensions in order to give indications of both methodological and domain-specific aspects within BPMN extension development.

1.3 Research Method

In order to find published BPMN extensions, a systematic literature review was conducted. We have applied the method of [12] that was configured as follows: The scope of our review was a broad analysis of BPMN extensions. According to [11] the review is conceptual, has a research outcome focus, aims to integrate existing results (to a classification schema), has an exhaustive coverage and addresses a general audience. Second, the topic was conceptualized by the definition of relevant search phrases and keywords (see [12]), such as "BPMN extension", "extend BPMN", "enhance BPMN", "extending BPMN", "domain-specifc BPMN" and "domain BPMN". Third, the literature search process was conducted [12]. Therefore, the journal and conference list of the german research organization *WKWI* was used [13]. Also, literature databases and search engines like *Google Scholar, Springer Link, Science Direct, AIS Digital Library* and the *IEEE Xplore Digital Library* were used. Besides, each found article was used for a backward search. This search procedure resulted in a set of 39 articles, whose content were reviewed. Publications, focusing on early BPMN extensions that are now part of the language (e.g., [14]) or articles that did not provide any conceptual advices on their extension (e.g., [15], [16]), were discarded and a set of 30 articles remain for in-detail analysis that was conducted subsequently. Therefore, a multi-perspective analysis framework has been designed in order to facilitate a comparison of the identified extensions. The systematization of all BPMN extensions and the derivation of the state of the art represent the synthesis of the review process. Finally, research gaps and aspects for further research were derived.

The structure of the article is as follows. Section 2 presents the extension analysis framework containing four main classes and all relevant criteria. In section 3, the results of the literature review are analyzed within the framework. Section 4 provides indications as a result of the classification. The article ends with a short summary.

2 BPMN Extension Analysis Framework

The reasonable analysis of BPMN extensions requires the definition of a description framework. In the context of BPMN, there are no comparable approaches, that could be leveraged for the derivation of such criteria. However, there are few research articles addressing a systematic overview or classification of extensions in the field of the workflow modeling language BPEL [6] and UML profiles [17]. [6] evolves a classification framework for BPEL extensions based on the analysis of 62 publications. Since their work focusses on workflow aspects, the reuse of the entire classification framework is not reasonable. Nevertheless, some criteria like standard conformity, extension purpose and basic characteristics are adapted in the context of BPMN. [17] provides a systematic review of UML profiles based on the analysis of 39 publications. Although the focus lies on the analysis of UML profiles, the consideration of extended meta classes (see [17], p. 413) is promising in the context of BPMN since both modeling languages are defined by the Meta Object Facility (MOF). Referring to the mentioned works and the research objective of this paper, the following classes for descriptive analysis of BPMN extensions were defined: "Basic attributes", "standard conformity", "applied method" and "extension". Each class, its containing criteria and all classification values are described in the tables subsequently. If necessary, detailed explanations of single criteria are given.

Table 1. Basic Attributes

Criterion	Description	Values
Authors	Authors of the publication	(reference)
Year	Year of publication	2007 - 2014
Version	Affected BPMN version	BPMN 1.x; BPMN 2.0 (since 2011)
Medium	Publication medium	J (journal); P (proceedings); O (others)
Title	Title of the extension	e.g., BPMN4WSN
Domain	Affected domain or area of discourse	e.g., Artifacts or Resources
Purpose	Derived purpose	D (descriptive); A (analytic); E (execution)

The criterion *Domain* describes the affected domain, the application fields or the general area of discourse of the extension. During analysis, similar domains (e.g., Security Management and Risk Management) were merged to single domains (e.g., Risk Management) in order to consolidate them. Criterion *Purpose* stands for the primarily purpose of the extension. An extension was classified as "descriptive" (D) if its focus lies on the description of a domain. It was classified as "analytic" (A) if the main purpose consists in facilitating some kind of analysis of existing BPMN models. If the extension aims to support process execution (e.g., supporting domain-specific transformation to BPEL), the extension was classified as "execution" (E).

Table 2. Standard Conformity

Criterion	Description	Values
Definition	Type of extension definition	Valid Ext; Own Ext; Own Ext Notation; None
Abstract Syntax	Definition of the meta model	e.g., UML, Ext MM (BPMN extension meta model)
Concrete Syntax	Definition of new notations	explicit; implicit (by example); none
Semantic Conflicts	Are there any semantic conflicts with the BPMN standard?	no; yes

The "Standard Conformity" class contains criteria regarding the syntactical and semantic correctness of the extension in the light of the BPMN standard (see section 1). Criterion *Definition* describes the way the extension is defined and explicated. "Valid Ext" stands for the definition as BPMN extension model. "Own Ext" outlines the application of a dedicated definition (e.g., UML model). "Own Ext Notation" stands for a solely graphical definition (e.g., by new icons).

Table 3. Method

Criterion	Description	Values
Requirements Analysis	Is there any analysis or consideration of requirements to the extension?	explicit; implicit; no
Semantic Fit Check	Is there any discussion of the semantic fit of domain concepts with BPMN elements for the identification of extension need?	yes; partly; no
Reuse of Artifacts	Many domains already provide some artifacts such as ontologies. The reuse and integration of them might be useful.	yes; partly; no
Process Model	Is any methodological approach applied (if yes, which one)?	STROPPI ET AL.; BPMN ext; yes (own); no

Further, the definition of customized or new graphical elements is considered by the criterion *Concrete Syntax*. Also, we have analyzed whether a single extension contains obvious semantic conflicts.

As stated at the beginning of the paper, the methodological development of BPMN extensions is important, but BPMN standard does not provide any guidance and only very few publications addressing this topic. Thus, both methodological and domain-analysis aspects are investigated within the class "Method". For instance, requirements analysis is perceived as essential for the development of artifacts. It might be reasonable to reuse existing domain artifacts for reasons of redundancy and communication with domain experts. Also, a discussion of the semantic fit with BPMN elements is necessary to constitute the need for extension elements.

The class "Extension" describes all extensions and customizations for the integration of domain-specific aspects in BPMN. The first part contains all newly added elements, relations, properties and diagrams. Therefore, first of all it was analyzed whether the extension was defined by a meta model. If not, we have

Table 4. Extension

Criterion	Description	Values
New elements		
Elements	New elements and enumerations (up to three example elements are stated)	(individual)
Count	Number of new elements (if the number is in brackets, a meta model is missing and the elements are derived logically; e.g., [18], [19])	(individual)
Size Class	Derived extension size class, based on the number of extension elements	Heavy (>17); large (11-17); light (6-10); tiny (<6)
Diagrams	Does the extension provide a new diagram?	yes; no
Extended or customized elements		
Relations	Extending a BPMN element by new navigable relations to or from the element	BPMN element(s)
Properties	New owned properties of a BPMN element	BPMN element(s)
Specialization	Adding new sub classes to a BPMN element	BPMN element(s)
Enhancement	Adding a new super class to a BPMN element	BPMN element(s)
Graphical Custom.	Specifying a BPMN element by a new graphical representation (see [7], p. 44)	BPMN element(s)
Count	Number of extended elements	(individual)
Extension Style	Identified extension styles	Codes from table 5

Table 5. Extension Styles

Code	Name	Description
Abstract Syntax		
AS-Sp	Specialization	Specialization of elements by inheriting from the standard element and extending it (e.g., by additional properties).
AS-A	Additive (various)	Set of both new elements and new relations or properties (both optional and mandatory). Thus, the meta model extension is largely integrated within the BPMN meta model.
AS-A-B	Additive (block)	Set of new elements that is related to the BPMN core model by only one or two relationships. Thus, the meta model extension looks like a well definable extension block.
AS-En	Enumeration	Domain-specific ranges in the form of enumeration elements.
Semantics		
Sem-Co	Concretisation	Specification of under specified elements (e.g., Lanes [7]).
Sem-Ch	Change	Dedicated change of some element's semantics, which is not permitted within BPMN.
Concrete Syntax		
CS-Dg	Diagram, view	Adding a new diagram or view to BPMN (e.g., resource diagram as complement of the collaboration diagram).
CS-Cu	Customization	Customization of graphical elements (e.g., data objects).
CS-Co	Color	Color highlighting of elements or parts with special semantics.
CS-Ah	Ad hoc	Elusive definition of an extension by graphical icons, without any abstract syntax.

tried to identify new elements based on explanations in the research article. Even though these explanations were missing, we looked for new, solely graphically defined elements (see *Graphical Custom.*). Criterion *Size Class* is a simple parameter for the number of new elements [1]. Further, the so-called extension styles of an extension were analyzed in order to get a better understanding of the way an intended extension was implemented and expressed. Therefore, ten extension styles were derived from the set of all 30 extensions inductively. Each extension style is assigned to one of the following classes that were adapted from method engineering: Abstract syntax, semantics and concrete syntax. Table 5 presents and describes all styles in detail. Each analyzed extension can have multiple extension styles.

3   BPMN Extension Classification

The conducted literature review resulted in a set of 30 BPMN extensions. Each extension was analyzed with respect to the abovementioned framework. Figure 1 presents the results of the analysis regarding to basic attributes, conformity to the standard and the applied method. Figure 6 presents the results regarding to the syntactical definition of the extensions.

3.1   Basic Extension Attributes

The majority of the considered extensions is related to BPMN version 2.0 (76,6%). Extensions are mainly published in conference proceedings (60,0%) or as research

---

[1] Size classes were generated by the application of the k-means algorithm over all element counts (k=4; euclidean distance).

Basic Attributes						Standard Conformity					Method			
Authors	Year	Version	Medium	Title	Domain	Purpose	Definition	Abstract Syntax	Concrete Syntax	Semantic Conflicts	Req. Analysis	Semantic Fit Check	Reuse of Artifacts	Process Model
Altuhhov et al.	2013	2.0	J	No title (Security Risk Management)	Risk Management	D	Own Ext Notation	UML	Explicit	No	implicit (ISSRM)	yes	yes (ISSRM)	no
Awad et al.	2009	2.0	O	No title (Ressource Allocation Constraints)	Ressource	E	Own Ext	UML, OCL	No	No	implicit (patterns)	no	no	no
Bocciarelli & D'Ambrogio	2011	1.x	P	PyBPMN	Performance Measurement	A	Own Ext	UML, OCL	No	No	no	no	yes (MARTE)	(yes)
Brambilla et al.	2012	2.0	P	No title (Social BPM)	Social BPM	D	Own Ext	(UML)	By example	No	no	no	yes	no
Braun & Esswein	2014	2.0	P	No title (Ressources in Engineering)	Resource	D	Ext MM	Ext MM	Explicit	No	implicit (ontology)	yes	yes (ResML)	yes: ext. of Stroppi et al.
Braun et al.	2014	2.0	O	BPMN4CP	E-Health	D	Valid Ext	Ext MM	By example	No	explicit	yes	yes (requirements)	yes: ext. of Stroppi et al.
Brucker et al.	2012	2.0	P	SecureBPMN	Risk Management	D	None	No	By example	No	no	no	yes (SecureBPM)	no
Charfi et al.	2010	2.0	J	AC4BPMN	Aspect Modelling	E	None	No	By example	No	no	no	partly (AOP elements)	no
Friedenstab et al.	2012	2.0	P	No title (Business Activity Monitoring)	Performance Measurement	A	Own Ext	UML	Explicit	No	implicit (descriptive)	no	no	no
Gagne & Trudel	2009	1.x	P	Time-BPMN	Time	A	None	No	By example	No	implicit (descriptive)	no	yes (time aspects)	no
Großkopf	2007	2.0	O	No title (Ressource Information Layer)	Resources	E	None	UML	Explicit	No	no	yes	yes	no
Kopp et al.	2012	2.0	J	BPMN4TOSCA	Cloud	D	None	No	By example	No	explicit (descriptive)	no	yes	no
Korherr & List	2007	1.x	J	No title (Performance Measures)	Performance Measurement	A	Own Ext	UML	By example	No	implicit (descriptive)	no	yes	no
Lodhi et al.	2011	2.0	P	No title (Process Evaluation)	Performance Measurement	A	Own Ext Notation	(UML)	By example	(No)	no	no	partly (eval. concepts)	no
Lohmann & Nyolt	2011	2.0	P	No title (Artifact-centric Modeling)	Artifacts	D	None	No	By example	No	no	no	no	no
Magnani & Montesi	2007	1.x	P	No title (Costs)	Performance Measurement	A	None	No	By example	No	no	no	no	no
Magnani & Montesi	2009	1.x	O	BPDMN	Artifacts	A	Own Ext Notation	No	Explicit	Yes	implicit (feature comparison)	no	yes (data flow, ERM)	no
Marcinkowski & Kuciapski	2012	2.0	J	No title (Risk Handling)	Risk Management	D	Own Ext	UML	By example	No	no	no	no	no
Müller-Wickop & Schultz	2013	2.0	P	No title (Process Audits)	Compliance and Audits	D	Valid Ext	Ext MM	Explicit	No	explicit	no	no	(yes) BPMN ext.
Natschläger	2011	2.0	P	Deontic BPMN	Deontic Analysis	A	None	No	No	No	no	no	yes (deontic items)	no
Pillat et al.	2012	2.0	P	BPMNt	Software Development	D	Own Ext	Ext MM	By example	No	implicit (description)	no	yes (SPEM 2.0)	(yes)
Rodriguez et al.	2007	1.x	J	No title (Security)	Risk Management	D	Own Ext	UML, OCL	Explicit	No	no	partly	yes (requirements)	no
Saeedi et al.	2010	2.0	P	No title (Serivce Quality Requirements)	Quality Management	D	Valid Ext	Ext MM	By example	No	implicit (description)	no	no	(yes) BPMN ext.
Saleem & Hassan	2012	2.0	J	No title (Security Requirements in SOA)	Risk Management	D	Own Ext	UML	Explicit	Yes	explicit	no	no	no
Schleicher et al.	2010	2.0	P	No title (Compliance Requirements)	Compliance and Audits	D	None	No	No	No	no	no	no	no
Stroppi et al.	2011	2.0	P	No title (Ressources)	Resources	E	Valid Ext	Ext MM	By example	No	explicit	no	yes	(yes) BPMN ext.
Sungur et al.	2013	2.0	P	BPMN4WSN	Sensors	D	Own Ext	UML	Explicit	No	explicit	no	no	no
Supulniece et al.	2012	2.0	P	No title (Knowledge)	Knowledge	D	None	No	Explicit	Yes	explicit	no	no	no
Wolter & Schaad	2007	1.x	P	No title (Authorization Constrains)	Authorization	A	Own Ext	UML	By example	No	no	no	yes (KMDL)	no
Zor et al.	2011	2.0	P	No title (Manufacturing)	Manufacturing	D	None	No	Explicit	Yes	explicit	partly	no	no

Fig. 1. Analysis of the extensions regarding their basic attributes, BPMN standard conformity and the applied extension approach or method

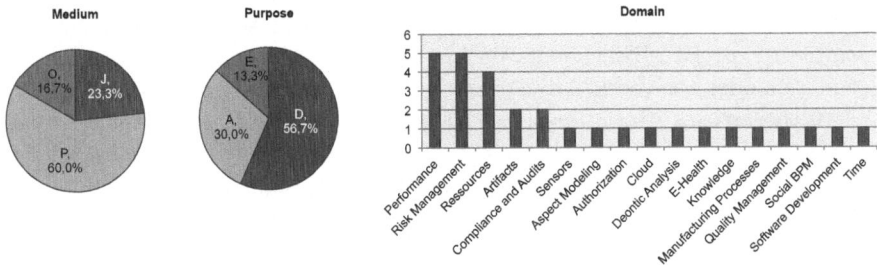

Fig. 2. Distribution of the observed extension attributes regarding the publication medium, the particular purpose and the addressd domain

reports (16,7%). Only every fourth extension is published in a journal, which could be interpreted as a lack of maturity in BPMN extension research (see figure 2). Also, we could not find any advice for cumulated research on single extensions. More than half of the publications reveal a descriptive purpose (56,7%) that aims to describe some domain (e.g., sensor networks [20]). 30% of the extensions aim to enrich BPMN for specific analytical purposes such as process cost [21]. 13,3% focuses run-time or execution-oriented issues like resource allocation constraints [22]. The targeted domains of the extensions are very heterogenous; altogether 17 domains were identified. Five publications address performance measurement [23], [24], [21], [25], [26], another five publications deal with issues related to risk management [27], [28], [29], [30], [31] and four extensions are designed for resource related issues [22], [32], [33], [34].

3.2   Standard Conformity

It is remarkable, that only 16,7% of the extensions are defined by the BPMN extension mechanism (see the first piechart in figure 3). Thus, four out of five extensions are not compliant with the BPMN meta model! These extensions are either defined by a dedicated meta modeling approach (36,7%) using UML or OCL expressions (e.g., [24], [23], [30]). Or these extensions do not have any meta model and are defined solely by new notation elements (10,0%) like [35]. 36,7% of the extensions do not present any definition! It has to be stated, that BPMN extension mechanism was introduced in version 2.0 in January 2011. Thus, actually all eleven extensions published before 2011 could not have any methodical support. However, the consideration of the 19 extensions published after 2011 reveals that only 21% were defined as BPMN extension meta models and still 32% do not provide any structured definition. It became obvious that the majority of extensions is not compliant with the BPMN standard.

Modeling language extensions generally requires the definition of customized or added notation elements (see [7], p. 44). 40% of the analyzed extensions present the extended concrete syntax be describing new graphics explicitly. Other 40% of the articles present new graphical elements implicitly within demonstration models. 20% of the extensions do not define or explicate any kind of graphical extension. Further, BPMN specification claims to not contradict the semantics of any BPMN element. Within the analysis process, not every part of each meta model was checked due to resource limitations and due to the fact that most of the articles were peer-reviewed before publication. However, we found semantic discrepancies in four extensions: [25] uses Pools and Lanes in order to express performances, although these elements are designated for organizational units, responsibilities or roles. [35] integrates data objects within the sequence flow, although they must not have any direct effect on it. In a similar way, [36] integrates non-flow elements within the sequence flow what is not permitted. [37] specializes gateways to material gateways and use them for material transformations what is not the scope of gateways. Despite these few irregularities, the majority of the extensions do not contain semantical errors.

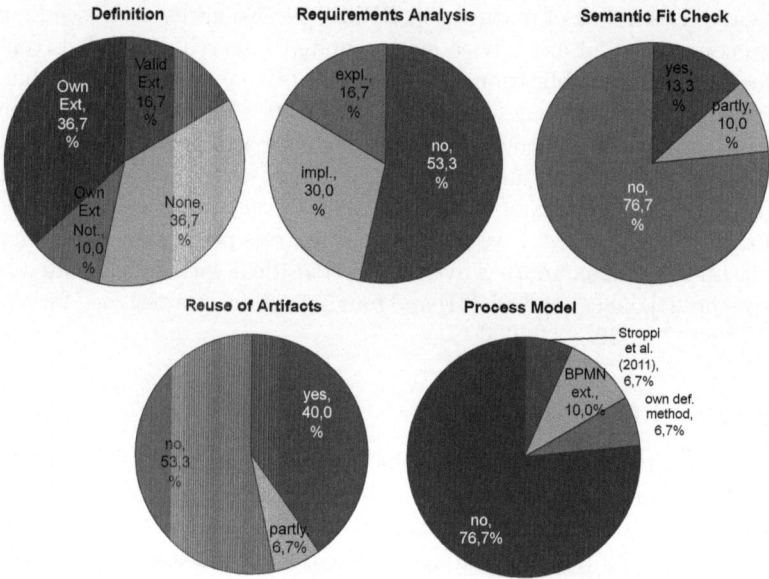

Fig. 3. Analysis of the extensions regarding their meta model definition and methodological aspects

3.3 Applied Method

As already shown in section 3.2, the BPMN extension mechanism is rarely applied. Nearly three out of four do not apply any method. These extensions are developed in an ad hoc manner, what impedes the assessment of the replicability and comprehensibility. 16,7% of the extensions were designed based on the BPMN extension model (five in total), whereby only two applied the process model of [8]: [32] and [38]. [38] extends the process model concerning a semantic equivalence check to ensure the necessity of extension. Another two extensions were designed based on individually outlined procedures [23], [39]. Regarding the criterion of requirements analysis, approximately one of two articles provide requirements to the extension. One third was stated explicitly (e.g., by a set of requirements R1 to Rn, [20]). The rest of these articles describe requirements implicitly within the introduction or the description of the application context (e.g., [40]). Three of four articles designed the particular extension without any deep consideration of the question, whether each requirement or extension demand needs necessarily an extension concept (see the middle piechart in figure 3). 13,3% conducted a discussion for every concept [27], [33], [32], [38]. Further, nearly half of the extensions make use of existing domain artifacts. For instance, UML profiles [23], [39], domain modeling concepts [27], [32], [36] or requirements [30] are reused within the extension design.

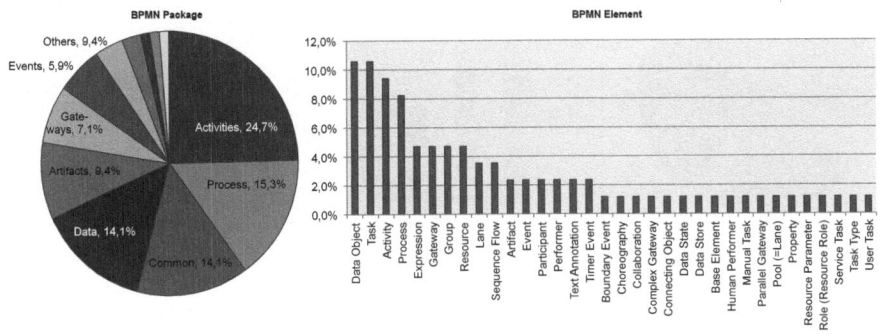

Fig. 4. Distribution of extended BPMN packages and elements

3.4   Domain-specific Extension

Within the extension analysis, only publications with at least one identifiable new element were considered. The number of new elements had a range between one and 35 elements; on an average of nearly eight elements (e.g., [41], [24]). Examples for particular new elements as well as the derived size classes can be found in figure 6. Although the definition of new diagram types is not considered within BPMN, some extensions also provide the definition of new diagrams like a Resource Structure Diagram [34] or a Secure Business Process Diagram [30], [31]. Next to the definition of new elements, BPMN elements are also extended or customized. As figure 4 shows, primarily Data Objects, Tasks, Activities and Processes are extended. This fact is also emphasized by the presentation of the extended BPMN packages: Elements from the Activity package, the Process package, the Common package (e.g., Resource, Sequence Flow or Expression) and the Data package are extended mainly. It could be concluded, that these elements are predestinated for domain-specific extensions. Especially,

Data Objects and Tasks are often specified within extensions (see figure 6, column "specialization"). The extension of standard BPMN elements is mainly realized by new relations (associations in the meta model) or specifications (inheritances). Generally, the new relations are passive. It means that they are not mandatory from the perspective of the extended element but rather optional; extending the dynamic range of the referencing element. New relations between standard elements are on rare occasions [24]. Also, the extension by owned attributes is implemented rarely (e.g., [32], [24], [40]), whereas the specification of (generic) BPMN elements by new domain specific sub classes seems to be a common means (e.g., [42], [43], [44], [29], [45]).

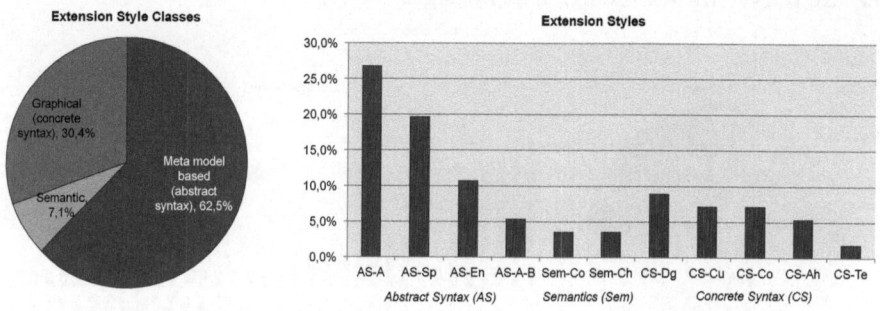

Fig. 5. Distribution of identified extensions styles (56 in total over all extensions)

Consequently, the distribution of the applied extension styles reveals that the *AS-Sp* style (specialization) is one of the most applied extension techniques (see figure 5). In total, 56 style applications could be identified within the extension definitions. 62,5% of them affect the abstract syntax (meta model), 30,4% are related to the graphical notation (concrete syntax) and 7,1% realize some extension by concrete or change some element's semantics. Unsurprisingly, the (more or less unspecific) *AS-A* style is applied the most. The enumeration technique (*AS-En*) for the domain-specific definition of ranges is used in more than 10% of all style applications. Within the area of graphical style, there is no dominating technique. Interestingly, *CS-Co* is not applied often, although BPMN explicitly emphasize this possibility for artifacts elements [7].

4 Implications

Several implications can be derived based on the analysis of existing BPMN extensions. We argue, that the following aspects should be considered in prospective research works on BPMN extensions.

Strict Use of the BPMN Extension Mechanism: As shown, only very few extensions are designed by applying the BPMN extension mechanism. However, such an implementation is indispensable for reasons of standard conformity,

Authors	New elements: Elements (sample)	Count	Class Size	New Diagram	Extended or customized elements: Relations	Properties	Specialization	Enhancement	Graphical	Extended Elements	Extension Style
Altuhhov et al.	Vulnerability Points, Lock, Association Flow	3	Tiny	-	Data Store, Data Object, Task	-	-	-	-	3	CS-Cu, CS-Co, AS-A
Awad et al.	Organizational Role, Profile, Case, ...	6	Light	-	Task, Process, Lane	-	Role	-	-	4	AS-A, CS-Co
Bocciarelli & D'Ambrogio	Ga Workload Event, Arrival Pattern, Pa Qualification, ...	11	Large	-	Collaboration, process (direction of association is not defined)	-	-	-	-	2	AS-A, CS-Te
Brambilla et al.	Social Monitoring, Social Behaviour, URl, ...	14	Large	-	-	-	Task	-	-	1	AS-Sp
Braun & Esswein	Human Resource, Material, Allocation States, ...	17	Large	-	Timer Event, Participant	Data Object	Property, Resource	-	-	5	AS-A, AS-Sp, AS-En, Sem-Co
Braun et al.	Medical Document, CPG Reference, Diagnosis Task, ...	14	Large	-	Activity, Group, Gateway, Process, Data Object	-	Data Object, Task, Parallel Gateway, Complex Gateway, Expression	-	-	9	AS-A, AS-Sp, AS-En, Sem-Co
Brucker et al.	Access Control, Separation of Duty, Binding of Duty, ...	(4)	Tiny	-	-	Activity, Process	-	-	-	0	AS-A
Charfi et al.	Pointcuts, Advice	(2)	Tiny	-	-	-	-	-	-	0	CS-Cu
Friedenstab et al.	Duration, Process Section, Quantitative Limit, ...	35	Heavy	(yes)	Data Object, Data State, Process, Expression, Sequence Flow	-	-	-	-	6	AS-A, AS-Sp, AS-En, CS-Dg
Gagne & Trudel	Time Date Expressions, Temporal Constraint Decorators	(2)	Tiny	-	(Temporal Dependencies, Temporal Constraint Attributes)	-	-	-	-	0	AS-A
Großkopf	Performer Role, Processor Role, Actor	3	Tiny	-	-	Activity	-	-	-	1	AS-A
Kopp et al.	TOSCA Node Management Task, TOSCA Script Task, TOSCA Data Object, ...	(4)	Tiny	-	-	-	Task, Data Object	-	-	2	AS-Sp
Korher & List	Waiting Time, Working Time, Process Goal, ...	12	Large	-	Pool, Process, Group, Event, Timer Event	-	-	-	-	5	AS-A-B
Lodhi et al.	Metric Values, Colors, Rules/Condition, Probability, Dimensional Attributes, Content/Structure	6	Light	-	Activity, Gateways, Connecting Objects, Artefacts, Lanes	-	-	-	-	5	AS-A, CS-Co, Sem-Ch
Lohmann & Nyolt	Placeholder container	(1)	Tiny	(yes)	-	-	Events, Choreographies (only graphically)	-	-	2	CS-Cu, (CS-Dg)
Magrani & Montesi 2007	Simple Costs, Cost Intervals, Average Costs	3	Tiny	-	Task, Gateway, Activity	-	-	-	-	3	CS-Ah
Magrani & Montesi 2009	Store, Entity, Relationship, ...	7	Light	-	-	-	-	-	Data objects	1	CS-Co
Marcinkowski & Kuciapski	Risk Factor, Risk Type, Risk Handler	9	Light	-	Sequence Flow, Resource, Participant	-	Artefact, Task	-	-	5	AS-Sp, AS-En
Müller-Wickop & Schultz	Account Entry, Debit And Credit, Account, Balance	4	Tiny	-	-	-	Data Object, Group, Text Annotation	-	-	3	AS-Sp
Natschläger	Deontic Task, O(Task), X(Task), P(Task), ...	(6)	Light	-	-	-	Task	-	-	1	AS-Sp
Pillat et al.	Tailored Base Element	1	Tiny	-	-	-	-	-	-	0	AS-Sp
Rodriguez et al.	Security Requirement, Integrity, Privacy, ...	13	Large	yes	-	-	Process (Business Process Diagram)	-	-	1	AS-A-B, AS-A, CS-Dg
Saeedi et al.	Reliability, Cost, Response Time, ...	7	Light	-	Activity	-	-	-	-	1	AS-A
Saleem & Hassan	Access Control, Authentication, Authorization, ...	8	Light	yes	-	-	-	-	-	0	AS-Sp, CS-Cu, CS-Dg
Schleicher et al.	Compliance Scope, Compliance Rule, Language Indicator	(3)	Tiny	-	-	-	-	-	-	0	AS-A-B
Stroppi et al.	Resource Privilege, Resource Base, Subsumption, ...	17	Large	yes	Resource, Resource Parameter, Element, Boundary Event, User Task, Human Performer, Expression	-	-	-	-	7	AS-A, AS-En, CS-Dg
Sungur et al.	WSN Task, tWSNOperation, tWSNPerformer, ...	7	Light	-	(Resource Assignment) Expression	-	Performer, Service Task	-	-	3	AS-Sp, AS-A, AS-En
Supulniece et al.	Data Object, Information Object, Knowledge	(3)	Tiny	-	Activity, Task Type, Role (Performer), Data Object	-	-	-	-	4	CS-Ah, (Sem-Ch)
Wolter & Schaad	Authorization Constraint	1	Tiny	-	Manual Task, Group (new relation, Lane	-	Text Annotation	Activity	-	4	AS-A, AS-Sp
Zor et al.	Parts Container, Machines and Tools Flow Connector, ...	10	Light	-	Gateway, Task, Resource, Sequence Flow	-	Gateway, Task, Resource, Sequence Flow	-	-	5	CS-Ah

Fig. 6. Analysis of the extensions regarding new and extended elements

comprehensibility, model exchange and tool support. For instance, model engineers fail in reusing the most BPMN extensions since they do not provide a valid BPMN extension model. Thus, it is necessary to transform the provided dedicated meta model into a BPMN conform model in order to integrate it within a BPMN tool. Also, the communication within the research community is hampered by this shortcoming. In the context of method engineering, it is also necessary to define the concrete syntax of each extension element explicitly to avoid misunderstandings. The semantics of a new element or its relations to BPMN elements should be described in detail in order to support its application.

Integrated Methodological Support Is Necessary: As stated at the beginning of this article, BPMN lacks in term of providing an extension process model. Thus, most of the considered BPMN extensions are not designed rigorously. There seems to be a gap between the domain-specific definition of extension requirements, their conceptualization and the implementation as valid meta model. The last aspect is successfully solved by [8] and few extensions make use of its proclaimed transformation procedure. However, the early phases of extension planning and design are still not guided. Therefore, we see the need for an integrated process model for BPMN extension development that focuses the domain analysis and conceptualization phase. For example, there should be a systematic support for the decision whether any domain concept can be represented within the "semantic scope" of a standard element or not. We suppose, that more than a few BPMN extensions do not exploit the entire expressiveness of BPMN. Besides, research on the integration of domain-specific artifacts within BPMN extensions and DSMLs in general should be intensified, since such artifacts (e.g., ontologies, taxonomies) provide well-defined domain knowledge that could complement domain expert knowledge.

BPMN Language and Extension Design: It became obvious, that specific aspects are often demanded. Especially, a better resource and data object modeling needs to be supported by BPMN, albeit BPMN will not be understood as any kind of a "data-flow language" ([7], p. 22). Referring to enterprise architecture frameworks, an extension of the BPMN regarding several views (e.g., resource perspective) is promising. Hereof, further research should consider the question, how to extend BPMN with new diagrams or views. Currently, such an extension is not designated. Also, based on our analysis of the so-called extension styles, a deeper analysis of extension patterns is necessary in order to provide specific patterns or guidelines for given extension purposes.

5   Conclusion

To the best of our knowledge, this is the first approach addressing the comparison and classification of BPMN extensions in order to present the current state of the art. Therefore, an extensive literature review of BPMN extensions was conducted that results in a set of 30 publications that were subjected an in-depth analysis. For the comparison and classification, a four-part extension analysis framework was designed containing criteria on the extension itself and the applied procedures. Based on the application of this framework, several implications were derived.

First, authors of BPMN extension should strictly use the BPMN extension mechanism in order to provide a valid extension and enable model exchangeability (currently less than 20% provide valid BPMN extensions). Second, we identified a need for an integrated methodological support of extension development, especially in terms of domain analysis and the comparison of domain elements with BPMN standard elements. Third, we have identified a recognizable need for the support of resource and data oriented modeling aspects within BPMN. In this context, especially the question of extending BPMN (or a modeling language in general) with new diagrams and views should be considered. Regarding to the identified extension styles, it might be promising to develop extension patterns (or at least guidelines) for specific extension needs in order to support the design process.

References

1. Chinosi, M., Trombetta, A.: Bpmn: An introduction to the standard. Computer Standards and Interfaces 34(1), 124–134 (2012)
2. ISO: Iso/iec 19510:2013 - International organization for standardization (iso) (2013)
3. Frank, U.: Outline of a method for designing domain-specific modelling languages. ICB Research Report 42, Universität Duisburg-Essen, Essen (2010)
4. Mohagheghi, P., Haugen, Ø.: Evaluating domain-specific modelling solutions. In: Trujillo, J., Dobbie, G., Kangassalo, H., Hartmann, S., Kirchberg, M., Rossi, M., Reinhartz-Berger, I., Zimányi, E., Frasincar, F. (eds.) ER 2010. LNCS, vol. 6413, pp. 212–221. Springer, Heidelberg (2010)
5. Lämmel, R., Ostermann, K.: Software extension and integration with type classes. In: Proceedings of the 5th International Conference on Generative Programming and Component Engineering, pp. 161–170. ACM (2006)
6. Kopp, O., Görlach, K., Karastoyanova, D., Leymann, F., Reiter, M., Schumm, D., Sonntag, M., Strauch, S., Unger, T., Wieland, M., et al.: A classification of bpel extensions. Journal of Systems Integration 2(4), 3–28 (2011)
7. OMG: Business Process Model and Notation (BPMN) - Version 2.0. Object Management Group (OMG) (2011)
8. Stroppi, L.J.R., Chiotti, O., Villarreal, P.D.: Extending BPMN 2.0: Method and tool support. In: Dijkman, R., Hofstetter, J., Koehler, J. (eds.) BPMN 2011. LNBIP, vol. 95, pp. 59–73. Springer, Heidelberg (2011)
9. Braun, R., Schlieter, H.: Requirements-based development of bpmn extensions – the case of clinical pathways. In: 1st International Workshop on the Interrelations between Requirements Engineering and Business Process Management (2014)
10. Hevner, A., Chatterjee, S.: Design science research in information systems. In: Design Research in Information Systems. Integrated Series in Information Systems, vol. 22, pp. 9–22. Springer, US (2010)
11. Cooper, H.M.: Organizing knowledge syntheses: A taxonomy of literature reviews. Knowledge in Society 1(1), 104–126 (1988)
12. Vom Brocke, J., Simons, A., Niehaves, B., Niehaves, B., Reimer, K., Plattfaut, R., Cleven, A.: Reconstructing the giant: on the importance of rigour in documenting the literature search process. In: ECIS 2009 Proceedings, Paper 161 (2009)

13. WKWI: Wi-orientierungslisten. Wirtschaftsinformatik 50(2), 155–163 (2008)
14. Decker, G., Puhlmann, F.: Extending BPMN for modeling complex choreographies. In: Meersman, R., Tari, Z. (eds.) OTM 2007, Part I. LNCS, vol. 4803, pp. 24–40. Springer, Heidelberg (2007)
15. Gao, F., Zaremba, M., Bhiri, S., Derguerch, W.: Extending bpmn 2.0 with sensor and smart device business functions. In: 2011 20th IEEE International Workshops on Enabling Technologies: Infrastructure for Collaborative Enterprises (WETICE), pp. 297–302. IEEE (2011)
16. Zor, S., Görlach, K., Leymann, F.: Using bpmn for modeling manufacturing processes. In: Proceedings of 43rd CIRP International Conference on Manufacturing Systems, pp. 515–522 (2010)
17. Pardillo, J.: A systematic review on the definition of UML profiles. In: Petriu, D.C., Rouquette, N., Haugen, Ø. (eds.) MODELS 2010, Part I. LNCS, vol. 6394, pp. 407–422. Springer, Heidelberg (2010)
18. Natschläger, C.: Deontic BPMN. In: Hameurlain, A., Liddle, S.W., Schewe, K.-D., Zhou, X. (eds.) DEXA 2011, Part II. LNCS, vol. 6861, pp. 264–278. Springer, Heidelberg (2011)
19. Schleicher, D., Leymann, F., Schumm, D., Weidmann, M.: Compliance scopes: Extending the bpmn 2.0 meta model to specify compliance requirements. In: 2010 IEEE International Conference on Service-Oriented Computing and Applications (SOCA), pp. 1–8. IEEE (2010)
20. Sungur, C.T., Spiess, P., Oertel, N., Kopp, O.: Extending bpmn for wireless sensor networks. In: 2013 IEEE 15th Conference on Business Informatics (CBI), pp. 109–116. IEEE (2013)
21. Korherr, B., List, B.: Extending the epc and the bpmn with business process goals and performance measures. In: ICEIS (3), pp. 287–294 (2007)
22. Awad, A., Grosskopf, A., Meyer, A., Weske, M.: Enabling resource assignment constraints in bpmn. Hasso Plattner Institute, Potsdam (2009)
23. Bocciarelli, P., D'Ambrogio, A.: A bpmn extension for modeling non functional properties of business processes. In: Proceedings of the 2011 Symposium on Theory of Modeling & Simulation: DEVS Integrative M&S Symposium, Society for Computer Simulation International, pp. 160–168 (2011)
24. Friedenstab, J., Janiesch, C., Matzner, M., Muller, O.: Extending bpmn for business activity monitoring. In: 2012 45th Hawaii International Conference on System Science (HICSS), pp. 4158–4167. IEEE (2012)
25. Lodhi, A., Küppen, V., Saake, G.: An extension of bpmn meta-model for evaluation of business processes. Scientific Journal of Riga Technical University. Computer Sciences 43(1), 27–34 (2011)
26. Magnani, M., Cucci, F.: BPMN: How much does it cost? An incremental approach. In: Alonso, G., Dadam, P., Rosemann, M. (eds.) BPM 2007. LNCS, vol. 4714, pp. 80–87. Springer, Heidelberg (2007)
27. Altuhhov, O., Matulevičius, R., Ahmed, N.: An extension of business process model and notation for security risk management. International Journal of Information System Modeling and Design (IJISMD) 4(4), 93–113 (2013)
28. Brucker, A.D., Hang, I., Lückemeyer, G., Ruparel, R.: Securebpmn: Modeling and enforcing access control requirements in business processes. In: Proceedings of the 17th ACM Symposium on Access Control Models and Technologies, pp. 123–126. ACM (2012)
29. Marcinkowski, B., Kuciapski, M.: A business process modeling notation extension for risk handling. In: Cortesi, A., Chaki, N., Saeed, K., Wierzchoń, S. (eds.) CISIM 2012. LNCS, vol. 7564, pp. 374–381. Springer, Heidelberg (2012)

30. Rodríguez, A., Fernández-Medina, E., Piattini, M.: A bpmn extension for the modeling of security requirements in business processes. IEICE Transactions on Information and Systems 90(4), 745–752 (2007)
31. Saleem, M., Jaafar, J., Hassan, M.: A domain-specific language for modelling security objectives in a business process models of soa applications. AISS 4(1), 353–362 (2012)
32. Braun, R., Esswein, W.: Extending bpmn for modeling resource aspects in the domain of machine tools. WIT Transactions on Engineering Sciences (87), 450–458 (2014)
33. Großkopf, A.: An extended resource information layer for bpmn. Hasso-Plattner-Institute for IT Systems Engineering, University of Potsdam (2007)
34. Stroppi, L.J.R., Chiotti, O., Villarreal, P.D.: Extended resource perspective support for bpmn and bpel. CIbSE, 56–69 (2012)
35. Magnani, M., Montesi, D.: BPDMN: A conservative extension of bpmn with enhanced data representation capabilities. arXiv preprint arXiv:0907.1978 (2009)
36. Supulniece, I., Businska, L., Kirikova, M.: Towards extending bpmn with the knowledge dimension. Enterprise, Business-Process and Information Systems Modeling, 69–81 (2010)
37. Zor, S., Leymann, F., Schumm, D.: A proposal of bpmn extensions for the manufacturing domain. In: Proceedings of 44th CIRP International Conference on Manufacturing Systems (2011)
38. Braun, R., Schlieter, H., Burwitz, M., Esswein, W.: Bpmn4cp: Design and implementation of a bpmn extension for clinical pathways. Research Report TU Dresden
39. Pillat, R.M., Oliveira, T.C., Fonseca, F.L.: Introducing software process tailoring to bpmn: Bpmnt. In: 2012 International Conference on Software and System Process (ICSSP), pp. 58–62. IEEE (2012)
40. Gagne, D., Trudel, A.: Time-bpmn. In: IEEE Conference on Commerce and Enterprise Computing, CEC 2009, pp. 361–367. IEEE (2009)
41. Charfi, A., Müller, H., Mezini, M.: Aspect-oriented business process modeling with ao4bpmn. Modelling Foundations and Applications, 48–61 (2010)
42. Brambilla, M., Fraternali, P., Vaca Ruiz, C.K.: Combining social web and bpm for improving enterprise performances: the bpm4people approach to social bpm. In: Proceedings of the 21st International Conference Companion on World Wide Web, pp. 223–226. ACM (2012)
43. Kopp, O., Binz, T., Breitenbücher, U., Leymann, F.: BPMN4TOSCA: A domain-specific language to model management plans for composite applications. In: Mendling, J., Weidlich, M. (eds.) BPMN 2012. LNBIP, vol. 125, pp. 38–52. Springer, Heidelberg (2012)
44. Lohmann, N., Nyolt, M.: Artifact-centric modeling using BPMN. In: Pallis, G., Jmaiel, M., Charfi, A., Graupner, S., Karabulut, Y., Guinea, S., Rosenberg, F., Sheng, Q.Z., Pautasso, C., Ben Mokhtar, S. (eds.) ICSOC 2011 Workshops. LNCS, vol. 7221, pp. 54–65. Springer, Heidelberg (2012)
45. Wolter, C., Schaad, A.: Modeling of task-based authorization constraints in BPMN. In: Alonso, G., Dadam, P., Rosemann, M. (eds.) BPM 2007. LNCS, vol. 4714, pp. 64–79. Springer, Heidelberg (2007)

Matching of Events and Activities - An Approach Based on Constraint Satisfaction

Thomas Baier[1], Andreas Rogge-Solti[2], Mathias Weske[1], and Jan Mendling[2]

[1] Hasso Plattner Institute at the University of Potsdam
Prof.-Dr.-Helmert-Str. 2-3, D-14482 Potsdam, Germany
`firstname.lastname@hpi.uni-potsdam.de`
[2] Wirtschaftsuniversität Wien, Welthandelsplatz 1, 1020 Vienna, Austria
`firstname.lastname@wu.ac.at`

Abstract. Nowadays, business processes are increasingly supported by IT systems that produce massive amounts of event data during the execution of a process. This event data can be used to analyze the process using process mining techniques to discover the real process, measure conformance to a given process model, or to enhance existing models with performance information. While it is essential to map the produced events to activities of a given process model for conformance analysis and process model annotation, it is also an important step for the straightforward interpretation of process discovery results. In order to accomplish this mapping with minimal manual effort, we developed a semi-automatic approach that maps events to activities by transforming the mapping problem into the optimization of a constraint satisfaction problem. The approach uses log-replay techniques and has been evaluated using a real process collection from the financial services and telecommunication domains. The evaluation results demonstrate the robustness of the approach towards non-conformant execution and that the technique is able to efficiently reduce the number of possible mappings.

Keywords: Process Mining, Event Mapping, Business Process Intelligence, Constraint Satisfaction.

1 Introduction

Organizations conduct business processes with the support of IT systems that typically log each step made by process participants or systems in the process. Individual entries in such logs represent the execution of services, the submission of a form, or other related tasks that in combination realize a business process. In order to improve business processes and to align IT process execution with existing business goals, a clear understanding of how processes are executed is necessary. Using the event data logged by IT systems, process mining techniques help organizations to get a better understanding of their processes by discovering and enhancing process models or by checking the conformance of the execution to the specification [1]. Yet, conformance checking and enhancement of process models have one important requirement: the mapping of log entries produced by

U. Frank et al. (Eds.): PoEM 2014, LNBIP 197, pp. 58–72, 2014.

IT systems to the corresponding process activities in the process models has to be known. Furthermore, such a mapping is not only necessary for conformance checking and process model enhancement, but it is also very helpful for discovery. The benefit of a discovered process model can only be fully exploited if the presented results use the same terminology that is known to the business analysts. Yet, such a mapping is often not existing as the logging mechanism of IT systems are usually not designed to log events for defined activities of a process model. In fact, it is often a tedious task to reconstruct a mapping from database column entries with cryptic names to the corresponding activities in the process models.

In this paper, we offer means to help the analyst to identify the mapping between a process model and events in an event log produced by an information system. Defining such a mapping is generally hard to do manually due to its combinatorial complexity. While there exist automatic techniques such as [2], they do not achieve precision and recall that would allow an analyst to accept the mapping proposal without double checking. Against this background, our contribution is a technique based on constraint satisfaction that drastically reduces the set of permissible mappings, which can be then efficiently inspected by the analyst. In contrast to recent approaches towards N:M mappings, it builds on the observation that events that are more fine-granular than model activities can be pre-processed with clustering, selection, and correlation [3,4], which makes the identification effectively a 1:1-match problem.

The remainder of this paper is structured as follows. Section 2 states the formal concepts and gives a formal definition of the mapping problem. Having laid the foundations, the matching technique is introduced in Section 3. In Section 4 the proposed approach is evaluated using an industry process model collection and simulated event logs. Related work is discussed in Section 5 and Section 6 concludes the work.

2   Preliminaries

Let S be a finite set of states, and A be a set of activities. A process model $M = (S, s_I, s_F, A, T)$ is a transition system that defines the allowed sequences of activity executions in a business process. Here, $T \in (S \times A \times S)$ is a finite set of transition relations modeling the allowed activities in a given state that result in a succeeding state. For example $(s_1, a, s_2) \in T$ implies that we can perform activity a in state s_1 and reach state s_2. A model has an initial state $s_I \in S$ and a final state $s_F \in S$.

The function $\tau : M \rightarrow \mathcal{P}(A^*)$ captures all execution sequences that start with the initial state s_I and end in the final state s_F and are allowed in T. Note that the number of these execution sequences is infinite if the model contains loops.   For example the model $M = (\{s_1, s_2, s_3\}, s_1, s_3, \{a, b, c\}, \{(s_1, a, s_2), (s_2, b, s_2), (s_2, c, s_3)\})$ has the execution sequences $\tau(M) = \{\langle a, c \rangle, \langle a, b, c \rangle, \langle a, b, b, c \rangle, \ldots\}$.

An execution sequence is also referred to as a process instance. Thus, we will use the terms execution sequence and process instance synonymously in this paper.

An IT system that supports process executions typically records events for each process instance in an event log [1]. Note that the relation of event instances to process instances might not be trivial in every practical setting. Yet, there is plenty of work on event correlation that tries to relate event instances to process instances (see e.g. [4,5]). In this work, we therefore assume that this relation is already given. Each process instance is represented as a sequence of events $\langle e_1, \ldots, e_n \rangle$, $e_i \in E$ and also referred to as a trace θ, where E denotes the set of all events. A labeling function $\alpha : E \to \Sigma$ assigns each event a label from the set of labels Σ. In this paper we denote traces as sequences of their labels, e.g. $\langle k, l, k, m \rangle$ is a trace with four consecutive events e_1, e_2, e_3, e_4 with $\alpha(e_1) = k$, $\alpha(e_2) = l$, $\alpha(e_3) = k$, and $\alpha(e_4) = m$. An event log L is a multiset of traces.

Confronted with a process model M and an event log L, the challenge is to derive the relation between the activities $a \in A$ and the event classes $e \in E$. In this paper, we assume a 1:1 relation. Thus, we are looking for the bijective function $\mu : \Sigma \to A$ that maps event labels to their corresponding activities.

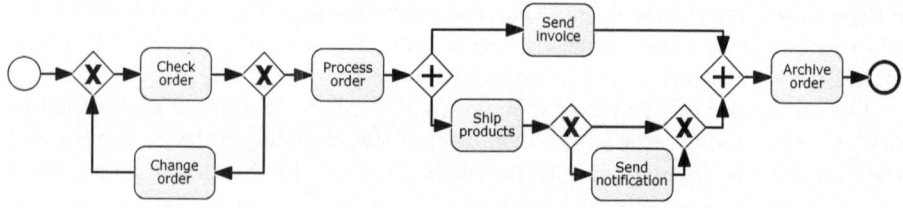

Fig. 1. Order process model in BPMN

Having laid the formal foundations, let us look at an example. Fig. 1 introduces a simple order process that will be used to illustrate the main concepts in Section 3. Table 1 shows an exemplary event log with 5 traces that have been produced by an IT system supporting the order process depicted in Fig. 1. Obviously, it is not straightforward to interpret the given event log as the event labels are cryptic database field names that cannot be easily matched to the names of the activities in the process model. Yet, once the mapping is established as shown in Table 2, we can use the event log to check conformance between the model and the log. For example, we are able to detect that there is a case in the log, in which the order has been changed after it has already been processed. It is critical for organizations to detect, and accordingly react to such non-conformant behavior [1]. Moreover, using process discovery techniques, a new process model that reflects the actual as-is process, including all deviations, can be automatically created. If the event log contains additional data, such as timestamps, even more techniques such as the prediction of remaining execution time for running instances [6] become possible.

Table 1. Event log (L) of order process (M)

	Label sequence
θ_1	O_CHK, O_PRC, I_SM, P_SP, O_ARC
θ_2	O_CHK, O_RCO, O_CHK, O_PRC, P_SP, P_NOT, I_SM, O_ARC
θ_3	O_CHK, O_PRC, O_RCO, P_SP, P_NOT, I_SM, O_ARC
θ_4	O_CHK, O_PRC, I_SM, P_SP, P_NOT, O_ARC
θ_5	O_CHK, O_PRC, P_SP, I_SM, P_NOT, O_ARC

Table 2. Mapping μ

Activity	Event
Check order	O_CHK
Change order	O_RCO
Process order	O_PRC
Send invoice	I_SM
Ship Products	P_SP
Send notification	P_NOT
Archive order	O_ARC

3   Mapping Event Log and Process Model Using Automatic Matching

This section introduces the approach for the mapping of events to given activities in a process model. The approach consists of three phases as depicted in Fig. 2.

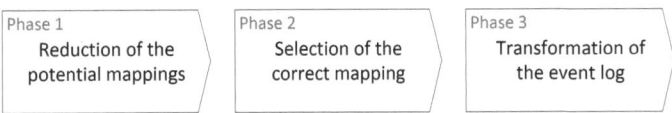

Fig. 2. Phases of the mapping approach

The first phase is an automated phase that builds and solves a constraint satisfaction problem to reduce the number of possible mappings between activities and events. The result of this phase is a set of potential event-activity mappings. During the second phase, the analyst is guided to select the correct mapping from the derived potential mappings. Finally, the last phase is used to automatically transform one or many event logs to reflect the activities in the process model. In the following sections, we will elaborate on each of the three phases.

3.1   Reduction of the Potential Set of Event–Activity Mappings

The first phase of our approach deals with the definition of a constraint satisfaction problem (CSP) that is used to restrain the possible mappings of events and activities. A CSP is a triple $CSP = (X, D, C)$ where $X = \langle x_1, x_2, \ldots, x_n \rangle$ is an n-tuple of variables with the corresponding domains specified in the n-tuple $D = \langle D_1, D_2, \ldots, D_n \rangle$ such that $x_i \in D_i$ [7]. $C = \langle c_1, c_2, \ldots, c_t \rangle$ is the t-tuple of constraints. We use predicate logic to express the constraints used in this paper.

The set of solutions to a CSP is denoted as $S = \{S_1, S_2, \ldots, S_m\}$, where each solution $S_k = \langle s_1, s_2, \ldots, s_n \rangle$ is an n-tuple with $k \in 1..m$, $s_i \in D_i$ and every constraint in C is satisfied.

To build the CSP, first, the activities and event labels need to be mapped to the set of variables and their domains. Therefore, a bijective function $var : A \rightarrow X$ is defined, which assigns each activity to a variable with the natural numbers $1..|\Sigma|$ as domain. Moreover, a bijective function $val : \Sigma \rightarrow 1..|\Sigma|$ is defined, which enumerates event labels, i.e., which assigns each event label a natural number in the range from 1 to the number of event labels. Table 3 and Table 4 show the mapping var and the mapping val respectively for the example given in Section 2.

Table 3. Mapping var			Table 4. Mapping val	

Activity $a \in A$	Variable $var(a) \in X$		Event $\alpha(e) \in \Sigma$	Value $val(\alpha(e)) \in 1..|\Sigma|$
Check order	x_1		O_CHK	1
Change order	x_2		O_RCO	2
Process order	x_3		O_PRC	3
Send invoice	x_4		I_SM	4
Ship Products	x_5		P_SP	5
Send notification	x_6		P_NOT	6
Archive order	x_7		O_ARC	7

Because we are looking at a 1:1 relationship between events and activities, a constraint that captures that no two activities can be mapped to the same event label can be specified. This constraint is defined as $c_1 \equiv \forall(x_i, x_j) \in X^2 : i \neq j \implies x_i \neq x_j$. It is available in most constraint solvers as the $allDifferent$ constraint. With the variables, domains, and the $allDifferent$ constraint defined, the solutions to the CSP reflect all possible mappings between events and activities, i.e., for n activities and events there are $n!$ solutions. For the example given in Section 2 this are be $7! = 5040$ possible mappings. In the following, we present an approach to tackle this complexity by combining the information available in the log with the knowledge of the process model structure.

To generate more constraints and thus be able to reduce the number of possible mappings, the next step of the first phase is the replay of the event log in the process model. Because the event log can contain multiple traces that encode the same ordering of events, the log is preprocessed to extract all unique variants of traces. The tuple $V = \langle v_1, v_2, \ldots, v_k \rangle$ contains all variants $v_i \in L$, $i \in 1..k$ and the tuple $W = \langle w_1, w_2, \ldots, w_k \rangle$ holds the number of occurrences for each variant, e.g., the variant v_1 is contained w_1 times in the log L. As the example log in Table 1 only contains unique traces, v_i refers to trace θ_i, and $w_i = 1$ for any $i \in 1..k$ in the following examples.

As the relation between events and activities is unknown at this stage, the replay of one trace variant v_i is essentially a mapping of each trace variant v_i to all possible execution sequences that have the same length as v_i. Therefore, we define the relation $vpi \subseteq V \times \tau(M)$ such that $vpi = \{(v_i, pi_j) \mid v_i \in V, pi_j \in \tau(M), |v_i| = |pi_j|\}$.

The relation vpi describes possible mappings between sequences of event labels and sequences of activities. In fact, we are interested in limiting the number of possible mappings to those that result in the highest number of traces with valid execution sequences, i.e., in the mapping that yields the *maximal conformance* when replaying the log with the mapped events. Each tuple in vpi reflects a replay of a trace variant in the model. For easier explanation of the procedure, let us first assume that all traces in the log are conformant to the model. First, a constraint $c_{i,j}$ is created for each tuple $(v_i, pi_j) \in vpi$. The constraint $c_{i,j}$ reflects a mapping of event labels to activities by assigning each event label to the activity at the same position in the sequence. Hence, $c_{i,j}$ has the form $\bigwedge_{k \in 1..|v_i|} var(a_k) = val(\alpha(e_k))$. Note that there can be several paths in the model that have the same length as the trace variant. In case of conformant execution, we need to ensure that for each trace variant v_i one of these constraints holds, i.e., that one of the defined mappings allows a valid replay of the trace variant in the model. Therefore, a constraint c_i is formulated for each trace variant. The constraint c_i has the form $\bigvee c_{i,j}, \forall j : \exists (v_i, pi_j) \in vpi$.

Consider the variant $v_1 = \langle$ O_CHK, O_PRC, I_SM, P_SP, O_ARC $\rangle$. There are two execution sequences in the model that have the same length as v_1. These are $pi_1 = \langle$ Check order, Process order, Send invoice, Ship products, Archive order $\rangle$ and $pi_2 = \langle$ Check order, Process order, Ship products, Send invoice, Archive order $\rangle$. Thus, we first create the two constraints $c_{1,1} : x_1 = 1 \wedge x_3 = 3 \wedge x_4 = 4 \wedge x_5 = 5 \wedge x_7 = 7$ and $c_{1,2} : x_1 = 1 \wedge x_3 = 3 \wedge x_5 = 4 \wedge x_4 = 5 \wedge x_7 = 7$. Given the two constraints $c_{1,1}$ and $c_{1,2}$, the constraint $c_1 : c_{1,1} \vee c_{1,2}$ is derived. By adding the constraint c_1 to the CSP, we already fix the mappings of "Check order", "Ship products" and "Archive order" and thereby limit the possible mappings from $7! = 5040$ to $(7 - 3)! = 24$. Once the constraint c_2 for trace variant v_2 has been built in the same manner and added to the constraint satisfaction problem, the number of solutions satisfying both constraints is reduced to a single one, which is the mapping as specified in Table 2.

Yet, adding the constraint c_3 for trace variant v_3 results in a CSP that has no solution. This is due to the fact that v_3 is not compliant to the model The CSP tries to satisfy all constraints and thus requires every trace variant to be conformant. Therefore, to handle non-compliant traces, the CSP is reformulated as an optimization problem. The optimal solution to the problem is a mapping in which the maximum number of traces is conformant to the model. It is important to note that we assume that there is a sufficient number of conformant traces in the log to be able to retrieve a correct mapping.

The constraint c_i, which has been built for each trace variant, is therefore used to define a boolean variable $validVariant_i$ for each trace variant as follows:

$$validVariant_i = \begin{cases} 1 & c_i = \text{true} \\ 0 & \text{otherwise.} \end{cases}$$

The variable $validVariant_i$ reflects whether trace variant v_i represents a valid execution sequence with the chosen mapping. Having defined the variable $validVariant_i$ for each trace variant, a new variable $validTraces \in 0..|L|$ is introduced that sums up all valid traces by multiplying the valid variants with the number of traces sharing the corresponding behavior:

$$validTraces = \sum_{i=1}^{|V|} validVariant_i \cdot w_i.$$

The variable $validTraces$ is set as the optimization goal that should be maximized when solving the CSP. This way, the CSP for the example can be solved with $validVariant_1 = 1$, $validVariant_2 = 1$ and $validVariant_3 = 0$, yielding $validTraces = 2$. The optimal solution is again the correct mapping as shown in Table 2. Hence, the approach is able to deal with non-compliant traces in the log. Furthermore, this shows that it is not necessary to have a complete log containing all possible behavior in order to construct an unambiguous mapping. Note however that there are cases where it is not possible to reduce the number of solutions to a single solution. In the next section, we discuss these cases and how we can handle them.

3.2   Selection of the Correct Event–Activity Mapping

The previous section introduced the approach for an automatic matching of event labels and activities. Still, there are cases for which no unambiguous mapping can be automatically derived. Basically, this is due to two common control flow constructs: choice and concurrency. Figure 3a and Fig. 3b depict the simplest forms of these two constructs. While it is impossible to unambiguously derive a mapping for activities "A" and "B" in these two cases, it is possible for the cases depicted in Fig. 3c and Fig. 3d. This is due to the fact that for case (a) and case (b) the branches are equivalent in their behavior, while they are not in case (c) and case (d). For case (c) there are two possible trace variants. Yet, a single trace is enough to unambiguously determine a mapping between corresponding events in a log and the activities in the model, if we assume that the available event labels are known. For example, we only need a trace with the two events corresponding to activities "B" and "C", or a trace with the event corresponding to activity "A". Regarding case (d), there are three possible trace variants. Still, two different traces are enough to unambiguously distinguish the activities from each other, because activity "A" is the only activity that can be first and last. Note that to reach an unambiguous mapping it is required to see at least one trace in which activity "A" was executed before, and another trace

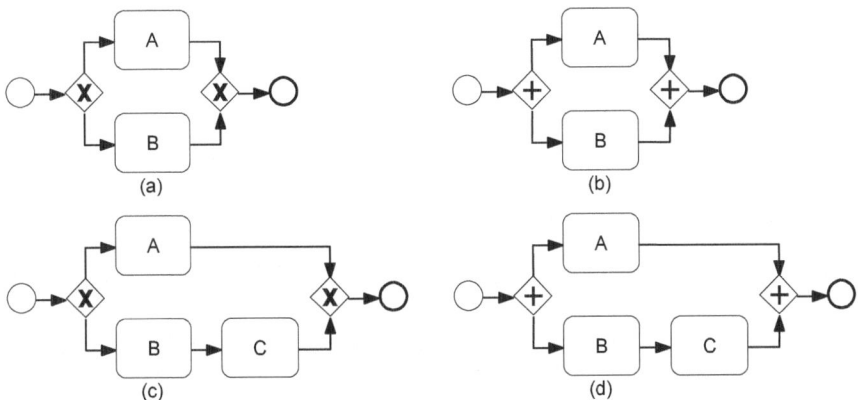

Fig. 3. Control flow patterns for choice and concurrency with different impact on potential mappings

where it was executed after the parallel activities "B" and "C". If this information is not contained in the log for any reason, a certain ambiguity remains in the automatically derived mapping.

Summing up, there are two main sources for ambiguities in the mapping. First, choices and parallel branches with identical behavior in the branches cause ambiguities. In this case, the number of the undistinguishable branches combinatorially increases the potential mappings. The second source for ambiguities is behavior that is possible in the model but not contained in the event log.

Ambiguous mappings, i.e., cases in which the CSP has multiple solutions, cannot be automatically resolved and require a domain expert to decide the mapping for the concerned events and activities. Nonetheless, this decision can be supported by the mapping approach. To aid the analyst with the disambiguation of multiple potential mappings, we introduce a questioning approach. The analyst will be presented one event label at a time with the possible activities to which this event label can be mapped. Once the analyst decided which of the candidate activities belongs to the event label, this mapping is converted into a new constraint that is added to the CSP. Consecutively, the CSP is solved again. In case there are still multiple solutions, the analyst is asked to make another decision for a different event label. This procedure is repeated until the CSP yields a single solution. The goal is to pose as few questions to the analyst as possible. To achieve this goal, we look into all solutions and choose the event label that is assigned to the maximal number of different activities.

To illustrate this principle, consider the example trace $\theta_1 = \langle k, l, m \rangle$. The events of which should be matched to the activities in the model in Fig. 3d. Building and solving the CSP for this example leads to three solutions: $S = \{\langle x_1 = 1, x_2 = 2, x_3 = 3 \rangle, \langle x_1 = 2, x_2 = 1, x_3 = 3 \rangle, \langle x_1 = 3, x_2 = 1, x_3 = 2 \rangle\}$. The value 2, which corresponds to event label "l" in this case, is assigned to all three variables, which correspond to the activities "A", "B" and "C". Opposed

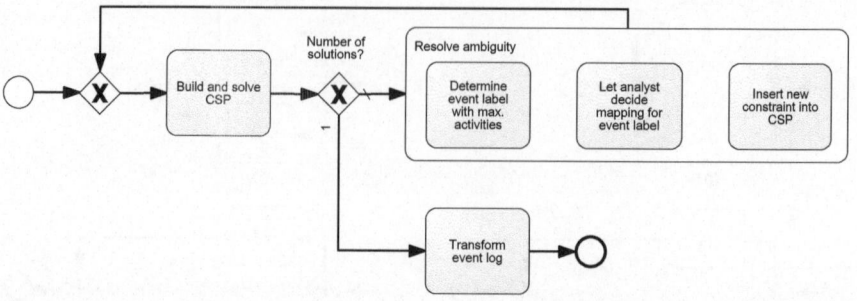

Fig. 4. Detailed flow of the matching approach

to this, the other two values are only assigned to a subset of the three variables. By deciding the matching activity for event label "l", the CSP contains only one solution. Deciding the matching for any of the other two event labels results in a CSP with two possible solutions.

3.3   Transformation of the Event Log

Having defined the procedure to build a CSP and iteratively resolve any ambiguities, the next step is to use the solution of the CSP to transform the event log. A single solution of the CSP can be interpreted as the mapping μ. The mapping μ can be used to iterate over all traces in the event log and replace each event label $\alpha(e_i)$ with the label returned by $\mu(\alpha(e_i))$. This results in an event log where each event carries the label of its corresponding activity. Such an event log can then be used as input for any process mining technique and other analyses of the process.

4   Evaluation

For the purpose of evaluation, the approach presented in this paper has been implemented as a plug-in in the process mining framework ProM[1]. The Petri net notation has been chosen as modeling language for the implementation of the approach, because it has well-defined semantics and can be verified for correctness [8]. Furthermore, most of the common modeling languages, as e.g. BPMN and EPC, can be transformed into Petri nets [9]. As solver for the constraint satisfaction problem, the java library CHOCO[2] has been used.

4.1   Experimental Setup

To evaluate our approach with real life business processes, we used the *BIT process library, Release 2009* that was analyzed by Fahland et al. in [10] and is

---

[1] See http://processmining.org
[2] See http://www.emn.fr/z-info/choco-solver/

openly available to academic research[3]. The process model collection contains models of financial services, telecommunications, and other domains [10]. First, the models have been transformed into Petri nets and checked for lifelocks, deadlocks and boundedness. Models that contained lifelocks, deadlocks or where not 1-bounded have been filtered out. Furthermore, models with disconnected activities (i.e., single activities or groups of activities that are not connected to the remaining process) have also been disregarded. After the filtering step, 796 models remained with which we tested our approach. There exist some models in the collection with very large state spaces due to massive parallelism. Fahland et al. [10] report that about 8.5 percent of the models they analyzed had state spaces of over 1 000 000 states, cf. [10, Table 2]. In our case, we start with an already reduced collection, where many of the models with large state spaces were filtered out, e.g., due to unboundedness. Of the considered 796 models, only less than 3 percent led to memory problems of our algorithm. Finally, we could use 779 processes for the evaluation of our approach. For these process models, we generated event logs by simulating the processes.

The purpose of our experiment is to evaluate (1) the *effectiveness* of our approach and (2) the *efficiency* of the method with regard to the required manual work by the process analyst. Therefore, we created two sets of event logs from the simulated processes. First, we randomly chose traces for each process to generate event logs with an increasing number of traces to show how the approach performs depending on the available number of trace variants. It is expected that the more different traces the algorithm is provided with as input, the more constraints are created on the possible mappings, which in turn make it easier for the analyst to select the correct mapping from the smaller set of resulting alternatives.

Second, to assess how the approach is able to deal with noise, we again randomly chose traces for each process, but fixed the number of traces for each process. The resulting logs were then used to create logs with different levels of noise by shuffling, duplicating and removing events for a different percentage of traces, i.e., we controlled the amount of noisy traces. For both log sets we evaluated (1) whether the approach is able to find the correct mapping, and (2) how many questions need to be answered by the analyst to arrive at the correct mapping. Moreover, we measured the runtime performance.

4.2 Evaluation of Effectiveness and Efficiency

Starting with the evaluation with logs of different sizes, we generated seven different event logs for each process, each event log with a specific amount of traces. Looking at (1) the *effectiveness* of our approach, it turned out that we were able to derive the correct mapping for all of the processes independent of the number of available traces. Figure 5a shows how many times we would have had to ask the analyst to decide to which activity an event belongs. For the set of event logs that entail only one trace, the approach is able to build the

---

[3] See http://www.zurich.ibm.com/csc/bit/downloads.html

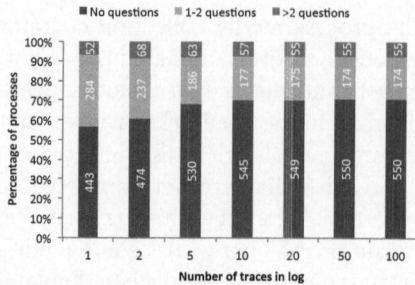 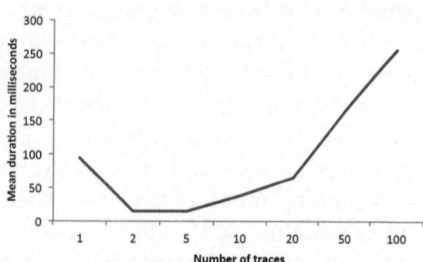

(a) Impact of the number of available traces on the number of necessary questions for conformant event logs.

(b) Mean duration of the mapping algorithm for different log sizes.

Fig. 5. Experiment results with varying number of traces

correct mapping for 443 (57 %) of the processes without any interaction with the analyst. For 284 (36 %) of the processes one or two decisions were necessary to be made manually, which is still very little effort. Only 52 (7 %) of the processes required more than two questions. The maximal number of questions for one process was six questions.

Furthermore, Fig. 5a depicts that with an increasing number of traces, the number of required manual decisions decreases until the saturation point is reached at 50 traces for all processes. Thus, it can be seen that for logs that only contain valid traces with respect to the model, our approach is both effective (i.e., it includes the correct solution even if only a small number of traces is provided as input to the algorithm) and efficient (i.e., it requires only limited interaction).

Regarding (2) the *efficiency* of the matching approach, we also measured the time that the approach takes to compute the solutions. Fig. 5b shows the mean durations for each of the evaluation sets with different log sizes. First of all, it can be stated that the approach runs conveniently fast, with a maximum average duration of 300 milliseconds. Moreover, it can be seen that there is an increase in speed depending on the trace size from one to two input traces. This increase in speed is due to the increased number of constraints, which help the constraint solver to reduce the search space. Nevertheless, the gain by the reduction of the search space is at some point outweighed with further increase of the log size as the construction of the constraints takes more time and the solver needs to evaluate a higher number of constraints that do not contribute to the reduction of the search space. Yet, the maximal duration we encountered was around 1 minute for 100 traces in the log. Hence, we argue that the approach runs fast enough in practical settings.

Turning to the evaluation with noise, we took a random set of 100 traces for each process model and randomly inserted noise into a fixed percentage of these traces. By continuously increasing the number of traces that contain noise, we evaluated the impact of noise to the effectiveness and efficiency of our approach.

As result of this evaluation it can be stated that the mapping results are not influenced by the noise up to a level of more than 90 percent of traces that contain noise. Still, the increasing noise level has a negative impact on the runtime of the mapping approach. While the mapping algorithm requires on average only 350 milliseconds for logs without noise, it takes more than 10 times as long for logs in which 50 percent of the traces contain noise.

4.3 Discussion

Summing up, it can be stated that the presented approach performs well in practical settings and requires none or only very little manual interaction for the majority of cases. Yet, it has to be noted that for the case that the event log and process model are not on the same abstraction level, further work will be necessary to establish the 1:1 relationship required by the matching approach. Future research should investigate the efficient usage of clustering, correlation and filtering techniques for the establishment of a 1:1 relationship for those cases where it is not yet in place.

A limitation of the presented approach is that it cannot deal with models that contain massive parallelism. In these cases, finding all potential execution sequences through the model with the same length as the input trace is costly and cannot be handled with reasonable computational resources. Yet, more than 97 percent of the filtered models we used (i.e., those that contain no lifelocks, deadlocks, and are 1-bounded) do not have massive state spaces and can be processed in reasonable computation time. This indicates that the approach is practicable for a large share of real-life process models.

In the next section, we discuss related work and the differences to our approach.

5   Related Work

Research related to this paper can be generally subdivided into approaches working on event logs and approaches working on process models. The work that focuses on event logs can be categorized into event log abstraction and event correlation. The related techniques that work on process models fall into one of three categories: process model abstraction, process model matching and process model similarity. In both main categories—work on event logs and on process models—there are a few hybrid approaches that take both an event log and a process model as input. Yet, these approaches always focus on either log or model when it comes to the objectives and the output of those techniques.

Looking at the approaches focusing on event logs, there are several approaches aiming at the abstraction of events to activities. Günther et al. introduce in [11] an approach that clusters events to activities using a distance function based on time or sequence position. Due to performance issues with this approach, a new means of abstraction on the level of event classes is introduced by Günther et al. in [12]. These event classes are clustered globally based on co-occurrence of related terms, yielding better performance but lower accuracy. A similar approach introducing semantic relatedness, N:M relations, and context dependence is defined by Li et al. in [3]. Another approach that uses pattern recognition and machine learning techniques for abstraction is introduced by Cook et al. in [13]. Together with the fuzzy miner, Günther and van der Aalst present an approach to abstract a mined process model by removing and clustering less frequent behavior [14]. While all these approaches aim at a mapping of events to activities, they are designed to automatically construct activities and not to match events to activities that have already been defined a-priori. In [2], we introduced an approach that aims at to mapping of events to pre-defined activities. Yet, this approach still required more manual work as the precision of matchings is not sufficiently high. In contrast, the approach presented in this paper requires only very little manual effort to match events to pre-defined activities.

The second branch of related approaches working on event logs are those works that deal with event correlation, as the work by Perez et al. in [4]. The main objective of event correlation techniques is to group events belonging to the same process instance. Typically, event attributes are investigated to find similarities. These techniques are similar to our approach in the fact that they also look at a relation between a set of events and a set of other entities. Yet, these approaches specialize in finding a 1:N mapping by clustering events of different types based on similarities and are therefore not suited to address the 1:1 mapping problem between events and predefined activities. In fact, we assume that the correlation of events to process instances is either already given, or can be established by an approach like [4].

Our work is also related to automatic matching for process models. While matching has been partially addressed in various works on process similarity [15], there are only a few papers that cover this topic as their major focus. The work on the ICoP framework defines a generic approach for process model matching [16]. This framework is extended with semantic concepts and probabilistic optimization in [17,18]. Further, general concepts from ontology matching are adopted in [19]. The implications of different abstraction levels for finding correspondences is covered in [20]. However, all these works focus on finding matches between two process models, not between events and activities.

6   Conclusion

In this paper we introduce a novel means for the mapping of events to activities that can be used as a preprocessing step to enable business process intelligence techniques (e.g., process mining). The approach uses behavioral information stored in existing business process models and the execution order of events generated by IT systems to establish a connection between conceptual process models and operational execution data.

The approach distinguishes from current works by establishing a 1:1 relation between events and a given set of activities in a process model. As we have shown in the evaluation in Section 4, the newly introduced matching technique performs well and requires very little manual intervention. It is also robust towards noise. Yet, there are a few processes that cannot be handled due to their very large state spaces. Future work needs to investigate, how such processes can be handled efficiently.

References

1. van der Aalst, W.M.P.: Process Mining: Discovery, Conformance and Enhancement of Business Processes. Springer (2011)
2. Baier, T., Mendling, J., Weske, M.: Bridging abstraction layers in process mining. Information Systems (2014)
3. Li, J., Bose, R.P.J.C., van der Aalst, W.M.P.: Mining context-dependent and interactive business process maps using execution patterns. In: Muehlen, M.z., Su, J. (eds.) BPM 2010 Workshops. LNBIP, vol. 66, pp. 109–121. Springer, Heidelberg (2011)
4. Pérez-Castillo, R., Weber, B., de Guzmán, I.G.R., Piattini, M., Pinggera, J.: Assessing event correlation in non-process-aware information systems. Software and Systems Modeling, 1–23 (2012)
5. Rozsnyai, S., Slominski, A., Lakshmanan, G.T.: Discovering event correlation rules for semi-structured business processes. In: Proceedings of the 5th ACM International Conference on Distributed Event-based System, pp. 75–86 (2011)
6. Rogge-Solti, A., Weske, M.: Prediction of remaining service execution time using stochastic petri nets with arbitrary firing delays. In: Basu, S., Pautasso, C., Zhang, L., Fu, X. (eds.) ICSOC 2013. LNCS, vol. 8274, pp. 389–403. Springer, Heidelberg (2013)
7. Freuder, E., Mackworth, A.: Constraint satisfaction: An emerging paradigm. In: Handbook of Constraint Programming. Foundations of Artificial Intelligence, vol. 2, pp. 13–27. Elsevier (2006)
8. van der Aalst, W.M.P.: Verification of workflow nets. In: Azéma, P., Balbo, G. (eds.) ICATPN 1997. LNCS, vol. 1248, pp. 407–426. Springer, Heidelberg (1997)
9. Lohmann, N., Verbeek, E., Dijkman, R.M.: Petri net transformations for business processes - a survey. T. Petri Nets and Other Models of Concurrency 2, 46–63 (2009)
10. Fahland, D., Favre, C., Koehler, J., Lohmann, N., Völzer, H., Wolf, K.: Analysis on demand: Instantaneous soundness checking of industrial business process models. Data & Knowledge Engineering 70(5), 448–466 (2011)
11. Günther, C.W., van der Aalst, W.M.P.: Mining activity clusters from low-level event logs. In: BETA Working Paper Series. Volume WP 165, Eindhoven University of Technology (2006)
12. Günther, C.W., Rozinat, A., van der Aalst, W.M.P.: Activity mining by global trace segmentation. In: Rinderle-Ma, S., Sadiq, S., Leymann, F. (eds.) BPM 2009. LNBIP, vol. 43, pp. 128–139. Springer, Heidelberg (2010)
13. Cook, D.J., Krishnan, N.C., Rashidi, P.: Activity discovery and activity recognition: A new partnership. IEEE T. Cybernetics 43(3), 820–828 (2013)
14. Günther, C.W., van der Aalst, W.M.P.: Fuzzy mining – adaptive process simplification based on multi-perspective metrics. In: Alonso, G., Dadam, P., Rosemann, M. (eds.) BPM 2007. LNCS, vol. 4714, pp. 328–343. Springer, Heidelberg (2007)
15. Dijkman, R.M., Dumas, M., van Dongen, B.F., Käärik, R., Mendling, J.: Similarity of Business Process Models: Metrics and Evaluation. Information Systems 36(2), 498–516 (2011)

16. Weidlich, M., Dijkman, R., Mendling, J.: The iCoP framework: Identification of correspondences between process models. In: Pernici, B. (ed.) CAiSE 2010. LNCS, vol. 6051, pp. 483–498. Springer, Heidelberg (2010)
17. Leopold, H., Niepert, M., Weidlich, M., Mendling, J., Dijkman, R., Stuckenschmidt, H.: Probabilistic optimization of semantic process model matching. In: Barros, A., Gal, A., Kindler, E. (eds.) BPM 2012. LNCS, vol. 7481, pp. 319–334. Springer, Heidelberg (2012)
18. Klinkmüller, C., Weber, I., Mendling, J., Leopold, H., Ludwig, A.: Increasing recall of process model matching by improved activity label matching. In: Daniel, F., Wang, J., Weber, B. (eds.) BPM 2013. LNCS, vol. 8094, pp. 211–218. Springer, Heidelberg (2013)
19. Euzenat, J., Shvaiko, P.: Ontology Matching. Springer (2007)
20. Weidlich, M., Dijkman, R., Weske, M.: Behaviour equivalence and compatibility of business process models with complex correspondences. The Computer Journal 55(11), 1398–1418 (2012)

A Look into Business Process Modeling Guidelines through the Lens of the Technology Acceptance Model

Isel Moreno-Montes de Oca[1], Monique Snoeck[2], and Gladys Casas-Cardoso[1]

[1] Department of Computer Science, UCLV, Santa Clara, Cuba
{Isel,GCasas}@uclv.edu.cu
[2] Faculty of Business and Economics, KU Leuven, Belgium
Monique.Snoeck@kuleuven.be

Abstract. Business process modeling is one of the first steps towards achieving organizational goals in the requirements engineering phase. This is why business process modeling quality is an essential aspect for the development and technical support of any company. Modeling experts rely mainly on their personal experience, and the tacit knowledge. In order to help less experienced modelers, many authors have formulated modeling guidelines as a mean to achieve better model quality. Our research goal is to assess the acceptance of these guidelines for teaching purposes through a survey. To achieve this objective we investigate usefulness, ease of use and the intention to use of a collected set of pragmatic guidelines according to the technology acceptance model by means of a survey amongst Cuban PhD students. Results reveal the "best" and "worst" guidelines as perceived by novice modelers. We also witnessed that perceived ease of use has an important influence on the perceived usefulness, and, at the same time, both influence the novice modelers' intention to use the guidelines. This implies that to ensure usage of the guidelines by junior modelers, they should be understandable and their utility should be well-motivated.

Keywords: Business process modeling, Quality guidelines, Technology acceptance model.

1 Introduction

Business process modeling has recently received considerable attention in information systems (IS) engineering due to its increasing importance in practice [1]. Although business process modeling has been around for many years, only lately research has started to examine quality aspects pertaining to it [2]. Business process modeling quality can be defined as "all desirable properties of a model are fulfilled to satisfy the needs of the model users" [3]. Pragmatic guidelines have been proposed by different authors as a way to provide useable and effective guidelines [4] to help modelers achieving better quality of models [5]. Many of these guidelines have resulted from experimental research that determines advised thresholds below which processes should be more understandable, correct, modifiable, maintainable, etc. While the practical importance of the guidelines is recognized by different authors in first place

U. Frank et al. (Eds.): PoEM 2014, LNBIP 197, pp. 73–86, 2014.

because of their applicability for novices and non-experts in practice, a first problem is that they remain scattered across different research works, leading to a fragmented and even potentially incoherent set of guidelines. For example, some studies propose modeling guidelines to support the builders of business process models (e.g. [6, 7]) base on empirical research, or present guidelines that results from discussions on how to apply concepts comparable to structured programming to business process models (e.g. [8]). Some other studies focus on how different factors affect model understanding (e.g. [9]), or perform studies that produce new knowledge from where it is possible to extract modeling guidelines (e.g. [10]). To tackle this problem, we performed a Systematic Literature Review (SLR) on the quality of business process modeling [11]. From that SLR we collected 30 pragmatic modeling guidelines. We describe the complete collected list in section 2.2.

On the other hand, designing high quality information systems is a difficult task that requires good skills to convert real business requirements into high quality conceptual models. According to [12], the knowledge of modeling concepts, of the modeling language and of the domain to be modeled are important key factors affecting the quality of a conceptual model and, more specifically, of a business process model. Teaching such knowledge and skills to novice modelers is a challenging task considering that system analysis is by nature an inexact skill. As a result, the effectiveness of novice modelers becomes an important aspect for IS education. A second problem we deal with in the current paper is that the usability of business process modeling guidelines for teaching purposes and their impact on the modeling process has not been researched so far. For this reason, our goal is to assess the acceptance of the collected guidelines for teaching purposes through a survey of the use of business process modeling guidelines by novice modelers. We use the technology acceptance model [13] to predict the usage of the guidelines in terms of their perceived ease of use, perceived usefulness and intention to use. We then examine empirically whether the perceived ease of use and the perceived usefulness of the guidelines are correlated with intention to use. We proceed as follows. In Section 2 we describe the research design. Section 3 presents the findings of the paper, section 4 discusses the results and section 5 concludes the paper.

2   Research Design

2.1   Technology Acceptance Model

A possible model to evaluate the usability of the guidelines is the technology acceptance model (TAM) proposed by Davis in [13]. Since its beginning TAM has served as the basis for research aiming at examining usage intentions and behavior of users of IS (e.g. [14]). Over time, different variants of the TAM were created, one being the Unified Theory of Acceptance and Use of Technology (UTAUT) [15] which integrates eight models used in IT acceptance research. Research on technology adoption shows that the UTAUT has the highest power in explaining behaviour intention and usage: the UTAUT explains 70% of acceptance while other models explain about 40% [16]. The question remain whether the use of a TAM which targets the use of a "product" applies to the use of a "method" as well. According to Moody [17], there are clear parallels between user acceptance of IS and practitioner adoption of methods. For this reason, a theoretical model used to explain and predict user acceptance of IS may be used to explain and predict the adoption of methods, like for example pragmatic modeling guidelines. In this context, pragmatic guidelines can be interpreted as technology and their perceived usefulness, ease of use and intention to use evaluation can be investigated through technology acceptance models. On the other hand Riemenschneider et al. [18] found that extending the boundaries of these models from the domain of products to methods has demonstrated their resilience in adapting to a new domain and the differences required by the new domain. Yet their research investigated the adaptation to a software development methodology, which tends to be mandatory rather than voluntary and radical rather than incremental. The use of modeling guidelines on the other hand, tends to be rather voluntary than mandatory and incremental rather than radical. In this respect, and in line with Moody's finding, we believe the acceptance model can be considered as model to predict the adoption of guidelines. There remains the question of which model to use. A key purpose of TAM is to provide a basis for tracing the impact of external factors on internal thinking, attitudes and intentions [19]. The two core constructs that underlie TAM are perceived usefulness and perceived ease of use, which both lead to behavioral intention. As defined by Davis in [13] perceived usefulness (PU) is "the degree to which a person believes that using a particular system would enhance his or her job performance" and perceived ease of use (PEU) is defined as "the degree to which a person believes that using a particular system would be free of effort". Ease of use is thought to influence the perceived usefulness of the technology. Another primary construct in TAM is the behavioral intention to use (BI). Behavioral intention to use is a measure of the likelihood a person will employ the technology. Finally the actual use (Usage) reflects the actual usage of the system [20].

The more extended UTAUT model adds to this several other constructs [15]. *Performance expectancy* is the degree to which an individual believes that using the system will help him to gain in job performance and therefore amounts to PU. *Effort expectancy* is the degree of ease associated with the use of the system and therefore matches PEU. *Social influence* is an additional construct about the degree to which an individual perceives that important others believe he should use the new system and *facilitating conditions* are another additional factor referring to the degree to which an individual believes that an organizational and technical infrastructure exists to support the use of the system. Facilitating conditions determine use. Social influence, performance and effort expectancy determine the intention to use a system. Behavioural intention in turn determines use. UTAUT also identifies moderating factors: gender, age, experience and voluntariness of use. The UTAUT suggests the following: (1) gender and age moderate the effect of performance expectancy on behavioural intention; (2) gender, age and experience moderate the effect of effort expectancy on behavioural intention; (3) gender, age, experience and voluntariness moderate the effect of social influences on behaviour intention and (4) age and experience moderate the effect of facilitating conditions on behavioural intention.

Another extension of TAM is the Model Evaluation Method (MEM) [17]. MEM combines two different but related dimensions of method "success": actual effectiveness and adoption in practice. The constructs of MEM are:

Actual Efficiency: the effort required to apply a method.
- Actual Effectiveness: the degree to which a method achieves its objectives.
- Perceived Ease of Use: the degree to which a person believes that using a particular method would be free of effort.
- Perceived Usefulness: the degree to which a person believes that a particular method will be effective in achieving its intended objectives.
- Intention to Use: the extent to which a person intends to use a particular method.
- Actual Usage: the extent to which a method is used in practice

Common factors between TAM, UTAUT and MEM are the Perceived Usefulness (PU), Perceived Ease of Use (PEU), Intention to use (IU) and actual use (Usage).

For our research, not all factors are required to be taken into account into the survey. Due to the use of the guidelines in a teaching context, some of the variables are constant across the entire population and hence do not need to be included in the survey. This applies to actual usage, voluntariness of use, age, experience, and facilitating conditions. The students were not free in their decision to use the guidelines or not. They were asked to at least try to apply each of the guidelines. As a result, we can only investigate future intention to use, and not actual use since the latter is the same for all students. Likewise, voluntariness of use will not vary across the population. *Facilitating conditions* are not available, since the guidelines were to be used without possibility of further guidance. The *age* is approximately the same for all students. Also the *experience* is the same for all students since none of them had prior education in business process modeling. As a result, the only factor that would be relevant to investigate on top of the basic TAM construct is the social influence by peers. Student may have perceived that the teacher believes (s)he should use the guidelines. We did not investigate to what extent this applies to the different subjects and how this might have affected their intention to use the guidelines.

2.2   Collected Modeling Guidelines

As a result from the previously performed SLR [11] we collected 30 pragmatic modeling guidelines that were spread over different studies. In those cases where guidelines overlapped, we chose the guideline taken from the most recent empirically validated work. For example, guideline "S1-do not use more than 31 elements" has been proposed in different formulations across different research works (e.g. [6, 7, 21]). We selected the guideline from the most recent empirically validated study which also suggests a precise number of elements by means of the threshold value (i.e. [7]). For the current study, we did not optimize the guidelines; we only grouped and presented them as they were collected from the literature. To make the paper self-contained, we list the guidelines below. For more details and sources of the guidelines, the reader is referred to [11] which classifies the collected papers on modeling guidelines along the different aspects of model quality (syntax, semantics, pragmatics, etc.).

- Size: The size of the model has undesirable effects on understandability and like-lihood of errors: larger models tend to be more difficult to understand [6]. For this reason, there are guidelines whose objective is to guide the modeler in the creation of small models. In this group we include five pragmatic guidelines.
  - S1: Do not use more than 31 elements.
  - S2: Keep the path from a start node to the end as short as possible.
  - S3: Use no more than two start and two end events in one process level.
  - S4: Distinguish success and failure end states with separate end events.
  - S5: Use no more than 12 gateways in your models.
- Modularity and Structuredness: Modularity is achieved by using subprocesses [22]. This entails reducing the size of the model at the top level in the model hierarchy to improve understandability of the model. There are various guidelines in the litera-ture that guide the modeler in the number of items from which the modularity should be included in the business process models and criteria for subprocess dis-covery [23]. Since model size is a prerequisite to introduce modularization, guide-line S1 is also related to modularity. The structuredness property on the other hand, has been discussed as a guideline to avoid errors, first in research on programming, and later also in business process modeling [24]. A business process model is structured if every split gateway matches a respective join gateway of the same type [8]. In this group we collected six guidelines.
  - M1: Model as structured as possible: every split gateway should match a respec-tive join gateway of the same type.
  - M2: Avoid deeply nesting structured blocks.
  - M3: Avoid decompositions into subprocesses with less than 5-7 activities.
  - M4: Good candidates for subprocesses are fragments of a model that are com-ponents with a single input and a single output control flow arc.
  - M5: Good candidates for subprocesses are those fragments of a model of which the nodes are more strongly connected by arcs to each other than the nodes out-side this collection.
  - M6: Avoid inclusion of many small process models.
- Complexity: According to several authors, there is a relationship between the com-plexity of a model and its understanding and error probability: more complex mod-els tend to be more difficult to understand and more prone to errors. That is why several research works advice to achieve the lowest as possible complexity in busi-ness process models [25]. This group contains eight quality guidelines.
  - C1: Minimize the routing paths per elements: no more than three (inputs + out-puts) per gateway).
  - C2: Minimize the heterogeneity of gateway types.
  - C3: Select the less complex alternative when modeling.
  - C4: Avoid redundancy in process models: use a subprocess instead of the same fragment several times.
  - C5: Avoid creation of multiple model variants for different scenarios: match process variants towards the creation of more generalized models.
  - C6: Avoid OR routing elements.
  - C7: Minimize parallelism in your process models.

   — C8: Avoid cycles.
- Layout and label style: This group collects guidelines pertaining to the visual presentation of the model. In order to improve the understandability of business process models the layout of the models proves an important aspect. Several pragmatic guidelines refer to the generalization and conceptualization of mechanisms to change the layout of a process model. In addition, an exploration of the label styles used in business process models demonstrated their importance in the understandability of the models. This group resulted in eleven pragmatic guidelines.
   — LS1- Use verb-object activity labels.
   — LS2- Use shorter activity labels.
   — LS3- Use a uniform style for names and flow descriptions.
   — L1- Minimize the number of crossings of connecting elements.
   — L2- Minimize the area of the drawing.
   — L3- Minimize the number of bends of connecting elements.
   — L4- Minimize the number of overlapping (connection) elements.
   — L5- Maximize the number of orthogonally drawn connecting objects.
   — L6- Maximize the number of connecting objects respecting workflow direction.
   — L7- Adapt the size of objects such that elements have enough space.
   — L8- Consider the use of partitions, e.g. pools and swimlanes.

2.3   Instrument

To collect evidence on the PU, PEU and BI of the guidelines, we administered a survey to a sample of 40 students enrolled in a pre-doctoral program at the Universidad de Ciencias Informáticas, in Havana, Cuba. 28 participants were male while 12 participants were female. They received around 50 hours of training in BPMN using Bizagi process modeling tool. We first asked the interviewees to model a medium sized business process case extracted from real systems using BPMN (3 pools with each 10-15 tasks). Then, we asked them to read carefully the collected guidelines and to consider their application to the obtained process model. The students were not free in their decision to use the guidelines or not. They were asked to at least try to apply each of the guidelines. They haven't shown practical implication on process models by the guidelines. After finishing the modeling task, we asked the interviewees to fill out a questionnaire based on TAM about every guideline. The questionnaire used in our study consisted of 9 items divided into three variables. The questions were taken from the original instrument developed by Davis and reformulated according to the context of evaluating guidelines. All items in each of these variables were measured on a five-point Likert Scale ranging from Strongly Disagree (1) to Strongly Agree (5). Each of these questions was scored for each of the 30 guidelines by each participant. Fig. 1 shows the items and the proposed relationship to be tested in our study.

3   Data Analysis

We first conducted Cronbach's alpha analysis to assess the reliability of the instrument used in this study. The Cronbach's Alpha value for each of the variables is well above the threshold of 0.7: perceived usefulness, 0.952; perceived ease of use, 0.953; and behavioral intention, 0.873. This confirms our confidence in our instrument.

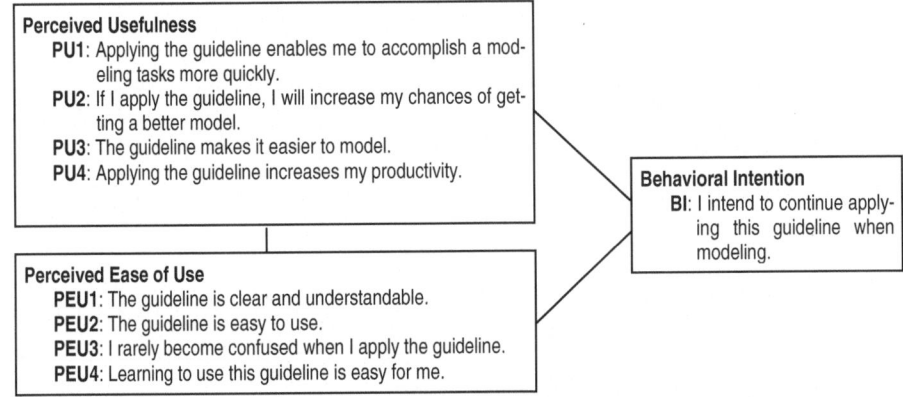

Perceived Usefulness
PU1: Applying the guideline enables me to accomplish a modeling tasks more quickly.
PU2: If I apply the guideline, I will increase my chances of getting a better model.
PU3: The guideline makes it easier to model.
PU4: Applying the guideline increases my productivity.

Behavioral Intention
BI: I intend to continue applying this guideline when modeling.

Perceived Ease of Use
PEU1: The guideline is clear and understandable.
PEU2: The guideline is easy to use.
PEU3: I rarely become confused when I apply the guideline.
PEU4: Learning to use this guideline is easy for me.

Fig. 1. Research model based on the TAM

3.1   Most and Least Useful Guidelines as Perceived by Novice Modelers

To investigate how novice modelers feel about the guidelines we calculate average, median and mode of the collected data from the survey. Table 1 shows the obtained results for each guideline. According to these values we can select the most easy to use, most useful and the highest intention to use guidelines as perceived by novice modelers. We highlighted those guidelines for which there is agreement on higher scores in all three constructs of TAM. Two of these guidelines belong to the complexity group while five belong to the layout and label style group. Size and modularity guidelines were not consistently highly scored by the participants. However, guideline S4 (i.e. distinguish success and failure end states with separate end events) received the highest score within the size guidelines. Also, guidelines M2 (i.e. avoid deeply nesting structured blocks) and M1 (i.e. model as structured as possible) received the highest score within modularity guidelines. Table 2 also shows the guidelines with the lowest scores for ease of use, usefulness and intention to use according to the survey participants. The highlighted guidelines are those that appear in all the three sets (i.e. the ones with lower scores). Among these guidelines three belong to modularity guidelines, three belong to complexity guidelines and one belongs to layout and label style guidelines.

3.2   Relationships between PEU, PU and BI

To assess whether a relationship exists between the different variables we computed Pearson's correlation coefficient. Fig. 2 shows the correlation between the variables and their significance. In order to further quantify the relationships amongst these variables we carried out a Principal Component Analysis (PCA). PCA is a useful statistical technique which supports the reduction of a complex data set to a lower dimension [26]. The Kaiser-Meyer-Olkin Measure of Sampling Adequacy and the Bartlett's Test of Sphericity indicate the adequacy of the analysis (see Table 3).

Table 1. Average, median and mode values for the modeling guidelines

	Average			Median			Mode		
	PEU	PU	BI	PEU	PU	BI	PEU	PU	BI
S1	4.325	3.912	4.175	4	4	4	5	4	4
S2	4.331	3.975	4.35	4	4	4	5	4	5
S3	4.287	3.806	3.95	5	4	4	5	4	4
S4	4.268	4.1	4.525	4	4	5	5	5	5
S5	4.118	4.106	4.3	4	4	4	4	4	4
M1	4.043	3.925	4.225	4	4	4	5	4	4
M2	3.975	4.187	4.225	4	4	4	4	4	4
M3	3.931	3.587	3.675	4	4	4	4	4	4
M4	4.018	3.756	3.85	4	4	4	4	4	4
M5	3.131	3.331	3.125	3	3	3	2	3	3
M6	3.95	3.962	4.125	4	4	4	4	4	5
C1	4.443	4.306	4.575	5	5	5	5	5	5
C2	4.168	3.993	4.025	4	4	4	5	4	5
C3	4.211	4.506	4.65	4	5	5	5	5	5
C4	4.531	4.7	4.65	5	5	5	5	5	5
C5	3.3	3.843	3.974	3	4	4	3	3	5
C6	3.337	2.85	2.810	3	3	3	4	3	2
C7	3.575	3.287	3.131	4	3	3	4	3	3
C8	4.125	3.915	4.075	4	4	4	5	4	4
LS1	4.9	4.525	4.9	5	5	5	5	5	5
LS2	4.580	4.318	4.55	5	4	5	5	4	5
LS3	4.656	4.602	4.65	5	5	5	5	5	5
L1	4.331	4.143	4.625	4.5	5	5	5	5	5
L2	4.506	4.093	4.4	5	4	5	5	5	5
L3	4.337	4.206	4.358	4	4	4	4	4	4
L4	4.241	4.156	4.575	4	4	5	4	4	5
L5	3.918	3.725	4	4	4	4	4	4	5
L6	4.331	4.237	4.5	4	4	5	5	5	5
L7	4.573	4.174	4.55	5	4	5	5	5	5
L8	4.420	4.443	4.525	5	5	5	5	5	5

Table 2. Guidelines with higher and lower PEU, PU and BI

	PEU	PU	BI
Higher Scoring Guidelines	S2, **C1**, **C4**, **LS1**, **LS2**, **LS3**, L1, L2, L3, L6, L7, **L8**	M2, **C1**, C3, **C4**, **LS1**, **LS2**, **LS3**, L3, L6, **L8**	S4, **C1**, C3, **C4**, **LS1**, **LS2**, **LS3**, L1, L4, L7, **L8**
Lower Scoring Guidelines	M1, M2, **M3**, M4, **M5**, M6, **C5**, **C6**, **C7**, L5	S1, S3, **M3**, **M4**, **M5**, **C5**, **C6**, **C7**, C8, **L5**	S3, **M3**, M4, **M5**, C2, **C5**, **C6**, **C7**, C8, **L5**

Three factors explaining 86.588% of the Total Variance Explained were computed, as shown in Table 4. Factors are listed in decreasing order of importance. The results of applying the Varimax Rotate Method are shown in Table 5, where a blank space represents low correlations values.

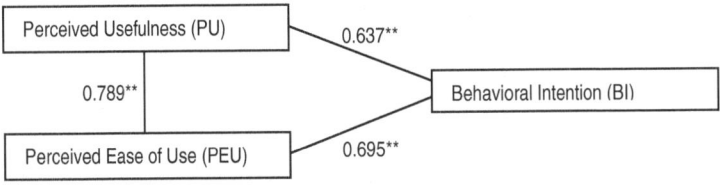

Statistical significance of path coefficients. ** p<0.01

Fig. 2. Structural path diagram for Pearson's correlation coefficient

Table 3. KMO and Bartlett's Test

Kaiser-Meyer-Olkin Measure of Sampling Adequacy.		.786
	Approx. Chi-Square	345.155
Bartlett's Test of Sphericity	df	36
	Sig.	.000

Table 4. Total Variance Explained

Component	Initial Eigenvalues		
	Total	% of Variance	Cumulative %
1	6.205	68.948	68.948
2	.933	10.362	79.310
3	.655	7.278	86.588
4	.407	4.528	91.116
5	.280	3.115	94.231
6	.225	2.500	96.731
7	.171	1.903	98.635
8	.084	.932	99.566
9	.039	.434	100.000

Factor 1 is the most important factor, explaining a 68.948% of variance. It coincides with "Perceived Ease of Use" because the four variables with higher correlations are PEU1, PEU2, PEU3, and PEU4. Factor 2 explains a 10.362% of the total variance. It coincides with "Perceived Usefulness" because the three variables with higher correlations are PU1, PU3, and PU4. Factor 3 explains a 7.278% of the total variance. It coincides with "Behavioral Intention (BI)" as the variable with highest correlation is BI. Notice that there are others variables with high correlation in this factor.

Analysis Per Guidelines. A more detailed analysis of the guidelines and their correlation values between PEU/PU and BI allows to asses which guidelines are more correlated and to know which groups they belong to. The correlation between PEU and BI was positive and significant for all the guidelines, except for guideline S1 (i.e. do not use more than 31 elements) and guideline S2 (i.e. keep the path from a start node to the end as short as possible) which belong to the size guidelines. For these two guidelines, there is a positive and significant correlation between PU and BI, while for PEU this is not the case.

Table 5. Rotated Component Matrix[a]

	Component		
	1	2	3
PU1		.815	
PU2			.737
PU3		.613	.576
PU4		.842	
PEU1	.626		.691
PEU3	.732		
PEU4	.854		
PEU2	.774		
BI			.894

Extraction Method: Principal Component Analysis.
Rotation Method: Varimax with Kaiser Normalization.[a]
a. Rotation converged in 9 iterations.

The Pearson correlation between PU and BI was positive and significant for all the guidelines except for guidelines LS1 (i.e. use verb object activity labels) and L1 (i.e. minimize the number of crossings of connecting elements). These guidelines belong to layout and label style. In the case of the guideline L1, some students disagree with the fact that using this guideline modelers will increase modeling speed. For guideline LS1, some students present neutral position when answering questions related to modeling speed, ease of use and productivity increment. However, they intend to use both of them when modeling a business process.

The Pearson correlation between PEU/PU and BI was positive and significant for all the Complexity and Modularity guidelines.

Analysis Per Questions. A further analysis of data per question allows to confirm that there exists a positive and significant correlation between understandability (PEU1), modeling speed (PU1), quality of the obtained model (PU2), modeling assistance (PU3), productivity (PU4) and BI. From these aspects, it seems that the improvement of the quality of the obtained model was an important factor for novice modelers when assessing intention to use the guidelines (i.e. the best correlation exists between PU2 and BI). This is followed by the understandability of the guidelines (i.e. PEU1 correlates very well with BI for almost all the cases).

4   Discussion Section

Our research has implications both for research and practice. For the practical contribution we present a collected set of pragmatic guidelines for business process modeling after performing a literature review by the authors. We presented them as they were collected from the literature, without further optimization. When having the collected guidelines assessed by the novice modelers we noticed that the most easy to use guidelines include complexity and layout-label style guidelines. Modularity guidelines never showed up in the most ease to use guidelines. Indeed, all the modularity guidelines appeared in the least perceived easy to use set. When looking at the different scores received for the modularity guidelines and PEU, we notice that students understand modularity guidelines (i.e. PEU1 has the highest score) but they realize they are difficult to apply to the model. This might signify that modularity guidelines need further refinement to make them easier to apply. For example, more details may be required on how modularity should be inserted into the process models; this could be something that eases their application. Modularity is a very important aspect to improve the understandability of business process models and a convenient set of guidelines that clarify modularity insertion into the business process models would be of great value. The behavior intention to use the guidelines is not as good as should be, probably due to the fact that students find them difficult to apply, according to our interpretation of the results.

Among the guidelines perceived as most useful we see all the categories (i.e. complexity, modularity and layout guidelines) appear, except for the size guidelines. Novice modelers do not perceive size guidelines as useful, especially for obtaining better quality models (PU2) or to assist them in the modeling process (PU3). They, however, believe size guidelines are easy to use, and they intend to use them. Another interesting aspect is that all label style guidelines appeared in the top 7 set of guidelines. These guidelines seem to be understandable by novice modelers and they also perceive them as useful and intend to use the guidelines.

When looking at the correlation coefficients found as a result of this study, we confirmed as expected that the Pearson correlation between perceived ease of use and perceived usefulness, between perceived ease of use and behavioral intention and between perceived usefulness and behavioral intention was positive and significant. This might indicate that perceived ease of use increases perceived usefulness and behavioral intention, and that perceived usefulness increases behavioral intention of the guidelines. The fact that perceived ease of use correlates with the behavioral intention to use is in line with what can be expected: when someone has just learned a new modeling technique and is asked to apply it, it seems reasonable that ease of use is the first parameter by which one is guided in order to decide to apply the technique in the future. It is only after some practice that a subject can leverage ease of use against usefulness. It makes therefore no sense to bestow guidelines onto people without giving them at least some guidance in applying the guidelines.

When looking into the finer details of the correlation analysis we notice some guidelines correlate better than other. That is the case for modularity and complexity guidelines, whose average correlations are positive and significant. Some size and layout guidelines did not correlate. In those cases we notice, in general, that modelers felt neutral when assessing PEU or PU of the guidelines and they however intend to use them. As a main conclusion we deduce that guidelines should be perceived as easy to use in first place to achieve their usage in the practice of modeling, and additionally, they should be well motivated.

5   Conclusion and Future Work

The increasing importance of business process models in practice demand an appropriate set of guidelines that assists modelers in the process of modeling. In this paper we have presented a set of pragmatic quality guidelines that were collected from different research works. Since "perceived efficacy" and "usage" are important measures of the "success" of a method and also of the impact of research in practice [17] we investigated how people feel about the guidelines through a survey. An analysis of the results brought the most/least useful, the most/least easy to use and the highest/lowest scored for intention to use guidelines according to the novice modelers' perception. According to the results, we conclude that layout and label style guidelines are perceived as the most useful, easy to use and receive the higher scores on intention to use from novice modelers. On the other hand, modularity guidelines were perceived as being the least useful, least easy to use and with lowest score of intention to use among the guidelines for novice modelers. Complexity guidelines appear in both resulting sets. Furthermore, results indicate perceived ease of use might increase the perceived utility of the guidelines, as well as perceived ease of use increase the behavioral intention to use the guidelines. Also, results show that perceived usefulness of the guidelines increase the behavioral intention to use.

Using students is not the same as using practitioners. In particular, given their experience in modeling, practitioners might evaluate the usefulness of guidelines in a different way. As future work we propose to replicate this survey on larger scale with expert modelers from the industry. This would allow to investigate the effect of age and experience on the appreciation of ease of use and perceived utility and their impact on intention to use. On the other hand, we can expect the same type of relationships between the variables as it was confirmed in [17] that relationships between variables are more generalizable between population (i.e. to practitioners) than, for instance, specific characteristics.

When looking into the business process modeling guidelines, different questions come to the surface after. According to this, we acknowledge this set of 30 guidelines is still vast and it needs further refinement. How should this set be in order to achieve its application in current practice of business process modeling? Does it need to be different for teaching purposes and for practitioners use? How should it be in order to help in obtaining high-quality business process models? In general, we believe that the "most intended to use set" of quality guidelines should be optimized in different ways. First, priorities could be defined amongst the guidelines according to targeted levels modeling quality (basic quality versus higher quality levels), or they could be partitioned according to envisaged quality goals such as understandability, correctness, maintainability, etc. of models. Second, the perceived usefulness of guidelines may not always match the utility of guidelines as established through research. The set of guidelines can be improved, e.g. by providing convincing motivations for each guideline. These motivations might be instrumental in teaching practice as they will foster a deeper understanding of modeling quality. The same holds for ease of use: the formulation of the guidelines should be enhanced such as to making them easy to apply, especially by inexperienced people who do not yet have sufficient insight in the consequences of modeling decisions in order to apply guidelines at the right moment and in the right way. Moreover, guidelines should be supported by empirical evidence. One direction of future work would be related to this, in order to make the modelers perceived the guidelines in such a way they have intention to use them.

Finally, from a theory-building perspective, it would be good to build this set of guidelines on quality frameworks fundaments (e.g. SEQUAL [27] or CMQF [12]). In future work, we intend to fill the gaps that still persevere in the research field with a new set of pragmatic guidelines that allows improvement of all desirable characteristics in the business process models. This could be seen as a contribution to the body of knowledge on the quality of business process models at a conceptual level.

References

1. Indulska, M., Recker, J., Rosemann, M., Green, P.: Business process modeling: Current issues and future challenges. In: van Eck, P., Gordijn, J., Wieringa, R. (eds.) CAiSE 2009. LNCS, vol. 5565, pp. 501–514. Springer, Heidelberg (2009)
2. Mendling, J., Reijers, H.A., Recker, J.: Activity labeling in process modeling: Empirical insights and recommendations. Information Systems 35(4), 467–482 (2010)
3. Bandara, W., Gable, G.G., Rosemann, M.: Factors and measures of business process modelling: model building through a multiple case study. European Journal of Information Systems 14(4), 347–360 (2005)
4. Wand, Y., Weber, R.: Research Commentary: information systems and conceptual modelling—a research agenda. Information Systems Research 13(4), 363–376 (2002)
5. Davies, I., et al.: How do practitioners use conceptual modeling in practice? Data Knowl. Eng. 58(3), 358–380 (2006)
6. Mendling, J., Reijers, H.A., van der Aalst, W.M.P.: Seven process modeling guidelines (7PMG). Information and Software Technology 52(2), 127–136 (2010)
7. Mendling, J., et al.: Thresholds for error probability measures of business process models. Journal of Systems and Software 85(5), 1188–1197 (2012)
8. Gruhn, V., Laue, R.: What business process modelers can learn from programmers. Science of Computer Programming 65(1), 4–13 (2007)
9. Reijers, H.A., Mendling, J.: A Study Into the Factors That Influence the Understandability of Business Process Models. Ieee Transactions on Systems, Man, and Cybernetics - Part A 41(3), 449–462 (2011)
10. Figl, K., Laue, R.: Cognitive complexity in business process modeling. In: Mouratidis, H., Rolland, C. (eds.) CAiSE 2011. LNCS, vol. 6741, pp. 452–466. Springer, Heidelberg (2011)
11. Moreno Montes de Oca, I., et al. A systematic literature review of studies on business process modeling quality. Information and Software Technology (2014), doi: 10.1016/j.infsof.2014.07.011
12. Nelson, H.J., et al.: A conceptual modeling quality framework. Software Quality Journal 20, 201–228 (2012)
13. Davis, F.D.: Perceived Usefulness, Perceived Ease of Use, and User Acceptance of Information Technology. MIS Quarterly 13(3), 319–340 (1989)
14. Lederer, A.L., et al.: The technology acceptance model and the World Wide Web. Decision Support Systems 29(3), 269–282 (2000)
15. Venkatesh, V., et al.: User acceptance of information technology: towards a unified view. MIS Quarterly 27(3), 425–478 (2003)
16. Venkatesh, V., Thong, J.Y.L., Xu, X.: Consumer Acceptance and Use of Information Technology: Extending the Unified Theory of Acceptance and Use of Technology. MIS Quarterly 36(1), 157–178 (2012)

17. Moody, D.L.: The method evaluation model: a theoretical model for validating information systems design methods. In: ECIS 2003 (2003)
18. Riemenschneider, C., Hardgrave, B., Davis, F.: Explaining software developer acceptance of methodologies: a comparison of ve theoretical models. IEEE Transactions on Software Engineering 28(12), 1135–1145 (2002)
19. Amoako-Gyampah, K.: Perceived usefulness, user involvement and behavioral intention: an empirical study of ERP implementation. Computers in Human Behavior 23, 1232–1248 (2007)
20. Turner, M., et al.: Does the technology acceptance model predict actual use? A systematic literature review. Information and Software Technology 52(5), 463–479 (2010)
21. Weber, B., et al.: Refactoring large process model repositories. Computers in Industry 62(5), 467–486 (2011)
22. Reijers, H.A., Mendling, J.: Modularity in process models: Review and effects. In: Dumas, M., Reichert, M., Shan, M.-C. (eds.) BPM 2008. LNCS, vol. 5240, pp. 20–35. Springer, Heidelberg (2008)
23. Reijers, H.A., Mendling, J., Dijkman, R.M.: Human and automatic modularizations of process models to enhance their comprehension. Information Systems 36(5), 881–897 (2011)
24. Laue, R., Mendling, J.: Structuredness and its significance for correctness of process models. Information Systems and E-Business Management 8(3), 287–307 (2010)
25. La Rosa, M., et al.: Managing Process Model Complexity via Concrete Syntax Modifications. IEEE Transactions on Industrial Informatics 7(2), 255–265 (2011)
26. Abdi, H., Williams, L.J.: Principal component analysis. Wiley Interdisciplinary Reviews: Computational Statistics 2(4), 433–459 (2010)
27. Lindland, O.I., Sindre, G., Solvberg, A.: Understanding quality in conceptual modeling. IEEE Software 11(2), 42–49 (1994)

Evaluating and Improving the Visualisation of CHOOSE, an Enterprise Architecture Approach for SMEs

Sarah Boone, Maxime Bernaert, Ben Roelens, Steven Mertens, and Geert Poels

Department of Management Information Systems and Operations Management
Faculty of Economics and Business Administration,
Ghent University, Tweekerkenstraat 2, B-9000 Ghent, Belgium
{SarahM.Boone,Maxime.Bernaert,Ben.Roelens,
Steven.Mertens,Geert.Poels}@UGent.be

Abstract. Enterprise architecture (EA) serves as a means to improve business-IT and strategy-operations alignment in an organisation. While it is a fairly mature domain in large enterprises, the need for EA in small and medium-sized enterprises (SMEs) has only been recently addressed. As SMEs have different characteristics and cope with specific problems, a different approach is essential to enable a successful adoption of EA. In order to meet these particular requirements of SMEs, the EA approach CHOOSE has been developed. In previous research, emphasis has been put on refining the method and metamodel of CHOOSE and on the development of supporting software tools. However, the visual notation of CHOOSE has not been investigated yet, while the form of representation has a great impact on the cognitive effectiveness of a diagram. This paper assesses the current visualisation of CHOOSE, describes alternatives and conducts an experimental comparison.

Keywords: Enterprise architecture, business architecture, small and medium-sized enterprises, CHOOSE, visualization.

1   Introduction

Enterprise Architecture (EA) is a structural approach to improve a company's business-IT and strategy-operations alignment [1]. Besides, it is a key instrument in controlling the complexity of an organisation [2]. This is achieved by creating a holistic overview of the organisation through describing and controlling the structure, processes, applications and technology in an integrated way [3]. Although EA is a fairly mature domain in large enterprises, the adoption in small and medium-sized enterprises (SMEs) is lagging behind due to the complexity involved in using the current EA approaches [4]. SMEs often lack the expertise required to implement these approaches and do not have the financial resources to hire consultants [5, 6]. In order to tackle this issue, Bernaert et al. have developed a new approach called CHOOSE, which is adapted to the needs of the target group (section 2.1) [2]. In previous research, the method and metamodel of CHOOSE have been refined and tool support has been developed [7-11]. These investigations have already put a lot of emphasis on

U. Frank et al. (Eds.): PoEM 2014, LNBIP 197, pp. 87–102, 2014.

the comprehensibility of the approach for inexperienced enterprise modellers. However, up to now the visual notation of CHOOSE has not been evaluated nor improved, while the form of representation has an important impact on the cognitive effectiveness of a diagram [12, 13]. This impact is especially crucial in the case of novice users, which makes it very worthwhile to investigate the visual notation of CHOOSE [12]. The research in this paper therefore focuses on how CHOOSE should be visualised in order to allow the users to interpret the diagrams in a cognitively effective way. Besides, the effect of the form of representation on the perceived ease of use, perceived usefulness and the intention to use is investigated as well. The result should enable effective and time efficient communication about the EA within SMEs.

Section 2 provides the theoretical background needed to conduct this research. First, the EA approach CHOOSE is briefly explained [7]. Next, Moody's Physics of Notations [12], a theory for visual notation design, is discussed. Last, related work is shortly summarized. The actual research consists of three major parts: first, the current visualisation is assessed based on the principles of the Physics of Notations (section 3) [12]. Second, alternative representations are developed (section 4). Third, an experiment is conducted to verify which visualisation has the best outcomes in terms of cognitive effectiveness on the one hand and perceived ease of use, perceived usefulness and intention to use on the other hand (section 5 and 6).

2   Background

2.1   CHOOSE for EA in SMEs

Implementing EA allows SMEs to create an overview of the company. In order to guide them in this process, Bernaert et al. have developed the CHOOSE approach [2]. CHOOSE is an acronym for 'keep Control, by means of a Holistic Overview, based on Objectives and kept Simple, of your Enterprise', which refers to the essential requirements for implementing EA in an enterprise [2]. Especially the term 'Simple' deserves some additional attention in the context of SMEs, because the word reflects six specific criteria an EA approach must satisfy in order to enable successful adoption in SMEs [7]:

1. The approach should enable SMEs to time efficiently deal with strategic issues.
2. A person with limited IT skills should be able to apply the approach.
3. It should be possible to apply the approach with little assistance of external experts.
4. The approach should enable making descriptions of the processes in the company.
5. The CEO must be involved in the approach.
6. The expected revenues of the approach must exceed the expected costs and risks.

The metamodel of CHOOSE incorporates these criteria, which means it enables SMEs to create simple, yet comprehensive models [7]. These models represent an overview of the business architecture layer, integrating elements of the information systems and technology layers [7, 10]. They consist of four viewpoints: goals (why), actors (who), operations (how) and objects (what) (Fig. 1).

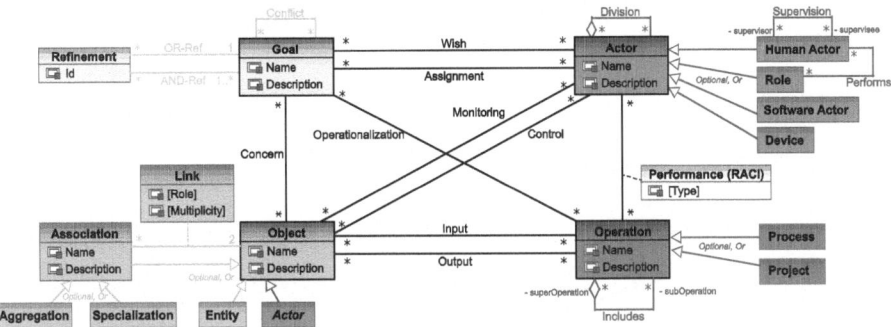

Fig. 1. CHOOSE metamodel [7]

An example of a model that has been created with CHOOSE is demonstrated in Fig. 2. As the content is rather straightforward, the reader is encouraged to analyse the diagram making use of the legend (see Appendix). At the same time, the example shows the current visual notation of CHOOSE. As will become clear in section 3, there is still a lot of room for improvement with respect to this visual notation.

2.2   Moody's Physics of Notations

Numerous papers cover the evaluation of a notation on the semantic level (e.g. [14, 15]). However, as stated in the introduction, the visual syntax of a notation has a great impact on the cognitive effectiveness of it as well [12, 13]. A couple of theories for evaluating the visual syntax of notations have been developed, such as the Cognitive Dimensions of Notations (CDs) framework [16], the semiotic quality (SEQUAL) framework [17] and Moody's Physics of Notations [12]. Genon et al. argue that the first two frameworks lack theoretical and empirical foundations concerning the visual aspects of notations [18]. Besides, in Moody's evaluation of the CDs framework, several additional shortcomings of that framework can be found [19]. Therefore, Moody's Physics of Notations is used as a basis for this research.

Moody states that a clear design goal needs to be identified before a visual notation can be developed [12]. Common design goals are e.g. simplicity and expressiveness. However, these goals are considered to be vague and subjective. A more objective and scientific goal is cognitive effectiveness, which is the speed, ease and accuracy with which a representation can be processed [13]. To enable designers to create cognitively effective visual notations, Moody has defined nine principles [12]. These are explained in the next paragraphs together with their relevance for this paper.

Semiotic Clarity. Each semantic construct should be represented by exactly one graphical symbol, and vice versa. Four kinds of anomalies can occur in a notation:
- *Symbol redundancy*: a semantic construct is represented by multiple symbols
- *Symbol overload*: one symbol represents more than one semantic construct
- *Symbol excess*: a symbol is created that does not represent any semantic construct
- *Symbol deficit*: there is no symbol provided for a certain semantic construct
This principle is incorporated in this paper with the intention to obtain an unambiguous notation that inherently avoids misconceptions.

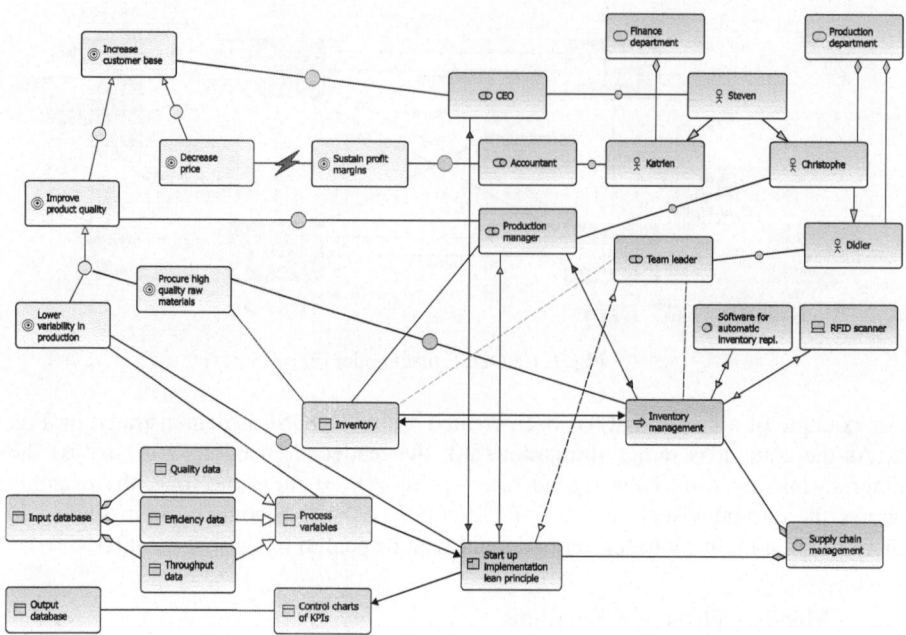

Fig. 2. Model created with the current visual notation of CHOOSE

Perceptual Discriminability. It should be possible to easily and accurately distinguish between different symbols. This is determined by the number of visual variables on which symbols differ, combined with the magnitude of the differences. A greater visual distance between symbols leads to a faster and more accurate recognition. Shape is a detrimental factor in distinguishing between symbols. Therefore, it should be used as the primary visual variable. Perceptual discriminability is very important in the case of CHOOSE, because this notation is used by novices and the requirements for discriminability are higher for novices than for experts.

Semantic Transparency. The representation of a construct should suggest its meaning. One way to design semantic transparent symbols is by using icons, which lead to a faster recognition and recall of the constructs. Besides, they especially enhance the comprehensibility of the notation for novice users, which makes it very worthwhile to incorporate this principle in this research.

Visual Expressiveness. This is determined by the number of visual variables used in a notation and the extent to which they are used. While perceptual discriminability is a measure for the pairwise discrepancy between symbols, visual expressiveness measures the diversity of the visual vocabulary as a whole. Colour is a strong mechanism for enhancing the visual expressiveness of a notation, as contrast in colour is seen faster than differences in other variables. However, it should only be used in a redundant way, because differences disappear when diagrams are printed in grayscale.

Complexity Management. Diagrammatic complexity is measured by the number of elements in a diagram. This type of complexity can be reduced in two ways. First, the diagram can be split into smaller sub diagrams, which is called modularisation. Furthermore, diagrams can be hierarchically structured to limit the levels of detail. This principle is very important in the case of CHOOSE, because novices have more difficulties dealing with complexity than experts [20].

Dual Coding. According to Moody, text can be used as a supplement for graphics. However, it is still important that symbols are distinguishable based on the graphics rather than the text. Labels can be used to distinguish between symbol instances, not between symbol types [12]. Therefore, this principle is somewhat less addressed here.

Cognitive Integration. The notation should enable integrating information from different diagrams. Although this principle should not be neglected, it is not incorporated in this research. As CHOOSE targets novices in enterprise modelling, one notation to model everything is preferred. Besides, when SMEs grow and more detail needs to be added to the EA models, it might be useful to map the CHOOSE models on the ArchiMate standard [21]. Bernaert et al. have already conducted a research on this [22], which makes it less relevant to include it in this paper.

Graphic Economy. The number of symbol types in a notation should be limited. This principle can be adopted in three ways. First, semantic constructs can be removed. However, the number of constructs in CHOOSE is already limited to the bare minimum. Second, symbol deficit can be introduced, but this harms the semiotic clarity of the notation (see above). Third, visual expressiveness can be used. Manipulating multiple visual variables reduces the need to lower the amount of symbols. In this research, this third action is applied in order to pursue graphic economy. Therefore, the principle by itself will not be individually investigated.

Cognitive Fit. Cognitively effective notations for novices might not be cognitively effective for experts, and vice versa. This principle therefore states that different audiences need different notations. CHOOSE targets SMEs, which is a very diverse audience in terms of expertise. However, this principle is not included in this research because in general most users of the target group are novices in enterprise modelling.

2.3   Related Work

Several visual notations such as UML [23], i* [24], BPMN [18] and UCM [25] have been evaluated based on the principles of the Physics of Notations. These studies constitute a useful basis for this paper, because they demonstrate a methodology to identify shortcomings in a notation. This methodology is also applied for evaluating the CHOOSE visualisation (section 3). However, the four articles have two limitations in common: the suggested improvements have not been thoroughly elaborated and the findings have not been empirically evaluated.

Gopalakrishnan et al. have compared two notation alternatives for process modelling by conducting a controlled experiment [26]. Although similar goals as in this research are pursued, they do not use the concept of cognitive effectiveness. Furthermore, Huang et al. have conducted an experiment to compare different graph visualisations, based on a cognitive load perspective [27]. Their research does not focus on visual notations, but several aspects of the test design provide useful insights for the experiment described in this paper.

3   Analysis of the CHOOSE Visualisation

In this section, the current visual notation of CHOOSE is evaluated based on five principles from Moody's theory. As mentioned in the previous section dual coding, cognitive integration, graphic economy and cognitive fit are not covered.

Semiotic Clarity. Currently, there is no symbol redundancy, excess or deficit. The only anomaly that occurs is symbol overload, which can cause misinterpretation [12]. For CHOOSE, the relationships *association*, *concern* and *control* are represented by the same symbol, which is also the case for *input* and *output* (see Appendix). For these latter two, the problem is not tremendous, since they represent the same content in the opposite direction. For *association*, *concern* and *control*, it is important to resolve this anomaly because the meaning of these relationships cannot be linked.

Perceptual Discriminability. Shape is a very important factor in distinguishing between different symbols. However, all ten entities are represented by one shape: a rounded rectangle. Besides, many relationships have equal shapes as well. For the total of 32 semantic constructs, only 12 different shapes are used. This is a crucial shortcoming that will have to be eliminated when designing alternative visualisations.

Semantic Transparency. There is clearly a lot of room for improvement regarding this principle. Only four symbols show a certain presence of semantic transparency, which are the symbols of *goal*, *conflict*, *human actor* and *device*. This means 28 symbols do not suggest the meaning of their construct at all.

Visual Expressiveness. In total, there are eight visual variables that can be modified: shape, size, colour, brightness, orientation, texture, horizontal and vertical position [12]. Currently, the variables shape, colour, brightness, horizontal and vertical position are used, which is better than most visual notations [24]. However, some of them are more adequately used than others. Constructs belonging to the same viewpoint are e.g. represented by one colour and they are grouped into the same corner. These variables are properly utilised. Brightness on the other hand is categorised as a used variable, because *informed* and *monitor* are represented in a slightly different grey. One could doubt whether the variable is utilised in the right context, because *informed* and *monitor* do not have any meaning in common.

Complexity Management. Currently, all information is modelled in one diagram. This means no mechanisms are provided for managing complexity. However, diagrams can quickly become too complex for novices [12]. Hence, integrating this principle would benefit the cognitive effectiveness of the notation. As the metamodel of CHOOSE clearly distinguishes between four viewpoints, it can be useful to apply the mechanism of modularisation and as such split the diagram into sub diagrams.

4   Alternative Visualisations Development

The evaluation of the current visual notation served as a basis for the development of three alternatives. During the establishment of the first alternative, special attention was paid to the principles of semiotic clarity, perceptual discriminability, semantic transparency and visual expressiveness. When, as a little exploratory research, the resulting diagram was presented to four CEOs of SMEs, the major remark was the lack of uniformity in style. Although this aspect is not incorporated in the Physics of Notations, the interview revealed that it should not be neglected. Besides, the research of Sonderegger and Sauer showed that aesthetics have a positive influence on the users' performance and the perceived usability [28]. It is therefore worthwhile to incorporate this in the visualisation. Hence, a second visualisation alternative was developed with the intention to achieve this uniformity in style. After this, complexity management was integrated, which resulted in a third visualisation alternative.

In the first alternative, some essential problems of the original notation are handled (Fig. 3). First of all, it is made sure that every semantic construct corresponds with exactly one graphical symbol, and vice versa. Only the relationships *input* and *output* are still represented by the same symbol, for reasons stated in section 3. Second, different constructs within one viewpoint are represented by symbols that have the same shape, while the shapes differ between the viewpoints. The contrast between the viewpoints is further enlarged by using clearly distinguishable colours. Third, icons are used in order to improve the semantic transparency of the symbols. *Operations* are represented by a gear, the relationship *monitor* by an eye, *control* by a steering wheel, etc. Last, visual variables are used in a consistent way. The variable brightness is only used when it can have a meaningful contribution. In the case of the symbols of *RACI*, relationships that involve a higher responsibility are represented by a darker colour.

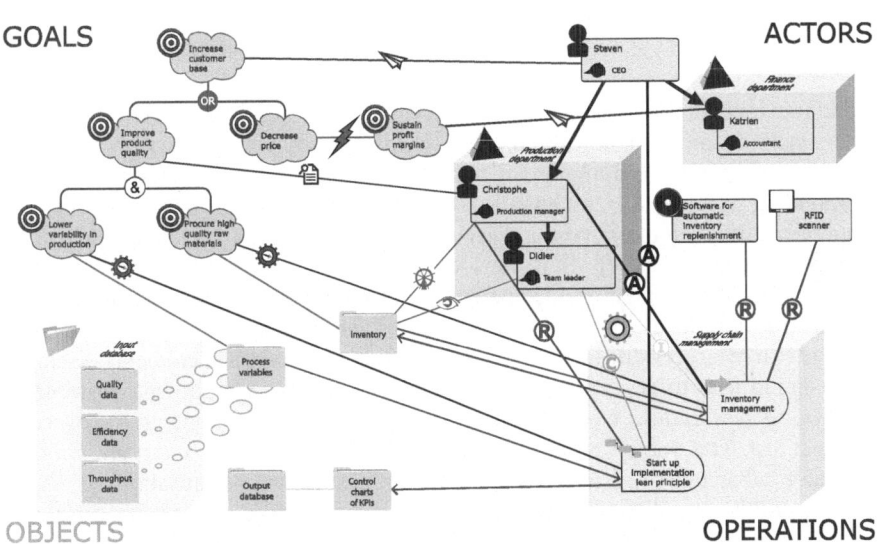

Fig. 3. Model created with the first alternative visual notation

In order to develop the second alternative visualisation, the first alternative is used as a starting point. This notation does not add any improvements in terms of Moody's principles. However, as explained above, it is developed in order to obtain uniformity in style. The result can be seen in Fig. 4.

GOALS   ACTORS

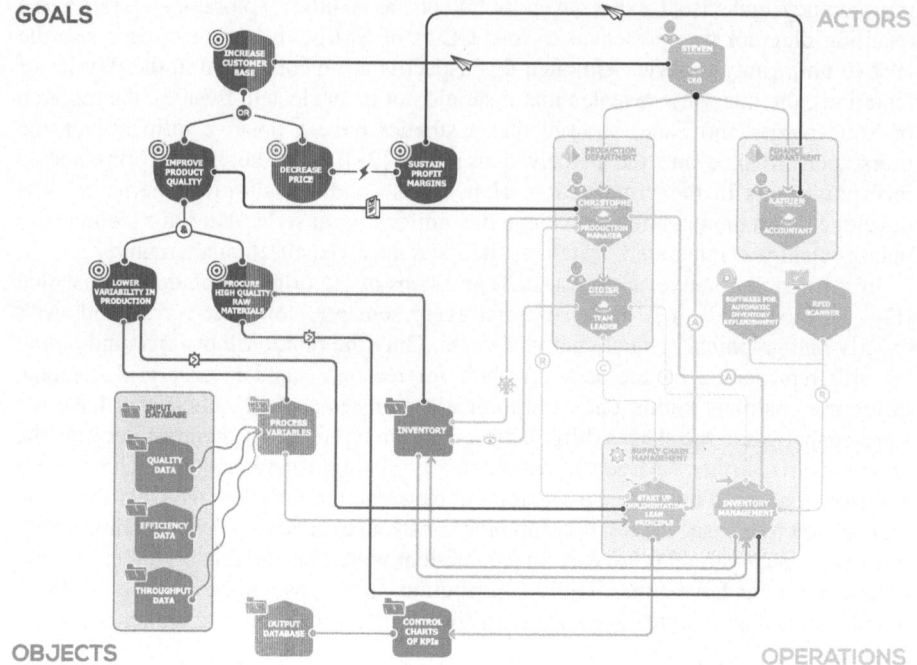

OBJECTS   OPERATIONS

Fig. 4. Model created with the second alternative visual notation

The previous alternatives display all information in one diagram. However, even for a small example as in the images in this paper, relationships between the viewpoints turn the diagram into a complicated maze of information. Therefore, incorporating mechanisms to enable complexity management might improve the comprehensibility of the notation. Several functionalities are hence applied on the previous alternative. First of all, it is made possible to interpret a single viewpoint at a time (Fig. 5). Second, relationships between viewpoints can be analysed in a diagram that only displays the elements of two viewpoints and their interconnections (Fig. 6).

These two measures drastically reduce the number of graphical elements displayed, which should lead to an easier and faster understanding of the content. However, if these two representations would be the only ways to access the content, the overview might get lost. This should be avoided because attaining a holistic overview is one of the major advantages of implementing CHOOSE in an organisation. It should therefore still be possible to access the entire diagram. Hence, a third functionality is added. When the entire diagram is displayed, and the user places the cursor on an element in the diagram, that specific element is highlighted together with all adjacent elements (Fig. 7). The combination of these three additional functionalities should lead to better results during the controlled experiment.

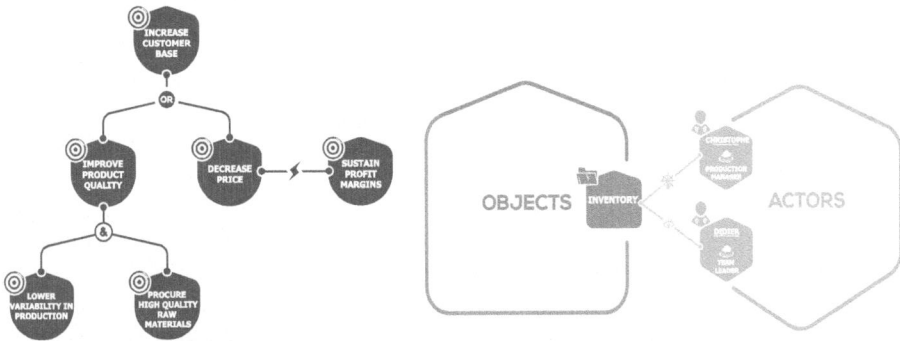

Fig. 5. Single viewpoint   **Fig. 6.** Pairwise relationships

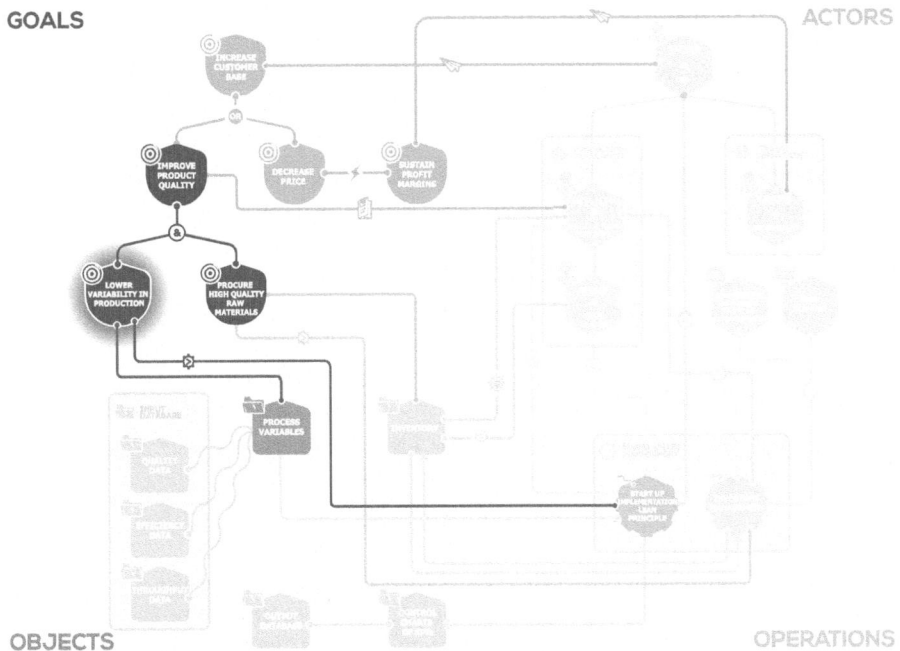

Fig. 7. Entire view with cursor on the goal 'Lower variability in production'

5   Evaluation

5.1   Test Design

In order to determine which representation of CHOOSE is the most comprehensive one, a controlled experiment is conducted. This approach is more appropriate than carrying out case studies because it would be impossible to compare different notations based on a real-life example of an SME without generating learning effects.

Yet, it is difficult to execute an experiment of this magnitude within the target group of CHOOSE (i.e. SMEs). Therefore, the test is conducted appealing to a homogeneous group of (on average) 20-year old business engineering students without enterprise modelling experience, as they have many similar characteristics.

Once this is known, the decision needs to be made whether a within-subjects or a between-subjects design is used. A major advantage of a within-subjects design is the need for fewer subjects [29]. However, this design would dramatically increase the duration of the survey, which could lead to a fatigue bias in the results. Therefore, a between-subjects design is applied. This means the students are divided into four groups, and each group receives the same survey but with another visual notation.

The goal of the survey is to examine whether the newly established visualisations result in a better cognitive effectiveness on the one hand and in improved perceived ease of use (PEOU), perceived usefulness (PU) and intention to use (IU) on the other hand. These last variables originate from the Technology Acceptance Model (TAM), which states that improvements in these variables increase the chance of adoption [30]. TAM is used in accordance to the research of Gopalakrishnan et al. [26].

As shortcomings are gradually managed within the developed visualisations, it is expected that each alternative outperforms the previous one. The overall hypotheses are described below. Null hypotheses are not mentioned due to limited space.

H_a: notation i outperforms notation i-1 in terms of cognitive effectiveness (i = 1 to 3)
H_b: notation i outperforms notation i-1 in terms of PEOU, PU and IU (i = 1 to 3)

Cognitive effectiveness (CE) is a variable composed out of three other variables: accuracy, time and mental effort. Accuracy (A) is expressed as the percentage of correct answers in the survey. Time (T) is expressed as the average time used to answer a question, while the subjects are asked to report the mental effort (ME) needed to answer a content question on a 9-point Likert scale [31]. Since these variables are expressed in different units of measurement, the variables are standardised before they are combined into the formula of cognitive effectiveness. Analogous to [32], CE is then calculated as follows:

$$Cognitive\ effectiveness = \frac{Z(A) - Z(T) - Z(ME)}{\sqrt{3}}$$

The survey[1] consists of three parts. In the first part, general questions are asked to verify the students' prior knowledge regarding enterprise architecture and conceptual modelling. As a between-subjects design is used, these questions are important to avoid an accidental group selection bias [26]. The second part comprises 12 questions to examine the understanding of the diagram(s), which are all accompanied by a question that inquires for the mental effort needed to answer the content question. The question groups (content + mental effort) are randomised in order to avoid obtaining overall better results for the last questions. The third and last part consists of 14 questions based on [26] that gauge the PEOU, PU and IU. The answers are measured on a 5-point Likert scale ranging from 'strongly disagree' to 'strongly agree'.

5.2   Experiment Results

In total, 120 useful observations can be analysed. Six results are omitted, because there are clear indications that those students have not conscientiously filled in the survey. The four sample sizes are slightly different, ranging from 29 responses to 32. Descriptive statistics for each variable can be found in Table 1.

Table 1. Descriptive statistics per group

Variable	Current notation (N=29)		Alternative 1 (N=30)		Alternative 2 (N=29)		Alternative 3 (N=32)	
	Mean	SD	Mean	SD	Mean	SD	Mean	SD
CE	-1.0353	0.9941	-0.4365	1.0696	-0.3956	1.0331	0.7080	0.8134
A	0.8276	0.1230	0.8810	0.1344	0.8916	0.1303	0.9665	0.0544
T	35.6616	8.6862	31.6336	6.3017	33.4239	5.7900	27.7378	4.6965
ME	3.3736	1.0176	3.4333	1.0941	3.1695	1.0323	2.7891	0.9499
PEOU	3.2690	0.3752	3.1533	0.4862	3.2138	0.6255	3.4375	0.4172
PU	3.6621	0.5017	3.6533	0.7482	3.5448	0.6277	4.0250	0.3619
IU	3.0776	0.7621	3.0750	0.7689	3.3707	0.5733	3.5625	0.5198

The variable CE satisfies all criteria to be analysed by means of an ANOVA. The other variables violate at least one of the assumptions. Therefore, these variables are examined with the Kruskal-Wallis test and the Mann-Whitney U test. These tests assume that the distributions of the different groups have equal shapes. It should be mentioned however that this assumption is not entirely satisfied for the variables ME and PEOU. Hence, these variables should be cautiously analysed. All analyses have been conducted with a significance level of 5%. The results in Table 2 demonstrate that the third alternative has a significantly higher cognitive effectiveness than the other visual notations, while the differences between the other notations are not significant. These results can be explained by analysing the component variables of cognitive effectiveness. All three alternatives have better scores for accuracy than the current notation, but alternative 3 outperforms alternative 1 and 2. Next to this, the average time needed to answer a question is tremendously lower for alternative three than for the other alternatives. And last, only for the third alternative, the mental effort required to interpret the notation is significantly lower than for the current notation. For the variable PEOU, the only significant result that can be observed is the difference between alternative 1 and 3. The boxplots reveal that alternatives 2 and 3 have a higher median than the current notation and the first alternative, yet the differences are not significant. Possibly, the true significance level has shifted due to the unequally shaped distributions [33]. Regarding PU, alternative 3 has significantly better results than the other notations. Finally, the IU is significantly better for alternative 3 than for the current notation and for 2 and 3 than for the first alternative.

Table 2. Test results of the pairwise comparisons

Variable	Test statistic	0 – 1	0 – 2	0 – 3	1 – 2	1 – 3	2 – 3
CE	MD	0.5988	0.6397	1.7433***	0.0409	1.1445***	1.1036***
A	U	311*	263**	128***	429	296**	279**
T	U	275**	337	182***	333	284**	214***
ME	U	406.5	370.5	310*	352	312.5**	379
PEOU	U	323.5	361.5	356.5	320	310.5**	382
PU	U	402	369	271**	373	365*	260**
IU	U	400.5	286.5	267.5**	286.5**	273**	360

Note: MD = mean difference (Tukey HSD); U = Mann-Whitney U
*P<0.05; **P<0.01; ***P<0.001.

6   Discussion

The experiment results demonstrate that the last visual notation is clearly the best alternative. First of all, this notation is cognitively more effective than the others. Besides, the respondents of this notation have indicated a high perceived usefulness and intention to use. It is therefore advised to implement this notation.

Several statements can be made in the context of this experiment:

1. When alternative 1 is compared to the current notation, the conclusion can be made that incorporating semiotic clarity, perceptual discriminability, semantic transparency and visual expressiveness improves the accuracy and speed of the answers. However, the change in cognitive effectiveness is not significant due to the variable mental effort, which is not significantly improved.

2. When, on top of these principles, complexity management is applied, an impressive difference can be observed. Adding this principle results in a significant increase in the cognitive effectiveness of the notation. This can be concluded when alternative 3 is compared to the other visualisations.

3. Enhancing the aesthetics of the notation does not improve the cognitive effectiveness of it, nor one of its component variables (alternative 2 vs. 1).

4. However, ameliorating the aesthetics does lead to a higher intention to use. The results for this variable are significantly better for alternative 3 compared to the current notation and for 2 and 3 compared to the first alternative.

5. Integrating all five considered principles leads to a higher perceived usefulness of the notation. As the PU is not improved when the first four principles are applied, the idea rises that complexity management causes the increase in PU.

Overall, it can be said that both Moody's principles and aesthetics have a positive influence on the notation, and this in a complementary way. Moody's principles improve the comprehensibility of the notation and lead to an increase in perceived usefulness. Aesthetics on the other hand augment the intention to use the notation.

7   Conclusion and Future Research

This research has investigated the visual notation of CHOOSE, which is an EA approach developed by Bernaert et al. with the aim to facilitate the implementation of EA in the context of SMEs [7]. The current visual notation has been evaluated and alternatives have been established, after which the different visualisations have been compared in an experiment. Based on this experiment, an advice has been made to implement one of the notations in the CHOOSE approach.

The result of the investigation facilitates a cognitively effective interpretation of CHOOSE diagrams on the one hand, and improves the perceived usefulness and the intention to use the notation on the other hand. In practice, this should lead to an effective and time efficient way to deal with EA and hence improve its adoption rate in SMEs. However, as the experiment is conducted appealing to students, this aspect is ought to be further analysed in future work by means of executing case studies or experiments in SMEs. Although the students subjected to the experiment have several characteristics in common with employees of SMEs – they have for example a keen interest in business topics and are novices in enterprise modelling – it is difficult to extrapolate the results of this investigation to the target group of SMEs.

Besides these practical implications, this paper also provides a validation for the Physics of Notations. The research reveals that applying its principles significantly improves the comprehensibility of the notation. On top of this, it becomes clear that aesthetics should not be neglected, as this increases the intention to use the notation.

At last, this paper suggests a methodology to evaluate visual notations and develop improved versions. Although this research is conducted in the context of CHOOSE, the positive outcome of this case might motivate researchers to consider following the same path.

References

1. Maes, R.: An Integrative Perspective on Information Management. In: Huizing, A., Vries, E.J. (eds.) Information Management: Setting the Scene, pp. 11–26. Elsevier, Oxford (2007)
2. Bernaert, M., et al.: Enterprise Architecture for Small and Medium-Sized Enterprises: A Starting Point for Bringing Ea to Smes, Based on Adoption Models. In: Devos, J., Van Landeghem, H., Deschoolmeester, D. (eds.) Information Systems and Small and Medium-sized Enterprises: State of art of IS research in SMEs, pp. 67–96. Springer (2013)
3. Lankhorst, M., et al.: Enterprise Architecture at Work. Springer, New York (2013)
4. Bhagwat, R., Sharma, M.K.: Information System Architecture: A Framework for a Cluster of Small- and Medium-Sized Enterprises (Smes). Production Planning Control 18(4), 283–296 (2007)
5. Dehbokry, S.G., Chew, E.K.: The Strategic Requirements for an Enterprise Business Architecture Framework by Smes. LNIT 2(1), 32–38 (2014)
6. Jacobs, D., Kotzé, P., van der Merwe, A., Gerber, A.: Enterprise Architecture for Small and Medium Enterprise Growth. In: Albani, A., Dietz, J.L.G., Verelst, J. (eds.) EEWC 2011. Lecture Notes in Business Information Processing, vol. 79, pp. 61–75. Springer, Heidelberg (2011)

7. Bernaert, M., et al.: Choose: Towards a Metamodel for Enterprise Architecture in Small and Medium-Sized Enterprises. Ghent University, K.U. Leuven, University of Antwerp (2013)

8. Ingelbeen, D., Bernaert, M., Poels, G.: Enterprise Architecture Software Tool Support for Small and Medium-Sized Enterprises: Ease. In: 19th Americas Conference on Information Systems (AMCIS 2013), Chicago, USA (2013)

9. Dumeez, J., Bernaert, M., Poels, G.: Development of Software Tool Support for Enterprise Architecture in Small and Medium-Sized Enterprises. In: Franch, X., Soffer, P. (eds.) CAiSE 2013 Workshops. LNBIP, vol. 148, pp. 87–98. Springer, Heidelberg (2013)

10. Bernaert, M., Maes, J., Poels, G.: An Android Tablet Tool for Enterprise Architecture Modeling in Small and Medium-Sized Enterprises. In: Grabis, J., Kirikova, M., Zdravkovic, J., Stirna, J. (eds.) PoEM 2013. LNBIP, vol. 165, pp. 145–160. Springer, Heidelberg (2013)

11. Zutterman, S.: Development of a Tool for Business Architecture Modeling in Eclipse. Ghent University (2013)

12. Moody, D.: The "Physics" of Notations: Towards a Scientific Basis for Constructing Visual Notations in Software Engineering. IEEE Transactions on Software Engineering 35(5), 756–778 (2009)

13. Larkin, J.H., Simon, H.A.: Why a Diagram Is (Sometimes) Worth Ten Thousand Words. Cognitive Science 11(1), 65–100 (1987)

14. Recker, J.C., et al.: Do Process Modelling Techniques Get Better? A Comparative Ontological Analysis of Bpmn. In: Campbell, B., Underwood, J., Bunker, D. (eds.) 16th Australasian Conference on Information Systems, Sydney, Australia (2005)

15. Opdahl, A.L., Henderson-Sellers, B.: Ontological Evaluation of the Uml Using the Bunge-Wand-Weber Model. Software & Systems Modeling 1(1), 43–67 (2002)

16. Green, T.R.G., et al.: Cognitive Dimensions: Achievements, New Directions, and Open Questions. Journal of Visual Languages & Computing 17(4), 328–365 (2006)

17. Krogstie, J., Sindre, G., Havard, J.: Process Models Representing Knowledge for Action: A Revised Quality Framework. European Journal of Information Systems 15(1), 91–102 (2006)

18. Genon, N., Heymans, P., Amyot, D.: Analysing the Cognitive Effectiveness of the BPMN 2.0 Visual Notation. In: Malloy, B., Staab, S., van den Brand, M. (eds.) SLE 2010. LNCS, vol. 6563, pp. 377–396. Springer, Heidelberg (2011)

19. Moody, D.: Theory Development in Visual Language Research: Beyond the Cognitive Dimensions of Notations. In: IEEE Symposium on Visual Languages and Human-Centric Computing, Corvallis, USA, pp. 151–154 (2009)

20. Sweller, J.: Cognitive Load Theory, Learning Difficulty, and Instructional Design. Learning and Instruction 4(4), 295–312 (1994)

21. The Open Group: Archimate 2.0 Specification. Van Haren Publishing (2012)

22. Bernaert, M., et al.: Bridging Ea for Smes to Ea for Large Enterprises: Mapping Choose on the Archimate Standard. Ghent University, K.U. Leuven, University of Antwerp (2013)

23. Moody, D., van Hillegersberg, J.: Evaluating the Visual Syntax of UML: An Analysis of the Cognitive Effectiveness of the UML Family of Diagrams. In: Gašević, D., Lämmel, R., Van Wyk, E. (eds.) SLE 2008. LNCS, vol. 5452, pp. 16–34. Springer, Heidelberg (2009)

24. Moody, D., Heymans, P., Matulevičius, R.: Visual Syntax Does Matter: Improving the Cognitive Effectiveness of the I* Visual Notation. Requirements Engineering 15(2), 141–175 (2010)

25. Genon, N., Amyot, D., Heymans, P.: Analysing the Cognitive Effectiveness of the UCM Visual Notation. In: Kraemer, F.A., Herrmann, P. (eds.) SAM 2010. LNCS, vol. 6598, pp. 221–240. Springer, Heidelberg (2011)
26. Gopalakrishnan, S., Krogstie, J., Sindre, G.: Adapting UML Activity Diagrams for Mobile Work Process Modelling: Experimental Comparison of Two Notation Alternatives. In: van Bommel, P., Hoppenbrouwers, S., Overbeek, S., Proper, E., Barjis, J. (eds.) PoEM 2010. LNBIP, vol. 68, pp. 145–161. Springer, Heidelberg (2010)
27. Huang, W., Eades, P., Hong, S.-H.: Measuring Effectiveness of Graph Visualizations: A Cognitive Load Perspective. Information Visualization 8(3), 139–152 (2009)
28. Sonderegger, A., Sauer, J.: The Influence of Design Aesthetics in Usability Testing: Effects on User Performance and Perceived Usability. Applied Ergonomics 41(3), 403–410 (2010)
29. Brown, S.R., Melamed, L.E.: Experimental Design and Analysis. SAGE, Newbury Park (1990)
30. Davis, F.D.: Perceived Usefulness, Perceived Ease of Use, and User Acceptance of Information Technology. MIS Quarterly 13(3), 319–340 (1989)
31. Paas, F.G.: Training Strategies for Attaining Transfer of Problem-Solving Skill in Statistics: A Cognitive-Load Approach. Journal of Educational Psychology 84(4), 429 (1992)
32. Tuovinen, J., Paas, F.: Exploring Multidimensional Approaches to the Efficiency of Instructional Conditions. Instructional Science 32(1-2), 133–152 (2004)
33. Skovlund, E., Fenstad, G.U.: Should We Always Choose a Nonparametric Test When Comparing Two Apparently Nonnormal Distributions? Journal of Clinical Epidemiology 54(1), 86–92 (2001)

A   Appendix

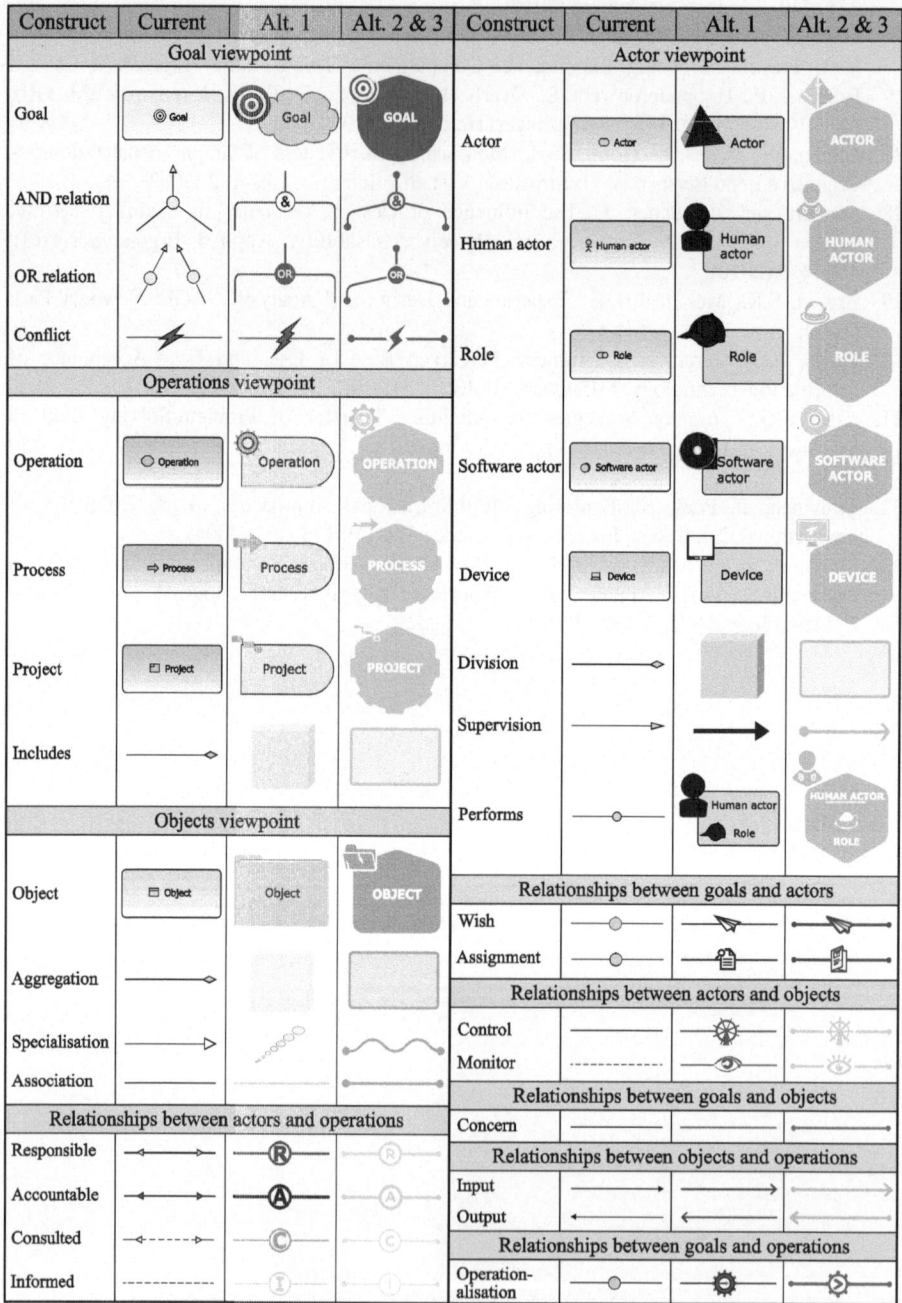

Fig. 8. Legend: symbols applied in the different visual notations

Simulation Preorder Semantics for Traceability Relations in Enterprise Architecture

Mika Cohen

Swedish Defence Research Agency (FOI)
Information and Aeronautical Systems
Decision Support Systems
Royal Institute of Technology (KTH)
School of Computer Science and Communication
Theoretical Computer Science

Abstract. The paper proposes a formal semantics for traceability relations in enterprise architecture. The proposed semantics requires that traceability relations should be simulation preorders, a requirement on abstraction relations widely used in program verification. The effectiveness of the proposed semantics is illustrated on a well-known enterprise architecture model from the military domain.

Keywords: Enterprise Architecture, Traceability, Verification.

1 Introduction

An enterprise architecture describes an enterprise through a sequence of abstraction layers, with each successive layer refining (implementing) the layer above. Model elements can be traced across abstraction layers via traceability relations that relate an element to its implementations (realisations) at lower, more concrete layers. Typically, the enterprise architecture modelling language provides only a weak formal semantics for its traceability relations; model elements at an abstraction layer may trace to model elements at higher abstraction layers in more or less arbitrary ways without violating the formal semantics. However, not every mapping between abstraction layers is intuitively reasonable given the internal connections within each abstraction layer. For example, it would be unreasonable to map two *interacting* technical system at a lower layer to two *independent* business functions at a higher abstraction layer. Since the semantics for traceability relations is (mostly) informal, verifying the traceability links in a model is a manual process, and as such can be both time consuming and error-prone, especially so for large models.

When looking for a formal semantics for traceability relations it is reasonable to consider *abstraction relations* [1] from program verification. Abstraction relations in program verification have the same intuitive semantics as traceability relations in enterprise architecture but come with a well-founded and much applied mathematical theory.

U. Frank et al. (Eds.): PoEM 2014, LNBIP 197, pp. 103–117, 2014.

In this paper we propose a formal semantics for traceability relations based on *simulation preorder*, the most widely used abstraction relation in program verification [2]. The formal semantics translates directly to an executable modeling guideline - in OCL, SQL, SPARQL, or other rule- and query language used in enterprise architecture modeling tools – that warns a user about problematic traceability links. We show its effectiveness (in identifying modeling errors) on a well-known architecture model from the military domain.

The proposed semantics might be too restrictive to be a mandatory part of a general-purpose enterprise architecture modeling language intended also for relaxed, imprecise modeling. However, a particular organisation or modeling project might adopt the proposed semantics as an executable part of their organization- or project specific modeling guidelines. In fact, the proposed semantics is already a part of a 'rule book' that FMV Swedish Defence Material Administration uses to verify enterprise architecture models.

The rest of the paper is organized as follows. Section 2 defines enterprise architecture models. Section 3 presents the formal semantics in the form of integrity constraints on enterprise architecture models. Section 4 shows how to implement the semantics in rule- and query languages. Section 5 presents a case study. Section 6 discusses related work. Finally, section 7 concludes.

2   Enterprise Architecture

In this section we define enterprise architecture models. The definition is simplified to avoid distracting detail in the following section. Informally, an enterprise architecture describes an enterprise through a sequence of abstraction layers, with each successive layer refining (implementing) the layer above; traceability relations link elements to their implementations (realisations) at lower, more concrete layers.

Example 1. [MODAF] As our running example we consider MODAF, an enterprise architecture modeling language developed by the UK Ministry of Defence. MODAF has three abstraction layers: green, blue and orange. The green 'strategic' layer specifies the intended business outcome and the capabilities these require, the blue 'operational' layer describes the processes and information flows needed to fulfill the capabilities specified at the green layer, and, finally, the orange 'system' layer detail the physical implementation of the processes and information flows from the blue layer. In this paper, we consider only a representative fragment of MODAF, shown in figure 1. Models (over this fragment) contain interdependent capabilities in the green abstraction layer; nodes that performs activities and exchange information in the blue abstraction layer; and, finally, resources that perform functions and exchange data in the orange abstraction layer. Traceability links (represented by dotted arrows in figure 1) connect nodes to capabilities, resources to nodes, functions to activities, resource interactions to information exchanges, and, finally, data elements to information elements. As a (toy) example model, figure 2 depicts a MODAF-model describing baby rearing.

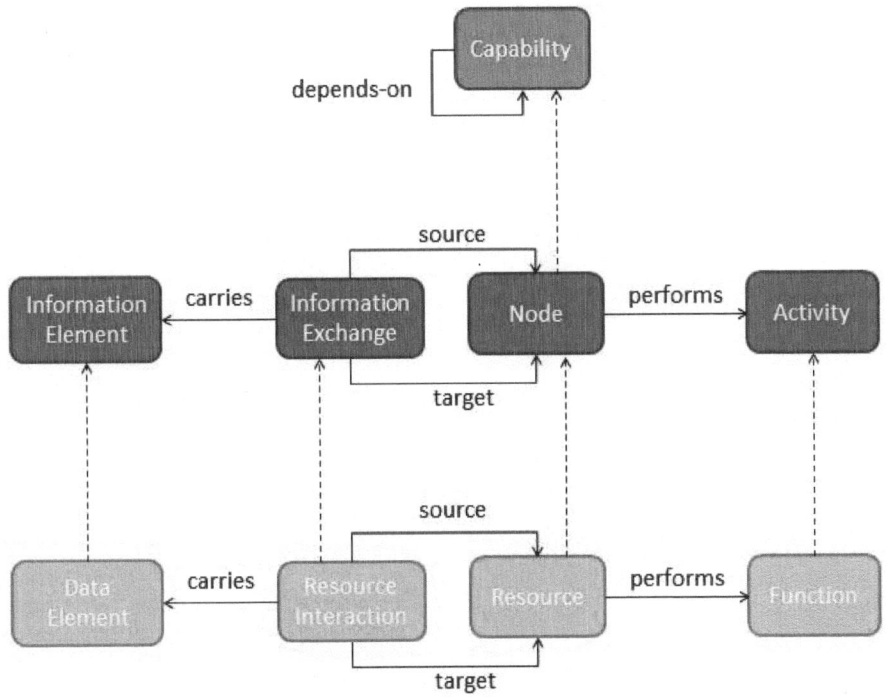

Fig. 1. MODAF fragment

Formally, an enterprise architecture modeling language, *language* for short, is a non-empty set O of unary predicates ('classes') and binary predicates ('relations'), including a special traceability relation, hereafter denoted *implements*.[1]

Example 2. Continuing the above example, the MODAF fragment O considered in this paper contains classes:

- *Capability* (from the green abstraction layer)
- *Node, Activity, InformationExchange, InformationElement* (from the blue abstraction layer)
- *Resource, Function, ResourceInteraction, DataElement* (from the orange abstraction layer)

and relations:

- *depends-on, performs, source, target, carries, implements*

Note that the MODAF abstraction layers are not explicitly captured in O.

Informally, a model M is a set of facts expressed with the given vocabulary in O. Formally, *facts* over a domain D (i.e., a non-empty set of elements) and

---

[1] For ease of presentation, we assume a single (un-typed) traceability relation.

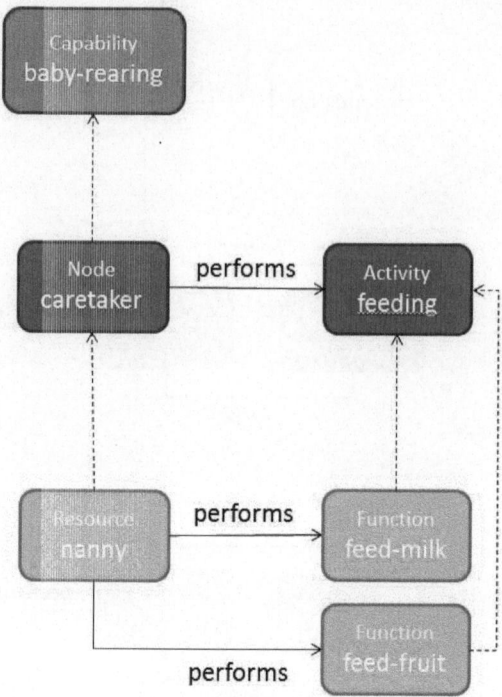

Fig. 2. MODAF model

a language O have either the form a: C or have the form a R a', where a and a' are elements from the domain D, and C and R are, respectively, classes and relations in O. Intuitively, a: C asserts that element a belongs to class C, while a R a' asserts that relation R relates element a to element a'. In particular, the fact a *implements* a' asserts that element a realises (implements, refines, supports) element a'.

Definition 1 (Model). *An enterprise architecture model, model for short, over a language O is a non-empty set M of facts over O and some domain D.*

Example 3. The model M from Example 1 and figure 2 contains the facts:

- *baby-rearing: Capability*
- *caretaker: Node, feeding: Activity, care-taker performs feeding*
- *nanny: Resource, feed-milk: Function, feed-fruit: Function, nanny performs feed-milk, nanny performs feed-fruit*
- *caretaker implements baby-rearing, nanny implements caretaker, feed-milk implements feeding, feed-fruit implements feeding*

The above definition of an enterprise architecture model is, of course, simplified. In particular, the definition does not explicitly capture abstraction layers

− explicit abstraction layers would unnecessarily complicate the presentation of the semantics in the next section. Moreover, the definition ignores the customary typing constraints inherited from UML class diagramming − these are both standard and straight forward .

3   Semantics for Traceability Relations

In this section we propose a formal semantics for traceability relations in enterprise architecture. Informally, a traceability relation links an element to its implementations (realisations) at lower, more concrete layers. To capture this intuitive semantics, we require that the traceability relation is a simulation preorder, a requirement on abstraction relations widely used in program verification.

Roughly, we require that an association between two elements at the lower abstraction layer is permitted only if there is a corresponding association between their abstractions at the higher abstraction layer; the structure at the higher abstraction layer thus constrains the possible solutions (realisations) at the lower abstraction layer.

Example 4. Continuing the earlier examples, the semantics proposed will enforce the integrity constraints on MODAF-models shown in figures 3a, 3b, 3c, and 4a, where *abstracts* is the inverse relation to the traceability relation (*implements*). The constraints are expressed in SBVR Structured English and should be self-explanatory. The diagrams should be interpreted as saying that the two thicker arrows jointly imply the existence of two thinner arrows.

In the above example, a relation R (*performs, target, source, carries*) at the higher abstraction layer corresponds to the same (identically named) relation R at the lower abstraction layer; for each move along R at the lower layer there must exist a corresponding move along R at the higher abstraction layer. However, a relation R at the higher abstraction layer may sometimes correspond to a differently named relation R' at the lower abstraction layer.

Example 5. Continuing the above examples, the semantics proposed will enforce the integrity constraint on MODAF-models shown in figure 4b. Here, the relation $R = $ *depends-on*, at the green strategic abstraction layer, corresponds to the relation $R' = $ *receives-from*, at the blue operational abstraction layer. The latter relation is a derived relation: *a node1 receives-from a node2 if there exists some information exchange that targets the node1 and that is sourced from the node2.*

From now on we assume that an enterprise architecture modelling language O comes with a counterpart function, i.e., a partial function $f: O \longrightarrow O$ that maps relations to their more abstract counterparts (if any).[2]

---

[2] For ease of presentation, we assume (somewhat sloppily) that O contains also derived relations, such as *receives-from* in the case of MODAF. For ease of presentation, we assume moreover that the traceability relation connects only between directly neighbouring abstraction layers.

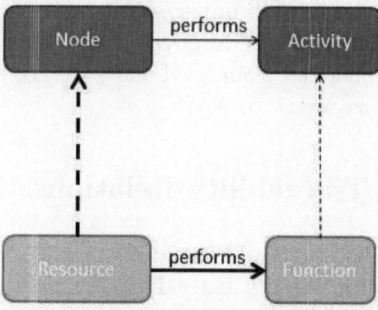

(a) *A node that abstracts a resource that performs a function, must perform an activity that abstracts the function*

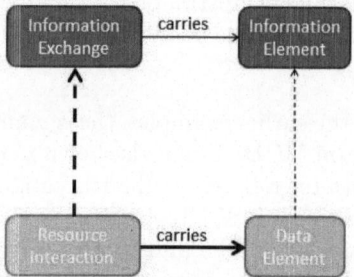

(b) *An information exchange that abstracts a resource interaction that carries a data element, must carry an information element that abstracts the data element*

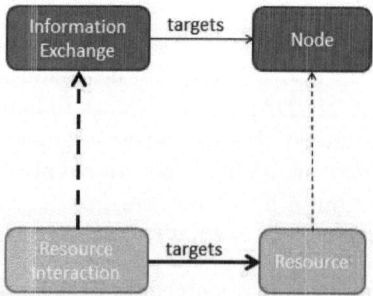

(c) *An information exchange that abstracts a resource interaction that targets a resource, must target a node that abstracts the resource*

Fig. 3. Integrity constraints enforced by the simulation preorder semantics

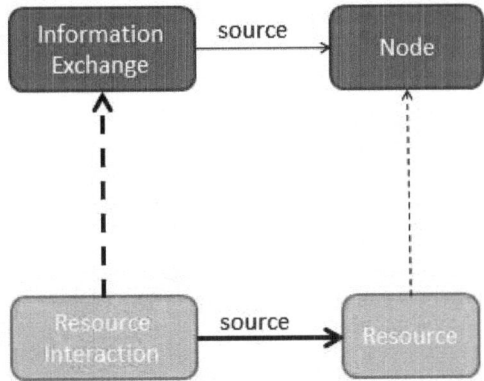

(a) *An information exchange that abstracts a resource interaction that is sourced from a resource, must be sourced from a node that abstracts the resource*

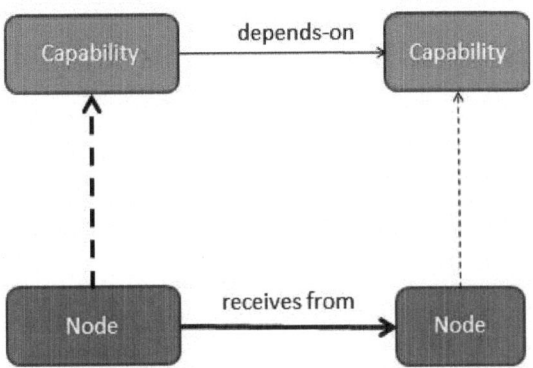

(b) *A capability1 that abstracts a node1 that receives from a node2, must depend on a capability2 that abstracts the node2*

Fig. 4. Integrity constraints enforced by the simulation preorder semantics

Example 6. Continuing Example 2, we assume the MODAF-fragment O comes with the following counterpart function f: $f(receives\text{-}from) = depends\text{-}on$, $f(performs) = performs$, $f(carries)=carries$, $f(source)=source$, $f(target)=target$

Of course, counterpart functions are not an explicit part of enterprise architecture languages, as found in the 'real world'. We believe, however, that they are there implicitly. Relations that correspond to each other will typically either be identically named or identically (stereo-)typed in the language meta-model. When this is not the case, informal modelling directives may indicate correspondences. As an example, the official MODAF handbook at the Swedish Armed Forces states: *'Dependencies between capabilities ought to lead to interaction between the instantiating nodes'* (*Handbok för försvarsmaktens tillämpning av MODAF*, Section 6.3.1.4.1, authors translation from Swedish). In other words, the relation $R = depends-on$ at the green strategic abstraction layer corresponds to the relation $R' = receives-from$ at the blue operational abstraction layer.

We are now in a position to formulate our proposed semantics for traceability relations. Assume a modeling language O with a counterpart function f, and let M be a model over O. Roughly, we require that for every arc in M at the lower abstraction layer there is a corresponding arc at the higher abstraction layer (see figure 5).

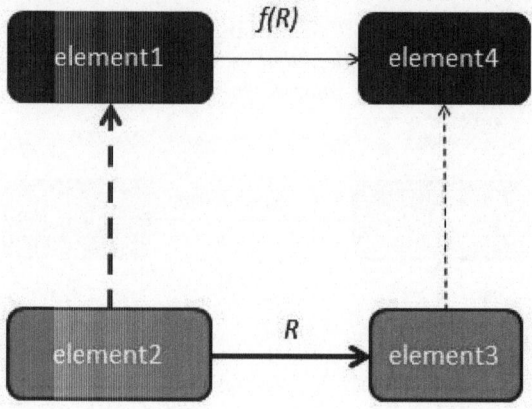

Fig. 5. Simulation preorder semantics. *An element1 that abstract an element2 that is R-related to an element3, must be f(R)-related to an element4 that abstracts the element3*

Definition 2 (Semantics for traceability). *We say that traceability relations are correct in M if the following condition holds for all elements a, b and a' in the domain and for all relations R in O such that f(R) exists: if M contains facts*

- *a R b*
- *a implements a'*

then there exists an element b' in the domain such that M contains facts

- *a' f(R) b'*
- *b implements b'*

Example 7. Continuing the above examples, traceability relations are correct in a model M (over our MODAF-fragment O) if the integrity constraints in figures 3a, 3b, 3c, 4a, and 4b hold. In particular, traceability relations are correct in the model over baby rearing (Example 3 and figure 2) since the functions the nanny performs are reflected in activities performed by the caretaker.

4   Implementation

The formal semantics proposed in the previous section translates directly to executable modeling guidelines in OCL, SQL, SPARQL, and other rule- and query languages used in modeling tools. In fact, the integrity constraints in SBVR-SE that instantiate the semantics in the previous section compile automatically to SQL with SBVR-compilers (c.f. [3,4]).

Example 8. The constraint in figure 3a translates to the following SPARQL-query that identifies traceability links (between resources and nodes) that violate the constraint:

```
SELECT ?resource ?node {
  ?resource a Resource.
  ?node a Node.
  ?function a Function.
  ?resource implements ?node.
  ?resource performs ?function.
  NOT EXISTS {
    ?activity a Activity.
    ?node performs ?activity.  ?function implements ?activity
  }
}
```

Of course, executable modeling guidelines should preferably produce appropriate warning messages, not merely list data.

Example 9. With SPARQL Inference Notation (SPIN), the SPARQL-query that identifies the constraint-violations can be associated with a custom error-message. E.g., the query-logic from the previous example can be associated with the error message:

```
CONCAT(
  ?resource, 'implements ', ?node,
  ' but ', ?resource, ' performs a function ', ?function,
  ' that does not implement some activity performed by ', ?node
)
```

Of course, the error-message that the executable modeling guideline produces need not necessarily point the finger at traceability links as the source of error. For some applications it might be more reasonable to assume that when a traceability link fails the simulation preorder semantics, the most likely cause of error is a mismatch between the higher- and lower abstraction layers, i.e., either a R-relation in the lower abstraction layer is unwanted or a correspondning $f(R)$-relation in the higher abstraction layer is missing.

Example 10. Continuing the above example, the implementation could accept the traceability links (between resources and nodes) as given and instead warn about illegitimate functions, i.e., functions not sanctioned by the higher abstraction layer:

```
CONCAT(
  ?resource, ' performs an illegitimate function ', ?function,
  ' that does not implement any activity performed by ', ?node
)
```

The proposed semantics has been implemented in MooD (as SQL-queries) and in MagicDraw (as OCL-constraints). The latter was used in the case study discussed in the next section.

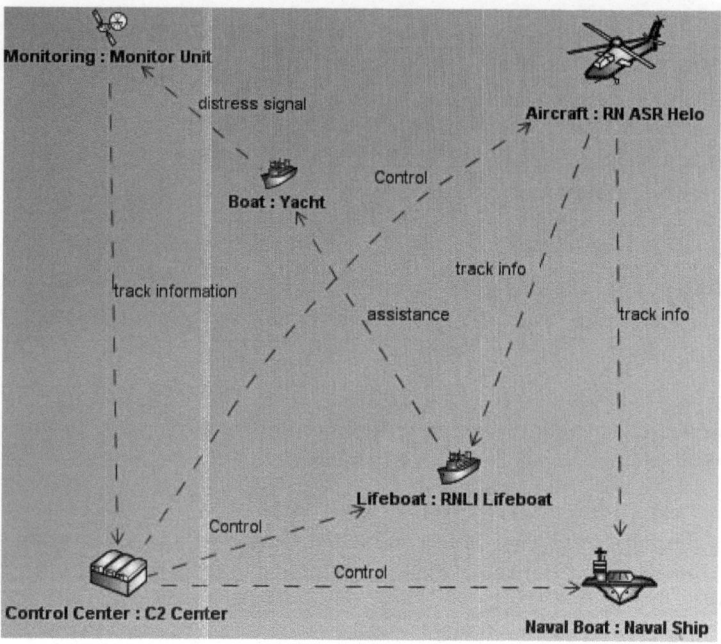

Fig. 6. SAR scenario (snippet)

5   Case Study

The semantics for traceability relations proposed above is part of a 'Rule book for MODAF' developed at FOI (the Swedish Defence Research Agency) and used at FMV (the Swedish Defence Material Administration) to verify MODAF models. Unfortunately, the models that have been verified at FMV are secret, and cannot be discussed in this paper. Instead, we illustrate the proposed semantics and its implementation in MagicDraw on the well-known SAR (Search And Rescue) model from the UK Ministry of Defence, a publically available MODAF model. The implementation identified numerous modeling errors. In this section, we consider two of the identified errors. To the best of our knowledge, neither of these errors has been identified in the MODAF-literature.

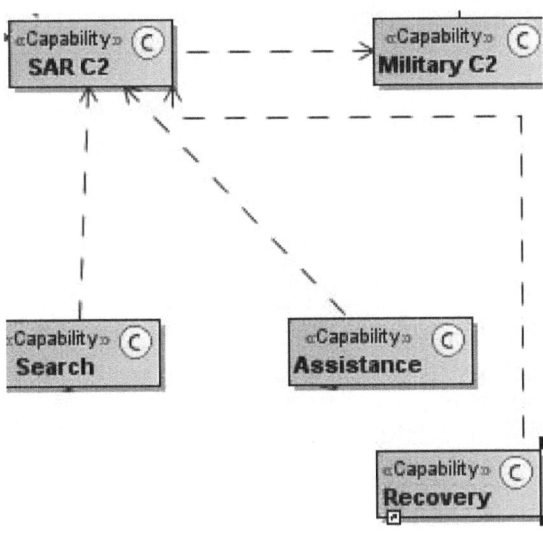

Fig. 7. Capability dependencies (snippet)

Figure 6 shows a scenario snippet from the SAR model in which a distressed yacht signals for help. The distress signals are caught by a rescue team consisting of a life boat (*RNLI Lifeboat*), a helicopter (*RN ASR Helo*) and other resources. The arcs between resources represent resource interactions. E.g., the lifeboat receives data (*track info*) from the helicopter .

Figure 7 shows another view from the same SAR model, this time from the more abstract green strategic layer. Here, the search and rescue capability is defined at a higher level of abstraction; the capability is decomposed into a number of simpler capabilities and dependencies (represented by dotted lines) between these. For example, the capability *Recovery* depends on the capability *SAR C2*.

The scenario in figure 6 is intended to realise the more abstract capability definition in figure 7; each resource in figure 6 implements some capability. E.g., the helicopter *RN ASR Helo* implements the capability *Search* while the lifeboat *RNLI Lifeboat* implements the capability *Recovery*. The traceability links between resources and capabilities are scattered at various places in the SAR model.

Are the traceability links between resources and capabilities correct? With the semantics for traceability relations implemented in our modeling tool (MagicDraw), we simply press a button to find out. After a few seconds the modelling tool produces a number warnings, among others: 'Resource interaction between *RN ASR Helo* and *RNLI Lifeboat* is not reflected in any capability dependency'. According to the warning, the helicopter *RN ASR Helo* exchanges data with the life boat *RNLI Lifeboat* (see figure 6) but there is no dependency between the capabilities these resources realise, *Search* and *Recovery* respectively, in the more abstract view, i.e., there is no dotted line between *Search* and *Recovery* in

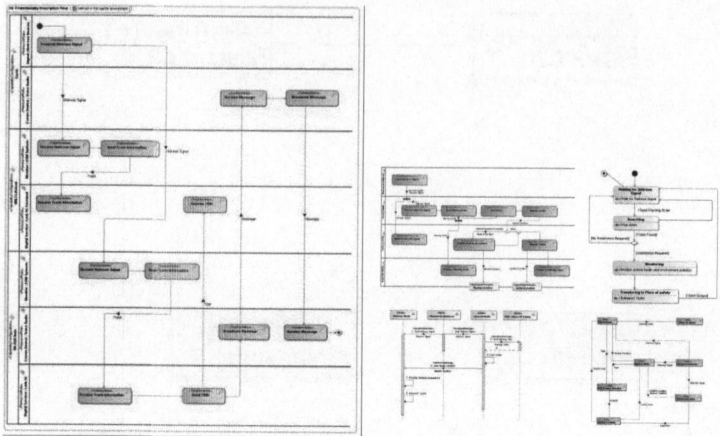

(a) Scenario realisation (miniature   (b) Abstract scenario (miniature
snapshot)   snap shots)

Fig. 8. Abstract scenario and realisation

figure 7; Note that the error message does not warn about an incorrect traceability links per se; rather it warns about a mismatch between the scenario view
in figure 6 and the capability view in figure 7.

Continuing, we consider next a more detailed scenario realisation at the orange system layer in the SAR model (figure 8a). The scenario starts when a
distressed yacht transmits distress signals (top swim lane in figure 8a) that are
eventually picked up (*Receive Distress Signal*, third swim lane from bottom) by
a monitoring system on the helicopter *RN ASR Helo*. The helicopter eventually
sends a message back to the distressed yacht (*Broadcast Message*, second swim
lane from bottom), the yacht receives the message (*Receive Message*, second
swim lane from top) and sends a reply (*Broadcast Message*, second swim lane
from top), and, finally, the helicopter receives the reply (*Receive Message*, second
swim lane from bottom).

The scenario in figure 8a is intended to realise a more abstract scenario definition from the blue, operational abstraction layer (figure 8b); resources and
functions from figure figure 8a implement, respectively, nodes and activities from
the blue abstraction layer (figure 8b). E.g., the resource *Yacht* maps to the node
Person in Distress, while the functions *Send Message* and *Broadcast Message*
both map to the activity *Send Distress Signal*. Again, the implementation-links
are scattered in the SAR model.

Are the traceability links correct? Again, we simply press a button to find out.
As before, the modelling tool warns us about a number of identified modelling
errors, among others the error: '*Yacht* performs illegitimate function *Receive
Message*'. According to this warning, the function *Receive Message* is not sanctioned by the more abstract scenario definition at the blue operational layer; the
integrity constraint from figure 3a is violated. In more detail, the yacht receives

messages while its abstraction at the blue layer, *Person In Distress*, merely sends distress signals (see figure 9). This might be a rather serious modeling error. The blue operational layer specifies a capability of rescuing a person in distress who sends distress signals. But the proposed physical realisation (figure 8a) assumes that the person in distress is reachable (can be contacted), an assumption which cannot be traced back to the scenario specification at the blue abstraction layer (figure 8b).

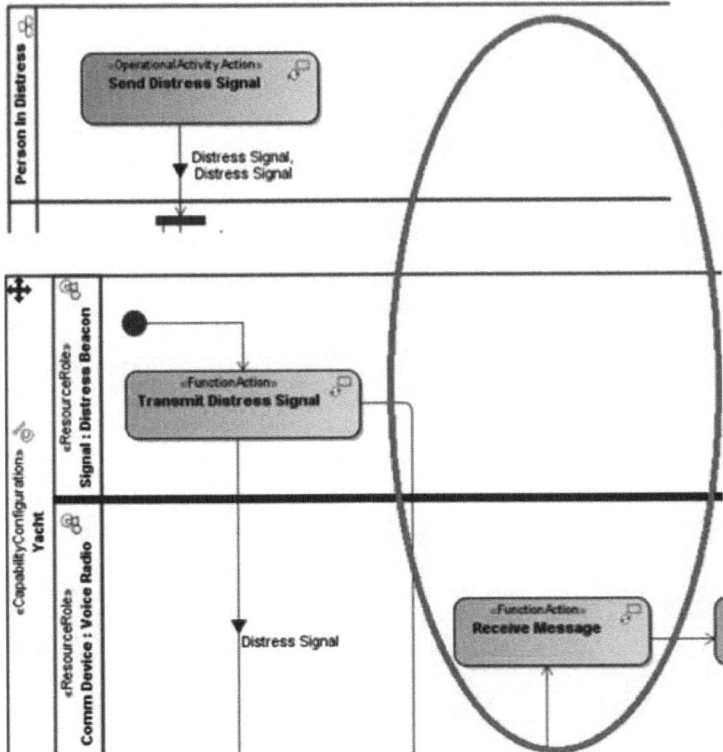

Fig. 9. Identified Error. The *Yacht* both transmits and receives but its abstraction, *Person In Distress*, only sends.

6   Related Work

Some enterprise architecture modeling tools enforce cardinality constraints on traceability relations. E.g., MagicDraw warns if e.g. a resource at the orange system layer in MODAF does not implement any node from the blue operational layer. Clearly, cardinality constraints alone constitute a weak semantics. In particular, none of the example modeling errors in the case study above fail such cardinality constraints.

[5] extends ArchiMate, a particular enterprise architecture modeling language, with inference rules that derive (numerical) data attributes in an element from other attributes in the same or related elements. The inference rules reflect empirically established correlations ('laws of causation') rather than an informal intuitive semantics, as do the integrity constraints in the present paper. [6,7] extend DoDAF and MODAF with inference rules capturing empirical correlations between high-level capabilities and attributes of the implementing technical systems.

Conditions similar to simulation preorder have been used as tools for debugging ontology mappings (cf. [8,9,10]). The approach in the present paper is similar: an informal, intuitive semantics for 'correspondences' is captured using mathematical constructions from theoretical computer science. However, the application in the present paper − traceability relations in enterprise architecture − is, to the best of our knowledge, novel.

7   Conclusion

Traceability relations trace model elements across abstraction layers in an enterprise architecture. Verifying traceability links is a manual, time consuming and error-prone process − existing formal semantics for traceability relations is weak (merely the cardinality constraints familiar from UML class diagrams).

The paper proposed a formal semantics for traceability relations in enterprise architecture. The proposed semantics required that traceability relations should be simulation preorders, a requirement on abstraction relations widely used in program verification. The effectiveness of the proposed semantics was illustrated on a well-known enterprise architecture model from the military domain.

Traceability relations play an important role not only in enterprise architecture but in model-based engineering more broadly. In the future, it would therefore be interesting to extend the semantics proposed to the model transformations in model-based engineering.

References

1. Cousot, P., Cousot, R.: Abstract interpretation: a unified lattice model for static analysis of programs by construction or approximation of fixed points. In: POPL (1977)
2. Clarke, E.M., Grumberg, O., Long, D.E.: Model checking and abstraction. ACM Trans. Program. Lang. Syst. (1994)
3. Minnock, M.: C-Phrase: A system for buidling robust natural kanguage interfaces to databases. In: DKE (2010)
4. Moschoyiannis, S., Marinos, A., Krause, P.: Generating SQL queries from SBVR rules. In: Dean, M., Hall, J., Rotolo, A., Tabet, S. (eds.) RuleML 2010. LNCS, vol. 6403, pp. 128–143. Springer, Heidelberg (2010)
5. Johnson, P., Ekstedt, M.: Enterprise Architecture: Models an analysis for information systems decision making (2007)

6. Franke, U., Flores, W.R., Johnson, P.: Enterprise Architecture dependency analysis using fault trees and Bayesian networks. Spring Simulation Multiconference (2009)
7. Franke, U., Johnson, P., Ericsson, E., Flores, W.R., Zhu, K.: Enterprise Architecture analysis using Fault Trees and MODAF. In: CAiSE Forum (2009)
8. Ghilardi, S., Lutz, C., Wolter, F.: Did I damage my Ontology? A case for conservatve extensions in description logics. In: KR (2006)
9. Bench-Capon, T., Malcolm, G.: Formalising ontologies and their relations. In: Bench-Capon, T.J.M., Soda, G., Tjoa, A.M. (eds.) DEXA 1999. LNCS, vol. 1677, pp. 250–259. Springer, Heidelberg (1999)
10. Cohen, M.: Semantics for mapping relations in SKOS. In: Faber, W., Lembo, D. (eds.) RR 2013. LNCS, vol. 7994, pp. 223–228. Springer, Heidelberg (2013)

Towards a Framework for Enterprise Information System Evolution Steering

Wanda Opprecht, Jolita Ralyté, and Michel Léonard

University of Geneva, Institute of Services Science
Battelle bâtiment A, 7 route de Drize, 1227 Carouge, Switzerland
{Wanda.Opprecht,Jolita.Ralyte,Michel.Leonard}@unige.ch

Abstract. Evolution is characteristic to every Information System (IS) because of continuing changes in its environment. It is also a necessary condition for guaranteeing IS fitness to the organizational needs and requirements. Nonetheless, each IS evolution presents several risks towards its sustainability and further changes, and steering IS evolution is indispensable for any organization. In this work we propose a framework that aims to guide the actors responsible for IS evolution steering. The framework allows to reduce the uncertainty, which is inherent in the IS evolution, by providing the information necessary to realise IS evolution activities and to simulate their impact. It is composed of several conceptual models representing different IS dimensions (information, activities, regulation). In this paper we detail the IS Steering Metamodel (IS-SM), which is the main element of our framework.

Keywords: Information System Evolution Steering, Steering Metamodel, Evolution Model, Evolution Steering Method.

1   Introduction

Information Systems (IS) evolution steering is today one of the key concerns of any organisation[1]. Indeed, evolution is inherent to every IS and evolving is its permanent condition. This is due to its ever-changing environment where contingency may arise from various dimensions such as: business activity (e.g. establishment of new business processes, re-organisation of business units, companies mergers or acquisitions), technology (e.g. introduction of new hard or soft technology), or regulation (e.g. law abrogation or modification, adoption of new industrial standards). In order to ensure IS sustainability (and hence, the information sustainability), its evolution must be understood and supported, i.e. steered.

The main challenge of the IS evolution steering is to cope with the uncertainty which is inherent to any IS change, while taking into consideration its complexity due to the entanglement of its multiple dimensions: regulation (laws and rules governing organisation activities), information (structure and provisioning), activity (business processes and activities), as well as the underpinning technology.

---

[1] In the following, we use the term 'organisation' to refer to any commercial enterprise, public governmental or non-governmental institution, or an unprofitable association.

U. Frank et al. (Eds.): PoEM 2014, LNBIP 197, pp. 118–132, 2014.

Information systems evolution is necessary but also presents several risks towards their sustainability and further changes. In particular, we can mention two important risks: the failure of IS to appropriately support business activities, and the failure to comply with the enterprise regulatory framework.

Usually, there are more than one IS to be taken into account in the same organisation. Either wholly (or partly) dependent or independent from each other, they support activities of the organisation at different organisational levels (i.e. strategic, tactic, operational). Some of them have been developed and evolve in silos and therefore testify to the consequences of the organisational restructuring (e.g. a merger of two businesses or a fusion of two departments), the evolution of the organisation activities (the development of a portfolio of B2B services for example), or the involvement of the organisation into new partnerships. This situation engenders important issues regarding IS interoperability at the information, technical and organisational levels, and it is particularly manifest when the organisation aims to adopt a service-oriented paradigm [13]. Therefore, in our research we assume that in every organisation several IS are potentially at stake during IS evolution steering.

The ultimate responsibility of the IS steering officer is to ensure IS sustainability at each step of its evolution. In order to support her in this challenging task, we focus on providing a framework that allows to reduce the uncertainty inherent to the IS evolution by exploiting different dimensions of the information available in the IS and by evaluating the impact of any planed IS change before its realisation. Our research assumptions acknowledge the following:

- the domain information is key element for the actors in charge of IS steering;
- the use of conceptual models is the sole and most reliable way to know the IS;
- the best IS steering system is the one based on its model.

We share the point of view of Olivé [17] who conveys the message that conceptual models (in [17] 'schemas') should be the centre of IS developments. In line with this statement, we argue that conceptual models should be the centre of IS evolution steering, too. IS and its evolutions are complex artefacts that can be expressed in a meaningful way with the help of conceptual models. This is particularly relevant for understanding the intertwinement of various IS dimensions [14] which cannot be undertaken otherwise.

The paper is organised as follows: in section 2 we provide the overview of our framework while section 3 is dedicated to the main metamodel of IS evolution steering. In section 4 we position our contribution with regards to the related works, and section 5 concludes the paper.

2   Overview of the Framework

We build our work on the assumptions that i) steering IS evolution requires understanding the underpinning IS domain, ii) the impact of IS evolution is difficult to predict and the simulation could help to take evolution decisions, and iii) the guidance for IS evolution steering is almost non-existent, and therefore needs to be developed. In particular, we propose a framework for IS evolution steering based on several models as shown in Fig. 1. We introduce each of them below.

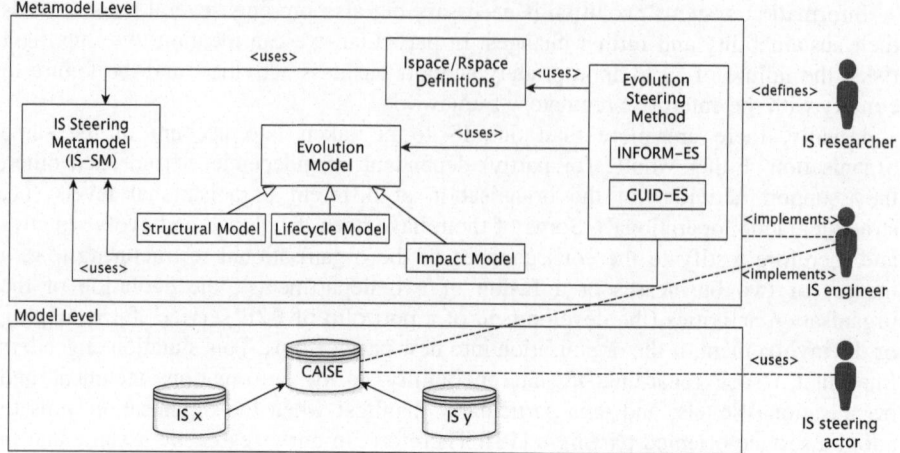

Fig. 1. Overview of the framework for IS evolution steering

2.1 IS Steering Metamodel (IS-SM)

The main element of our framework is the metamodel for IS evolution steering (IS-SM) which homogeneously integrates the activity, regulation and information dimensions (the technology dimension is out of scope of this paper) and seeks to treat their diverse elements in a sufficiently homogenous manner to be taken as a whole. IS-SM represents an information kernel, generic to any organisation, and supporting the evolution steering of several IS in the organisation. On the one hand, IS-SM allows to define the models of the evolution, and, on the other hand, it helps to simulate the evolution and to analyse its effect. IS-SM is further detailed and illustrated in the next section.

2.2 Evolution Models

The purpose of the evolution modelling is manifold. First and foremost, it helps to understand the IS evolution – the concepts at stake and their relationships that represent fundamental elements for IS steering. Secondly, it serves to build a complex artefact with multiple views to facilitate a collaborative work. Third, it supports the decision-making related to the project of evolution. Finally, with a set of models based on information, the evolution realisation is facilitated in each IS dimension with information as a 'common language'.

In order to understand IS evolution and to identify its potential impacts on the organisation, we develop three models, namely *structural*, *lifecycle* and *impact*.

The structural model defines the schema of an evolution. Indeed, an evolution is composed of several parts; each one is itself an evolution too. Therefore, the structural model allows to capture the complexity of an evolution, to identify the evolution chains, to provide evolution scenarios, and to delimit responsibilities. It is based on the concept of atomic primitive (i.e.: *create()*, *update()*, *activate()* and *inactivate()*).

The lifecycle model allows to represent different possible states of an evolution (e.g.: ready, triggered, succeeded, failed) together with the conditions (transactions) allowing the evolution to pass from one state to another. In case of a failure, it allows to identify its cause (at the primitive level) and to support the choice of the structural model (with an inter-component coordination).

The impact model represents the IS elements that are at stake in an evolution at hand, i.e. directly or indirectly impacted by the evolution. With this model, the evolution can be simulated and potential informational conflicts can be detected.

The three models can be applied for any type of planned IS evolution, regardless the evolution granularity (the whole IS, a particular service, an information element or a mixed granularity), the IS context (with or without a service level, with one or several IS), the trigger (organisation, information or regulation) and the span of the consequences (local to a particular services, local to a particular IS, or global). Moreover, these models do not rely on a determined steering metamodel. They can be easily adapted to any other steering metamodel than IS-SM.

2.3   Ispace/Rspace

The impact analysis of an evolution is often too challenging to conduct due to the number of entities and possible points of view it implies. The use of IS-SM allows concentrating the attention on the main evolution stakes – to identify all the entities that are directly or indirectly concerned by the evolution. Thus, it contributes to reduce the risks [23] of information overload, which could lead the steering actors to paralysis, to misleading estimations, or to inappropriate decisions. However, too much and too complex information is still at stake.

In order to reduce the complexity of the information space concerned by a particular evolution and, therefore, to facilitate the IS evolution impact analysis, we define a model named Ispace/Rspace. In particular, the role of Ispace/Rspace is to reflect the notion of responsibility in IS evolution steering.

Our assumption is that responsibility is a key concept for the impact analysis of an evolution. Inspired by [9] and [12], we define responsibility as a set of information entities that represents the accountabilities and the capabilities of an actor (or group of actors) to perform a task.

With Ispace/Rspace, we create sub-sets of information that allow informing the steering actors about the changes caused by an evolution affecting the responsibility. Two perspectives are taken into account: the information perspective, named Ispace, represents the responsibility over information elements, and the regulatory perspective, named Rspace, represents the responsibility over regulatory elements.

Ispace and Rspace are defined on the basis of the IS-SM and allow to simulate IS evolutions and to identify potential risks.

2.4   Evolution Steering Method

The last, but not least, component of the meta-method level of our framework is the *Evolution Steering Method* that aims to guide the actors in charge of IS evolution steering in order to support their activity.

Evolving implies for an IS to move from a known to an expected, but at the same time unknown, situation. Actors steering this evolution are responsible for the decision making under a certain level of uncertainty. This situation is characterised by risks that are either positive or negative deviations from the expectations. Consequently, guidance is a way to help IS steering actors in identifying risks, taking decisions about their handling and finally handling them.

Furthermore, IS evolution may fail due to its complexity caused by its various aforementioned dimensions. Guidance for IS evolution steering is essential for understanding and taking into account the various and interrelated components that constitute the complexity of the evolution situations.

Our Evolution Steering Method includes two interrelated models: the product model named Information Model for Evolution Steering (INFORM-ES) and the process model named Guidance for Evolution Steering (GUID-ES). INFORM-ES is based on the IS-SM, Ispace/Rspace and the evolution models; it includes concepts necessary to serve the purposes of GUID-ES. GUID-ES is an intention-driven process model providing semi-formal guidelines for IS evolution steering. In particular, it is composed of four ordered intentions, namely *Build evolution*, *Assess risks*, *Do the transition* and *Operate the evolution* and provides guidelines to reach these intentions. The set of guidelines altogether form a situational process model that can be adapted to each specific IS evolution situation and could be easily supported by a tool as introduced below.

2.5   CAISE

The formalisation of our framework allows to build a Computer-Aided Information Steering Environment (CAISE) – a powerful tool allowing to guide the steering actors in the IS evolution process. It would, for example, provide a step-by-step navigation from large-grainer to finer guidelines as well as an information space for evolution impact simulation.

To conclude this overview, we claim that our framework provides a concrete guidance for steering IS evolution, which is applicable to any type of organisation. It unveils the strong potentialities of IS models exploitation where information represents a means to address strategic concerns of IS evolution and to provide related operational support for decision-making.

2.6   Running Example: Split of a Faculty

We now introduce an example that will be used to illustrate different parts of our framework in the following section. It is inspired from a real, but rather unusual, situation – a University decides to split one of its faculties (let's say the Faculty of

Economics and Social Sciences (ESS)) into two new ones (Faculty of Economics and Business (EB) and Faculty of Social Sciences (SS)). The Faculty of ESS was founded a century ago and offers more than twenty programs of initial education (Bachelors, Masters and PhDs) and the same amount of continuing education. It is clear that such an important evolution of the University organisation has impact on its activities, people (students, professors, administrative staff) and information systems, and cannot be done without a thorough consideration and steering. In our work, we claim that most of the information regarding organisation's activities, roles and rules lies in its information systems. The Faculty of ESS exploits several information systems and in particular: *StudentsIS* for the enrolment of students in different faculty programs, *ProgramsIS* for the design and updates of the education programs, *CoursesIS* for the registration of students to different courses and exams and managing their evaluations, and *RoomsIS* for booking rooms for courses.

The split of the faculty is a complex and planed organisational evolution that leads to inevitable changes in the underpinning IS. University IS cannot be put on hold or easily replaced. Students must be able to continue to register to courses, professors still have obligation to give courses and evaluate students and the administrative staff are responsible for booking rooms for courses in each of the two new Faculties.

3   IS Steering Metamodel

The *IS Steering Metamodel (IS-SM)* embodies the foundation of our framework for IS evolution steering. It is composed of three inter-related models: *Activity*, *Regulatory* and *Information*. The IS-SM components and their relationships are shown in Fig 2.

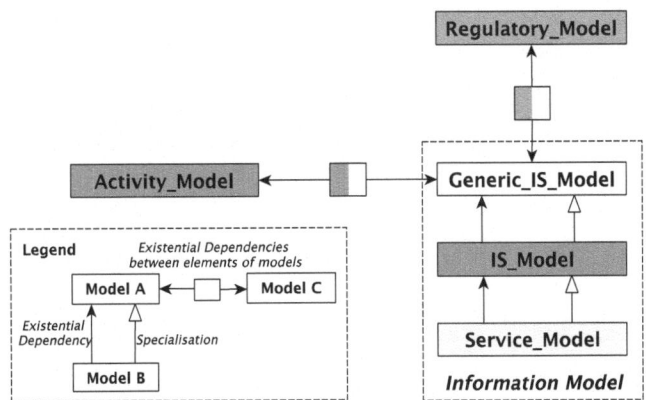

Fig. 2. The structure of the IS Steering Metamodel (IS-SM)

3.1   The Activity Model

The *Activity Model* intents to represent the interpretation of a perception [21] on the organisation of business activities. These activities can be carried out at the operational level (e.g. creating a new Master program), tactical level (e.g. planning the split of the faculty) or strategic level (e.g. developing a vision for the new faculties). They are specific to a given organisation (e.g. a company, a non-profit association or a governmental agency, a university in our case).

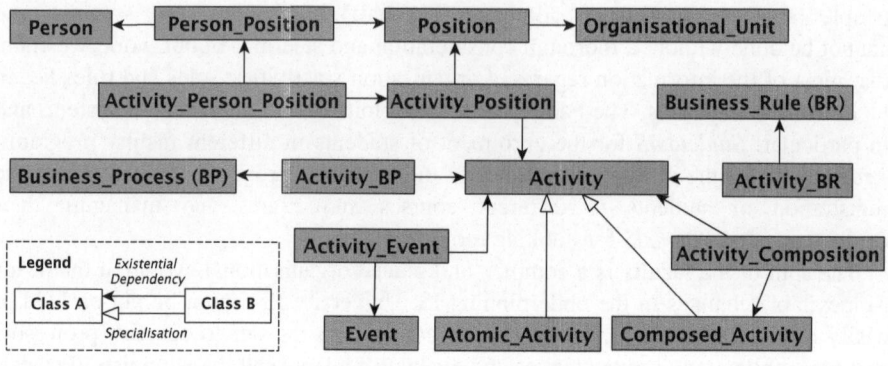

Fig. 3. Metamodel of Activity Model

As shown in Fig. 3, the activity model defines how organisational *activities*, that can be atomic or composed, are related to *business processes* and *positions* held by *persons* in different *organizational units*. A person holding a position may be responsible for a set of activities defined for the position. Activities are governed by *business rules* and may trigger or be triggered by *events*.

For example, the activity model allows to structure the following information (see Fig. 4): John Doe is a person who holds the position of professor in the Faculty ESS. Among the activities of this position, he is in charge to lead a Master program on Business Administration.

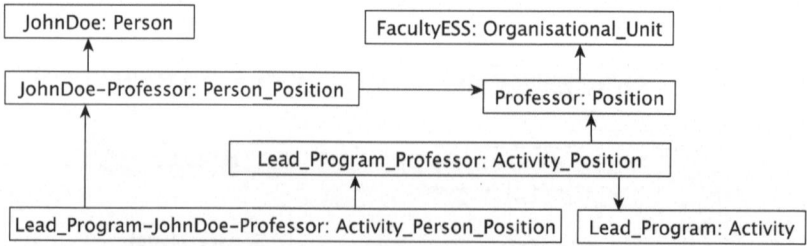

Fig. 4. An excerpt of the activity model describing University activities, roles and responsibilities

3.2   The Regulatory Model

The *Regulatory Model* allows to specify the necessary, unquestionable and invariant concepts and their relationships identified in laws, policies and other regulations (e.g. SOX[2], ISO 9001[3], a particular regulation of the organisation) that govern organisation's activities and to which the organisation must/decides to comply.

The metamodel depicted in Fig. 5 defines the regulatory model. A *regulatory source* is a legal base or industrial standard which is used as a common base for the IS development. A *fragment* of a regulatory source may be a law article, or a paragraph of a standard. A *regulatory element* may be a *concept*, a *regulatory role* or a *regulatory rule*. It originates from one or several regulatory fragments. A regulatory concept is an abstract construct defined in a regulatory source (e.g. scientific committee). A regulatory role represents a set of necessary responsibilities, authorities and capabilities, expressed in laws, to perform the execution of activities or to supervise the execution of activities performed by other roles. A regulatory rule represents a rule defined in a regulatory source governing organisation's activities.

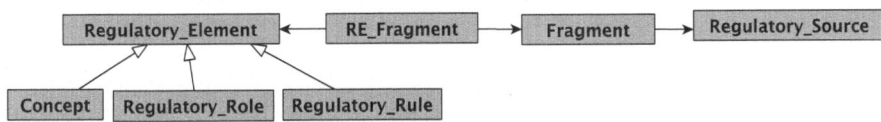

Fig. 5. Metamodel of Regulatory Model

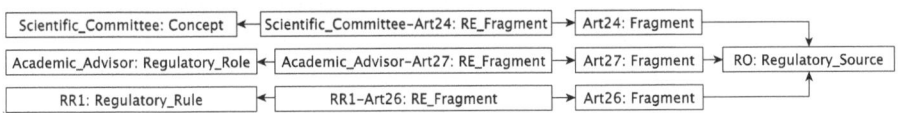

Fig. 6. An excerpt of the University regulatory model

The example in Fig. 6 shows that the Faculty ESS is ruled by the *Rule of Organisation*[4], where the concept *Scientific_Committee* (art. 24), the regulatory role of *Academic_Advisor* (art. 27) and the regulatory rule *RR1* regarding the creation of a new program (art. 26) are extracted.

3.3   The Information Model

The *Information Model* is composed of three models: the *Generic IS model*, *IS model* and *Service model* (see Fig. 2).

The purpose of the *Generic IS metamodel* is to represent an integrated view of the IS level which can consist of several IS. It allows inter-relating the Information model with the Activity and Regulatory models. Fig. 7 depicts a small part of this metamodel; it defines the generic concepts such as *class*, *role* and *treatment*. A role is

---

[2]   Sarbanes-Oxley Act,
http://www.govtrack.us/congress/bills/107/hr3763/text
[3]   ISO   9001,   http://www.iso.org/iso/home/standards/management-standards/iso_9000.htm
[4]   Règlement d'organisation http://www.unige.ch/ses/telecharger/faculte/ro2012.pdf

a responsibility pattern that may be assumed by several actors. It is associated to a class and/or to a treatment in order to specify the authorisations that the role has over the class objects or treatments.

For example, the generic role *Program_Director* has responsibilities over the class *Program* and over the treatment *Offering_Program*. It can be implemented in one or several IS of the Faculty ESS (see Fig. 8).

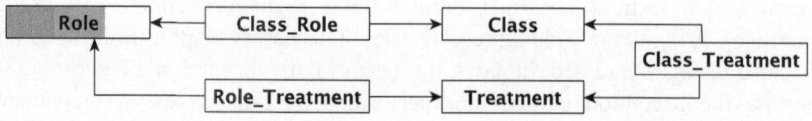

Fig. 7. An excerpt of the metamodel of Generic IS Model

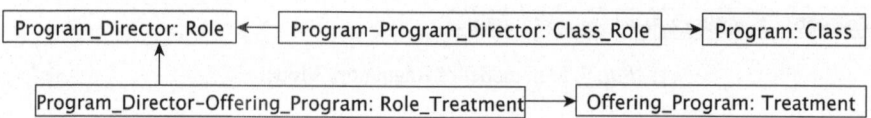

Fig. 8. An example of instantiation of Generic IS Model

The *IS level metamodel* has been built upon the Generic level metamodel in order to add to it the information elements relating to the IS level. From now on, an IS defines itself as a restriction of the generic level previously described. Indeed, two or more IS may support the activities of an organization. For example, as mentioned above, the activities of the Faculty ESS are enabled trough several IS such as *StudentsIS*, *ProgramsIS*, *CoursesIS* and *RoomsIS*. They may share some of their information elements (classes, methods, treatments, etc.), i.e. related to the same generic element. Fig. 9 shows a small excerpt of the IS level metamodel named IS-Model, and its links with the Generic IS Model.

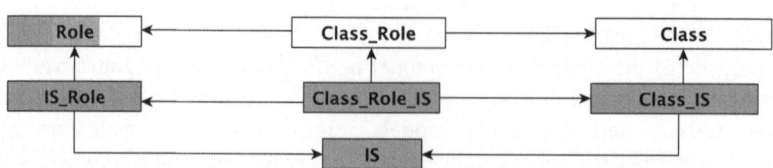

Fig. 9. An excerpt of the metamodel of IS-Model

To illustrate the instantiation of the IS-Model we can mention that the generic role *Program_Director* exists in the IS *ProgramsIS*, where it is responsible for the class *Program* (see Fig. 10).

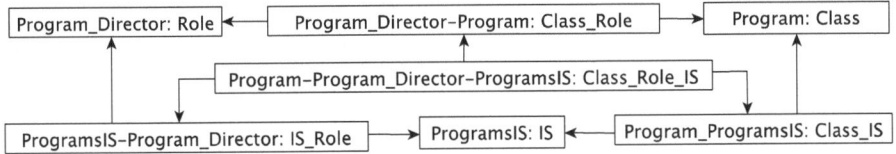

Fig. 10. An example of instantiation of IS model representing an IS role

Finally, the *Service level metamodel,* named *Service-Model,* defines the elements of an information service[5]. In our approach, a service shares the same metamodel as an IS. A service is a specialised IS which is based on one or several IS. Fig. 11 shows only very small part of the service level metamodel that allows to identify the information systems used by a service.

Fig. 11. An excerpt of the metamodel of Service-Model

For example, Fig. 12 shows the service *Master_Admission* that has been built on two IS, *StudentsIS* and *ProgramsIS,* in order to support the process of the admission to the master programs more efficiently. It allows for the applicants to send their application files directly to the administrative staff, the program director and the scientific committee, to evaluate the application.

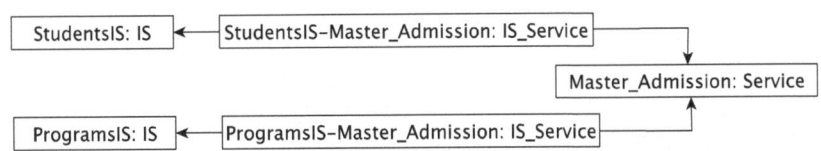

Fig. 12. An excerpt of service model representing a service built on two IS

Altogether the models constituting the IS-SM aim to reduce the uncertainty pertaining to the situation of IS evolution. In particular, they help to identify and understand the elements at stake when steering a particular IS evolution (inform the evolution), and to specify, via simulation, direct and indirect impacts of this evolution (analyse the evolution simulation).

Let us take as example the Evolution *E1* illustrated in Fig. 13, which, because of the split of the Faculty ESS, consists in the creation of a new organisational unit (*FacultyEB*). This creation implies other actions like the creation of the position of professor in this new Faculty and the related activity of leading a program. John Doe who used to be professor in *FacultyESS* is now affected to *FacultyEB*. In this new position, he takes the lead of a program and receives the new role of

---

[5] Hereafter, the term service is used for 'information service'.

DesignerEBProgram, which enables him to add and remove courses to/from this program in the *ProgramIS*.

In the simulation environment, this evolution is processed on the IS-SM data, which have been extracted from the actual University IS. The resulting IS-SM data are then analysed and related risks may be identified[6].

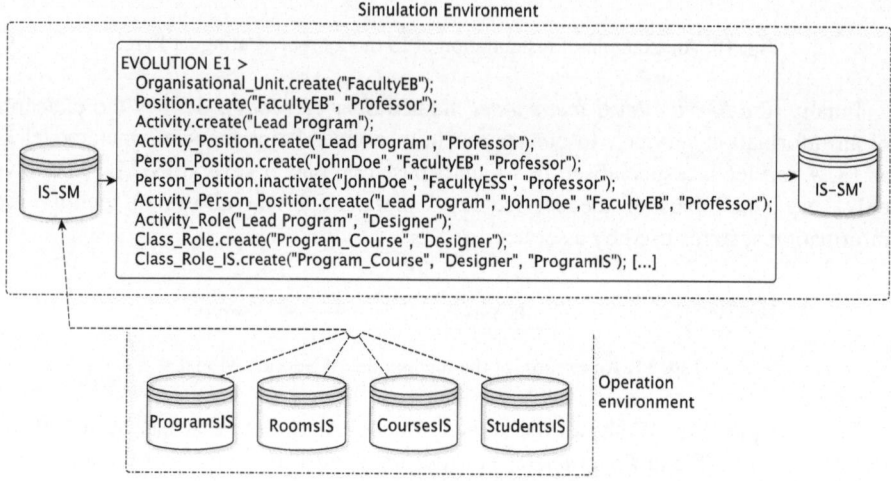

Fig. 13. Example of simulation of the Evolution E1

4   Related Works

The literature review reveals that there is no consensus on the definition, goals, models and methods of IS evolution steering. This domain is at the crossroads of several IS research areas such as: Enterprise Architecture (EA), Enterprise Modelling, Business/IT alignment, IS Governance and Risk Management. Below we discuss a few related approaches, which contribute to the understanding of the IS evolution steering stakes.

4.1   Enterprise Architecture Models

Many Enterprise Architecture (EA) frameworks have been proposed since 1987 when Zachman created the 'Zachman Framework' [28]. Some of them originate from industry (e.g. TOGAF[7] [19]), other from research projects (e.g. GERAM[8] [5], CIMOSA[9] [2], PERA[10] [27], GRAI-GIM [8], EKD-CMM[11] [4]) or even from

---

[6] The method for analysing the simulation and identifying the evolution risks are not presented here due to the space limit.

[7] TOGAF: The Open Group Architecture Framework.

[8] GERAM: Generalised Enterprise Reference Architecture and Methodology.

[9] CIMOSA: Computer Integrated Manufacturing Open System Architecture.

governments (e.g. the Finnish GEA[12] [25], the US FEA[13] [18], the US Department of Defense DodAF[14] [7]).

However, despite a large number of approaches, there is no common agreement on the definition of EA, because it can be approached from a number of viewpoints [16] such as products (especially structural models), services (such as architectural guidance), processes (e.g. creating and updating EA products), outcomes (e.g. systems or processes implemented according to EA) and benefits (e.g. improvement of business-IT alignment). Most of the frameworks acknowledge the need for multiple views in order to manage complexity, separate concerns and address different life spans of the architecture elements [3]. These approaches often expose best practices and generic principles, but fail to offer a formal steering method. Moreover, they do not exploit information as a 'common language' between different IS dimensions that we do with our IS evolution steering model.

4.2   Business/IT Alignment

Business/IT alignment has been one of the main concerns for both IS practitioners and researchers since two decades, particularly in the domain of IT/IS Governance [15, 26] and in the discipline and practice of EA. It consists in the design, restoration and evolution of the alignment between business activities and the IS enabling them. According to Henderson and Venkatraman [10], business/IT alignment aims to reach a degree of strategic fit and functional integration between enterprise business and IT (their respective strategies and infrastructures and processes). Reich and Benbasat [22] define business/IT alignment as a degree to which the information technology mission, objectives and plans support (and are supported by) the business mission, objectives and plans. Most of the time, the alignment implies two entities and therefore, is bivariate [10]. But, it can also imply several entities and be cross-domain [10] or multivariate. Usually, one of these entities corresponds to the business domain and the other to the IT domain. The systematic review of alignment presented in [24] suggests four directions for the study of the alignment process: the business strategy, business structure, business culture and social directions.

As an answer to the integration of multiple IS dimensions, there is a large amount of works suggesting business/IT alignment. However, none of them, to our knowledge, includes three IS dimensions: information, regulation and activity, neither takes into account multiple IS at once. Furthermore, these approaches often fail to take into account the inherent characteristic of the IS level – the permanent evolution of its entities. Besides, the IS model is not used as a source of the integration of different IS dimensions.

---

[10] PERA: Purdue Enterprise Reference Architecture.
[11] EKD-CMM: Enterprise Knowledge Development - Change Management Method.
[12] GEA: Government Enterprise Architecture.
[13] FEA: Federal Enterprise Architecture.
[14] DodAF: Department of Defense Architecture Framework.

4.3   IS Evolution Metamodels

The techniques of evolution in IS and software engineering are mostly based on models [1, 6, 11, 20]. These research works mainly address the problem of structural evolution (e.g. changing a hierarchy, adding a class) [20]. Their intention is to support the change propagation in order to allow the automation of data migration, to evaluate the impact of metamodel changes on models, to support forward-, reverse-, and re-engineering techniques or to record the model history. Some works are language-dependent (for example UML, EMF, MOF), while others are not. However, these models are not designed for IS evolution steering purposes and are not considered as means to support decision making in IS evolution, which is the purpose of our framework for IS evolution steering.

To sum-up this literature review, we claim that, to our best knowledge, there is no another holistic approach supporting IS evolution steering that the one we propose in this paper.

5   Conclusion

Every change in enterprise organisation, business activity, or regulation inevitably entails a chain of evolutions of its information systems and services. Actors, responsible for IS evolution steering, have to take important decisions those impact on the enterprise business and IS can be devastating. To be able to make these decisions, they must have a thorough knowledge of the situation, and we claim that this information can be extracted from enterprise information systems.

In this paper, we present an overview of a framework dedicated to support enterprise IS evolution steering and to help IS steering actors to take critical decisions. The framework aims to address IS sustainability issues by proving clear and complete information allowing to simulate IS evolution and to assess the impact of its changes. Especially, it allows to reduce the uncertainty that the actors responsible for IS steering are facing at each IS change, and to guide them in such a hazardous task.

The framework is composed of several models that represent different and complementary IS evolution perspectives such as: related information structure, evolution lifecycle, impact of the organisation and its IS, and responsibility, and provides guidance to exploit these models. The main part of the framework, the IS steering model (IS-SM) that captures the fundamentals of the approach, is detailed and illustrated in this paper.

Our main future research perspective concerns the integration of the technology dimension into our framework. It starts with the extension of IS-SM with software and hardware infrastructure components. It could lead the steering actors to identify potential security risks caused by an evolution.

Our framework paves the way to the building of a novel Computer Aided Information Steering Environment (CAISE) dedicated to support the activities of IS evolution steering led by information. It unveils the strong potentialities of IS models exploitation for reducing the uncertainty inherent to the evolution steering, and for allowing the actors of multiple IS dimensions to collaborate, which is the most promising approach for the pursuit of a sound and sustainable IS evolution.

References

1. Aboulsamhl, M.A., Davies, J.: A Metamodel-Based Approach to Information Systems Evolution and Data Migration. In: 5th International Conference on Software Engineering Advances (ICSEA), Nice, France, pp. 155–161 (2010)
2. AMICE: Open Systems Architecture for CIM, 2nd. Revised and Extended Version. Springer, Berlin (1993)
3. Armour, F.J., Kaisler, S.H., Liu, S.Y.: A big-picture look at enterprise architectures. IT Professional 1(1), 35–42 (1999)
4. Barrios, J., Nurcan, S.: Model Driven Architectures for Enterprise Information Systems. In: Persson, A., Stirna, J. (eds.) CAiSE 2004. LNCS, vol. 3084, pp. 3–19. Springer, Heidelberg (2004)
5. Bernus, P., Nemes, L.: A framework to define a generic enterprise reference architecture and methodology. Computer Integrated Manufacturing Systems 9(3), 179–191 (1996)
6. Burger, E., Gruschko, B.: A Change Metamodel for the Evolution of MOF-based Metamodels. In: Proc. of Modellierung, vol. 161, pp. 285–300. GI (2010)
7. DoDAF: DoD Architecture Framework Version 2.02. US Dep. of Defence (2010), http://dodcio.defense.gov/dodaf20 (accessed July 2014)
8. Doumeingts, G., Vallespir, B., Chen, D.: Decision modelling GRAI grid. In: Handbook on architecture for Information Systems, pp. 313–337. Springer, Heidelberg (1998)
9. Feltus, C., Petit, M., Dubois, E.: ReMoLa: Responsibility Model Language to Align Access Rights with Business Process Requirements. In: 5th IEEE International Conference on Research Challenges in Information Science (RCIS 2011), pp. 1–6. IEEE, Guadeloupe (2011)
10. Henderson, J.C., Venkatraman, N.: Strategic Alignment: Leveraging Information Technology for Transforming Organizations. IBM Systems Journal 32(1), 4–16 (1993)
11. Kchaou, D., Bouassida, N., Ben-Abdallah, H.: A Mof-Based Change Meta-Model. In: Proceedings of the 13th International Arab Conference on Information Technology (ACIT 2012), Zarq, Jordan (2012)
12. Khadraoui, A., Feltus, C.: Service specification and service compliance: How to consider the responsibility dimension? Journal of Service Science Research 4(1), 123–142 (2012)
13. Khadraoui, A., Opprecht, W., Léonard, M., Aïdonidis, C.: Service specification upon multiple existing information systems. In: 5th IEEE International Conference on Research Challenges in Information Science (RCIS 2011), pp. 1–11. IEEE, Guadeloupe (2011)
14. Léonard, M.: Modèle dans le domaine des systèmes d'information. In: Encyclopédie de l'informatique et des systèmes d'information, pp. 1396–1411. Vuibert, Paris (2006)
15. Luftman, J.: Assessing business-IT alignment maturity. Communications of the Association for Information Systems 4(14), 1–51 (2000)
16. Niemi, E., Pekkola, S.: Enterprise Architecture Quality Attributes: A Case Study. In: Proceedings of the 46th Hawaii International Conference on System Sciences (HICSS), pp. 3878–3887 (2013)
17. Olivé, À.: Conceptual schema-centric development: A grand challenge for information systems research. In: Pastor, Ó., Falcão e Cunha, J. (eds.) CAiSE 2005. LNCS, vol. 3520, pp. 1–15. Springer, Heidelberg (2005)

18. OMB: Federal Enterprise Architecture (FEA). US White House Office of Management and Budget (2012), http://www.whitehouse.gov/omb/e-gov/fea/ (accessed July 2014)
19. The Open Group: TOGAF version 9.1, An Open Group Standard (2012), http://pubs.opengroup.org/architecture/togaf9-doc/arch/ (accessed July 2014)
20. Pons, C., Kutsche, R.-D.: Model evolution and system evolution. In: V Congreso Argentino de Ciencias de la Computación, La Plata, Argentina (1999)
21. Proper, H.A., Van der Weide, T.P.: Modelling as Selection of Interpretation. In: Modellierung 2006, Innsbruck, Austria, LNI, pp. 223–232. GI (2006)
22. Reich, B.H., Benbasat, I.: Measuring the Linkage between Business and Information Technology Objectives. MIS Quarterly 20(1), 55–81 (1996)
23. Sherer, S.A., Alter, S.: Information system risks and risk factors: are they mostly about information systems. Communications of the Association for Information Systems 14(2), 29–64 (2004)
24. Ullah, A., Lai, R.: A Systematic Review of Business and Information Technology Alignment. ACM Transactions on Management Information Systems 4(1), 1–30 (2013)
25. Valtonen, K., Seppanen, V., Leppanen, M.: Government Enterprise Architecture Grid Adaptation in Finland. In: Proc. of the 42st Hawaii International Conference on Systems Science (HICSS 42), Waikoloa, Hawaii, pp. 1–10 (2009)
26. Van Grembergen, W., De Haes, S., Guldentops, E.: Structures, processes and relational mechanisms for IT governance. In: Strategies for information technology governance, pp. 1–36. Idea Group Inc., Hershey (2004)
27. Williams, T.J.: The Purdue enterprise reference architecture. Computers in industry 24(2), 141–158 (1994)
28. Zachman, J.A.: A Framework for Information Systems Architecture. IBM Systems Journal 26(3), 276–292 (1987)

Capturing Design Rationales in Enterprise Architecture: A Case Study

Georgios Plataniotis[1,2,4], Sybren de Kinderen[3,4], and Henderik A. Proper[1,2,4]

[1] Public Research Centre Henri Tudor, Luxembourg, Luxembourg
[2] Radboud University Nijmegen, Nijmegen, The Netherlands
[3] University of Luxembourg, Luxembourg
[4] EE-Team, Luxembourg, Luxembourg*
{georgios.plataniotis,erik.proper}@tudor.lu,sybren.dekinderen@uni.lu

Abstract. We aim for rationalizing Enterprise Architecture, supplementing models that express EA designs with models that express the decision making behind the designs. In our previous work we introduced the EA Anamnesis approach for architectural rationalization, and illustrated it with a fictitious case study.

In this paper we evaluate our approach in terms of its ability to capture design rationales in the context of a real life case study. Together with stakeholders from the business and IT domains of a Luxembourgish Research and Technology Organization, we captured the design rationales behind the introduction of a new budget forecast business process. Our case study shows that EA Anamnesis can reflect the design rationales of the stakeholders, also linking business and IT concerns. Furthermore our study shows that, for this particular case, the stakeholders often used heuristics (commonsensical "short cuts") to make their decision, or even made decisions without considering alternative choices. Finally, we discuss what the lessons learned from this case imply for further research.

Keywords: Enterprise Architecture, Design Rationale, Design Decisions, Case Study.

1   Introduction

As architects create blueprints for (re-)designing buildings, enterprise architects use EA modeling languages for (re-)designing organizations [1]. They do so by relating the business and IT concerns of an organization. For example, EA modeling languages can be used to design an IT application landscape suitable for a particular business process. Prominent examples of EA languages are the Open Group standard ArchiMate [2], and the recent OMG standard Unified Profile for DoDAF/MODAF (UPDM) [3], an UML profile for describing enterprise architecture in accordance with the enterprise architecture frameworks DoDAF/MODAF.

---

* The Enterprise Engineering Team (EE-Team) is a collaboration between Public Research Centre Henri Tudor, Radboud University Nijmegen and HAN University of Applied Sciences (www.ee-team.eu)

U. Frank et al. (Eds.): PoEM 2014, LNBIP 197, pp. 133–147, 2014.

Yet, EA modeling languages describe the EA designs, but not the reasoning behind these designs.This also holds for the recent motivation extension of the EA modeling language ArchiMate [2]. While the motivation extension allows for expression stakeholder intentions, it lacks well-established decision making concepts such as criterion, used decision making strategy and more. Moreover, in some cases practitioners have a different understanding even for the same EA model because they interpret the meta-conceptual constructs with different ways [4].

Experience from the field of software architecture shows that leaving design rationales implicit leads to 'Architectural Knowledge vaporization' (cf. [5]). This means that, without design rationale, design criteria and reasons that lead to a specific design are not clear. Also, alternatives that were considered during the design process are not captured.

Among others, a lack of transparency regarding design decisions can cause design integrity issues when architects want to maintain or change the current design [6]. This means that due to a lacking insight of the rationale, new designs are constructed in an ad-hoc manner, without taking into consideration constraints implied by past design decisions. Furthermore a survey on EA rationalization amongst EA practitioners [7] suggests the relevance of architectural rationalization for motivating design decisions, and for architectural maintenance. However, the same survey shows that practitioners often forego the use of a structured template/approach when rationalizing an architecture. Instead they capture decision characteristics in an ad hoc manner, and do so largely in plain text.

In our earlier work [8,9,10] we introduced the EA Anamnesis approach for architectural rationalization. EA Anamnesis captures decision characteristics such as decision criteria and used decision making strategy, and shows the relation between business-level and IT-level decisions. Furthermore, EA Anamnesis allows for a formal linkage to metamodel-based EA artifacts, thus allowing for a bridge between languages for EA design (basically ArchiMate) and the corresponding design rationale.

Thus far, EA Anamnesis has been developed with the aid of a fictitious case study, and with a survey amongst practitioners [7]. The fictitious case helped for idea development, while the survey provided us a first practical assessment of the EA Anamnesis's rationalization concepts. However, none offered us an *in-depth* assessment of the practical applicability of EA Anamnesis. In particular, we lack substantial insight into the extent to which EA Anamnesis can express real life decisions.

As a response, in this paper we apply our approach to a real world case in a Research and Technology Organization. Together with two stakeholders, from the financial and IT domain respectively, we extracted the design rationales behind the introduction of a new budget forecasting business process. This helps us identify how practitioners perceive the concepts of EA Anamnesis for capturing and understanding enterprise architectures. Moreover we observe that, for this particular case, practitioners select among alternatives by using simple decision making processes. Even more so, practitioners do not consider alternatives during their decision making process.

This paper is structured as follows. Section 2 presents the EA Anamnesis approach, Section 3 introduces the Research and Technology Organization Case Study and discusses the case study protocol we followed, the limitations and the capturing of design rationales with our approach. Section 4 presents lessons learned. Section 5 concludes.

2   EA Anamnesis Approach

Fig. 1 presents the EA Anamnesis metamodel as discussed in [8,9,11]. With this metamodel we allow for (1) contextualizing the decision making process of a single decision in terms of cross cutting/intertwining decision relationships, and (2) a comparison of decision outcomes to the original decision making process.

For comprehension purposes the concepts of our metamodel will be introduced in 3 subsections: decision properties (Subsect. 2.1), decision making process concepts (Subsect. 2.2) and decision relationships (Subsect. 2.3).

2.1   Decision Properties

EA Decision: We define decision as the choice made between alternative courses of action in a situation of uncertainty [12]. Moreover, an enterprise architecture (EA) decision names the decision that is made in the context of an Enterprise Transformation [13]. Regarding the distinction between made decision and alternative decision, see the decision relationship "alternative".

EA Issue: Similar to the concept of an issue from [14], an EA issue represents the architectural design problem that enterprise architects have to address during the Enterprise transformation process.

EA Artifact: An EA artifact (similar to concept of an architecture element [6]) is either the direct result produced from a set of executed EA decisions, or a representation of this result. For now, we use an EA artifact to refer to architectural representations. Specifically, we use it as a bridging concept towards the EA modeling language ArchiMate, whereby an EA artifact allows us to link EA decisions to concepts from ArchiMate.

Layer: In line with the ArchiMate language [2], an enterprise is specified in three layers: *Business, Application and Technology*. Using these three layers, we express an enterprise *holistically*, showing not only applications and physical IT infrastructure (expressed through the application and technology layers), but also how an enterprise's IT impacts/is impacted by an enterprise's products and services and its business strategy and processes.

Observed Impact: The observed impact concept signifies an *unanticipated* consequence of an already made decision to an EA artifact. This opposes to anticipated consequences, as indicated by relationships such as translation or decomposition. Observed impacts can be positive or negative.

In current everyday practice, architects model *anticipated* consequences using what-if-scenarios [1]. Unfortunately, not every possible impact of made EA

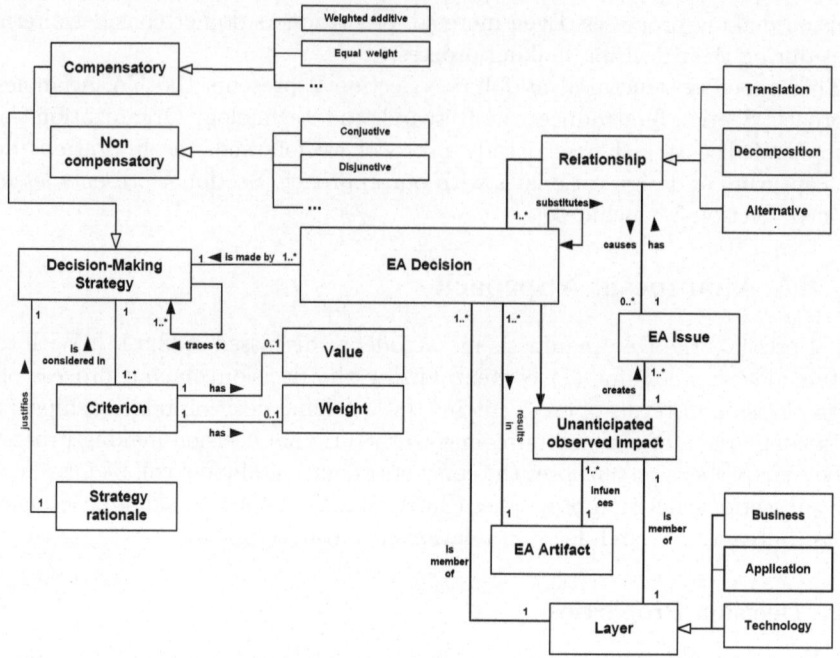

Fig. 1. EA Anamnesis metamodel

decisions can be predicted. This is especially true for enterprise architecture, where one considers impacts across the enterprise rather than in one specific (e.g. technical) part. The outcome of EA decisions can be observed during an ex-post analysis of the architecture [13]. Some of the consequences of EA decisions are revealed during the implementation phase, or during the maintenance of the existing architecture design. These unanticipated consequences are captured exactly by the concept of an observed impact.

For us the main usefulness of capturing observed impacts is that they can be used by architects to avoid decisions with negative consequences in future designs of the architecture.

2.2   Decision Making Process Concepts

The decision making process concepts of our metamodel focus on capturing (1) decision making strategies that were used during the architectural design process for a specific EA decision, (2) the rationale behind this specific decision strategy choice, and (3) available alternatives and criteria that were taken into account. Below we provide the description of these concepts.

Decision-Making Strategy: This concept captures the decision making strategy used by the enterprise architect to (1) evaluate the alternatives, and make the actual EA decision. As we analyzed in our previous work [8], decision strategies are characterized as compensatory, noncompensatory, or as a hybrid of these two. A hybrid decision strategy is also supported by our metamodel. The relationship 'trace to' signifies the combination of two or more decision strategies during the decision making process.

Criterion: Criteria play an important role in our metamodel. Depending on the decision strategy that was used for the evaluation process, criteria can be compensatory or noncompensatory. For example, if a disjunctive strategy was used, the criteria that were used for the evaluation with this strategy are disjunctive. Furthermore, the concepts **value** and **weight** of criterion are included in our viewpoint. The value concept represents the value that the decision maker assigns to this criterion during the evaluation process. The weight concept represents the importance of this criterion, and is typically used in WADD strategies.

Strategy Rationale: In a decision making process, the architect not only has to choose amongst some alternatives (actual decision making process), but has also to select the decision strategy that satisfies his current evaluation needs. Actually, this concept represents the rationale for the decision strategy that was selected for the evaluation process. This is what is referred as metadecision making, decision making about the decision process itself [15].

2.3 EA Decision Relationships

The role of relationship concepts is to make the different types of relationships between EA decisions explicit. Based on ontologies for software architecture design decisions [16,17], we define four types of relationships:

Translation Relationship: Translation relationships illustrate relationships between decisions/EA issues that belong to different layers/EA artifacts. Architects translate the requirements that new EA artifacts impose (EA issue) to decisions that will support these requirements by means of another EA artifact [18].

Decomposition Relationship: The Decomposition relationship is in line with 'Comprises (Is Made of, Decomposes into)' of Kruchten's ontology [17]. Decomposition relationships signify how generic EA decisions decompose into more detailed design decisions in the context of a specific EA artifact.

Alternative Relationship: This relationship type [17] illustrates the EA decisions that were rejected (alternatives) in order to address a specific EA issue.

Substitution Relationship: A substitution relationship explicates how one EA decision repairs the negative outcome of another EA Decision.

3 Research and Technology Organization Case Study

In this section we describe the application of our approach to a case study of a Research and Technology Organization in Luxembourg (LuxRTO).

3.1 Case Study Setup

Objectives and Setup: The main objective of this case is to review to what extent our approach is able to capture design rationales in the context of a *real life* enterprise transformation.

To this end, we study one particular transformation: the introduction of a new budget management business process at LuxRTO. We organized interviews with two key stakeholders that were involved in the transformation: The financial officer, and the IT architect. Both these stakeholders provided a good starting point for the domain knowledge that we had to capture. On the one hand, the financial officer possessed significant business expertise on this enterprise transformation project. Being involved from the start of the transformation project, she had knowledge about the drivers that initiated this transformation and how the business process design evolved over time. On the other hand the IT architect had significant IT expertise on the transformation project. Furthermore, the stakeholders provided us with the documentation of this transformation project (text documents, presentations, emails).

We started our case study by presenting the EA Anamnesis approach to the financial officer and the IT architect. We explained the goals and challenges of our case study, and we illustrated our approach using an example case. This example case helped the stakeholders to understand our approach.

After the presentation of EA Anamnesis, we conducted a collaborative modeling exercise with the two stakeholders. The goal of this exercise was to see to what extent our approach was able to capture the design rationales of this transformation. Furthermore we also identified the perception of stakeholders regarding the concepts of EA Anamnesis.

Note that the setup above is inspired by the main steps for doing case study research set out in [19]. For example: prior to the collaborative modeling we explained our approach to practitioners. This is in line with [19], who advices to prepare for data collection prior to the collection of evidence.

Limitations: In this subsection we discuss limitations that have potentially played a role in the application of our approach in LuxRTO and in the interpretation of the results of this study.

The first limitation is that the actual enterprise transformation was held around two years before the case study. This implies that stakeholders may had a bias in what information they captured during the case study (colored memory) or they may have forgotten certain things. Another limitation is the number of stakeholders that participated in the case study. Normally, multiple stakeholders participate in an enterprise architecture transformation. In our case we interviewed two stakeholders (one from business domain and one from IT). We are aware of this restriction but in the current stage of our research we focused on how our approach captures design rationales and not on the support of multiple stakeholders decision making.

3.2   Budget Forecasting at a Research and Technology Organization

Here we present the introduction of a new budget management business process and how this process was supported by information systems in the context of an enterprise architecture transformation.

During the last years, the Luxembourgish government introduced stricter rules on the budget spending of research institutions. This policy had to be incorporated by the research institutions, meaning that the institutions should be able to establish long term financial projection plans. This would give to institutions a better awareness regarding the availability of resources and in turn the planning of future projects and personnel hiring.

LuxRTO did not have an established business process for the budget estimation. Stakeholders from the management side of LuxRTO had to design this new business process. Their initial objectives were that this business process should provide a clear view on human resources and projects coverage, an input for the future hiring plan, comparison between the forecasted and valuable budget, and in general robustness of the organization's financial data. Last but not least, a training for the users of this new business process should be organized.

3.3   Enterprise Transformation

In this part we describe how the enterprise design was changed in order to support the new budget estimation business process. For expressing the EA Design of the budget forecast project we used the ArchiMate EA modeling language. Not that LuxRTO had already established IT systems that were supporting other types financial, project and human resources business processes. Before we present the transformation we briefly describe the new business process and the already established IT systems.

Budget Forecast Business Process: The main objectives of this business process are the estimation and the planning of resources to ensure the planning activities, the assessment of the need for additional resources, the estimation of the associated budgets and the checking of the forecast in relation to the available budget in LuxRTO. The role of the business process is to provide annual budget estimates, which should be validated and approved by the finance department.

IT Systems: Application A is the main financial application of the organization. The main functionalities of this application is the management of procurements, traveling costs, personal costs, overhead costs calculation, salaries payment and project dashboard. The user access to this application in controlled and only allowed to financial officers.

Application B is the human resources management application. Tasks like resource allocation, start/end dates of work contracts, weekly calendar, different types of leaves (sickness, vacation etcetera) are executed by this application.

Application C is the project management application of the organization. The actual hours assigned per project in the organization are maintained in this application.

First Iteration of the Transformation: Fig. 2 depicts the EA model after the incorporation of the budget forecast business process. From this model we can realize that the business process was supported by the interaction and collaboration among Applications A, B, C and a spreadsheet application. However, due to some problems (which can not been described by the EA model), stakeholders had to do some additional changes in the EA design.

Second Iteration of the Transformation: Fig. 3 depicts the final iteration of the enterprise transformation. With this iteration stakeholders managed to address the aforementioned problem. Instead of using spreadsheets for entering the budget data, a new application interface was added in the financial application A.

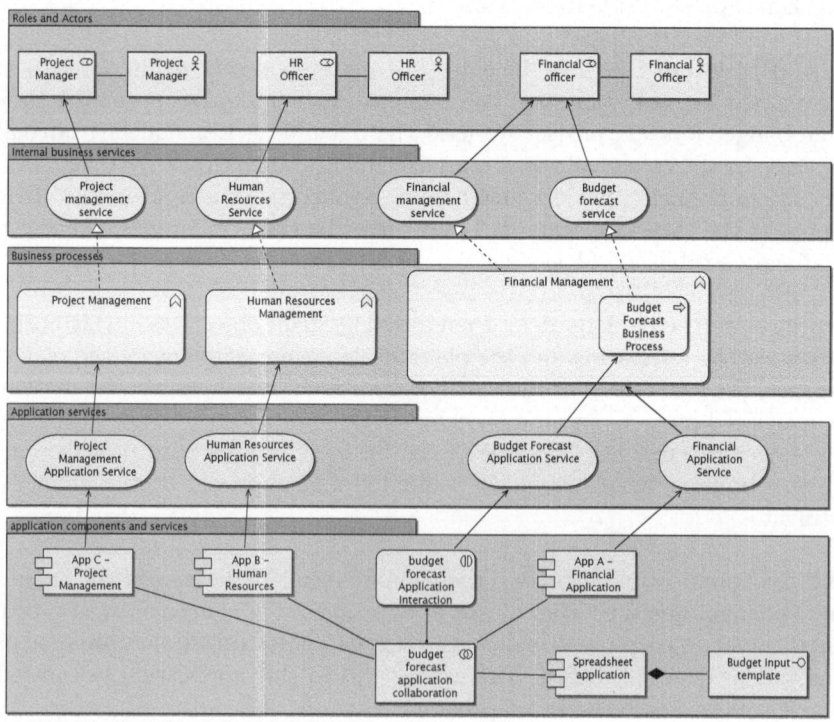

Fig. 2. LuxRTO enterprise transformation - First iteration

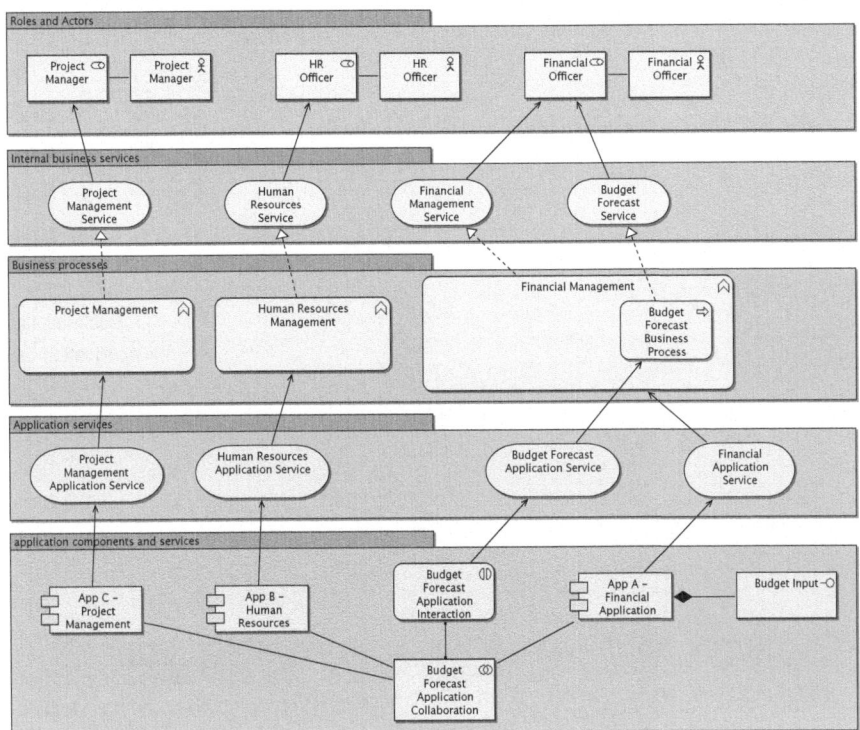

Fig. 3. LuxRTO enterprise transformation - Second iteration

3.4   Capturing the Rationale behind the Budget Forecast Design

In the previous subsection we described the changes happened in the enterprise architecture design in order to support the new budget forecast business process. However, the rationale behind this design is not captured by the EA models. Based on the case study we could potentially ask these questions:

Why these IT systems were selected for the realization of the business process? Were there any other alternatives? What were the unanticipated consequences of these decisions in the enterprise architecture?

The answers to these questions provide a useful insight in the understanding of the EA design and can not be answered just by examining EA models. This is exactly the point where EA Anamnesis approach intervenes.

Our approach uses two elements for capturing and representing design rationales. The visualization of Fig. 4 is a design decision graph which is constructed while design rationale is captured. The graph represents design decisions and how they are interrelated with other design rationale concepts (issue, observed impact etc) of the EA Anamnesis approach. The graph is accompanied with Table 1 which provides a summarization of the design rationale information.

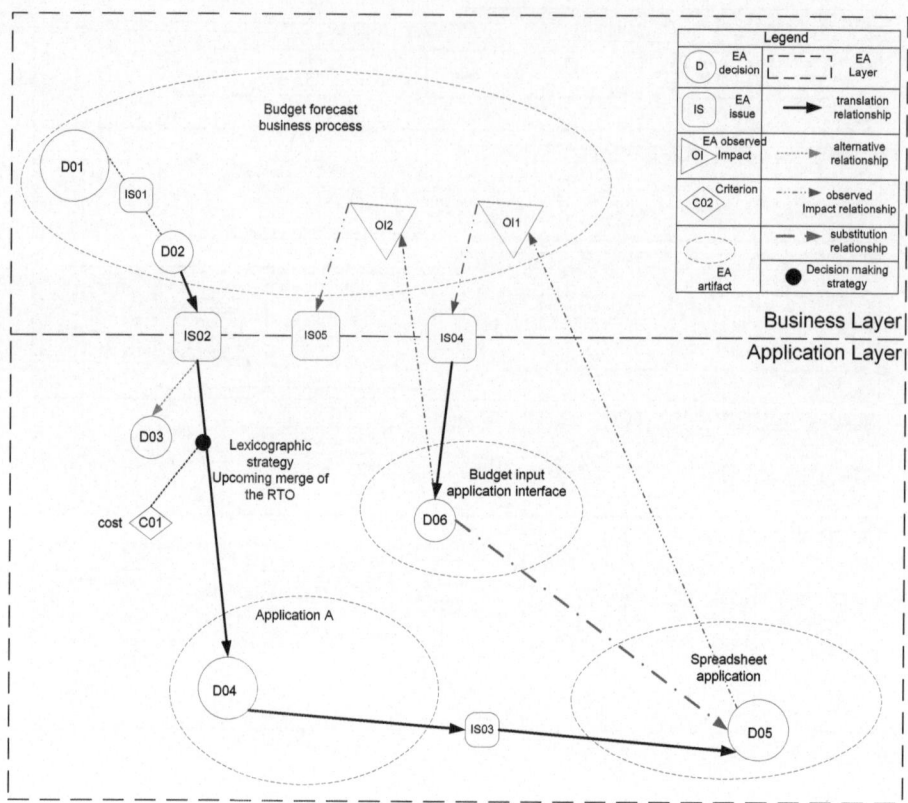

Fig. 4. Budget forecast design decision graph

We start by capturing the design decisions of the EA artifact "Budget forecast business process". EA artifacts are depicted in the decision graph as circles with dashed lines. At the same time the EA artifact "Budget forecast business process" is depicted in the EA models of Figures 2 and 3. This helps us trace design decisions, since we can start examining EA artifacts and then zooming (using the graph) in the design rationale behind the specific EA artifacts.

Decision 01 (D01) "Create budget forecast business process" is the decision that initiated the transformation. Reasons behind this decision is the business goal of having budget forecast in the long term. The execution of D01 triggered amongst others a new enterprise architecture architecture issue (IS01) "Storing budget estimation frequency". This means that the business stakeholder should define a certain frequency of storing the budget estimation per year. This issue was addressed by a newer decision (D02) "Storing budget estimation once per year". Since these two design decisions belong to the same EA design artifact they are interrelated with a *decomposition* relationship.

Table 1. Design rationale summarization table

D01	Create budget forecast business process
IS01	Storing budget estimation frequency
D02	Storing budget estimation once per year
IS02	Find solution for storing and processing budget
D03	COTS Application A
D04	Upgrade application A
IS03	How to upload budget data
D05	Create budget spreadsheet
OI1	Each department created its own excel form, resulting in incompatible information
IS04	How to upload budget data
D06	Build budget input interface
OI2	Errors in the calculation of the budget forecast. The application does not detect mistakes
IS05	Extend the application with business logic rules

The new design decision (D02) created the EA issue (IS02) "Find solution for storing and processing budget". This means that stakeholders should find a way to store the budget information. Stakeholders decided to support this need in the application level. More specifically with D04 "Upgrade application A" they decided to upgrade the existing financial application A in order to store and process the financial information. A *translation* relationship between D02 and D04 signifies how the design issue in the business layer was addressed by a design decision in a different artifact/layer of the enterprise. The alternative was the acquisition of a COTS application which is depicted by D03 "COTS Application A" and is represented with an *alternative relationship* from IS02 to D03. This signifies that D03 is a rejected design decision.

So, what was the reason that stakeholders chose the upgrade of the existing financial application? By interviewing the stakeholders we understood the context which influenced their decision making: during the execution of the enterprise transformation another high level decision from the Luxembourgish government had to be applied in the organization. The government decided that LuxRTO had to be merged with another national Research and Technology Organization. This implied the need for serious changes in the organizational structure since some departments of LuxRTO had overlapping roles with departments of the other organization. Moreover new business models should be defined based on the exchange of research expertise of research groups.

The upcoming merge of the organization posed some serious design challenges on the involved stakeholders of the budget estimation business process. On the one hand they had ambitious design goals considering the realization of this business need, while on the other hand they had to compromise because of the merge. It was not clear how the financial departments and business processes would be merged, therefore the risk of wasting budget for significant business and IT development was high.

Consequently, despite the fact that the initial plan of the stakeholders was the acquisition of a new COTS application, budget restrictions led stakeholders to the decision of upgrading the in house applications. We captured and depicted the budget restriction by using criterion C01 "cost" on our decision graph. Furthermore, by explaining to stakeholders the different types of decision making strategies we identified that they used a "lexicographic strategy", which means that they rejected alternatives by just using the "cost" as the most important criterion without examining other quality characteristics. The rationale behind this strategy was, as we mentioned before, the "upcoming merge of LuxRTO".

D04 created some additional issues in the application layer. The financial application was able to support the storage of the financial data but this information should somehow entered in the system (IS03). Stakeholders, by having in mind again the budget restiction, decided to use a spreadsheet standardized template (D05). This template was distributed by the financial department to different departments of LuxRTO. The users of the other departments had to fill the spreadsheet template and send it back to the financial department for further processing. This flow of EA design decisions and issues comprises the underlying rationale of the EA model of Fig. 2.

However, several unanticipated consequences occurred after the execution of these decisions. The use of spreadsheet templates for the insertion of budget data was problematic. More specifically, the users of each department started modifying the template and the order of the data fields. The financial officer who was receiving the input budget data had serious problems on the processing of this information and in turn on the calculation of the budget forecast. The usability of the budget forecast business process was deteriorated. The observed impact (OI1) "Each department created its own excel form, resulting in incompatible information" captures and represents this problem.

In order to solve the problem the stakeholders decided to upgrade further the financial application A with a budget input application interface (D06). EA Decision D06 "Build budget input interface" solves the unanticipated consequences of D05. This is also represented by a *substitution* relationship between D06 and D05. The resulting EA model after these modifications is depicted in Fig. 2. Despite the fact that this EA model represent the final outcome of this enterprise transformation, other EA issues were still open. After the incorporation of the budget input application interface another problem arose in the budget forecast business process and it was not addressed. This application module lacks business logic error checking functionality during the data entry of the budget input. The problem is depicted in OI2 "Errors in the calculation of the budget forecast. The application does not detect mistakes" and users of this application who are not familiar with financial parameters can create serious mistakes on the calculation of budget forecast. A new EA issue was created (IS05) "Extend the application with business logic rules". Despite the fact that stakeholders were aware of the problem, they were not able to take additional decisions because of the upcoming merging. The EA issue remained unresolved.

Without rationalization the above reasons behind the architecture designs of Figures 2, 3 remain implicit. Yet clearly such rationalization is useful. For example: by using rationalization one explicates the negative observed impact of diverging spreadsheets as a result of the introduction of the new business process. As a result this negative observed impact can be anticipated on for future similar decisions.

4   Lessons Learned

This section presents the lessons learned of applying EA Anamnesis to a real life case study.

Lesson 1: EA Anamnesis can reflect the decisions made by the budget forecasting practitioners. As was stated in Sect. 3, the main objective of this study was the evaluation of our approach in terms of its ability to capture and represent design rationales of Enterprise Architecture designs.

As stated in Sect. 3, the design rationale was created together with the involved stakeholders. Their perception was that the approach was adequate in terms of expressivity of reasoning and decision relationships. They were able to trace their design decisions and to realize what were the cross cutting implications of their decisions. For example: using our approach, the stakeholders could express that the IT-application layer decision to create a budget spreadsheet has the business process layer impact of having different, and incompatible, spreadsheets from each department.

Lesson 2: Stakeholders use simple selection processes, or decide without examining alternatives. This reduces overall capturing effort Our approach is designed to cover a variety of decision making strategies, compensatory or non compensatory. Our findings, at least for this case, show that actually designers use simple techniques to eliminate alternatives from their choice set. For example, in Sect. 3 we have seen that "cost" is the only criterion for the decision "Upgrade Application A". Even more, sometimes stakeholders solved an EA issue without examining alternative choices. The main reason for not considering alternatives is that experienced stakeholders make decisions based on previous experiences from similar cases.

Advanced techniques like multiple-criteria decision analysis (MCDA) were not used for any of the captured design decisions.

We argue that this finding actually supports the applicability of our approach in practice since it is easier in terms of capturing effort for the designer to capture the underlying decision making strategies.

Lesson 3: By modeling decisions in EA Anamnesis, stakeholders became aware of decision making strategies. We had to educate the stakeholders and make them understand how they actually decide. Implicitly, they were using decision making processes. However, the stakeholders did so *without being aware of this*. The awareness of different types of decision making strategies enabled them to better structure and analyze the decision problem. This means that they were able to explicitly describe how they decided (decision making strategy) for a certain decision problem and what evaluation criteria they used.

Lesson 4: EA Anamnesis insufficiently reflects that decision making can be ongoing, with open issues. As can be observed from EA issue 05 "Extend the application with business logic rules" (Fig. 4) some EA issues were not resolved. Reasons such as lack of resources (budget, time) sometimes prevent designers from addressing open issues.

This is currently not reflected in EA Anamnesis, which assumes that decision making is a past rather than an ongoing activity. We feel that, in a future iteration, ongoing issues should be captured explicitly by our approach. This is because awareness of unresolved issues gives the ability of better justification of EA designs. For example, by capturing open issues a stakeholder of the RTO organization can justify a lacking usability of the budget forecast business process due to a lack of business logic control mechanisms in the application layer.

5   Conclusions and Future Work

In this paper we presented the application of EA Anamnesis approach on a real world enterprise architecture transformation. By conducting case study research we testified the capability of our approach to capture and represent adequately design rationales. The approach captures sufficiently design rationales for EA. Furthermore, during the application of our approach, some important lessons derived from this case. The decision making strategies used by the stockholders of this case were much more simpler than initially perceived. This can reduce further the capturing effort of our approach and in turn improve its usability in practice.

For future research, we intend to confront decision models of our approach to enterprise architecture practitioners. An example of such an evaluation is to divide participating practitioners in two groups, whereby one group receives an architectural design and the other group receives an architectural design and an EA Anamnesis rationalization thereof. Subsequently, we could ask both groups the same questions about the architectural design, and observe to what extent and how EA Anamnesis aids the architects on the understanding of the EA design.

Acknowledgments. The authors would like to thank Nathalie Bonnel and Frédéric Klein for their valuable contributions to this case study.

This work has been partially sponsored by the *Fonds National de la Recherche Luxembourg* (www.fnr.lu), via the PEARL programme.

References

1. Lankhorst, M.: Enterprise architecture at work: Modelling, communication and analysis. Springer (2009)

2. The Open Group: ArchiMate 2.0 Specification. Van Haren Publishing (2012)
3. OMG: Unified profile for DoDAF and MoDAF (UPDM), version 2.1 (2013)
4. van der Linden, D., Hoppenbrouwers, S., Lartseva, A., Molnar, W.: Beyond termi-
   nologies: Using psychometrics to validate shared ontologies. Applied Ontology 7,
   471–487 (2012)
5. Jansen, A., Bosch, J.: Software architecture as a set of architectural design decisions. In: 5th Working IEEE/IFIP Conference on Software Architecture, WICSA
   2005, pp. 109–120. IEEE (2005)
6. Tang, A., Jin, Y., Han, J.: A rationale-based architecture model for design traceability and reasoning. Journal of Systems and Software 80, 918–934 (2007)
7. Plataniotis, G., de Kinderen, S., van der Linden, D., Greefhorst, D., Proper, H.A.:
   An empirical evaluation of design decision concepts in enterprise architecture. In:
   Grabis, J., Kirikova, M., Zdravkovic, J., Stirna, J. (eds.) PoEM 2013. LNBIP,
   vol. 165, pp. 24–38. Springer, Heidelberg (2013)
8. Plataniotis, G., de Kinderen, S., Proper, H.A.: Capturing decision making strategies in enterprise architecture – A viewpoint. In: Nurcan, S., Proper, H.A., Soffer,
   P., Krogstie, J., Schmidt, R., Halpin, T., Bider, I. (eds.) BPMDS 2013 and EMM-
   SAD 2013. LNBIP, vol. 147, pp. 339–353. Springer, Heidelberg (2013)
9. Plataniotis, G., der Kinderen, S., Proper, H.A.: Relating decisions in enterprise
   architecture using decision design graphs. In: Proceedings of the 17th IEEE International Enterprise Distributed Object Computing Conference (EDOC)(2013)
10. Plataniotis, G., de Kinderen, S., Proper, H.A.: Ea anamnesis: An approach for
    decision making analysis in enterprise architecture. In: International Journal of
    Information System Modeling and Design (IJISMD) (2014)
11. Plataniotis, G., de Kinderen, S., Proper, H.A.: Ea anamnesis: towards an approach
    for enterprise architecture rationalization. In: Proceedings of the 2012 workshop
    on Domain-specific modeling, DSM 2012, pp. 27–32. ACM, New York (2012)
12. Eilon, S.: What is a decision? Management Science 16, B–172-B–189 (1969)
13. Harmsen, F., Proper, E., Schalkwijk, F., Barjis, J., Overbeek, S. (eds.): PRET
    2010. LNBIP, vol. 69. Springer, Heidelberg (2010)
14. Tyree, J., Akerman, A.: Architecture decisions: Demystifying architecture. IEEE
    Software 22, 19–27 (2005)
15. Mintzberg, H., Raisinghani, D., Theoret, A.: The structure of unstructured decision
    processes. Administrative Science Quarterly, 246–275 (1976)
16. Kruchten, P.: An ontology of architectural design decisions in software intensive
    systems. In: 2nd Groningen Workshop on Software Variability, pp. 54–61 (2004)
17. Kruchten, P., Lago, P., van Vliet, H.: Building up and reasoning about architectural
    knowledge. In: Hofmeister, C., Crnković, I., Reussner, R. (eds.) QoSA 2006. LNCS,
    vol. 4214, pp. 43–58. Springer, Heidelberg (2006)
18. Op't Land, M., Proper, H.A.: Impact of principles on enterprise engineering. In:
    ECIS 2007 Proceedings (2007)
19. Runeson, P., Host, M.: Guidelines for conducting and reporting case study research
    in software engineering. Empirical Software Engineering 14, 131–164 (2009)

A Comparative Analysis of Selected Enterprise Modeling Approaches

Alexander Bock, Monika Kaczmarek, Sietse Overbeek, and Michael Heß

Chair of Information Systems and Enterprise Modelling
Institute for Computer Science and Business Information Systems (ICB)
Faculty of Business Administration and Economics, University of Duisburg-Essen,
Universitätsstraße 9, 45141 Essen, Germany
{alexander.bock,monika.kaczmarek,sietse.overbeek,m.hess}@uni-due.de

Abstract. Complexity inherent to the management of organizational action recommends the use of instruments that support the structured description and analysis of organizations. A variety of enterprise modeling (EM) methods have been developed to serve these purposes. To contribute to the elucidation of their conceptual differences, overlaps, and focal points, this paper analyzes four selected EM methods based on a designed analysis framework. It includes an assessment of the methods' key goals and purposes, central assumptions, and concepts. The paper concludes with a suggestion of future research topics.

Keywords: Enterprise modeling method, comparative analysis.

1 Introduction

Enterprise modeling (EM) is commonly regarded as the construction and use of conceptual models to describe, analyze, and (re-)design different aspects of an organization (e.g., [1, pp. 942-943], [2, p. 1]). Enterprise models are built from modeling concepts [3, p. 251], defined in modeling languages, which constitute abstractions of organizational aspects (organizational action systems) and information systems (IS) [1, p. 942]. Examples of enterprise modeling methods include ArchiMate [4], Architecture of Integrated Information Systems (ARIS) [5], Business Engineering (BE) [6], Design and Engineering Methodology for Organizations (DEMO) [7,8], For Enterprise Modeling Method (4EM; formerly Enterprise Knowledge Development) [9,10], Multi-Perspective Enterprise Modeling (MEMO) [1,11,12], Semantic Object Model (SOM) [13], The Open Group Architecture Framework (TOGAF) [14], and Work System Theory (WST) [15].

Conceptual overlaps between these methods can be assumed, as in general, they all aim at the development of structured descriptions of enterprises. The methods are not identical, though, as they emerged from different backgrounds, were developed with different purposes in mind, and are based on different assumptions. As each method, moreover, is using its own terminology, similarities and distinctions between the methods are not obvious. Assessing the methods

U. Frank et al. (Eds.): PoEM 2014, LNBIP 197, pp. 148–163, 2014.

with respect to the requirements of different application contexts becomes a challenge, and integration benefits for both the usage and evolution of EM methods may remain unexploited. To contribute to the consolidation, integration, and evolution of EM methods, and, possibly, to advance the field of EM, a need emerges to comparatively analyze existing EM methods [16, p. 1-3], [3, p. 250].

The main goal of this paper is to analyze a set of EM methods to contribute to understanding the range of conceptual and foundational similarities and differences between existing EM methods. The analysis aims to answer the following questions: What are the main similarities and distinctive features of the selected EM methods? What are their focal points? Finally, which areas could be further investigated in order to potentially advance research and practice of EM?

In order to answer these questions, we devise an analysis framework and conduct a comparative analysis that places focus on the identification of the essential characteristics of a limited set of EM methods. According to a scheme proposed by [16, p. 111], we conduct a 'vertically dominant' analysis. As an exemplary selection, four EM methods are chosen for our analysis: ArchiMate, DEMO, MEMO, and WST. These methods are deliberately selected such as to achieve a variety in background, underlying theoretical references, and key application scenarios. Further, already performed comparisons (e.g., between ARIS, BE and SOM [17]) have been taken into account, and only more mature approaches being in the development for at least one decade have been considered.

The paper is structured as follows. First, related work is shortly described in Sect. 2. In Sect. 3, the utilized analysis framework is presented. A conceptual analysis and comparison of the methods based on the defined framework is conducted in Sect. 4. The results are discussed in Sect. 5. Concluding remarks and an outlook on possible future research directions are provided in Sect. 6.

2   Related Work

The comparison of alternative modeling methods (i.e., of "alternative suggestions to (re-)construct the world" [18]) is an important challenge in the IS field. This is reflected in related work in two ways. Firstly, there is literature concerned with the approaches to evaluating modeling methods. Secondly, there is a range of work conducting concrete comparative analyses or evaluations of EM methods.

Literature yields some work specifically dealing with approaches to analyzing and evaluating modeling methods. In [3, pp. 251-260] different techniques for evaluating modeling methods are classified and discussed. In [16, pp. 98-120], a classification of approaches to comparing (modeling) methods is proposed. More specifically, in [19], a particular framework for evaluating object-oriented modeling methods is presented. In [20], an evaluation technique is presented that builds on computing metrics for language specifications.

When it comes to specific examples of analysis, a comparative assessment of several EM methods is performed in [1, pp. 957-960]. The evaluation schema is based on a conception of EM set forth in the same paper [1, pp. 943-946]. The assessment includes several methods and criteria considered here as well, but the main goal of the paper is the elaboration of a particular EM method. In [17], an in-depth comparison of three EM methods is offered, taking into account architectures, meta models, and process models. None of the methods considered here is assessed in this work. In [20, pp. 3403-3406], different modeling methods (the scope is not limited to EM) are compared based on 'formal aspects'. The aim of this analysis does not correspond with the one of our paper, because it focuses on the degree of formalization with which syntax and semantics of modeling methods are specified.

With a focus on enterprise architecture (EA), an overview of the state of the art is provided in [21]. The overview also includes a comparative summary of different EA and EM methods [21, pp. 294-295], but it does not point out particularities of the underlying modeling languages. A comprehensive analysis of 22 different EA approaches is offered in [22]. Each approach is summarized and discussed in detail [22, pp. 21-112]. However, the approaches are not contrasted with respect to the offered modeling concepts. Less comprehensive high-level overviews of EA frameworks and methods are offered in, e.g., [23, pp. 11-41] and [24, pp. 65-73]. Neither one of the overviews provide a concrete juxtaposition of the methods. In addition to the mentioned overviews and comparisons, literature yields various contrasting discussions of specific pairs of methods (e.g., [25], [26]) while not including any further discussions of the state of the art in EM.

This paper distinguishes itself from the existing work with respect to three points. Firstly, it focuses on EM methods exclusively. It covers several current and distinct EM methods, which provide conceptual means for describing different aspects of organizational action systems and IS. This excludes more general (EA) frameworks. Secondly, the paper makes use of an analysis scheme that is explicitly defined in order to reach the defined goal. Thirdly, emphasis is placed on outlining and discussing conceptual and paradigmatic overlaps and distinctions between the considered EM methods. Thus, the paper contributes to harnessing complementary benefits in the further use, development, and integration of EM methods.

3   Analysis Framework

To conduct a comparative analysis of EM methods, we define and utilize an analysis framework (see Tab. 1) that accounts for the particularities of such methods. Considering the literature, we develop a framework in two steps. First, we relate our framework to the classifications suggested by [3, p. 251-260] and [16, pp. 111-113] in order to define its general orientation. In the next step, a particular analysis framework consisting of a set of categories (to delineate focal points of the analysis) and of particular criteria for each category is defined.

According to the classification proposed by [3, pp. 251-260], our analysis partly exhibits characteristics of a 'feature comparison' and a 'theoretical and conceptual investigation'. An 'empirical evaluation' is not conducted. 'Feature comparison' describes an evaluation technique that makes use of predefined checklists of criteria [3, p. 251]. We use predefined criteria, but we do not regard them as

Table 1. Analysis framework

Criterion	Explanation
Way of thinking	
Background of the method	What was the initial motivation to develop the method? From which context did the method emerge?
Key goals and purposes	What are the key goals and purposes stated for the EM method?
Central assumptions	What are the fundamental assumptions of the EM method?
Way of modeling	
Concept specification	What are the mechanisms used to define modeling concepts?
Modeling concepts	Which central modeling concepts are defined?
Representation of modeling concepts	How can modeling concepts be represented (concrete syntax)? Are prototypical representation forms defined?
Way of working	
General approach to modeling	What is the general approach to applying the modeling method?
Process models and guidelines	Are any process models, procedural specifications, guidelines etc. available to guide users in applying the method?

checklist items. Instead, we use them to structure what is called 'theoretical and conceptual investigations' by [3, p. 251].

A classification scheme for analysis frameworks based on sets of criteria is proposed in [16, p. 98]. It can be used to explain the general orientation of our framework. Essentially, it is argued that analysis frameworks can be designed along two basic dimensions [16, pp. 102-105]. The first dimension relates to the criteria of a framework. The definition of criteria can vary with respect to their number and granularity [16, pp. 102-105]. The second dimension relates to the methods that are intended to be compared. The selection of methods can vary with respect to their number as well as the degree of their homogeneity [16, p. 105]. Based on these two dimensions, an analysis framework can be regarded as 'horizontally dominant' or 'vertically dominant' [16, pp. 111-113]. A 'horizontally dominant' framework takes into account a high number of criteria and methods [16, p. 111]. In contrast, a 'vertically dominant' one takes into account a low number of coarse criteria and homogeneous methods [16, p. 111]. The focus of a 'vertically dominant' comparison lies on identifying the essential characteristics of a set of methods [16, pp. 111]. As this focus is in line with our goal, the analysis framework devised below is aimed to be 'vertically dominant'.

Building on this general orientation, we can particularize the analysis framework that will guide our comparison. The proposed framework consists of two levels: Criteria categories and concrete criteria. Table 1 indicates the considered categories and criteria. For each criterion, questions are provided that explain their intended scope. The criteria categories are adopted from a high-level view of IS development methods suggested in [27, pp. 13-25]. This view consists of the 'way of thinking', 'way of modeling', 'way of working', 'way of controlling', and 'way of supporting' [27, p. 13]. The categories defined by this view are also used to structure discussions and evaluations of modeling methods elsewhere (see, e.g., [24, pp. 76-78], [23, pp. 51-52]). In line with the goals of this paper, our focus lies on the 'way of thinking', 'way of modeling', and 'way of working'. The 'way of thinking' perspective is related to the *"salient aspects [...]* of a specific method" [27, p. 22]. It is supposed to embrace "starting points", "basic objectives", and "major assumptions underlying a certain approach" [27, p. 22]. The 'way of modeling' "structures the models which can be used in information systems development" [27, p. 14]. It thus pertains to modeling languages and modeling concepts defined by them. The 'way of working' corresponds with what is commonly referred to as the 'process model' or 'procedure' of a method (cf. [27, pp. 17-18]). 'Way of controlling' and 'way of supporting' are not within the scope of this paper, as the former is concerned with practical issues of the "management of a development process" [27, p. 20] and the latter relates to existing "collection of tools" [27, p. 24].

4   Comparative Analysis

4.1   Way of Thinking

Background. *ArchiMate's* development started in 2002 within a project conducted by several Dutch companies, governmental organizations, and research groups [23, p. v], [4, p. xviii] with the aim to define a modeling language to be used in the context of EA management [23, p. x]. Its first version was described in 2004 [23, pp. ix-x], the most recent one in 2013 by The Open Group. Its design is oriented towards specifications of TOGAF [4, pp. 1-2, 14-15].

DEMO stems from an academic project started in the early 1990s [7,8,28]. It is motivated by the conviction that means for supporting business process design should focus on modeling their 'essentials', instead of the particular ways they are performed [7, p. 352]. Its design is inspired by language-related research strands in philosophy and other fields [28, pp. 237-247].

MEMO's development started as academic research in 1989 and aimed at offering means for an integrative account of business-related and technological aspects to support the design, implementation, and use of IS [11, pp. 162-163]. It was motivated by the conviction that it is valuable to obtain different 'perspectives' on the business context of IS to be developed [11, pp. 163-169]. An object-oriented modeling framework was proposed [11, pp. 162-163], whose structure and focus has been adapted over time [12,1]. MEMO is progressively extended with domain-specific modeling languages (DSMLs) and methods (e.g., [29,30]).

WST is not explicitly labeled as an EM or EA approach, but it is based on similar considerations. It has been been discussed and modified over the past two decades (e.g., [15,31,32,33]). WST's development is driven by a dissatisfaction with (theoretical) conceptualizations of core terms in the IS field [31, pp. 1-3], [32, pp. 299-300], [15, p. 73]. WST regards a 'work system' as the central concept for considering possibly IT-supported systems in organizations [31, p. 7], [15, pp. 75-76]. Building on WST, the work system method (WSM) has been proposed to support the design and analysis of 'work systems' [15, pp. 83-84].

Key Goals and Purposes. *ArchiMate's* goal is to define a modeling language for "the representation of enterprise architectures [...] as well as their motivation and rationale" [4, p. 2]. This reflects in the requirement that the language should offer concepts for describing "main elements" of different organizational domains and relations between them [23, pp. 76-77]. It is stated that the language is aimed to be "as small as possible" [4, p. 4]. ArchiMate is not meant to replace detailed modeling languages for specific domains [23, p. 77]. As one key purpose, it is supposed to permit the creation of models, which are used as deliverables required by EA frameworks such as TOGAF [4, pp. 14-15].

DEMO is intended to support the '(re-)design' and '(re-)engineering' of organizational business processes [7, p. 360]. As a distinctive goal, it is stated that DEMO is aimed to enable the creation of an 'essential model' or 'ontological model' of organizational operations [7, p. 360], [8, p. 127]. Such a model is supposed to abstract "fully from the informational/documental as well as from the organizational (structural) realization" [7, p. 360]. The advantage of this approach is seen in that it enables to "look through the distracting and confusing appearance of an enterprise right into its deep kernel" [8, p. 12].

MEMO's general goal is to bridge language-related gaps between stakeholders from business and IT-related domains [11, p. 162], [1, pp. 943, 945]. Initially, the focus was placed on supporting the development of IS that are "well integrated with a company's strategy and its organization" [12, p. 73]. Currently, MEMO is also seen as a foundation for the construction of modeling methods in support of various domains [1, p. 950]. MEMO models are supposed to convey a non-deterministic view of action systems [1, p. 946]. At the same time, they are aimed to be transformable to implementation level code [1, p. 943]. MEMO aims to offer comprehensive tool support for model creation and use [12, p. 3], [1, p. 946].

WST: The key goal of WST and WSM is to support the design and analysis of what is considered, in a given situation, to be a 'work system' [15, pp. 83-84]. The application of WSM may be initiated by any kind of problem or opportunity noted for a 'work system', and may result in changes related to, e.g., business activities, participants, or software [15, p. 116].

Central Assumptions. *ArchiMate* implicitly follows assumptions linked to EA management, as it is proposed as a dedicated EA modeling language [4, pp. 1-2] [23, p. 75]. Explicitly, it is assumed that a set of generic concepts can be defined as generalizations of elements from all 'layers' of an enterprise (namely 'business', 'application', and 'technology') [23, pp. 78-79]. Also, it is assumed that 'service' is a suitable metaphor for describing "outputs" of elements from each layer, e.g., organizational units and applications [23, pp. 77-78]. Finally, it is assumed that limiting the number of concepts contributes to language usability, and that the current specification covers "most [EA] modeling tasks" [4, p. 4].

DEMO is stated to be based on the "single assumption" that "communication between human beings in organizations constitutes a necessary and sufficient basis for developing a theory of organizations" [34, p. 303]. This is detailed in a set of 'axioms' [8, pp. 81-125]. At first, it is assumed that operations of an organization are composed of 'coordination' (language-based interaction) and 'production' (realizing products or services) acts of human actors [8, pp. 80-88]. It is assumed that these activities can be assigned to one of three clearly distinguishable levels: 'Forma' acts relate to handling data; 'informa' acts relate to interpreting information [8, pp. 106-114]. 'Performa' acts, on the coordination side, are stated to involve human commitments [8, pp. 106-114]. This view is inspired by, e.g., the speech act theory (Searle) and the theory of communicative action (Habermas) [7, pp. 352-354]. On the production side, the 'performa' level refers to the ability to "establish new original things" [8, p. 114]. An 'ontological' model of an organization, then, is defined to relate to the 'performa' level exclusively [8, pp. 106, 127]. To create such a model, it is consequently assumed that the state space and its possible transitions relating to relevant human 'performa' acts can be captured fully and formally [8, pp. 173-184]. Lastly, it is posited that starting from an 'ontological' model, implementation models regarding the operations and IS of an organization can be consistently 'engineered' [8, pp. 74-77].

MEMO's main assumption is that organizational action and information systems should be analyzed and designed conjointly [1, p. 943], necessitating communication between different groups of organizational actors [1, p. 943], and that therefore integrated models are helpful that offer different 'views' or 'perspectives' on an enterprise [11, pp. 163 ff.], [12, p. 942]. It is assumed that the design of corresponding modeling languages can and should be based on detailed reconstructions of technical languages of the targeted actor groups [1, p. 945]. Similarly, it is assumed that (visual) notations being associative for targeted actors promote model acceptance and understandability [1, p. 943] [35, p. 55].

WST's central assumption is that the concept 'work system' is suitable for thinking about, analyzing, and improving relevant sections of organizations [31, p. 7], [15, p. 75]. It is defined as a "a system in which human participants and/or machines perform work [...] using information, technology, and other resources to produce specific products/services for specific internal and/or external customers" [15, p. 83]. It is thus assumed that for the targeted problem cases in organizations meaningful definitions of concrete 'work systems' can be found.

4.2 Way of Modeling

Concept Specification. *ArchiMate:* Modeling concepts are introduced using several meta models [4, pp. 5, 17, 49, 63]. The underlying meta modeling language is not specified. The meta models do not specify all valid relationships between concepts [4, p. 18]. A complete definition of relationships is given in the form of additional tables [4, pp. 188-194]. Every relationship end features '0..*' cardinalities [4, p. 5]. The specification of concepts does not include attributes. These are regarded as 'profiles' to be added on demand [4, pp. 137-138]. To explain concept semantics, textual descriptions are provided [4, pp. 18 ff.]. Extensions are specified using the same mechanisms [4, pp. 137-181]. It is noted that further extensions can be added on demand [4, pp. 9-10].

DEMO: The modeling concepts are defined using the Extended Backus-Naur Form (EBNF) and example diagrams [36, p. 2]. A complete meta model is not provided. The concept specifications do not include attributes. In [8, pp. 159-214], modeling concepts are introduced by means of an application scenario.

MEMO: Modeling concepts, their attributes, and relationships for each MEMO DSML are introduced using meta models presented in different publications. All meta models are defined using the MEMO meta modeling language (MML) [37]. Based on this common meta modeling language, relationships between concepts from different meta models are defined, leading to an integrated language architecture. As a result, concepts from all MEMO DSMLs can be used to create a comprehensive, integrated (enterprise) model.

WST does not define a modeling language, but uses glossaries to define concepts for describing nine core 'elements' related to work systems (e.g., [31, pp. 18-24], [15, pp. 79-81]). Additionally, textual 'consistency rules' for using the concepts are offered [15, p. 86]. Recently, a meta model has been published, defining and augmenting the core concepts. Attributes are not defined [26, p. 4].

Modeling Concepts. All investigated EM methods define specific sets of modeling concepts to address their stated goals. Due to the different concept specification mechanisms underlying each method, the semantics of the provided specifications are not fully comparable. Furthermore, concepts in different methods are conceptualized differently, even if they are denoted using the same name. Taking further into account that the total number of concepts is quite high (in particular, MEMO encompasses more than 150 concepts), a full comparison of all concepts and their details (i.e., attributes and relationships) is not in the scope of this paper. Instead, we provide in Table 2 a structured overview of (selected) modeling concepts of each method, which may be used to create models (thus, only non-abstract, i e., instantiable, concepts are considered). The table has been constructed as follows. For ArchiMate, all 43 non-abstract concepts defined in [4] are listed, including those defined as part of two extensions [4, pp. 137-181]. Custom extensions are not considered, as they are not part of the official specification. For DEMO, the listed concepts have been derived from [36]. Because ENBF definitions and exemplary diagrams are used to define the language, some definitions can be interpreted as either concepts, attributes, or relationships. According to the best of our knowledge, and guided by the described key diagram types, we identified 17 conceptual definitions as core modeling concepts. The other definitions have been regarded as attributes, relationships, and further (syntactical) constraints. MEMO encompasses more than 150 concepts, therefore, only selected core concepts from recent MEMO DSMLs have been included in the table. References are provided that point to the full specifications. For WST, all 52 concepts defined in the most recent meta model [26, p. 4] are included. Concept names in Table 2 are taken literally from the specifications (names containing commas appear in quotation marks). The resulting list of concepts has been assigned to a coarse categorization of 'areas'. The areas have resulted from interpreting and structuring the selected concepts. They serve purposes of clarity and abstraction solely, and are not proposed as a reference taxonomy. The area 'Business aspects and resources' is particularly broad, embracing traditional concepts from business administration (ArchiMate, MEMO, WST) as well as more general ('ontological') state and transition concepts used to describe (business) domains (DEMO) [36, p. 4]. Finally, it should be kept in mind that even if a method does not feature a concept directly assigned to a certain area, this area could still be addressed implicitly. For example, highly general concepts such as 'Fact Kind' in DEMO can be used to model aspects related to various areas.

Representation. *ArchiMate* defines iconographic symbols to represent the concepts [4, pp. 46-47, 61, 75-76]. The symbols mostly consist of elementary

Table 2. Selected concepts of the analyzed EM methods

ArchiMate	DEMO	MEMO	WST
Area: Goals and strategies			
Value, Goal, Requirement, Driver, Assessment,		EngagementGoal, SymbolicGoal, GoalConfiguration (further concepts related to goals in [29]), Strategy [1]	Value Constellation, Value for Customer, Goal, Strategy, Enterprise Strategy, Department Strategy, Work System Strategy, Motive
Area: Business aspects and resources			
Business Object, Product, Contract, Business Service, Business Interface, Meaning, Representation, Constraint, Principle	Fact Kind, Derived Fact Kind, Product Kind, Scale	Product [29], Cost, Direct Cost Allocation, Proportional Cost Allocation, Unit-Based Cost Allocation, Cost Assessment, Agreement (further concepts related to costs in[30]), HumanResource, PhysicalResource, CompositeResource, TransportationResource (further concepts related to resources in [38])	Customer, Product/Service for Customer, Product/Service from Activity, Resource, Other Resource, Physical Entity, Time, Resource from Environment, Organizational Culture, 'Laws, Standards, Regulations, Policies', Other Env. Resource, Resource from Shared Infrastructure, Shared Human Resource, Shared Informational Resource, Shared Technical Resource
Area: Dynamic abstractions and human actions			
Business Process, Business Event	Transaction Kind, Aggregate Transaction Kind, Coordination Act, Production Act, Coordination Fact, Production Fact, Process Step, Discussion Step, Action Rule	BusinessProcess, ControlFlowSubProcess, Event, EventMerger, ProcessMerger, Exception, Branch, Branching, Fork, RegularSynch, ExclusiveSynch, MultiSynch (further concepts related to business processes in [39]), Decision, DecisionProcess, Stimulus (further concepts related to decisions in [40,41])	Business Process, Work System Activity
Area: Organizational structures, actors, and roles			
Business Function, Business Interaction, Business Collaboration, Location, Business Actor, Business Role, Stakeholder	Elementary Actor Role, Composite Actor Role, Scope of Interest, Responsibility Area	Organisation, OrganisationalUnit, Superior, Position, LocalUnitType, PrototypicalPosition, PositionShare, PositionCategory, Board, Committee, Role, Task, Interaction (further concepts related to organizational structures in [35]).	Work System (WS), Other Work System, Customer Work System, Enterprise, Participant, Actor Role, Skill/Capability, Knowledge/Expertise, Role in Customer Work System, Customer Participant, Non-Customer Participant
Area: Information systems and IT			
Application Service, Application Function, Application Interaction, Application Component, Application Collaboration, Application Interface, Data Object, Software System, Infrastructure Service, Infrastructure Interface, Infrastructure Function, Artifact, Node, Communication Path, Device, Network		Information System, IT Service, IT Functionality, IT Utilisation, IT Involvement, Software, Application Software, Database Management Software, Operating System Software, Cluster, Server, Personal Computer, Fax, Printer, Multi Device, Access Point, Router (further concepts related to IS and IT in [30])	Technological Entity, Tool, Transaction Record, Informational Entity, 'Plan, Forecast, or Commitment', 'Guideline, Rule, or Structure', Precondition, Trigger, Other Information, Document, Video, Image, Message, Conversation
Area: Risks, measurement, and indicators			
		Indicator, IndicatorCategory, Risk, Chance, Assignment, MeasureImpact (further related concepts in [42,43,30])	Performance Metric
Area: EA and EM processes and projects			
Plateau, Gap, Deliverable, Work Package			

graphical shapes augmented with small graphical metaphors (e.g., arrows). ArchiMate defines several so-called 'viewpoints', which describe how to select and arrange concepts to support certain 'concerns' [4, pp. 97-135].

DEMO models are represented using iconographical symbols, tables, and textual representations [36]. The graphical symbols consist of elementary geometrical shapes. For each kind of model, one or several representation forms (e.g., iconographical diagram types or table structures) are defined.

MEMO models are represented using iconographical elements, some of which are designed by a professional graphic artist [35, p. 55] [43]. The design of the notation is stated to be oriented towards recommendations proposed by [44]. For each DSML, at least one diagram type is specified [1, p. 947].

WST proposes a table structure ('work system snapshot') to represent descriptions of particular work systems [33, pp. 16-18], [15, p. 86]. No specific representation form for the specialized concepts in the meta models is defined.

4.3   Way of Working

General Approach. *ArchiMate* is to be applied as a part of more comprehensive enterprise architecture management processes [23, p. 75]. The general idea is to successively create and modify models of EAs (however conceptualized in particular settings) [23, pp. 4-6]. A corresponding prototypical 'architecture life cycle' should consist of the phases 'design' (encompassing the creation and analysis of models), 'use', 'management', and 'idea' [23, pp. 4-6].

DEMO: The general approach of applying DEMO is to develop an 'ontological' model of the business processes of an organization (or a part of it) and to use this model as the basis for various ongoing (re-)design and (re-)engineering efforts [8, pp. 74-77]. Since the aim of an 'ontological' model is to abstract from implementation and realization issues, it can be implemented in terms of different concrete activities or technological means [7, p. 362], [8, pp. 74-75]. Deriving more implementation-related models from an 'ontological' model is regarded as 'engineering' [8, p. 74]. Changing aspects of the 'ontological' model is regarded as 'designing'. [7, p. 361]. 'Engineering', in contrast to 'designing', is understood as "not a matter of creativity but of craftsmanship" [8, p. 74].

MEMO: The general approach of MEMO is to create, maintain, and extend a comprehensive 'multi-perspective' enterprise model, and utilize this enterprise model for different purposes. Depending on the given needs, all or a subset of the existing MEMO modeling methods may be applied. It is assumed and suggested that a comprehensive enterprise modeling cannot be build ad hoc, but must be developed over time (e.g., [30, p. 382]). Once a (temporary version of an) enterprise model has been developed, it is proposed that a range of problems can be addressed [1, p. 950]. For example, it is suggested to perform goal planning processes [29], to support IT cost management [30], or to develop software systems from an existing enterprise model [45].

WST: The general approach of WSM is to investigate a particular work system, at a given point in time, to deal with identified problems or opportunities [32, pp. 21-22]. It is thus not the intent of WSM to develop and maintain more comprehensive models over a longer period of time. As essential parts of analyzing a particular work system, it is proposed to create an 'as-is' and a 'to-be' snapshot of the work system under consideration [15, pp. 85-86, 114-116].

Process Models and Guidelines. *ArchiMate's* specification does not include a process model or direct guidelines for applying the language. Instead, it is suggested that ArchiMate can be used in conjunction with the language-agnostic Architecture Development Method (ADM) defined by TOGAF [4, pp. 14-15]. Other publications contain some high-level guidelines and exemplary analysis techniques using ArchiMate, e.g., [23, pp. 115 ff., 189 ff.].

DEMO: A process model consisting of six steps is specified, which guides the general application of DEMO [8, pp. 144-158]. This process model is to be applied in an iterative manner. In addition to that, various general guidelines or and heuristics are available (e.g., [8, pp. 71-77]).

MEMO: For each MEMO modeling method, a specific process model is provided that guides the application of the language (e.g., [30, pp. 381-450]). In addition, various general guidelines are offered [11, pp. 337-342], [12, pp. 5-9]. Furthermore, a method guiding the development of new DSMLs is provided [43]. However, there is currently no overarching process model that guides the application of all existing MEMO methods in combination.

WST provides various specifications to guide the conduct of the WSM. The application of the method is described in detail in [33, pp. 21-32] and encompasses a process model consisting of several steps and elements, prototypical questions to be asked, and general guidelines. Further specifications include an overview of the suggested process model in the form of a business case template [15, p. 85] and a prototypical analysis schema [15, p. 116].

5   Discussion

Based on the preceding analysis, several similarities and distinctions between the considered methods can be identified.

Key Goals and Purposes. While the methods pursue similar goals on a basic level, their focal points vary. DEMO concentrates on a few elementary—'ontological'—organizational aspects and is associated with the intention to 'engineer' an enterprise [8, p. 74]. This claim is not raised by other methods. Contrarily, MEMO emphasizes that an engineering point of view is not sufficient for shaping organizations, because, as is emphasized by organizational studies, organizations can be seen to emerge through social construction [1, p. 946]. MEMO, ArchiMate, and WST nevertheless intend to support organizational (re-)design efforts. WST is distinct in that its application is typically limited to a particular organizational (sub-)system [15, p. 83]. ArchiMate and MEMO both strive for creating comprehensive enterprise models. They differ, however, as ArchiMate is oriented towards use with existing EA frameworks and practices, whereas MEMO aims at supporting diverse organizational domains by providing dedicated DSMLs [1, p. 950]. In addition, as a distinct feature, MEMO models are aimed to be transformable into implementation level artifacts [1, p. 950].

Central Assumptions. The methods differ with respect to the degree that underlying assumptions are explicated and with respect to the research areas that serve as an inspiration or their basis. ArchiMate states only a few assumptions, mostly based on the EA literature [23, pp. 11-74]. DEMO refers to an explicit set of assumptions ('axioms' [8, pp. 81-125]), inspired by ontological philosophy and speech act theory [8, pp. 45-46, 83-85]. MEMO, in addition to fundamentals of (object-oriented) conceptual modeling [11, pp. 75-158], assumes the importance of taking into account several 'perspectives' on an enterprise and thus suggests considering insights and technical languages from different domains and research areas [1, pp. 944-945]. WST is based on assumptions building primarily on IS and business research [15, pp. 75-81]. In general, however, it appears that no method provides an exhaustive account of all underlying assumptions. To some degree, justifications, assumptions, and referenced theories are described in a partly selective manner, distributed over different publications. Moreover, when comparing all methods, we could not identify a common and coherent theoretical underpinning. For instance, while the importance of language is emphasized by DEMO and MEMO, it is not well elaborated upon which mechanisms are involved in the process of (linguistic) sense-making through EM, and the way that natural and modeling languages mutually influence and shape each other.

Concept Specification. The methods use different specification mechanisms to define modeling concepts. This is due to different backgrounds. Also, the meta modeling languages are not always made explicit, which threatens to impede the interpretation of formal semantics. Heterogeneous concept specification mechanisms limit the possibilities to analyze and integrate language specifications.

Modeling Concepts. The methods, firstly, vary with respect to the covered domains. Some domains are covered by all analyzed methods, e.g., operational business processes. DEMO, through the lens of language acts, even takes business processes as its prime focus. Here, emphasis lies on rigid routine operations in organizations. Other domains, such as indicators and risks (MEMO) or EA projects (ArchiMate), are covered only by some methods. In addition, some methods provide concepts that relate to less rigid, social or 'meaning-giving' facets of action in organizations (e.g., 'SymbolicGoal' in MEMO or 'Organizational Culture' in WST). Such concepts, however, do not seem to be widely adopted yet. Secondly, the methods vary with respect to the semantic richness of concepts. ArchiMate, DEMO, and WST favor a language design with fewer concepts and attributes, while MEMO intends to provide comprehensive reconstructions of the technical languages that prospective users are familiar with. This seems to point at an essential conflict regarding the design of modeling methods. On the one hand, a modeling language can be regarded as an analysis instrument, which suggests providing elaborate concepts that enable differentiated representations. On the other hand, a modeling language should be easy to use, which recommends using a small set of concepts that allow for a wider range of interpretations.

Representation. ArchiMate, DEMO, and MEMO all define iconographic symbols to graphically represent enterprise models. The symbols by ArchiMate and DEMO limit themselves mainly to basic shapes and figures, whereas MEMO aims to offer visually richer symbols. DEMO, in addition to iconographic symbols and tables, also uses a textual representation. WST utilizes tables exclusively.

6   Conclusions and Future Research

In this paper, four EM methods have been analyzed using a configured framework. Based on the obtained results, we have pointed at their main similarities, distinctive features, and focal points. Obtained findings, on the one hand, contribute to the understanding of conceptual and foundational similarities and differences between the investigated methods. On the other hand, they allow us to suggest the following challenges that could be addressed in the future.

Comparative Analysis of Goals. Considering the variety of goals addressed by the investigated methods, an attempt could be undertaken to identify, structure, and compare goals that can possibly be addressed by EM methods, and means applied to achieve them. In particular, presumptions and world views underlying each goal could be pointed out, e.g., 'engineering' vs. 'designing' social systems.

Analysis and advancement of theoretical underpinning. Considering the heterogeneous assumptions and research strands associated with EM methods, it seems beneficial to clarify the theoretical underpinning of EM, and to enhance it with further insights from research areas such as the philosophy of language, organizational studies, and sociology. Particular attention could be devoted to the role and relation of natural languages and modeling languages to support bringing the design of EM methods yet closer to human (linguistic) perceptions of organizations. Furthermore, with some exceptions, the focus of current EM methods lies on more rigid aspects of organizing (i.e., operational processes and structures). It seems worthwhile to investigate which further insights from organizational studies (e.g., insights related to social aspects of organizing, or dealing with non-routine situations) could be considered in EM.

Common Meta Modeling Foundation. The analyzed methods utilize different concept specification mechanisms. To foster interpretation, comparability, and, consequently, a potential integration and extension of EM methods and research results, the usage of a common mechanism could be considered.

Language Expressiveness vs. Ease of Use. As there seems to be a conflict between method ease of use and support for differentiated analyses, an attempt could be undertaken to investigate approaches to mitigating this conflict.

Cognitive Perception. EM methods have different goals, target partly different user groups, and make use of different concrete syntaxes. This could suggest investigating the suitability of different graphical representation forms, especially generic vs. context-specific visualizations, for different purposes and user groups.

To gain a more thorough view of the current state of EM, however, a more comprehensive analysis with a more detailed analysis framework is necessary. Such an analysis remains on our research agenda.

References

1. Frank, U.: Multi-Perspective Enterprise Modeling: Foundational Concepts, Prospects and Future Research Challenges. SoSyM 13(3), 941–962 (2014)
2. Stirna, J., Persson, A.: Evolution of an Enterprise Modeling Method – Next Generation Improvements of EKD. In: Sandkuhl, K., Seigerroth, U., Stirna, J. (eds.) PoEM 2012. LNBIP, vol. 134, pp. 1–15. Springer, Heidelberg (2012)
3. Siau, K., Rossi, M.: Evaluation techniques for systems analysis and design modelling methods – a review and comparative analysis. ISJ 21(3), 249–268 (2011)
4. The Open Group: ArchiMate 2.0 specification: Open Group Standard. Van Haren, Zaltbommel (2012)
5. Scheer, A.W.: ARIS - Modellierungsmethoden, Metamodelle, Anwendungen, 4th edn. Springer, Heidelberg (2001)
6. Hubert, Ö., Robert, W. (eds.): Business Engineering. Auf dem Weg zum Unternehmen des Informationszeitalters, 2nd edn. Springer, Berlin (2003)
7. Dietz, J.L.G.: Demo: Towards a discipline of organisation engineering. EJOR 128(2), 351–363 (2001)
8. Dietz, J.L.G.: Enterprise Ontology: Theory and Methodology. Springer, Berlin (2006)
9. Rolland, C., Nurcan, S., Grosz, G.: Enterprise knowledge development: the process view. Information & Management 36(3), 165–184 (1999)
10. Sandkuhl, K., Wißotzki, M., Stirna, J.: Unternehmensmodellierung: Grundlagen, Methode und Praktiken. Springer, Heidelberg (2013)
11. Frank, U.: Multiperspektivische Unternehmensmodellierung: Theoretischer Hintergrund und Entwurf einer objektorientierten Entwicklungsumgebung. Oldenbourg, München (1994)
12. Frank, U.: Multi-Perspective Enterprise Modeling (MEMO): Conceptual Framework and Modeling Languages. In: Proceedings of the 35th HICSS (2002)
13. Ferstl, O.K., Sinz, E.J.: Modeling of Business Systems Using the Semantic Object Model (SOM). In: Bernus, P., Mertins, K., Schmidt, G. (eds.) Handbook on Architectures of Information Systems, pp. 339–358. Springer, Berlin
14. The Open Group: TOGAF Version 9.1. Van Haren, Zaltbommel (2011)
15. Alter, S.: Work System Theory: Overview of Core Concepts, Extensions, and Challenges for the Future. JAIS 14(2), 72–121 (2013)
16. Strahringer, S.: Metamodellierung als Instrument des Methodenvergleichs. Eine Evaluierung am Beispiel objektorientierter Analysemethoden. Shaker, Aachen (1996)
17. Leist-Galanos, S.: Methoden zur Unternehmensmodellierung. Vergleich, Anwendungen und Integrationspotentiale. Logos, Berlin (2006)
18. Frank, U.: Essential Research Strategies in the Information Systems Discipline: Reflections on Formalisation, Contingency and the Social Construction of Reality. The Systemist, 98–113 (1998)
19. Frank, U.: Ein Bezugsrahmen zur Beurteilung objektorientierter Modellierungssprachen – veranschaulicht am Beispiel von OML und UML. Technical Report 6, Universität Koblenz-Landau, Koblenz (1997)
20. Bork, D., Fill, H.G.: Formal Aspects of Enterprise Modeling Methods: A Comparison Framework. In: Proceedings of the 47th HICSS, pp. 3400–3409 (2014)
21. Aier, S., Riege, C., Winter, R.: Unternehmensarchitektur – Literaturüberblick und Stand der Praxis. Wirtschaftsinformatik 50(4), 292–304 (2008)

22. Buckl, S., Schweda, C.M.: On the State-of-the-Art in Enterprise Architecture Management Literature (2011)
23. Lankhorst, M.: Enterprise Architecture at Work: Modelling, Communication and Analysis, 3rd edn. The Enterprise Engineering Series. Springer, Heidelberg (2013)
24. Land, M.O., Proper, E., Waage, M., Cloo, J., Steghuis, C.: Enterprise Architecture: Creating Value by Informed Governance. Springer, Berlin (2009)
25. Ettema, R., Dietz, J.L.G.: ArchiMate and DEMO – Mates to Date? In: Albani, A., Barjis, J., Dietz, J.L.G. (eds.) CIAO! 2009. LNBIP, vol. 34, pp. 172–186. Springer, Heidelberg (2009)
26. Alter, S.: Potentially Valuable Overlaps between Work System Theory, DEMO, and Enterprise Engineering. In: 1st Workshop on Enterprise Engineering Theories and Methods, IEEE Conference on Business Informatics 2014, Geneva, pp. 1–8 (2014)
27. Wijers, G.M.: Modelling Support in Information Systems Development. PhD thesis, Technische Universiteit Delft, Delft and Netherlands (1991)
28. Dietz, J.L.G., Widdershoven, G.A.M.: Speech acts or communicative action? In: Bannon, L., Robinson, M., Schmidt, K. (eds.) Proceedings of the 2nd ECSCW 1991, pp. 235–248. Kluwer, Dordrecht (1991)
29. Overbeek, S., Frank, U., Köhling, C.: A language for multi-perspective goal modelling: Challenges, requirements and solutions. CSI 38, 1–16 (2015)
30. Heise, D.: Unternehmensmodell-basiertes IT-Kostenmanagement als Bestandteil eines integrativen IT-Controllings. Logos, Berlin (2013)
31. Alter, S.: A general, yet useful theory of information systems. CAIS 1(13), 1–70 (1999)
32. Alter, S.: Work Systems and IT Artifacts - Does the Definition Matter? CAIS 17(14), 299–313 (2006)
33. Alter, S.: The Work System Method: Connecting People, Processes, and IT for Business Results. Work System Press, Larkspur (2006)
34. Dietz, J.L.G.: The atoms, molecules and fibers of organizations. Data & Knowledge Engineering 47(3), 301–325 (2003)
35. Frank, U.: MEMO Organisation Modelling Language (1): Focus on Organisational Structure. ICB-Research Report 48, University of Duisburg-Essen (2011)
36. Dietz, J.L.G.: Demo-3: Models and representations, version 3.7 (2014)
37. Frank, U.: The MEMO Meta Modelling Language (MML) and Language Architecture. 2nd Edition. ICB-Research Report 43, University of Duisburg-Essen (2011)
38. Jung, J.: Entwurf einer Sprache für die Modellierung von Ressourcen im Kontext der Geschäftsprozessmodellierung. Logos, Berlin (2007)
39. Frank, U.: MEMO Organisation Modelling Language (2): Focus on Business Processes. ICB Research Report 49, University of Duisburg-Essen (2011)
40. Bock, A., Kattenstroth, H., Overbeek, S.: Towards a modeling method for supporting the management of organizational decision processes. In: Proceedings of the Modellierung 2014. LNI, vol. 225, pp. 49–64. Gesellschaft für Informatik, Bonn (2014)
41. Heß, M., Schlieter, H., Täger, G.: Modellierung komplexer Entscheidungssituationen in Prozessmodellen – Anwendung am Beispiel der Tumorklassifikation bei Weichteilsarkomen. In: Thomas, O., Nüttgens, M. (eds.) Dienstleistungsmodellierung 2012, pp. 268–290. Springer, Wiesbaden (2012)
42. Strecker, S., Heise, D., Frank, U.: RiskM: A multi-perspective modeling method for IT risk assessment. ISF 13(4), 595–611 (2011)

43. Frank, U.: Domain-specific modeling languages: Requirements analysis and design guidelines. In: Reinhartz-Berger, I., Sturm, A., Clark, T., Cohen, S., Bettin, J. (eds.) Domain Engineering, pp. 133–157. Springer, Berlin (2013)
44. Moody, D.L.: The Physics of Notations: Toward a Scientific Basis for Constructing Visual Notations in Software Engineering. IEEE TSE 35(6), 756–779 (2009)
45. Gulden, J.: Methodical Support for Model-Driven Software Engineering with Enterprise Models. Logos, Berlin (2013)

Component-Based Method Development: An Experience Report

Kurt Sandkuhl[1,2,3] and Hasan Koç[1]

[1]The University of Rostock, Institute of Computer Science
Chair Business Information Systems, Albert-Einstein-Str. 22, 18059 Rostock, Germany
{Kurt.Sandkuhl,Hasan.Koc}@uni-rostock.de
[2]Jönköping University, Box 1026, 55 111 Jönköping, Sweden
[3]ITMO University, St. Petersburg, Russia

Abstract. A method defines a systematic process for problem solving including the required aids and resources. This paper aims at contributing to the area of method development and in particular to practices and experiences in this field by reporting on a case from conceptual modelling and reflecting on lessons learned in it. The contributions of the paper are (1) an application case from method development in a distributed team, (2) the actual method development process integrating work procedure, cooperation principles and notation, and (3) experiences and lessons learned from developing a method component for context modeling.

Keywords: method component, method engineering, method development, enterprise modeling, conceptual modeling.

1 Introduction

In very general terms, a method defines a systematic process for problem solving including the required aids and resources. Many engineering disciplines use methods as means to capture proven practices and to formalize best practices. In computer science and business information systems, methods do not only address solution development processes or parts thereof, but also the construction of specific artefacts, like various kinds of models. The development of methods usually is a complex process since methods have to be grounded in solid experiences, elaborated with an adequate level of detail and ideally validated in many application cases in order to reach a sufficient maturity level. Although there is a rich body of knowledge in the field of method engineering, the number of experience reports from actual method engineering projects is limited (see section 2).

This paper aims at contributing to the area of method development and in particular to practices and experiences in this field by reporting on a case from conceptual modelling and reflecting on lessons learned in it. The case considered is the development of a component-based methodology in the area of information systems development. The contributions of the paper are (1) an application case from method development in a distributed team, (2) the actual method development process integrating work procedure,

U. Frank et al. (Eds.): PoEM 2014, LNBIP 197, pp. 164–178, 2014.

cooperation principles and notation, and (3) experiences and lessons learned from developing a method component for context modeling.

The remaining part of the paper is structured as follows: the background for the work from method engineering is briefly introduced in section 2. Section 3 presents the application case constituting the frame for this research. An overview to the method development process is given in section 4. Section 5 discusses the different phases of the process with experiences and lessons learned. Conclusions and future work are discussed in section 6.

2   Background

Work from the areas of method engineering and related work regarding experiences in method development will be summarized in this section.

2.1   Method Engineering

The research area of method engineering offers a rich body of knowledge how to systematically develop, introduce and adapt "methods". Methods often are considered as prescriptive since they are supposed to provide guidance for problem solving or for performing complex tasks. This requires that a method includes what activities to perform, how to perform them (procedure), what results (artefacts) to develop and how to capture these results (notation) [23]. All methods build on perspectives, values, principles, and categories (with definitions), which are expressed in the method and its elements and which show its underlying theories and rationality.

Different conceptualizations of the term "method" and related terms have been proposed. If there is a close link between procedure, notation, and concepts, the term method component is used [13]. The concept of method component is similar to the concept method chunk [14] and [15] and the notion of method fragment [16]. Methods often consist of an integrated set of several method components, which also could be referred to as methodology [17]. These different method components together form a structure called a framework.

In this paper we focus on the process of a component based method development as a part of the EU-FP7 project "Capability as-a-Service in Digital Enterprises" (CaaS). CaaS proposes to design a business service explicitly considering its delivery context and supports modeling both, the service as such and the application context to facilitate service configuration.

An often used and acknowledged approach in method development is situational method engineering (SME), which basically promotes to adapt methods to the project situation at hand [22]. We argue that our efforts in method development in CaaS Project (see section 3) has overlapping aspects with SME since the general phases of an engineering process were adapted to the specific needs of the application case. Moreover, the initial CaaS methodology, also called the "base methodology", has been constructed for the specific demands and situation of the project [11]. Finally, due to the component based development approach the component relevant for a specific tasks can be selected "on demand" from a repository and applied correspondingly.

2.1   Experience Reports

This section summarizes experience reports in situational method engineering area and experience reports in method engineering in general. Reflecting on the practices of method application and presenting the usefulness of the applied methods in projects is a decisive and necessary activity. In the literature there are only a few publications reporting from the topics of method engineering experiences, such as method application, realized business value, stakeholders of the method as well as the development process of the method itself [10].

Most of the work in the field of practices from method engineering is being carried out in situational method engineering area, which *encompasses all aspects of creating a development method for a specific situation* [11]. In this respect [7] outlines both the theory of situational method engineering as well as its application in terms of industrial case studies and evaluates possibilities of applying SME with method fragments from OPEN Process Framework (OPF) repository. Likewise [8] reports on experience in the application of a method engineering approach in practice by constructing a situation specific method for a small company. The study shows that not only big enterprises need methods but also small companies benefit from method application and model-based documentation. Finally, in [9] different articles report on the works and experiences gathered by applying the situational method engineering.

Apart from the practices of method engineering, literature reveals several experience reports on applying frameworks and methods in projects. [4] aligns two reference architecture frameworks, TOGAF and NATO architecture framework (NAF) and reports from the implementation experiences in Norwegian Army Forces. Based on the i* framework [5] defines a method and presents experiences on the usage of the framework in large projects from the stakeholder and modeler point of view. Finally [6] reports results from the application of Enterprise Knowledge Development (EKD) Method in various domains and discusses next generation method improvements based on the observations [6].

3   Application Case

Work in this paper is based on the methodology development which is a part of the EU-FP7 project "Capability as-a-Service in Digital Enterprises" (CaaS). The main goal of the CaaS project is to facilitate a shift from the service-oriented paradigm to a capability delivery paradigm. The CaaS project aims to facilitate configuration of business services and development of executable software to monitor the fitness of purpose of these services to evolving business contexts. The CaaS project will deliver the Capability Driven Development (CDD) approach which is supposed to include methodology, tools and runtime environment. In order to ease adaptation of business services to new delivery contexts, changes in customer processes or other legal environments, the CaaS approach is to explicitly define (a) the potential delivery context of a business service (i.e. all contexts in which the business service potentially has to be delivered), (b) the potential variants of the business service for the delivery context and (c) what aspect of the delivery context would require what kind of variation or adaptation of the business service. This requires development of a new methodic framework supporting capability-driven design in the three industrial cases in CaaS. The CaaS methodology for capability-driven design and development will consist of various components addressing different modelling aspects, such as context modelling, business services modelling, pattern modelling and capability modelling.

According to the definition developed in CaaS (see [18]), a capability is the ability and capacity that enable an enterprise to achieve a business goal in a certain context. Thus, a capability always is defined by specific business services, a defined application context for these business services and goals of the enterprise to be reached. Technically, the model of a capability consists of

- Strategic objectives or business goals related to the capability or motivating the creation of the capability. These objectives should be specified in a precise, measurable and accepted way, for example by using enterprise modelling techniques and by elaborating a goal model.
- The business service(s) offered to customers within the capability. In CaaS, the business service(s) have to be specified using a model-based approach. Currently, the focus is on process-oriented approaches.
- The specification of the potential application context where the business service is supposed to be deployed. This specification also has to capture at what points in the process what variation will have to happen. The specification of the capability's potential deployment contexts is captured in a context model.
- An IT-based solution for executing the business service in the defined context, including all variations of the solution for different context instances. The context only defines the switching between variants and potential parameterization, but not the generation of new variants.
- Patterns specifying reusable design-time or run-time elements for reaching business goals under specific situational contexts. The run-time patterns are also called capability delivery patterns. The CaaS methodology will provide a method component for identification, elicitation and representation of patterns.

The CaaS methodology has to cover development of all the above parts of a capability model. Methodology development in CaaS is performed in a dedicated work package with four academic partners responsible for different methodology parts. The CaaS methodology will be developed in several versions:

- CaaS base methodology: the main purpose of the initial CaaS methodology, also called "base methodology", is to support the industrial use cases in developing initial capability models, i.e. the business services to be considered in the use cases including their context. For this purpose, the base methodology will cover only selected ways of capability modelling and provide method components supporting these selected ways.
- CaaS methodology: the "regular" CaaS methodology will support a wider selection of capability development processes and extend the base methodology also towards capability delivery and runtime adaptation
- CaaS method extensions: each of the industrial cases in CaaS are supposed to develop extensions of the regular CaaS methodology

- Final CaaS methodology: one of the final results of the CaaS project will be a final version of the CDD methodology including the method extensions and packaged for use outside the CaaS project.

The report about the method development process in section 4 and the experiences presented in section 5 originate from work on the base methodology in the CaaS project.

4   Method Development Process

Within the application case described in section 3, the process for development of the CaaS method and its components roughly follows the general phases of an engineering process: scope setting, requirements analysis, design, implementation and test - with several iterations included in these phases. However, all these phases are adapted to the specific needs of the application case and heavily influenced by the method conceptualization used (see section 5.1). Moreover, the scope of the method development so far is limited to the CaaS base methodology, i.e. future work on other method versions (see section 3) will probably lead to more experiences and refinements of the phases. This section gives an overview of the overall method development process, while section 5 describes the most important phases in detail.

The process was started with organizational and technical preparations as depicted in Fig. 1. The organizational preparations had the purpose to initialize the method development and included formation of the development team, defining the responsibilities of the team members, agreeing on schedule and clarifying available resources. Most of these organizational issues were included in the description of the CaaS methodology work package and confirmed in a kick-off meeting for the method development. The technical preparations were directed to identifying and agreeing on frame conditions. For CaaS, this included the purpose of the method, a set of requirements and the capability meta-model, which were a result of the previously completed requirements work package. The requirements work package also defined four principles which the base methodology has to follow [18]:

- The methodology should not be a monolithic block but component-oriented in order to allow for flexible and situative use of selected method components
- Integration of existing methods or method components should be given preference before substituting them
- CaaS should not develop a single methodology mandatory for all business cases but a reference methodology ready-to-use and pathways from this reference methodology to proprietary methodologies
- All types of models, i.e. pattern, context, process and enterprise models, should be based on the same meta-model

After these preparations, the actual work on the method started with discussing different method conceptualizations and agreeing on one conceptualization to use. The selected conceptualization has a component-oriented method view and is described in section 5.1 in more detail. The decision in favor of a component-oriented method view mainly was motivated by the fact that many different parts has to be

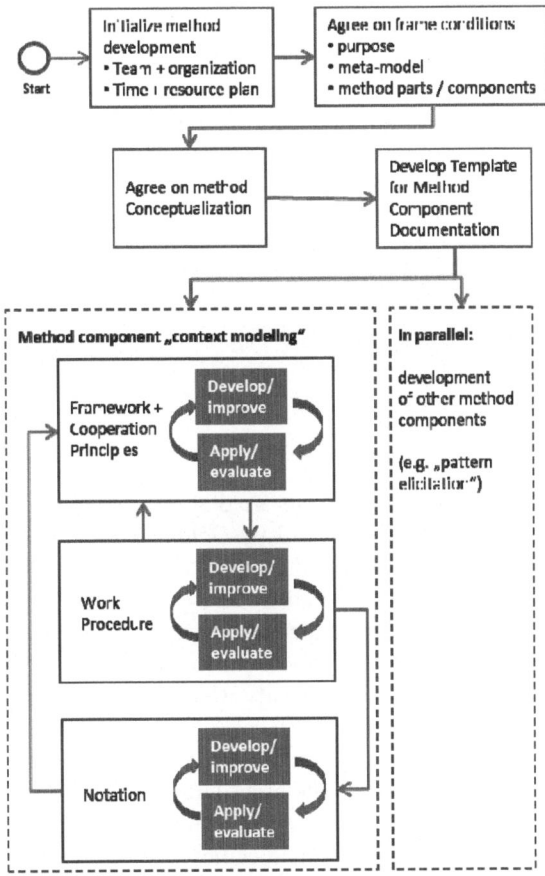

Fig. 1. Method development process

accommodated in the CaaS methodology, as described in section 3. In order to provide an aid for developing the different method components, a template for documentation of method components was developed. The template basically is a document with pre-defined chapters and short descriptions of the content supposed to be described in these chapters. The template was supposed to ease the coordination between the different distributed method component developers.

The development process for the different method components happened in different parallel activities performed by different groups from the method development team. This paper will focus on the development process for the context modeling component only. For this component, the framework and the cooperation principles were developed first. Afterwards, the work procedures for the different steps defined in the framework were elaborated. The last step was to elaborate the notation. All the three steps included several iterations of develop/improve and apply/evaluate activities.

The background for developing the context modeling method component was two-fold: on the one side there were the experiences of the development team members in context modeling from previous projects and the knowledge of the state of the art in this area. Unfortunately, the term "context" is used in different meanings in computer science[12]. Hence, there is no single established practice for context modeling in general. On the other side, practical experience in CaaS context modeling was gathered in the CaaS use cases. The first modeling attempts were a more explorative study which concepts from other context modeling areas could be reused; the later attempts were more systematic and resulted in the initial method idea.

5   Development Steps and Experiences

This section will describe the method development steps performed and the experiences gathered during this development.

5.1   Agree on Method Conceptualization

The way methods and method components are described within CaaS is an extension of the method conceptualization proposed by Goldkuhl et al. [19]. Goldkuhl et al. state that a comprehensive method description should describe the perspective, framework, cooperation principles and all method components. Fig. 2 illustrates how these elements of the method conceptualization are related.

- Method components: A method component should consist of concepts, a procedure and a notation. The concepts specify what aspects of reality are regarded as relevant in the modeling process, i.e. what is important and what should be captured a model. These relevant concepts should be named in the method component and explained if necessary. The procedure describes in concrete terms how to identify the relevant concepts in a method component. It may also cover prerequisites and resources. The notation specifies how the result of the procedure should be documented. As a rule, this must provide appropriate expressions for each concept and for the potential relationships between them. In graphic notations, these are the symbols to be used.
- Framework: the method framework describes the relationships between the individual method components, i.e. which components are to be used and under what conditions, as well as the sequence of the method components (if any).
- Forms of cooperation: many modeling tasks require a range of specialist skills or cooperation between different roles. These necessary skills and roles must be described, along with the division of responsibilities between the roles and the form of cooperation. The cooperation form also includes who will take responsibility for each task or method component, and how the collaboration will be organized.
- Perspective: every method describes the procedure for the modeling process from a particular perspective, which influences what is considered important when developing a model. This perspective often is related to the aims and purpose of the method.

The extensions made for CaaS were made with the intention to further operationalize the use of the above method conceptualization. The discussion in the method development team, which included two members familiar with Goldkuhl's conceptualization and five members not familiar with this approach, showed that some terms

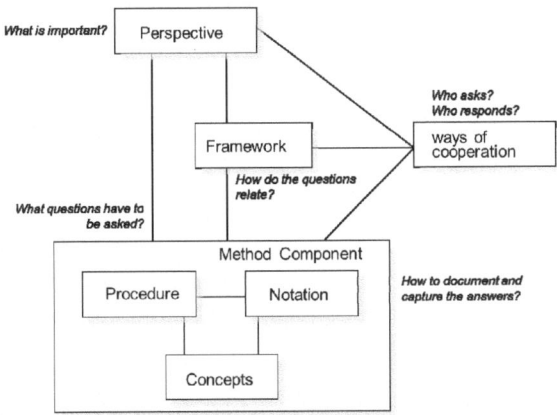

Fig. 2. Method components according to Goldkuhl et al. [19]

needed clarification. The following modifications and extensions were made based on the results of these discussions:

- The term „perspective" sometimes confuses method users. This is why the template contains the „purpose" of the method instead.
- Instead of using the term "framework" as proposed by Goldkuhl, we use "overview to method components". The reason for this change is that many of the envisioned method users found the term "framework" misleading.
- The procedure within a method component has been further refined. It contains steps with input, output and tool support
- A method component often includes a number of work steps and sometimes it even contains other method components. Thus, we assume that a method component can include method components, which can be described in the same structure as a complete method: purpose (perspective), framework, cooperation principles and method (sub-)components.

5.2   Define Method Documentation Template

In order to prepare for a uniform or at least similar way of describing the different method components, a template for documenting method components was defined. The document template is based on the agreed method conceptualization (section 5.2) and defines structure and content of the method documentation. The following structure of the method template was defined:

- Chapter 1 Introduction: Overview to the CaaS methodology in general and brief summary of the method or method component described in the document
- Chapter 2 Purpose and Preconditions: introduction to the purpose of the method and the preconditions required for using it
- Chapter 3 Overview to method components: overview to the different method components and recommended sequence of using them

- Chapter 4 Cooperation principles: Competences, roles and organization structures needed to use the method
- Chapter 5 Method component: one section for each method component describing procedure of working, notation to document the results and important concepts. The procedures consist of steps with inputs, outputs and tool support.
- Chapter 6 Example: an example showing the results of each method component and the overall method

When using the template for documenting a CaaS method all chapters should be with content according to the instructions and guidelines given in these chapters.

5.3   Develop Work Procedures

Development of the work procedures can be classified into three phases. Before the actual development concerning the context modeling began, some effort had been done in the area of modeling context and interpretation of the term within the CaaS Project [12, 21] which basically summarized the relevant work up-to-date. The results of these investigations have been used in the *Preparation* phase for different purposes such as extracting the important terms and concepts in the domain of context and context modeling (see Fig. 3). By conducting this activity the project team realized the first steps towards the identification of the method scope since only the concepts are included, which are closely related to the method application context. Likewise, the excluded concepts helped to limit the method scope.

The important terms have been classified and specified as context dimensions, which later on helped to formulate questions that the method should answer. The core of the development process included three main activities that have been executed recursively in the *Initial Development* phase as illustrated in Fig. 3. The first activity defined the questions that are relevant for method application and grouped them in accordance with their focus, i.e. for designing a context model different question sets are applied. The answers to the questions are transformed into tasks to be executed while grouping the questions has supported us to specify the boundaries of these tasks and to define the components of the context modeling method. The last activity in the initial development phase was to identify how to represent important terms and concepts, i.e. what notation to use when executing the tasks. Results of this phase were presented to the CaaS project team responsible for different methodology parts. After collecting the feedbacks a new iteration has begun and a process oriented method has evolved, which is depicted in Fig. 4. Fig. 4 shows on the left-hand side the components (find variation, design context, operationalize context, monitor & use context) and on the right-hand side the procedure included in these components.

At that time, the project team agreed on the frame conditions of the method and on the method conceptualization as described in section 5.1. Moreover a method development template has been made available that supports the documentation of different method components in a standardized way. In *Conceptualization* phase the artifacts that have been developed in the last iteration are classified as method components, which comprised of procedures, concepts and notations. Following this the prerequisites and purpose of the method have been formulated. Defining the cooperation principles,

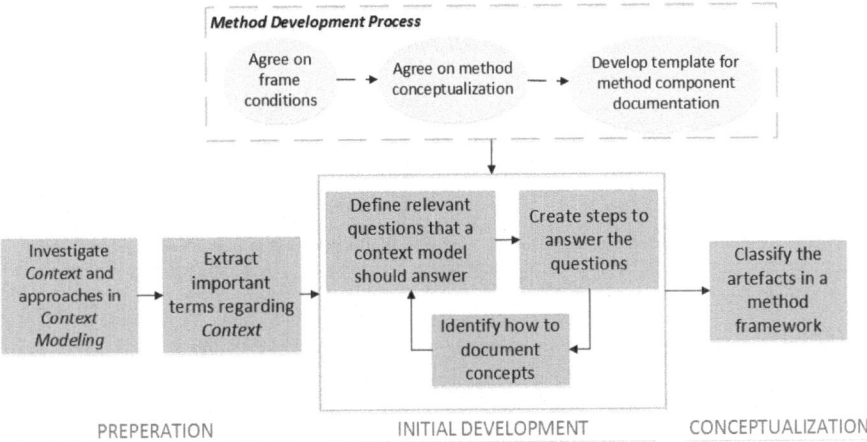

Fig. 3. Phases of Developing the Work Procedure

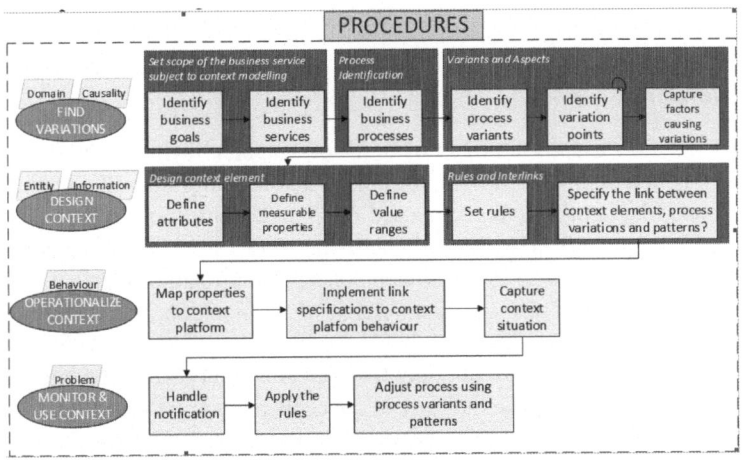

Fig. 4. Important terms, concepts and procedures: A process oriented view

i.e. describing the structures and roles within the team using the method, and the enterprise or organization where the method is applied for modeling was a hard task since we had no experience in developing context models.

Hence, we were able to describe the competence profile of the context modeler applying the method. The result of this phase was the presentation and discussion of the initial method. An exemplary method component "Find Variations" is illustrated in **Fig. 5**. It should be mentioned that we used placeholders for the method components that need to be further investigated in the following versions of the method. Detailed information on the context modeling method component can be found in [20].

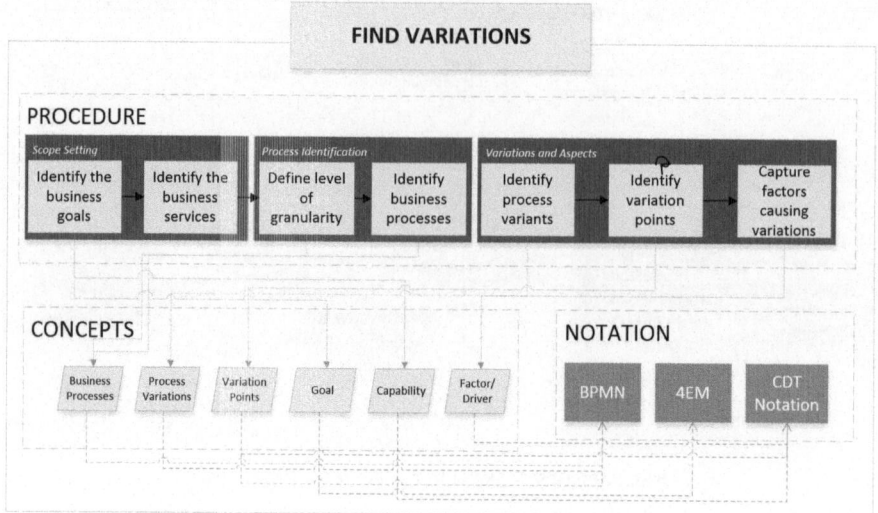

Fig. 5. Initial method: An exemplary method component

5.4   Develop Notation

A visual notation usually consists of a set of graphical symbols, definitions of the meaning of each symbol and compositional rules defining how the symbols may be arranged and diagrams may be composed [2]. The development of the visual notation was an iterative process consisting of alternating elaboration and validation steps. The first elaboration step was to define which concepts and relationships have to be established in the notation. From the first version of the notation, the elaboration process used the principles proposed by Moody [2] for the design of notations. Moody explicitly states that the principles are not only for evaluating and comparing but also for constructing visual notations. The majority of concepts including the relevant relationships could be taken from the meta-model which is presented in [3]: context type, context set, context element, context element range, and measurable property. When developing the context modeling method component (see section 5.3), two additional concepts were defined: variation aspect and variation point. Most relationships between these concepts to be covered by the visual notation also originate from the meta-model:

- Context type <defines> context element
- Context element <is measured by> measurable property
- Context element <has> context element range
- Context set <consists of> context element ranges
- Variation aspects <is related to> variation point
- Context element <causes> variation aspect

The above list of concepts and relationships form the semiotic constructs to be represented in the visual notation. The notation was initially developed by one member of the method development team who is experienced in method development and use of visual modeling languages. This initial development included the creation of shapes for the semiotic constructs and to assign colors and textures to these shapes. Furthermore, the principles proposed by Moody [2] were applied by checking if the initial development was meeting the principles and – if not – how they had to be adapted. The result is summarized in Table 1.

Table 1. Moody's principles and their use during notation development

Moody's principles	How the principles were taken into account
1: Semiotic clarity (1:1 correspondence between semantic constructs and graphical symbols)	All concepts have an own symbol; there are no redundant symbols and no symbol overload
2: Perceptual Discriminability (clearly distinguishable symbols)	Different shapes, colors and textures were used to make concepts discriminable
3: Semiotic Transparency (visual representations suggesting their meanings)	Spatial relationships (subset, hierarchy) indicating their meanings were used
4: Include mechanism for dealing with complexity	For context sets and variation aspects, abstraction levels were introduced into the notation
5: Cognitive Integration of information from different diagrams	Variation aspects were integrated into business process models
6: Use full range of visual variables	Besides shape, color and texture also the position (horizontal/vertical) was used for content element range – context element and for variation aspect – variation point relations
7: Dual Coding (use text to complement graphics)	All concepts show the concept name in addition to their specific shape
8: Number of symbols should be cognitively manageable	The number of different semiotic constructs is 7. This is only slightly above the recommended number 6.
9: Different visual dialects for different tasks and audiences	Not supported.

The first validation step was internal validation in the method development team, i.e. the other team members checked the proposed notation using Moody's principles and their own experiences with visual notations. The second validation step involved a practitioner from industry with 20 years of experience in software modelling. The practitioner was familiar with the concepts of the CaaS meta-model, the purpose of context modeling and the work procedure recommended. The result of this step was a minor adjustment in the color of the variation aspect symbol.

Afterwards, the proposed notation was handed over to the developers of the modeling tool, which in the CaaS project includes off-the-shelf components for business process modeling and newly developed functionality for enterprise modeling with the 4EM method and context modeling. The tool developers on the one hand side checked the implementability of the notation and on the other side the compatibility to their understanding of the operational semantics of the CaaS meta-model. The latter resulted in an adaptation of the notation regarding the mechanisms dealing with complexity.

Not only context elements but also context element ranges should be part of the context set, since context elements are according to the meta-model only part of the context set since they are only related to context element range.

6   Summary and Future Work

Based on the development of a method component for context modeling in a distributed team, this paper reported on the way of working and experiences collected in method engineering. This section will summarize recommendations and lessons learned.

The first recommendation is related to the overall organization of the method development process. In a distributed team of developers we strongly recommend to treat the method development task like a project and define clear role and task structures. The roles needed are the overall method development responsible and the responsible actors for different method components, which in project management could be considered as project manager and work package managers. Furthermore, there should be an expert for the selected method conceptualization supporting the method component development and the developers as such. To develop a method documentation template and define it as mandatory for all method component also proved valuable. However, we recommend complementing this with additional training for all method developers in how to use the method conceptualization. We expect this to contribute to more consistent component documentation.

Moody's principles for visual notations also proved very valuable but more for the evaluation than for the construction of the notation. The construction of a notation to some extent is a creative process for designing an orchestrated set of semiotic symbols. The process of how to do this is not addressed by Moody's work. The key competence for this creative part from our view is in-depth knowledge of other visual notations and their semiotic symbols, semantics and way of achieving good usability. At least for defining the context modeling notation this was important. One aspect not taken into account by Moody is the implementability of the developed visual notation with the software development environment for the modeling tool. This aspect could be considered as out of scope for the visual notation but nevertheless is crucial for projects attempting to apply the notation in industrial settings. Thus we recommend to use Moody's principles for evaluating and improving visual notations and to add the aspect of implementability.

The method conceptualization by Goldkuhl et al with the extensions and renaming described in section 5.1 proved to be suitable and applicable. The method developers perceived the conceptualization and its way to decompose a method into different elements as helpful in the overall development process.

The overall method development process described in section 4 worked nicely for our project, but we cannot claim that it is recommendable for all method development projects. The design of this process was based on experiences in previous projects and had rather a pragmatic than a scientific view on method development. We think the approach has the potential to become what in knowledge management is called a good practice. Good practice in this context has the meaning of a proven procedure for reliably completing a defined task [1]. More application cases would be needed to achieve this.

Furthermore, future work will have to focus on improving both, the development process in general and the context method component as such. In the method engineering literature, there is much information on development of method chunks and fragments [24] which most likely also is useful for method components. This aspect needs further investigation. Moreover, the practical use of the CaaS methodology and the context modeling method component will result in a clearer picture about potential other sequences of the method components and the influence of method components on pre/post-conditions of other method components. This will probably lead to adjustment requirements of the approach presented in this paper.

Acknowledgements. We wish to thank the anonymous reviewers for their many comments and recommendations helping us to improve the paper.

This work has been performed as part of the EU-FP7 funded project no: 611351 CaaS – Capability as a Service in Digital Enterprises. This work was also partially supported by the Government of Russian Federation, Grant 074-U01.

References

1. Davenport, T.H., Prusak, L.: Working Knowledge. Harvard Business School Press, Boston (1998)
2. Moody, D.L.: The "Physics" of Notations: Toward a Scientific Basis for Constructing Visual Notations in Software Engineering. IEEE Transactions on Software Engineering 35(6), 756–779 (2009)
3. Zdravkovic, J., Stirna, J., Henkel, M., Grabis, J.: Modeling Business Capabilities and Context Dependent Delivery by Cloud Services. In: Salinesi, C., Norrie, M.C., Pastor, Ó. (eds.) CAiSE 2013. LNCS, vol. 7908, pp. 369–383. Springer, Heidelberg (2013)
4. Jørgensen, H.D., Liland, T., Skogvold, S.: Aligning TOGAF and NAF - Experiences from the Norwegian Armed Forces. In: Johannesson, P., Krogstie, J., Opdahl, A.L. (eds.) PoEM 2011. LNBIP, vol. 92, pp. 131–146. Springer, Heidelberg (1980)
5. Carvallo, J.P., Franch, X.: On the Use of i* for Architecting Hybrid Systems: A Method and an Evaluation Report. In: Persson, A., Stirna, J. (eds.) PoEM 2009. LNBIP, vol. 39, pp. 38–53. Springer, Heidelberg (2009)
6. Stirna, J., Persson, A.: Evolution of an enterprise modeling method – next generation improvements of EKD. In: Sandkuhl, K., Seigerroth, U., Stirna, J. (eds.) PoEM 2012. LNBIP, vol. 134, pp. 1–15. Springer, Heidelberg (2012)
7. Henderson-Sellers, B.: Method Engineering: Theory and Practice. In: 5th International Conference ISTA 2006, Klagenfurt, Austria, pp. 13–23. GI (May 2006)
8. Ralyté, J.: Situational Method Engineering in Practice: A Case Study in a Small Enterprise. In: CAiSE 2013 Forum at the 25th CAiSE, Valencia, Spain, June 20, pp. 17–24. CEUR-WS.org (2013)
9. Ralyté, J., Brinkkemper, S., Henderson-Sellers, B.: Situational Method Engineering: Fundamentals and Experiences, Proceedings IFIP WG 8, Geneva, Switzerland, September 12-14, vol. 244. Springer, Heidelberg (2007)

10. Hidding, G.J., Odell, J.J., Parkinson, J., et al.: Panel: Method Engineering: Experiences in Practice. In: Brinkkemper, S., Lyytinen, K., Welke, R.J. (eds.) Method Engineering, pp. 319–320. Springer, US (1996)

11. Henderson-Sellers, B., Ralyté, J.: Situational Method Engineering: State-of-the-Art Review. J. UCS 16(3), 424–478 (2010)

12. Koç, H., Hennig, E., Jastram, S., Starke, C.: State of the Art in Context Modelling – A Systematic Literature Review. In: Iliadis, L., Papazoglou, M., Pohl, K., et al. (eds.) CAiSE Workshops 2014. LNBIP, vol. 178, pp. 53–64. Springer, Heidelberg (2014)

13. Röstlinger, A., Goldkuhl, G.: Påväg mot en komponentbaserad metodsyn (in Swedish). Presented at "VITS Höstseminarium 1994, Linköping University, Linköping, Sweden (1994)

14. Ralyté, J., Backlund, P., Kühn, H., Jeusfeld, M.A.: Method chunks for interoperability. In: Embley, D.W., Olivé, A., Ram, S. (eds.) ER 2006. LNCS, vol. 4215, pp. 339–353. Springer, Heidelberg (2006)

15. Mirbel, I., Ralyté, J.: Situational method engineering: combining assembly-based and roadmap-driven approaches. Requirements Eng. 11, 58–78 (2006)

16. Brinkkemper, S.: Method engineering: engineering of information systems development methods and tools. Information and Software Technology 1995, 37 (1995)

17. Avison, D.E., Fitzgerald, G.: Information Systems Development: Methodologies, Techniques and Tools. Berkshire. McGraw Hill, England (1995)

18. Bērziša, S., Bravos, G., Gonzalez Cardona, T., Czubayko, U., España, S., Grabis, J., Jokste, L., Kuhr, J.-C., Koc, H., Kampars, J., Llorca, C., Loucopoulos, P., Juanes Pascual, R., Sandkuhl, K., Simic, H., Stirna, J., Zdravkovic, J.: Deliverable D1.4 - Requirements Specification for CDD. CaaS Deliverable (February 2014)

19. Goldkuhl, G., Lind, M., Seigerroth. U.: Method integration: the need for a learning Perspective. IEE Proceedings, Software (Special issue on Information System Methodologies) 145(4) (1998)

20. Koc, H., Sandkuhl, K.: Task Report 5.2: CaaS Method Component for Context Modeling. CaaS – Capability as a Service for Digital Enterprises, FP7 project no 611351. Rostock University, Germany (2014)

21. Bērziša, S., España, S., Grabis, J., Henkel, M., Jokste, L., Kampars, J., Koç, H., Sandkuhl, K., Stirna, J., Valverde, F., Zdravkovic, J.: Task Report 5.1: State-of-the-art in Relevant Methodology Areas. CaaS – Capability as a Service for Digital Enterprises, FP7 project no 611351. Rostock University, Germany (2014)

22. Ralyté, J., Deneckère, R., Rolland, C.: Towards a generic model for situational method engineering. In: Eder, J., Missikoff, M. (eds.) CAiSE 2003. LNCS, vol. 2681, pp. 95–110. Springer, Heidelberg (2003)

23. Seigerroth, U.: Enterprise Modelling and Enterprise Architecture – the constituents of transformation and alignment of Business and IT. International Journal of IT/Business Alignment and Governance (IJITBAG) 2(1), 16–34 (2011)

24. Henderson-Sellers, B., Ralyté, J., Ågerfalk, P.: Matti Rossi: Situational Method Engineering. Springer, Berlin (2013)

Organizational Adoption of Enterprise Modeling Methods – Experience Based Recommendations

Anne Persson[1] and Janis Stirna[2]

[1] University of Skövde, Informatics Research Centre, P.O. Box 408,
SE-541 28 Skövde, Sweden
anne.persson@his.se
[2] Department of Computer and Systems Sciences, Stockholm University, Forum 100,
SE-1644 0, Kista, Sweden
js@dsv.su.se

Abstract. Organizations normally begin using Enterprise Modeling (EM) within the context of a development project of some sort, where an outside vendor and/or consultant provide the method and related IT tool usage competence. If an organization uses EM sufficiently frequently it may be motivated to develop in-house EM competence and to acquire and adopt an EM method. The paper is an experience paper. It defines what it means to adopt an EM method in an organization and describes the process of adopting and institutionalizing EM as an organizational strategy to support continuous improvement and development. The process consists of three activities: deciding that an EM method should be adopted as part of the organization's set of institutionalized methods, electing a suitable method and implementing the method.

Keywords: Enterprise Modeling, method adoption.

1   Introduction

Enterprise Modeling (EM) is a process where an integrated and negotiated model describing different aspects of an enterprise is created. An Enterprise Model consists of a number of related "sub-models", each describing the enterprise from a particular perspective, e.g., processes, business rules, goals, actors and concepts. There are three main reasons for organizations to use EM [1].

To develop the business. This entails, e.g., developing business vision, strategies, redesigning business operations, developing the supporting information systems, etc. Business development is one of the most common purposes of EM. It frequently involves change management – determining how to achieve visions and objectives from the current state in organizations. Business process orientation is a specific case of business development – the organization wants to restructure/redesign its business operations.

To ensure the quality of the business operations. This purpose primarily focuses on two issues: 1) sharing the knowledge about the business, its vision, and the way it operates, and 2) ensuring the acceptance of business decisions through committing the

U. Frank et al. (Eds.): PoEM 2014, LNBIP 197, pp. 179–192, 2014.

stakeholders to the decisions made. Two important success factors for ensuring quality are that stakeholders understand the business and that they accept/are committed to business decisions. Knowledge Management (KM) is often integrated with day-to-day business processes in organization. KM systematically deals with creating, maintaining and disseminating organizational knowledge between stakeholders. Sharing business knowledge becomes instrumental, e.g., when organizations merge or collaborate in carrying out a business process. A key aspect of this is terminology. EM has a role to play here as it aims to create a multifaceted "map" of the business as a common platform for communicating between stakeholders. One KM perspective is keeping employees informed with regard to how the business is carried out. Most modern organizations consider that the commitment of stakeholders to carry out business decisions is a critical success factor for achieving high quality business operations. Differences in opinion about the business must hence be resolved, requiring that communication between stakeholders be stimulated. EM, particularly using a participative approach, can be effective in obtaining such commitment.

To use EM as a problem solving tool. In this case EM is only used for supporting the discussion among a group of stakeholders trying to analyze a specific problem at hand. In some cases making an EM activity is helpful when capturing, delimiting, and analyzing the initial problem situation and deciding on a course of action. In such cases EM is mostly used as a problem solving and communication tool. The enterprise model created during this type of modeling is used for documenting the discussion and the decisions made. The main characteristics of this purpose are that the company does not intend to use the models for further development work and that the modeling activity has been planned to be a single iteration. In some cases the situation evolves into one of the other EM purposes because the organization sees EM as beneficial or the problem turns out to be more complex than initially thought and more effort is needed for its solution.

EM usually is organized in the form of a project or it is a part of a larger project targeting, e.g., organizational or information system (IS) development.

Organizations normally begin using EM within the context of a development project of some sort, where an outside vendor and/or consultant provide the method and related IT tool usage competence. If an organization uses EM sufficiently frequently it may be motivated to develop in-house EM competence and to acquire and adopt an EM method.

Authors have reflected on the use of enterprise models in organizations from a practical perspective (see e.g. [2]). However, research is scarce into how organizations systematically should proceed to adopt EM. Therefore, the aim of this paper is to discuss the process of adopting EM as an institutionalized way of working and to provide a baseline for further research. It does so based on experiences from a large number of observations from projects using EM as a method. For examples of projects that the authors have been involved in, see, e.g., [3].

The remainder of this paper is organized as follows. Section 2 defines the meaning of organizational EM adoption and institutionalization. The experience base of the paper is described in Section 3. The process of adopting an EM method in an organization is described in Section 4. In section 5 the notion of a modeling department is discussed. The paper ends with some concluding remarks in Section 6.

2   Experience Base

This paper is based on a number of projects carried out since beginning of the 1990-ies:

- Development of the Enterprise Knowledge Development (EKD) EM method [3] (recently refined into the 4EM Method [4]),
- Extensive field work applying versions of EKD to a variety of problems,
- Interview studies involving experienced EM consultants and method developers.

The most influential application cases were, for the most part, carried out within international research projects financed by the European Commission. An overview of the cases is given in Table 1.

Table 1. Overview of main application cases

Organization	Domain	Problems addressed
British Aerospace, UK	Aircraft development and production	Requirements Engineering
Telia AB, Sweden	Telecommunications industry	Requirements validation Project definition
Volvo Cars AB, Sweden	Car manufacturing	Requirements engineering
Vattenfall AB, Sweden	Electrical power industry	Change management, Process development, Competence management
Riga City Council, Latvia	Public administration	Development of vision and supporting processes for knowledge management
Verbundplan GmbH, Austria	Electrical power industry	Development of vision and supporting processes for knowledge management
Skaraborg Hospital, Sweden	Health care	Capturing knowledge assets and development of a knowledge map of a knowledge repository.
SYSteam AB, Sweden	Management consulting	Development of a vision for an employee knowledge management portal

Their processes and their outcome were observed and analyzed. Collected data and experiences from method development, fieldwork and interviews were analyzed. In addition, EKD and its earlier versions have also been used in a number of problem solving and organizational design cases at organizations such as e.g. Strömma AB (Sweden), Ericsson (Sweden), Livani District (Latvia), Riga Technical University (Latvia), University of Skövde (Sweden) and RRC College (Latvia).

3   The Meaning of EM Adoption and Institutionalization

In this section we take one step up from the single EM project and consider projects to be part of an organizational strategy to use EM for supporting continuous organizational improvement, i.e., EM becomes institutionalized.

The EM lifecycle can then be outlined according to the following steps [5]. It is also depicted in Figure 1.

1. Something triggers the need to investigate a potential change in the organization. This trigger can be a business opportunity, a challenge, a problem or a symptom of a problem. A choice is made to use EM in the investigation and potentially also to design a change to business operations and/or the IT systems that support business operations.
2. The EM project is initiated and executed.
3. The implementation of the resulting models is planned and executed and the models now become part of the day-to-day business processes.
4. Continuous organizational improvements are made. EM could support some of these improvements. Changes of greater importance will most likely cause the process to start over from step 1.

The outcome or effect of the implementation of models is very much dependent on the following two aspects:

-   How the EM project is planned and executed. Management of modeling and model quality is one aspect here as well as the many facets of managing the EM project as a whole.
-   How the implementation and continuous improvement of the resulting models is planned and executed over time.

Effectively managing quality throughout the project will ensure that the intended effects of EM and the resulting models will materialize, not only from a short-term perspective but also long-term perspective.

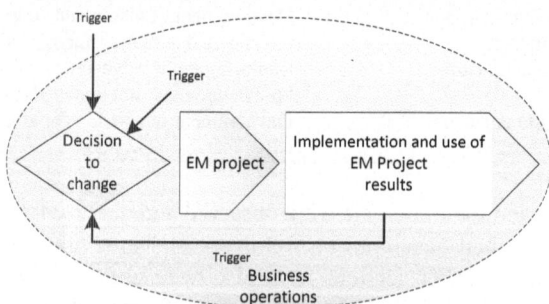

Fig. 1. EM in the context of continuous improvement [5]

When a future state process is implemented following an EM project, a responsible process owner is preferably in control. Measurements are in place and used for continuous follow-up, subsequent rewarding of good process performance and identification of triggers for continuous improvement of organizational operations is made. New opportunities and threats emanating from external or internal sources will challenge or ask for attention and potential new developments, some needing support from EM.

The complete "map" of existing enterprise models will function as important input to future improvement and development projects. This way unnecessary modeling work can be avoided. Even if the organizational context has changed slightly, the existing models will provide a good starting point. Since models will be extensively reused, it is essential that their quality is high. The reuse of models will also require good tool-support that enables change management of models.

The effect of adopting this approach, where EM has an important role, i.e., is institutionalized, is that the process of continuous improvement is kept alive and that external and internal triggers for change are properly analyzed and acted upon.

In order to properly capitalize on the opportunities that this brings, an organization needs be systematic about their approach to adopting EM as an organizational strategy while being aware on the challenges of the adoption process. The EM adoption process will be discussed in the following section.

4   The Adoption Process

In the previous section, an example was given of how EM can become an integral part of an organization's continuous improvement work. In this section we provide an overview of the process of adopting an EM method as part of such an improvement approach. In the following sections, the different steps of the adoption process are discussed in turn.

Despite the advancements in the areas of EM methods and tools, their impact in practice is largely dependent on how they are adopted and institutionalized. EM usage often follows the phases of initial interest, pilot project, and subsequent institutionalization. The most challenging is the final one because at this stage the organization should presumably have enough competence to perform modeling without external support. In cases when this is not so, EM struggles to make positive impact and is gradually forgotten. Therefore, the process of adopting a method should be given the proper attention and resources, in order to be reasonably successful.

In addition, the application of EM is heavily influenced by a large number of situational factors, one of which is the intentions behind its use. We argue that knowledge about these intentions is essential when making decisions about which method, way of working, tool support etc. is appropriate in order for those intentions to be fulfilled.

In [6] we described how the purpose of EM influences the choice of EM language, modeling process, tools etc. (see overview in Table 2.).

The table suggests that if more than one purpose is intended, both the selection process and the adoption process itself becomes inherently difficult, needing tradeoffs to be made between the different purposes.

In some cases it may even be necessary to adopt more than one complementing method to cater for anticipated needs. This in itself requires that the two methods are integrated and that their tool support is also accordingly integrated. This last aspect is a challenge in itself.

Table 2. Requirements on EM [6]. Model types from the 4EM method [4]

Purpose of EM	Input models and documentation	Models to be developed	EM language requirements	EM process requirements	EM tool requirements	Model quality requirements
Develop the business						
Develop visions and strategy	Existing models and other business "blueprints"	Business oriented models, e.g. Goal Model (GM), Concept Model (CM), Business Proc. Model (BPM), Actor Model (AM), inter-model links	Notation that domain stakeholders understand	Participatory	Plastic wall[1], simple documenting tools	Understandability, correctness, simplicity, flexibility
Design/ Redesign the business	Vision and strategy models and other kinds of business "blueprints"	Business oriented models, e.g. as above as well as inter-model links	Established notation that domain stakeholders understand	Participatory involving multiple stakeholder groups	Plastic wall, EM tools that makes it possible to seamlessly move to requirements analysis and IS design	Completeness, correctness, flexibility, integration, understandability, usability
Develop IS	Business oriented models	IS architecture models as well as links with business oriented models	Enough formality and precision to allow modeling of complex facts	Partly participatory and partly analyst driven	Plastic wall, EM tools or CASE tools depending on the development approach	Completeness, correctness, flexibility, integration, usability
Ensure the quality of business operations						
Ensure acceptance for business decisions	Various types of business "blueprints" (e.g. Balanced Scorecard)	Business oriented models (GM, CM, BPM, ARM, BRM) as well as inter-model links	Notation that domain stakeholders understand	Participatory involving knowledge bearers and users	Plastic wall, simple tools, tools for presentation of models	Completeness, correctness, integration, simplicity, understandability, usability
Maintain and share knowledge about the business	Business models (GM, CM, BPM, ARM, BRM), inter-model links	"Cleaned" models that make sense to a wider audience	Simple and intuitive modeling language	Partly participatory, partly analyst driven	EM tools with web interface	Correctness, integration, understandability, usability
Use EM as a business problem solving tool						
To analyze and solve a specific problem or task	Initial problem statement and other relevant documentation	Business oriented models (GM, CM, BPM, ARM, BRM) & inter-model links	Notation that domain stakeholders understand	Participatory involving multiple stakeholder groups	Plastic wall, simple documenting tools	Correctness, flexibility, understandability

---

[1] Plastic sheet on the wall where the emerging model is visible to all modeling participants.

The general process of adopting an EM method in an organization consists of the following phases:
-   Deciding that an EM method should be adopted as part of the organization's set of institutionalized methods
-   Selecting a suitable method
-   Implementing the method in the organization

4.1 Deciding that an EM Method Should be Acquired and Adopted

The decision to adopt an EM method as a part of the organization's set of institutionalized methods often originates from the organization having been involved in projects where external consultants have used EM for various purposes, as indicated in the introduction of this paper. This often generates an interest, particularly if the results from such projects have been successful, and a decision to acquire and adopt a method may follow.

4.2 Selecting a Suitable EM Method

The terms modeling method and modeling language are sometimes in practice used as synonyms, which can be confusing. Furthermore, the modeling language itself is not enough to achieve the goals of EM. The user of a modeling language needs guidance for *how* to use the modeling language in a practical context.

Therefore, an EM method is, according to the understanding of the authors of this paper, not an EM method if it does not have two components:

1.   An EM language, with a defined syntax, semantics and notation, i.e., the building blocks of an enterprise model. Examples of EM languages can be found, for instance, in [7, 8, 9, 10, 4]
2.   An EM process, with a set of recommended elicitation approaches, a set of tools and a project approach which defines how a project using the EM method can be set up and carried out.

We claim that there are very few EM methods that follow this definition, but there are examples, for instance, the AKM approach [7], and the 4EM method [4]. In practice, it may well be the case that the organization is first acquainted with an EM language and wants to adopt it. However, sustainable and successful adoption of EM requires that the organization not only adopt an EM language, with some supporting tool, but also considers and plans for how the modeling process will be managed and also how modeling projects will be organized.

4.2.1 Selecting a Modeling Language

The core of EM is the modeling language because that determines which aspects of a certain problem that can be addressed.

In most cases a certain problem to be addressed can be modeled by using several EM languages/notations. Even within one modeling language the modelers often define "dialects" and sub-notations, i.e., they add elements of secondary notation such as comments, groupings of modeling components, as well as include modeling components from other languages.

The choice of modeling language is to a large extent dependent on the purpose for which EM will be used (see Table 2). The more specific the purpose, the more specialized the language can be. A broad range of intended purposes makes it more difficult to find a language that perfectly fits all purposes. However, there is often room in a language to make adjustments to fit the situation.

When an organization decides to adopt EM as a general method and not only for carrying out a specific project it may be appropriate to select more than one language to cater for intended purposes. E.g. using an EM method for developing visions and strategies and as a general problem-solving tool can require a different level of formality compared to using EM for developing information systems. As a general rule, languages originally intended for developing information systems, e.g. UML, are often more difficult for non-modeling-experts to understand and work with, which suggests that they may not be the optimal choice for problems less formal.

In cases where more than one language is selected, the issue of integration between the languages comes into play. E.g., process models are often part of many EM languages. In projects dealing with information systems development decisions need to be made about which models will be used in the more business oriented part of a project, where understandability is essential, and how these will be used in the more systems oriented part. Adopting more than one modeling language also influences the choice of tools, more specifically computer-based tools. One of many issues here is how models created by using one tool can be integrated with models created by using another tool.

4.2.2   Selecting a Modeling Process

A general process for carrying out an EM project is described in [11]. It contains a number of activities according to Table 3.

Table 3. Activities in the EM process [11]

Define scope and objectives of the modeling project
Plan for project activities and resources
Plan for modeling session
Gather and analyze background information
Interview modeling participants
Prepare modeling session
Conduct modeling session
Write meeting minutes
Analyze and refine models
Present the results to stakeholders

Some steps in the process can be omitted and some may be added. This means that an organization may adopt more than one general modeling process. In any case they should be documented and made easily available to the organization in order to support the modeling experts and business stakeholders in their work and to standardize the process between specific projects. Such standardization will save time for modeling experts. It will also familiarize business stakeholders with the modeling process and by that make them feel more secure in their participation throughout the various projects that they will be involved in. The introduction of newly employed modeling experts into the way of working of the organization will also be smoother if the process is documented and easily available.

An important decision to be made is which elicitation approach that is most appropriate for the organization. The authors of this paper recommend a participatory approach to EM as a general rule, based on previous research and a great deal of own experience. There are two main arguments for using the participatory approach, if possible [12]:

-   The quality of a model is enhanced if the models are created in collaboration between stakeholders, rather than resulting from a consultant's interpretation of interviews with domain experts.
-   The adoption of a participatory approach involves stakeholders in the decision making process, which facilitates the achievement of acceptance and commitment. This is particularly important if the modeling activity is focused on changing some aspect of the domain, such as its visions/strategies, business processes and information system support.

Although this is the recommended way of working, a less participatory approach such as interviewing and observation can be appropriate under specific circumstances, e.g. if the organizational culture does not allow for different views and opinions being expressed in a group setting.

4.3 Implementing the Method

As indicated, implementing a method in an organization is the most difficult and time-consuming part of the adoption process. There are many issues that need to be addressed in the process, e.g. how to acquire a method, whether or not to adapt the chosen method, acquiring competent modeling experts, acquiring modeling tools, starting to use EM. Evaluation and making adjustments to the implementation should not be neglected as well.

4.3.1   Acquiring a Method

An EM method consists of a modeling language and a modeling process (see Section 3.2). Some methods, like 4EM [4] come with a predefined modeling process but most methods do not. Therefore, the process of acquiring a method should also include selecting one or more ways of working, both in terms of the overall process of carrying out an EM project and in terms of elicitation approaches within a project (see Section 4.2.2). The chosen elicitation approaches will most certainly influence which competence that will be needed. More regarding EM competence can be found in Section 4.3.3 and in [12].

EM languages can be commercially available or they can be research based. When acquiring a modeling language it is important to consider its long-term sustainability, in addition to the fitness for purpose. Commercially available languages come at a price but on the other hand they may be more widely accepted and their long-term development and support taken care of by the supplier. The ownership of the method is in such cases clear. Research based languages may very well be suited for their intended purpose(s) but the organization needs to ensure that they have been tested properly and that the method documentation is freely available.

4.3.2   Adapting the Method

Sometimes adaptation to the method needs to be made, particularly if the chosen EM method is intended to integrate with other methods, e.g. systems development methods. However, it is advisable only to make the really necessary adaptations in the beginning. After a few pilot projects (see Section 4.3.4) an evaluation can be carried out and further adaptations can then be introduced, if necessary. However, too many local adaptations to a method will make the method more difficult to maintain over time. It will also cause problems and additional costs in terms of adaptation of computer-based tools.

4.3.3   Acquiring In-house Modeling Competence

Most probably the organization will not have competent EM experts among its employees. This means that they will have to be hired. The different levels of EM competence is described in [11] should be considered here, i.e., ability to model, ability to facilitate modeling session, and ability to lead modeling projects. In [12] these competences were also related to the purposes of EM.

It should be noted here, that in order for an organization to be able to handle modeling projects on their own, the last two abilities are critical. Unfortunately it may be difficult to hire people who already have these abilities, because they take a long time to acquire. Hiring people on the highest level of competence may even be impossible. In those cases the organization may start out with a few simple projects with less experienced modeling experts that are hired from outside. The following quote from an interview with an experienced modeling expert illustrates the challenges:

"We interviewed 73 or 74 potential facilitators. Out of these we chose 15 who we thought were at least reasonably good. Towards the end we had seven left. This is the real situation. We lost some on the first level. They didn't really have the ability to model. Some we lost on the second step. They didn't have the ability to facilitate modeling sessions. Then we lost some because ... well, all facilitators are exhibitionist prima donnas ... but some had too many co-operation problems."

An alternative to hiring modeling experts is to train employees who have shown an interest in EM and let them start working with some simple modeling projects, preferably under the supervision and mentorship of external experienced consultants. These projects should be evaluated from a competence perspective. Additional training activities can then be initiated based on the evaluation.

It is clear that training to become a skilled participatory EM method expert involves acquiring knowledge that is provided in the literature or by taking courses. However, most of the training must be focused on practice, in order to become more and more skilled. It can, however, be difficult to organize "learning by doing", with feedback loops in a systematic and practical way, for a large group of people. A complicating factor here is that the person being trained needs to be subjected to a variety of situations, in order to be prepared for future assignments. In addition, the situation in real projects is often sensitive leaving no room for critical mistakes. This means that the number of skilled participatory modeling experts increases very slowly.

A practical way is to work together with more experienced facilitators. Novices should never facilitate alone, since the errors made during modeling will negatively influence the outcome of the process where modeling is used. With reference to the maturity levels of method experts, a common mistake that novices make is that they believe that just because they have learned to master a modeling language, they will be able to carry out a participatory modeling process.

Since modeling expertise takes a long time to build it is essential to allocate resources for competence assessment and development during a number of years. Also, planning for continuous exchange of experiences and mentoring between modeling experts will decrease the vulnerability of competence since it can help easing the dependence on individual modeling experts and allow individuals to develop from one competence level to the next.

4.3.4   Carrying out Pilot Projects

When an organization starts to carry out its own modeling projects some pilot projects should be initiated that are designed to test the modeling language, the modeling process, the modeling tools as well as the modeling competence. Evaluation criteria should be carefully defined. The series of pilot projects should be selected to reflect the different purposes for which the organization intends to use EM.

Most probably the organization will need to hire consultants to supervise the pilot projects and also to set up and carry out the evaluation.

4.3.5   Evaluation and Adjustment of the Method

In order to ensure that the chosen method will be useful over time, the organization also needs to document it and to organize its maintenance.

The maintenance of the method entails not only changing the documentation when the method evolves over time (and it probably will) but also setting up an evaluation process targeting modeling projects that are carried out in the organization. The criteria for selecting the modeling language and modeling process should be used in the evaluation, together with evaluation of the outcome of modeling projects.

Based on the results of the evaluation, different adjustments to the method may be needed. However, care should be taken so that these are not made hastily and frequently because it will cause unnecessary uncertainty and instability in the organization. It is advisable that any adjustments are based on at least 2-3 projects and that they are documented in detail and also communicated to the organization. The communication aspect is particularly important, since people tend to stick to old practices of modeling.

The evaluation can also show that the competence of method experts needs to be enhanced (see Section 4.3.3). Different training activities and exchange of experiences between method experts should then be initiated accordingly.

5   Organizational Structure to Support EM – The Modeling Department

In the previous sections we have discussed the activities that lead to adopting an EM approach in an organization. The result of these activities should be a pool of competent employees that can be used in EM projects, which in many cases may require creating a supporting organizational unit dedicated to modeling – a modeling department.

The following roles should be considered for inclusion in a modeling department:

- Facilitator – the modeling facilitator leads and advises the modeling participants during participatory modeling sessions.
- Method expert – organizations that have been more successful in using EM all had one or several persons who were very knowledgeable about the modeling method (or several methods) used in their organization. They were also very enthusiastic about the modeling way of working. Their enthusiasm also motivated their colleagues' support and engagement in modeling. We call them "method experts" while actually "method champions" would be more correct. These people have often been the first in their organizations who tried to "sell-in" the modeling way of working to their organization. Another responsibility of method experts is the development and maintenance of the modeling method used within the organization and if necessary integration with other methods and approaches.
- Tool expert – in order to use an EM method efficiently, a modeling tool is needed and, hence, the organization should also have in-house competence concerning the modeling tool(s) used. E.g., the different integration possibilities with other tools and configurable information systems, presentation possibilities on the web, collaboration support, tool versions and upgrades, etc. Depending on the actual methods and tools used and background of the people involved, the method and tool expertise can be combined and fulfilled by the same person(s).
- Model maintenance and presentation expert – modeling maintainers are required if the company wants to keep their business models up to date. In larger organizations where many different EM activities take place at the same time, modeling facilitators may not have the time needed to fine-tune the models, for instance, to the levels of presentation quality required for publishing the models on the intranet. Hence, the modeling department may include staff experienced in documenting models for various purposes – e.g. for presentation, for inclusion in reports, requirements specifications, etc.

The building of a modeling department depends on the organization's intentions regarding the long-term use of EM. If the organization wants to model without external consultants or keep models "alive" then it has to develop its own in-house EM competency. Such a task cannot be accomplished "overnight" – time is needed for the personnel to learn the EM method, to develop modeling skills, to develop in-house modeling guidelines and procedures, as well as to accumulate experience (see Section 4.3.3). An organization attempting to do this should also be aware that developing and sustaining a modeling department requires considerable resources.

6   Discussion and Concluding Remarks

The method adoption process can be seen as a process of knowledge transfer. Back-lund, Hallenborg and Hallgrimsson [13] discuss the process of adopting a method in an organization from this perspective (Figure 3).

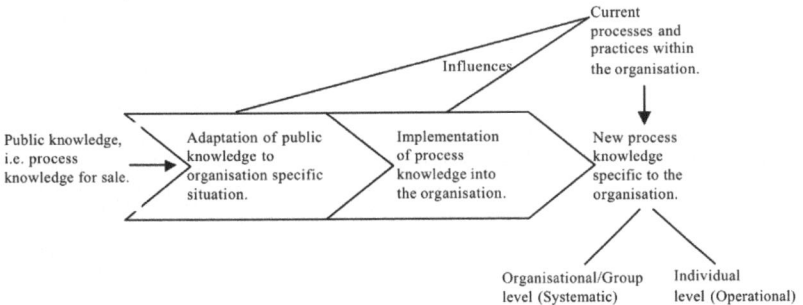

Fig. 2. The method adoption process, a knowledge transfer perspective [13]

A method encapsulates process knowledge, in the case of this paper the knowledge about how to carry out EM. In the process of adopting an EM method in an organiza-tion, this knowledge is transferred from the method constructor to the organization and is internalized by the employees of the organization. In the internalization process, the organization's current knowledge and practices meets the knowledge encapsulated in the new method. The current knowledge influences the adoption process and sometimes requires the new method to be adapted.

For a method to be truly adopted, all employees concerned should have embraced the new method and carry out their work according to it, a change that can take consi-derable time. This suggests that making a management decision about adopting a new method is just the beginning of the adoption process. In this paper we have discussed the adoption process from a fairly instrumental perspective, but the social mechan-isms and the culture of an organization will heavily influence the process. This aspect of the adoption process has not been addressed in this paper, but it will be included in future work.

References

1. Persson, A., Stirna, J.: An explorative study into the influence of business goals on the practical use of Enterprise Modelling methods and tools. In: Tenth International Confe-rence on Information Systems Development (ISD 2001), September 5-7. University of London, Royal Holloway (2001)
2. Wesenberg, H.: Enterprise Modeling in an Agile World. In: Johannesson, P., Krogstie, J., Opdahl, A.L. (eds.) PoEM 2011. LNBIP, vol. 92, pp. 126–130. Springer, Heidelberg (2011)

3. Stirna, J., Persson, A.: EKD - An Enterprise Modeling Approach to Support Creativity and Quality in Systems and Business Development. In: Halpin, T., Proper, E., Krogstie, J. (eds.) Innovations in Information Systems Modeling: Methods and Best Practices, pp. 68–88. IGI Global (2009) ISBN 978-1-60566-278-7

4. Sandkuhl, K., Stirna, J., Persson, A., Wißotzki, M.: Enterprise Modeling – Tackling Business Challenges with the 4EM Method, Springer (2014), ISBN 978-3-662-43724-7

5. Höglund, J., Persson, A.: Up-Stream and Down-Stream Quality in Enterprise Modeling Practice – Supporting Model Driven Continuous Improvement in Organizations. In: Sandkuhl, K., Seigerroth, U., Stirna, J. (eds.) PoEM 2012. LNBIP, vol. 134, pp. 148–159. Springer, Heidelberg (2012)

6. Bubenko Jr, J.A., Persson, A., Stirna, J.: An Intentional Perspective on Enterprise Modeling. In: Salinesi, C., Nurcan, S., Souveyet, C., Ralyté, J. (eds.) An Intentional Perspective on Enterprise Modeling, pp. 978–973. Springer (2010) ISBN 978-3-642-12543-0

7. Lillehagen, F., Krogstie, J.: Active knowledge modeling of enterprises, Springer, Heidelberg (2008)

8. Josey, A.: The Open Group. In: Haren, V. (ed.) ArchiMate 2.0—A Pocket Guide (2012) ISBN 978-9087536961

9. Scheer, A.-W., Nuttgens, M.: ARIS architecture and reference models for business process management. Springer, Heidelberg (2000)

10. Frank, U.: Multi-perspective enterprise modeling: foundational concepts, prospects and future research challenges, software and systems modeling. Software & Systems Modelling 13(3), 941–962 (2013), http://link.springer.com/article/10.1007/s10270-012-0273-9

11. Persson, A., Stirna, J.: Towards Defining a Competence Profile for the Enterprise Modeling Practitioner. In: van Bommel, P., Hoppenbrouwers, S., Overbeek, S., Proper, E., Barjis, J. (eds.) PoEM 2010. LNBIP, vol. 68, Springer, Heidelberg (2010)

12. Stirna, J., Persson, A.: Purpose Driven Competency Planning for Enterprise Modeling Projects. In: Ralyté, J., Franch, X., Brinkkemper, S., Wrycza, S. (eds.) CAiSE 2012. LNCS, vol. 7328, pp. 662–677. Springer, Heidelberg (2012)

13. Backlund, P., Hallenborg, C., Hallgrimsson, G.: Transfer of Development Process Knowledge Through Method Adaption and Implementation. In: ECIS 2003 Proceedings, Paper 19 (2003), http://aisel.aisnet.org/ecis2003/19

Requirements Engineering
for Capability Driven Development

Jelena Zdravkovic[1], Janis Stirna[1], Jan-Christian Kuhr[2], and Hasan Koç[3]

[1] Department of Computer and Systems Sciences, Stockholm University, Forum 100,
SE-16440, Kista, Sweden
`jelenaz@dsv.su.se,js@dsv.su.se`
[2] SIV Software-Architektur & -Technologie GmbH, DE-18184 Roggentin, Germany
`jan-christian.kuhr@siv.de`
[3] University of Rostock, Institute of Computer Science
Albert-Einstein-Straße 22, 18059 Rostock, Germany
`hasan.koc@uni-rostock.de`

Abstract. Lately, the notion of capability has emerged in IS engineering as an instrument to context dependent design and delivery of business services. Representing core business functionalities of an organization, capabilities, and capability driven IS development can be seen as both – a shift beyond and complement to the widely established service-oriented engineering paradigm where needs of customers form the leading modeling and design perspective. To ensure the needs of business stakeholders for variety of business contexts that an organization faces, and thus facilitate successful systems delivery, capability-driven development needs a well-defined method for requirements engineering, as well as its confirmation in practices. In this paper a process for specifying requirements capabilities and their designs is proposed. An application of the proposed approach to the area of business process outsourcing (BPO) services is carried out for the German company SIV.

Keywords: Requirements Engineering, Requirements Engineering Process, Enterprise Modeling, Capability Modeling.

1   Introduction

Organizations are facing the need to adapt their business services according to various situations in which their applications need to be used. To this end an ongoing EU FP7 project "Capability as a Service in digital enterprises" (CaaS) has been conceived [1]. The ethos of the project is support of the capture and analysis of changing business context in design of information systems (IS) using the capability notion.

Capability as a concept originates from competence-based management and military frameworks, offering a complement to traditional Enterprise Modeling (EM) approaches by representing organizational knowledge from a result-based perspective.

In the specification and design of services using business planning as the baseline, capability is seen as a fundamental abstraction to describe what a core business does

U. Frank et al. (Eds.): PoEM 2014, LNBIP 197, pp. 193–207, 2014.
© IFIP International Federation for Information Processing 2014

[2] and, in particular, *as an ability and capacity for a company to deliver value, either to customers or shareholders, right beneath the business strategy* [3,4].

The key rationale behind the CaaS initiative of developing a capability driven approach to development is to make IS designs more accessible to business stakeholders by enabling them to use the capability notion to describe their business needs more efficiently. The prevailing Model Driven Development (MDD) paradigm for IS development mostly relies on the models defined on a relatively low abstraction level. In contrast, EM captures organizational knowledge and provides the necessary motivation and input for designing IS. Our intention is to enable a holistic approach to model-oriented IS development starting from EM supporting both – the business and technological perspective.

As we have envisioned it in [5] and [6], Capability Driven Development (CDD) requires a number of concepts to be specified, such as business goals, processes, resources, Key Performance Indicators (KPIs), as well the parameters describing business contexts for different capabilities. It is therefore important to define Requirements Engineering (RE) for capability, to ensure a proper specification of the models in consideration and thus facilitate successful development of IS that are able to run and switch between changing operating contexts.

The objective of this paper is to analyze relevant theories and best practices in RE Process and to propose an approach to elicit, analyze, specify and manage the requirements for capabilities and their patterns within the life-cycle of an entire development methodology. A requirement in this context refers to a documented business functional need that the subsequent capability design must be able to support through executable processes and services.

To ensure a cross-industry applicability of the CDD, we have followed action research methodology, by introducing requirements engineering process for capability modeling in company SIV.AG [7] – an independent software vendor in the utility industry.

The rest of the paper is organized as follows. Section 2 briefly describes the theory of the RE process, as well as the Capability Meta-model and the current version of Capability Development Life Cycle. Section 3 defines the RE process for capability and capability patters, which is illustrated in section 4 with a case of the company SIV. Section 5 presents a brief discussion, conclusions and future work.

2   Theoretical Foundations and Related Work

In this section brief overviews of the topics and the results related to the research of this paper are presented.

2.1   Requirements and RE Process

In the business analysis community, a requirement is seen as a condition describing the current or a future state of any aspect of an enterprise. A basic objective is to ensure that requirements are visible to and understood by all stakeholders [8]. As IS have become the norm for supporting functionalities of enterprises, many of initial business requirements once refined to lower level of details become system-related, and eventually end-up as software solutions.

From a development life-cycle perspective, RE is considered critical to avoid wrong, incomplete, or ambiguous requirements which will be as such delivered to a next development phase. Hence, it is a common practice to use a process to steer successful management of requirements. Although the activities of the RE process in literature differ from practice, the following are widely accepted as the major [9, 10]:

- *Requirements Elicitation*: in this activity where stakeholders and their requirements are identified using different elicitation techniques (e.g., interviews, focus groups, documentation, etc.).
- *Requirements Analysis*: the elicited requirements are analyzed individually for feasibility, conflicts, ambiguity, redundancy, priority, etc., and they are negotiated with stakeholders for acceptance.
- *Requirements Validation*: the activity concerns checking that the documented requirements specification is understandable, consistent, complete, and meets stakeholder needs.
- *Requirements Management*: this activity is performed to record and track changes to requirements at any time of development.
- *Requirements Documentation*: it is a supportive activity of elicitation, analysis, validation and management, where each requirement is modeled and represented in the way that is understood by relevant stakeholders.

In complex IS development the above activities of the RE process may interweave, and they are performed incrementally and iteratively, i.e. during each iteration more details are elaborated [10].

The traditional way of RE process, where each of the outlined activities have been often performed sequentially and documented in details, has been challenged by the needs of rapidly changing business environments. Consequently, agile methods for system development have emerged [11]. They have set a focus on working software over comprehensive documentation, interactions over processes, responsiveness to change, etc. The methods hence include practices such as short iterations, frequent releases, simple design, minimal documentation in the form of user stories or meeting minutes, implementing requirements as new evolve or existing change, and test cases [12]. In contrast to a few well-established methodologies for agile software development such as XP and Scrum, effective and agile ways for RE are less conclusive than traditional, in terms of theories and practices [13]

2.2   Capability Driven Development

The capability meta-model (CMM) presented in Figure 1 is developed on the basis of industrial requirements and related research on capabilities. It provides the theoretical and methodological foundation for the CDD [5, 6]. The meta-model has three main sections: a) *Enterprise modeling* representing the organizational designs with the *Goals, KPIs, Processes* (with concretizations as *Process Variants*) and *Resources*.

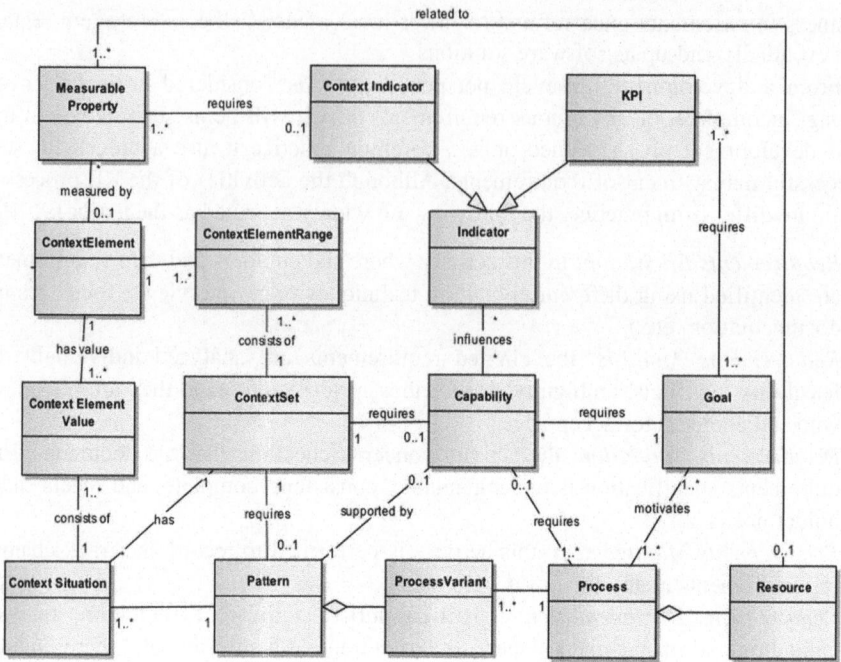

Fig. 1. A Meta-model supporting Capability Driven Development

b) *Context modeling* represented with *Situational Context* instantiating a set of elements under which the solutions should be applied including *Context Indicators* for measuring the context properties (*Measuring Property*); and c) *Patterns* for delivering *Capability* by reusable solutions for reaching business goals under different situational contexts. The context defined for the capability should match the context in which the pattern is applicable. The presented meta-model is a foundation for developing capability-oriented software applications driven by *capability development life cycle process* (Figure 2).

The process starts with EM for capturing business change and required capability, for instance, in order to re-configure existing or to create new goals and business processes to, combined with captured business contexts, elicit required capabilities and patterns. This is followed by development and deployment of the capability delivery application requiring composition and integration of the technologies supporting defined models. During the execution of the application the changes of context are monitored, and run-time adjustments algorithms are used to calculate if the changes are become such to require another capability pattern. Monitoring of defined KPIs facilitate capability refinement and pattern updating.

In the next section we will elaborate the beginning part of the CDD life cycle utilizing the principles of RE to elaborate how required capabilities and corresponding patterns can be elicited, represented, and managed with incoming business changes.

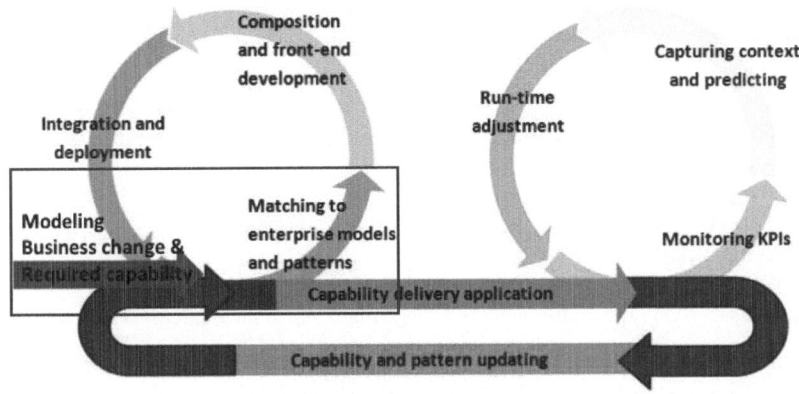

Fig. 2. Capability Driven Development, the life cycle process

3   A Capability-Oriented Requirements Engineering Process

In our view, capability-oriented RE should be facilitated through an efficient process for discovering and defining capabilities of an enterprise acting in varying business contexts. Following the traditional as well as recent views on the RE process and the presented aim for development of capability driven applications, we have elicited a number of objectives for the RE process and the means to achieve them (Table 1). The rest of this section will present in detail our views on the activities of an RE process for capability specification.

Table 1. The main objectives of the RE process for capability specification

Objective	Means
Support specification of concept-wide requirements inherited from EM, and of varying business situations; facilitate specification of patterns of capability delivery that are meant to be sufficiently general and reusable in long-term.	Apply the principles and the activities of the RE process to systematically collect and manage the requirements.
Integrate EM and MDD to overcome inconsistencies between the final software application and the requirements for capability.	Use a model-oriented approach and an integrated tool platform for documenting the requirements as well as for application development.
Facilitate rapid application development and efficient support for requirements change.	Apply incremental and iterative RE, as well as agile practices.

3.1   Elicitation

The objective of the elicitation phase is to iteratively draft requirements for new capabilities according to the CMM. The tasks are (1) identify relevant stakeholders and (2) to elicit capabilities by identifying the sub-models from the CMM.

Stakeholders' identification: the knowledge to be elicited according to the Capability Meta-Model involves several types of included sub-models and a number of concepts: Enterprise Models with a focus to Goal- and Business Process- Models with Process Variants and Resources; Context Models for specifying potential context situations of the capability; and Patterns for specifying reusable capability elements. Table 2 shows relevant stakeholder roles that have been identified.

Table 2. Stakeholder roles in RE for capability

Stakeholder	Responsibility
Business analyst	Identify new, or change/improve existing enterprise sub-models, i.e. goals, processes, resources, and KPIs.
Context analyst	Identify the context-sub model.
Requirements engineer	Has the knowledge of CDD
Customer	Has benefits of delivered capabilities
Capability user	Is directly involved in the interactions of a delivered capability

Any of the roles in Table 2 will be further refined in the beginning of the elicitation process to: a) "localize" the roles for a concrete business model – e.g., in a model where goods from a seller are delivered to a customer by an intermediary delivery company, when eliciting goals of the business, both the Business Analyst of the seller and the deliverer may be considered for this stakeholder role; b) "instantiate" the roles – the roles are to be specified for concrete people, and/or organizations.

Capability elicitation: three strategies are proposed to cover different starting perspectives in capability elicitation – *goal-first, service-first, and context-first.*

Goal-first elicitation strategy is used when the organization has decided to fulfill the goals following an overall business strategy, and/or where the organization's enterprise model is elaborated, including actors, business concepts and rules, goals, processes, etc.. The starting focus is to consider existing business goals, and if needed, defining new goals. The iteration tasks are the following:

— A goal-pathway is elicited from a top goal and completed to leaf goals.
— KPIs are defined for the goals, and mandatory for the leaf goals.
— For each leaf goal, zero or more capabilities are identified (for example the goal "To optimize case throughput" identifies the capability "Dynamic business service provider support", see section 4.1). If for a goal it is concluded that there is no a feasible capability, then it is left for a future consideration.

Each identified capability is further elicited in a separate iteration to:

— Identify the process variant models enacting the capability
— Identify all relevant context elements from the context sub-model of CMM, and relate them to the variation points of the processes.

After an elicitation iteration is completed, a next one is initiated with a focus to another possible goal pathway; the process is continued until the goal model is fully analyzed. The stakeholders from Table 2 are engaged according to their responsibilities in the form of focus groups, for each of the tasks. Business Analyst is the key stakeholder role in this strategy.

Service-first elicitation strategy is used when the customer needs are of the highest importance. Capabilities are therefore identified to support these needs, which are often articulated as top business services. The iteration tasks are the following:

— A desired customer need (i.e. business service), supported by a number of organization's business processes is described as a new capability. For example, the members of a municipality may request "marriage registration e-service", which in turn will lead to the elicitation of a candidate capability "marriage registration" further specified by the tasks below.
— The goals of the capability are elicited, where at least one goal must be elicited with a corresponding KPI.
— The process variant models enacting the capability are identified and improved.
— Identify all context elements from the context sub-model of CMM, and relate them to the variation points of the processes.

After an elicitation iteration as above is completed, a next one is initiated with a focus to another customer need/service; the process is continued until all possible services are exhausted. Customer is the key stakeholder role in this strategy.

Context-first elicitation strategy is chosen when the coverage of wide range of the business contexts of the organization is the most important. E.g. the first main outcome: one or more defined capabilities. The iteration tasks are the following:

Initially observed contexts are analyzed and refined to as many as possible context sets. These are then matched with goals to elicit a new capability, and needed processes are (re)designed accordingly. E.g. if a company offers its services in several countries the local legislations (how heavily regulated it is) are relevant contexts.

— A context set is identified and mapped to a new capability. E.g. in the area of business process outsourcing one might consider two capabilities – one for heavily regulated business environments, and one for more loosely regulated.
— The goals of the capability are elicited, where at least one goal must be elicited with a corresponding KPI.
— The process variant models enacting the capability are identified and improved, variation points are set to match the identified context sets.

After an elicitation iteration as above is completed, a next one is initiated with a focus to another context set; the process is continued until all possible business contexts are exhausted. Context Analyst is the key stakeholder role in this strategy.

The overall way of working according to these elicitation strategies is envisioned to be incremental and iterative. In this sense the capability modeling follows the principle of multi-perspective EM approaches where different modeling perspectives, such as goals, processes, and concepts are modeled in dedicated sub-models. The sub-models are not elicited sequentially, i.e. starting with one sub-model, completing it, moving on to the next one, and so on. Modeling in this way would lead to sub-models that are poorly integrated, inconsistent, and some their parts end up as not addressing the actual goal of the project because the focus of the modelers may shift unintentionally. At some point, to rectify this problem, the modelers would need to "stitch" the model together by identifying gaps and introducing inter-model links.

To avoid this from happening goal, context, and process sub-models of CMM are elicited iteratively and incrementally (and hence analyzed and documented similarly), by switching the focus of modeling among different sub-models. I.e. a CMM model is specified reasonably "in balance" – as proposed in the 3 strategies above, i.e. an iteration is driven to elicit a single capability with corresponding sub-models' parts.

3.2   Analysis

The objective of the requirements analysis is to assess if the elicited capabilities are correct following the criteria outlined in section 2.1. Table 3 shows the criteria for the context in discussion.

Table 3. Main analysis criteria for capability specification

Parameter	Action
Necessity	Is the elicited capability needed in respect to the given goals? The CMM mandates at least one goal for a capability, ensuring a motivation to exist. Another assessments relate to the existence of at least one business context in which the capability will bring a value to the customer, or at least one requested business service that would be supported by the capability.
Feasibility	An elicited capability is through a feasibility study checked by stakeholders to ensure that it can be developed in the context of economic, time, technical and other constraints set for the development project.
Redundancy	When a new capability is about to be elicited, stakeholders need to get the knowledge on the existing capabilities; the supporting mechanism is the single development environment containing the models of existing capabilities, and the repository of all the capability patterns with descriptions.
Consistency	An elicited capability should not be contradictory, ambiguous or in a conflict with other existing capability. The first two criteria can be assessed by examining the consistency of the CMM sub-models of the capability, and their completeness. Possible conflicts need to be examined on different levels – e.g. if they exist in the goal model of the capability, or in the process resources, or if any of the context elements are in conflict.

The accepted capabilities from the analysis can also be negotiated among stakeholders in order to prioritize them, which is a common practice in RE [10]. From an agile perspective, both the analysis and prioritization of capabilities can be done during elicitation – the single and integrated development platform (Table 1) enables these activities to be done concurrently, and especially when the relevant stakeholders are able to continuously or frequently collaborate (Table 2).

For each capability that is successfully analyzed, a candidate capability pattern is assigned (see Figure 1) either by selecting it from a pattern repository or by developing a new pattern from the existing business solutions (e.g. process variants). Patterns require dedicated activities for elicitation, analysis, documentation, validation and management shown by the bottom loop in Figure 2, which we consider outside the scope of this paper.

3.3   Documentation

The intention of CDD is to facilitate a holistic and integrated approach to model-oriented IS development starting from enterprise modeling. Therefore,

- Documentation should be done in a tool environment using modeling languages,
- Natural-language annotations are used for descriptions of models, elements, etc.
- Development environment is open to the use of any modeling language for specifying requirements for goals, processes, context, and patterns.
- Intra- and inter-model links can be defined for traceability purposes.
- Documented requirements can be searched, or navigated.

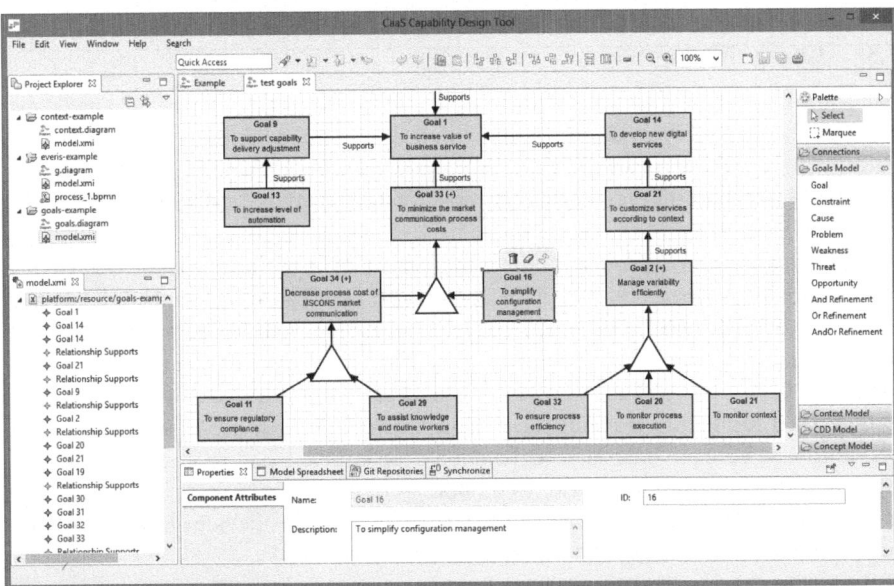

Fig. 3. Documenting Capability according to CMM; goal modeling (center pane), the language (right pane), descriptions (bottom pane), navigation (left pane), and search (top pane)

Requirements documented in the tool are further transformed to development artifacts by augmenting the descriptions of the models with technology-related data – for example, business process can be modeled with BPMN2 where the modeling details can be added in any of the development phases.

3.4   Validation

In contrast to analysis where the assessment is set to the correctness of individual capabilities, the objective of the validation in the traditional view is to examine the quality of the requirements specification *as a whole*, where the major criteria are outlined in section 2.1; considering them, as well as the advices from agile practices for using iterative-type of actions we propose the validation of a capability as following:

— Use review meetings for validation after each or every few iterations, and involve developers in addition to the main RE stakeholders (Table 2). During the meeting, the specified capabilities are demonstrated from the tool, and Q&A on their quality and usefulness are used to obtain feedback and to emphasize problems early. In addition, the demonstration has the objective to increase customer trust and confidence to the current results.

— Use expert reviewing to assess the quality of the current models in terms of, e.g. understandability, completeness, and consistence, as well as the links for traceability among them. The reviewing is organized as a session in conjunction with the main meeting, and where the models are given to individual experts (Table 2) for assessment and proposals for improvements for next iterations.

3.5   Change Management

In contrast to traditional way of managing changes in requirements, where formal requests for change are submitted and a well-documented analysis of the change is performed by specially assigned roles, agile practices recommend to consider changes in requirements simply as new requirements which will be according to priorities elaborated in one of the regular iterations.

Following the agile approach, the management of a business change depicted in Figure 2) is considered as it occurs. Depending on the cause of the change (such as inference of a new context element), the key stakeholder will be the main responsible to assess the importance and priority for the change; thereafter changes in the sub-models of CMM will be elicited, where the traceability of intra- and inter- model links will be used to identify the influenced models and concepts. For example, if for the previously mentioned "marriage registration" capability, a new context element "period" is added because of a heavier load during springs than in winters, consequently a process model within the capability has to change to include needed variation points, as well as needed variants of execution.

4   An Application Case at SIV

The CaaS partner SIV is a Germany-based independent software vendor (ISV) and a business process outsourcing (BPO) provider for the utilities industry. SIV has developed a domain-specific ERP platform kVASy® that supports all relevant value-added processes of market players. All BPO services offered to SIV's customers – mostly grid access providers and balance suppliers – are based on the functionalities of kVASy®. SIV's business goal is to deliver a maximum of business value to its customers by to combining best practice business processes with compliance to the market's ever changing business rules and regulatory requirements.

4.1   Requirements Engineering for Capabilities in SIV

In SIV's approach, key capabilities are elicited following the principle of the *Goals first* strategy, i.e. the RE process starts by defining goals for offering BPO services

(Figure 4). The reason for choosing this approach lies in the fact that over the years the company's role in the market has arrived at a mature stage, where the ERP platform kVASy® is well established in the industry. Therefore, the challenge of keeping existing and acquiring new customers in a highly competitive utility market is a top priority. Performing an enterprise-level analysis with a clear focus on business goals, and linking them to appropriate BPO capabilities is a way to deliver business value to kVASy® users, thereby sustainably strengthening SIV's market position.

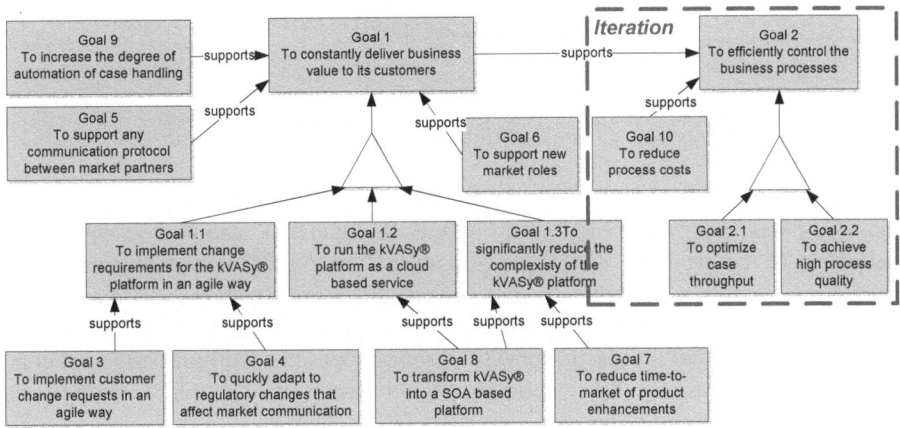

Fig. 4. The goal model of SIV

The goals of the industrial use case are modeled using the 4EM approach. Due to the relationship between SIV and its customers, a distinction was made between customer goals and SIV goals, i.e. customer goals are more *operational* whereas SIV follows *strategic* business goals, since SIV has no operative business. For SIV's customers, however it is of prime importance running their business processes as efficiently as possible, thus keeping process costs low. Therefore, these organizations are predominantly driven by operative factors such as workload, backlog, and the availability of human resources. By contrast, SIV is more oriented to strategic goals, such as to constantly meet the customer's requirements and to exploit opportunities of the market. Thus, there are two aspects in the overall goal model that are distinct, yet not separable. In this respect, the main goal of SIV is *to deliver constant business value to its customers,* thereby supporting the customer's goal *to efficiently control business processes.* Also, goals can be refined into sub-goals, forming a hierarchically organized goal model. To efficiently control business processes, customers aim to *optimize case throughput and to achieve a high process quality.* Both can be considered as subordinate goals in the use case.

Elicitation: Following the guidelines of the *Goal-first* approach, the objective for business analysts of the utility companies and of SIV was to iteratively analyze the goals to identify capabilities. In an iteration, a single goal-pathway is elicited, such as for example Goal 2 supported by Goal 1, further requiring the achievement of Goal 2.1 and Goal 2.2. According to the CaaS approach, achievement of business goals requires specific capabilities. In the following we exemplify the linkage of capabilities to goals, using Goal 2.1 *"To optimize case throughput"*. Enabling customers to optimize their case throughput, requires SIV to deliver capabilities to route their processes in accordance with the workload. For the industrial case at hand, *"Dynamic business service provider (BSP) support"* is identified as a key capability that supports this goal. This connection is illustrated in Figure 5.

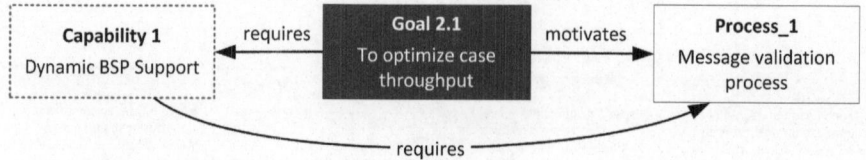

Fig. 5. Specification of a capability from a goal, supported by a process

The capability comprises the business process triggered when partner A sends a message about energy consumption to partner B (Figure 6). The process involves a validation of the message, and a processing step. The purpose of validation is to ascertain the message is syntactically and semantically correct with respect to an underlying informal data model. Upon validating the message, exceptions can occur, triggering in turn another process to remedy this exception. If a faulty message could be remedied, the processing step may be successfully re-executed. If this is not the case, then the process has to be aborted.

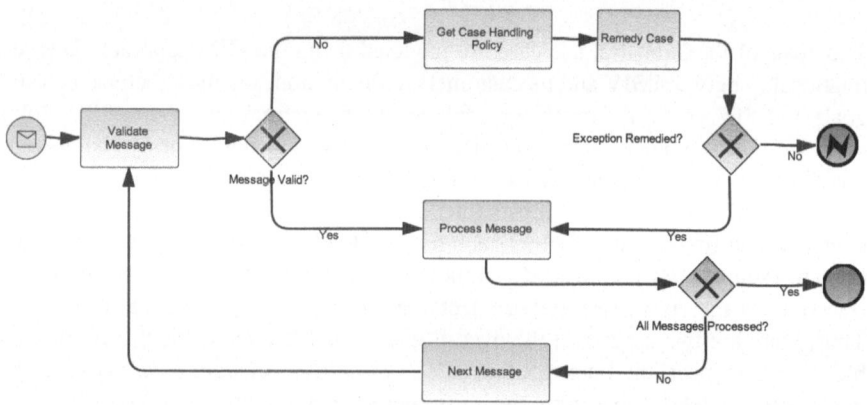

Fig. 6. "Message Validation" business process

To implement the *"Dynamic BSP support"* capability, which is required by the "To *optimize case throughput"* goal of the customer, SIV must offer instruments enabling customers to automatically route individual process instances to an external business service provider in order to achieve the desired case throughput. Since such routing decisions depend on many operational factors such as the customer's workload, the current backlog size and exception type, he associated capability requires evaluation of complex situations, which are represented by context models. Depending on the concrete context situation, the task "Remedy case" can be dynamically routed to the external business service provider (BSP), or left with the customer. This accordingly leads to the elicitation of two process variants: either the customer handles the faulty case on his own, or the case is treated by the BSP's highly trained experts (Figure 7).

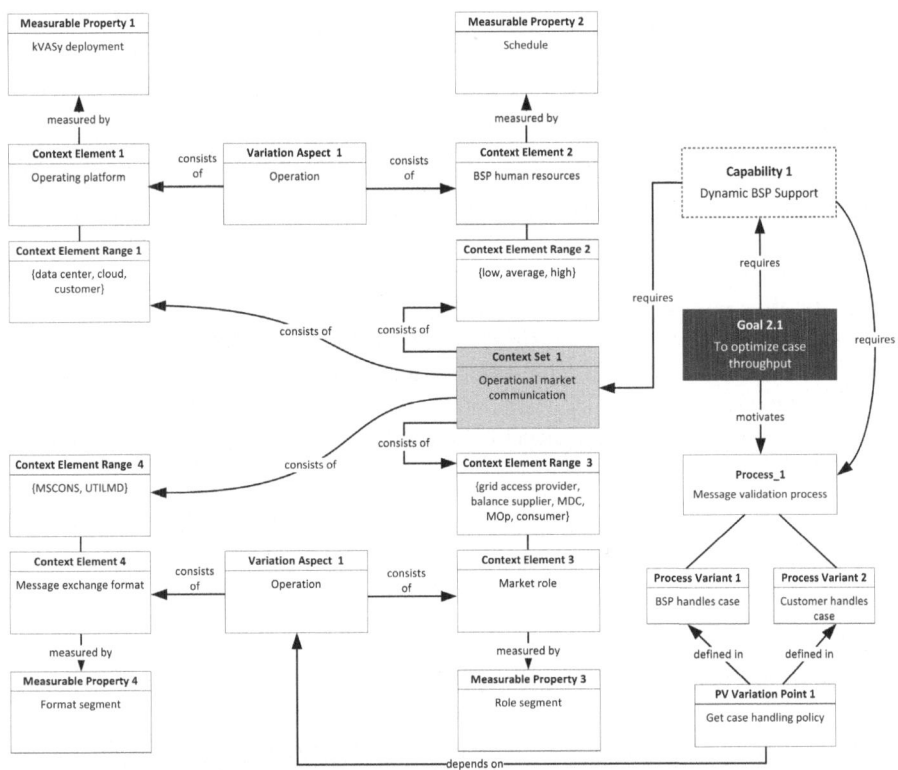

Fig. 7. Context model for the *Dynamic BSP Support* capability

As a result, the process variation point is located in *"Get case handling policy"* process. The decision which variant must be executed depends on the business context. Acquisition of such situation during runtime has to take place for each individual case to feed the decision logic component with sufficient input data to enable a correct routing scenario for the case in question. Three main business drivers are identified, which cause variations and thus provide stimulus for changes. The first business driver is the contractual aspect, which specifies parameters such as backlog threshold as well as the process variant to be implemented regarding the backlog size, such as "if the backlog size exceeds the agreed threshold, then the case is routed to customer". The second business driver, payload aspect, includes information of the service call such as the market role, the faulty message and the exception type etc. The last driver, the operational aspect, is related to both SIV Services personnel deployment plan and the kVASy-operating environment. These are captured as variation aspects, which are further elaborated to identify context elements. A capability offered by an enterprise requires an application context and this is captured as a context set. "Operational market" communication context set is required by the capability and comprises of the possible ranges of four context elements such as operating platform, BSP human resources, market role and message exchange format.

With the completion of context elicitation, the capability becomes specified. As illustrated in Figure 5 and motivated above, the elicited capability is needed in respect to the business goals. Delivering such capability is context-dependent, i.e. dynamic BSP support capability brings value to the customer in a specific situation that is captured with Operational market communication context set.

Analysis. Although we have not conducted a feasibility study, the stakeholders perceived the development of such capability in given project conditions in a positive manner and collaborated actively on the development activities both in workshops and in distributed project teams. It is still early to make statements about the consistency of the capability models since at the time being we have developed only one capability. We are expecting in the future more observations on this.

Documentation has been successfully done in the integrated modeling environment (section 3), with the outcomes represented in the figures above. The tool uses natural language annotations for model descriptions and allows for linking different parts of the enterprise models such as connecting a business process model to a goal and to a capability. It was also possible to apply a notation to represent the context model, which have been created and developed following the principles of Moody [14].

Validation has been performed in an extended expert group, in the form of reviews as explained in section 3. Change management has not yet been practiced, because there was not any business change occurring during the period of requirements' specification.

5   Conclusions and Future Work

We have proposed an approach for Requirements Engineering for Capability Driven Development, which specifies the notion of capability and related concepts and integrates organizational analysis with IS development taking into account changes in the organization's business context.

The main objective of the process is to facilitate the specification for capability requirements in an integrated way following the multi-perspective views defined in the CMM to enable efficient application development. Therefore the proposed process consists of guidelines for systematic management of requirements combined with agile principles of working and model based documentation of requirements. The requirements are proposed to be elicited starting either from business goals, services, or from relevant business contexts. In any of the three strategies, both the functionality and the quality aspects of capability are captured, where the first are dictated by the CM, and latter by the setting of the goals and KPIs.

The proposed process and its guidelines were tested in a real case concerning business process outsourcing (BPO) services carried out within the company SIV. The results have confirmed the functionality of the process, where both its systematic and agile aspects have been practiced. The model-based documentation of requirements for capabilities using the presented tool has been widely accepted by the stakeholders. Efficiency in communication, rapid specification and analysis, and effective validation principles, were the key aspects to accept the process, even over traditional, text-oriented and more sequential way of doing RE

For the future work, we plan to define a process for managing the requirements for capability patterns. A composite structure of the patterns requires specific guidelines and a language for their specification, storing, search, combining, etc. Another challenge to address concerns the elicitation of capabilities in the situations where a supporting base of software services has been previously developed, and capability requirements need therefore to consider these services as existing "IT capabilities".

References

1. EU FP7 CaaS Project. Capability as a service for digital enterprises., `http://caas-project.eu/`
2. Ulrich, W., Rosen, M.: The business capability map: Building a foundation for business/it alignment. Cutter Consortium for Business and Enterprise Architecture (2012)
3. OPENGROUP TOGAF - enterprise architecture methodology, version 9.1 (2012), `http://www.opengroup.org/togaf/`
4. OPENGROUP Archimate - modelling language for enterprise architecture, v2.0 (2012), `https://www2.opengroup.org/ogsys/catalog/c118`
5. Stirna, J., Grabis, J., Henkel, M., Zdravkovic, J.: Capability Driven Development – An Approach to Support Evolving Organizations. In: Sandkuhl, K., Seigerroth, U., Stirna, J. (eds.) PoEM 2012. LNBIP, vol. 134, pp. 117–131. Springer, Heidelberg (2012)
6. Zdravkovic, J., Stirna, J., Henkel, M., Grabis, J.: Modeling Business Capabilities and Context Dependent Delivery by Cloud Services. In: Salinesi, C., Norrie, M.C., Pastor, Ó. (eds.) CAiSE 2013. LNCS, vol. 7908, pp. 369–383. Springer, Heidelberg (2013)
7. SIV. AG `http://www.siv.de/` (last accessed July 16, 2014)
8. International Institute of Business Analysis (IBA). A Guide to the Business Analysis Body of Knowledge® (BABOK® Guide) Version 2.0 (2009), `http://www.theiiba.org`
9. Dorfman, M., Thayer, R.H.: Software Requirements Engineering. IEEE Computer Society Press, Los Alamitos (1997)
10. Kotonya, G., Sommerville, I.: Requirements Engineering: Process and Techniques. John Wiley and Sons, New York (2002)
11. Fowler, M., Highsmith, J.: The agile manifesto. Software Development 9(8), 28–35 (2001)
12. Ramesh, B., Cao, L., Baskerville, R.: Agile requirements engineering practices and challenges: an empirical study. Information Systems Journal 20(5), 449–480 (2007)
13. Leffingwell, D.: Agile software requirements: Lean Requirements Practices for Teams, Programs, and Enterprise. Addison-Wesley (2011) ISBN-10: 0321635841
14. Moody, D.L.: The "Physics" of Notations: Toward a Scientific Basis for Constructing Visual Notations in Software Engineering. IEEE Transactions on Software Engineering 35(6), 756–779 (2009)

Integrating Security Patterns with Security Requirements Analysis Using Contextual Goal Models

Tong Li, Jennifer Horkoff, and John Mylopoulos

University of Trento, Trento, Italy
{tong.li,horkoff,jm}@disi.unitn.it

Abstract. Security patterns capture proven security knowledge to help analysts tackle security problems. Although advanced research in this field has produced an impressive collection of patterns, they are not widely applied in practice. In parallel, Requirements Engineering has been increasing focusing on security-specific issues, arguing for an upfront treatment of security in system design. However, the vast body of security patterns are not integrated with existing proposals for security requirements analysis, making them difficult to apply as part of early system analysis and design. In this paper, we propose to integrate security patterns with our previously introduced goal-oriented security requirements analysis approach. Specifically, we provide a full concept mapping between textual security patterns and contextual goal models, as well as systematic instructions for constructing contextual goal models from security patterns. Moreover, we propose a systematic process for selecting and applying security patterns, illustrated with a realistic smart grid scenario. To facilitate the practical adoption of security patterns, we have created contextual goal models for 20 security patterns documented in the literature, and have implemented a prototype tool to support our proposal.

Keywords: Security Patterns, Security Requirements Analysis, Contextual Goal Model.

1 Introduction

Dealing with security concerns for complex software systems is a laborious and knowledge-intensive process. Security patterns encapsulate reusable security knowledge that can support analysts with little security knowledge. Much work has been done to collect and document such patterns, resulting in several security pattern repositories, such as [1,2,3]. However, such security patterns have not been integrated with existing security requirements analysis techniques, making them difficult to apply as part of early system analysis and design. Analysis using security patterns mainly focuses on "how" to tackle a particular security problem, but does not address "why" a security problem needs to be treated. Effective application of security patterns requires a systematic analysis method, which is currently lacking among existing proposals.

U. Frank et al. (Eds.): PoEM 2014, LNBIP 197, pp. 208–223, 2014.

Requirements Engineering (RE) has been increasingly focusing on security-specific issues, arguing for an upfront treatment of security in software system design. Goal-oriented modeling techniques constitute an effective way to capture and analyze stakeholder intentions. Proposals such as Secure Tropos [4], Secure-i* [5], and STS analysis [6], have been used by multiple authors to analyze security requirements. In this paper, we argue that integrating goal-oriented requirements analysis with security pattern analysis can benefit both types of analysis. Goal models capture the rationale for applying security patterns and facilitate selection among alternatives, while the application of security patterns can efficiently operationalize security requirements into specific security solutions.

Our previous work deals with security requirements for socio-technical systems using a three-layered approach [7]. Our proposed framework does make use of security patterns to assist goal-based security requirements analysis. However, several challenges were revealed during that work, hindering the integration of security patterns and security requirements analysis. Firstly, there is normally more than one security pattern candidate that can potentially treat one security requirement, and analysts have to manually choose the best pattern to apply, a highly non-trivial task. Moreover, the complexity of security pattern selection grows with the number of security requirements. Secondly, creating security patterns in terms of goal models is non-trivial and time-consuming, requiring the analyst to have a full understanding of a security pattern she is about to use. Preliminary steps towards tackling these challenges have been described in a short workshop paper, which proposes to model security patterns as contextual goal models by introducing an initial concept mapping between them [8]. However, the concept mapping was incomplete, as only six security patterns had been analyzed by that time. Also, this work lacks a detailed methodology for selecting and applying security patterns.

In this paper, we significantly improve our previous work [8] in order to seamlessly integrate security patterns with our three-layer security requirements analysis approach [7]. In particular, this paper makes the following contributions:

1. Offers a complete concept mapping between the constituent concepts of security patterns and contextual goal models, as well as a detailed process for constructing contextual goal models from security patterns.
2. Proposes a systematic process for selecting the most appropriate security pattern and applying it to security goal models. The process is illustrated with a realistic smart grid scenario.
3. Sketches a prototype tool, which helps to build contextual goal models and interactively check context. We have built contextual goal models for 20 security patterns adapted from [3] by using this tool.

In the reminder of this paper, we first describe our research baseline on security patterns, contextual goal models, and our previous work in Section 2. In Section 3 we present a smart grid scenario used throughout the paper to illustrate our proposal, while in Section 4 we describe how to transform textual security patterns into contextual goal models. In Section 5, we present a systematic process to select and apply security patterns. We briefly introduce the prototype tool in Section 6, and then describe related work in Section 7. Finally, conclusions and future work are presented in Section 8.

2   Background

2.1   Security Patterns

Security patterns capture proven security solutions to known security problems. Much work has gone towards identifying security patterns [9,10], while other work focuses on summarizing catalogues of security patterns [11,2,3]. In total, there are more than 100 security patterns.

In this work, we adopt the security patterns presented in [3], which provides detailed specifications of 68 security patterns. In particular, security patterns in [3] are documented in the POSA (Pattern-Oriented Software Architecture) template [12] with predefined sections. Among these sections, there are four essential sections as highlighted in [12]: *Context, Problem, Force,* and *Solution.* Table. 1 shows the *Intrusion Detection System (IDS)* pattern [3], which contains all four essential sections, as well as the *Consequence* section, which is also analyzed in our approach. In addition to this book, we also took into account several security patterns presented in [2] to cover more security aspects.

2.2   A Goal-Based Contextual Requirements Framework

Stakeholder requirements may vary from context to context. Ali et al. [13] and Lapouchnian et al. [14] argue that requirements should be analyzed in a way that reflects context settings. They propose goal-based frameworks for contextual requirements modeling and analysis, in which they relate goals and contexts.

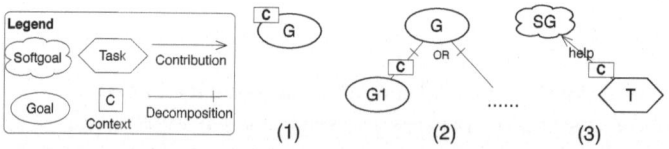

Fig. 1. Goal models with contexts

We use here the proposal by Ali et al. [13], which extends Tropos [15] with context-related concepts. In particular, contexts are treated as labels that can be attached to specific goal model elements, such as what is shown in Fig. 1. Moreover, they define semantics for contexts that are modeled within goal models. For example, in the first case of Fig. 1, goal G represents a requirement if and only if context C applies. In the other two parts of the figure, a link between two goals is part of the goal model only when context C applies. We follow their method to model contexts, but also extend it to suit our purposes.

Table 1. The specification of the Intrusion Detection System pattern [3]

Context:
Nodes for local systems that need to communicate with each other using the Internet.
Problem:
An attacker may try to infiltrate our system through the Internet. We need to know when an attack is happening and take appropriate response.
Force:
• *Incomplete security*. Security measures such as encryption, authentication and so on may not protect all our systems, because they do not cover all possible attacks. • *Non-suspicious users*. Request coming from a non-suspicious address (permitted by a firewall) could still be harmful and should be monitored further. • *Flexibility*. Hard-coding the type of attack can be done easily. But it will be hard and time-consuming to adapt to attack patterns that change constantly.
Solution:
Each request to access the network is analyzed to check whether it conforms to the definition of an attack. If we detect an attack, an alert is raised and some counter-measures may be taken.
Consequence:
• *Non-suspicious users*. A request coming from a non-suspicious address (permitted by a firewall) is further inspected and analyzed. • *Flexibility*. The detection information can be modified to include new attacks. • There is some overhead in the addition of IDSs to a system.

2.3 A Three-Layer Security Requirements Analysis Framework

Our previous work proposed a three-layer security requirements analysis framework that aims to address security issues at the business layer, software application layer, and physical infrastructure layer [7]. Our framework is designed to support analysis of both security issues within one layer and influences across layers, offering a holistic approach to security analysis.

We use the concept *Security Goal* to represent security requirements. A security goal is specified in a template, *<Importance><Security Property>[<Asset>, <Interval>]*, as shown in Fig. 2. Our approach iteratively carries out security requirements analysis in each of the three layers. In particular, we iteratively refine security goals to "operationalizable" ones, among which we identify critical security goals that need to be treated. Then we operationalize critical security goals into specific security mechanisms, which can fulfill the security requirement being analyzed. Finally, we transfer related influences of selected security mechanisms into the next layer down, and further analyze security requirements in that layer.

We leverage existing security patterns [2,3] to help analysts without security knowledge to operationalize security requirements. In particular, we assign each security pattern a tag, which specifies the security property that a security pattern can potentially tackle. Thus, by matching the security property specified within a critical security goal and the tag of a security pattern, we can identify

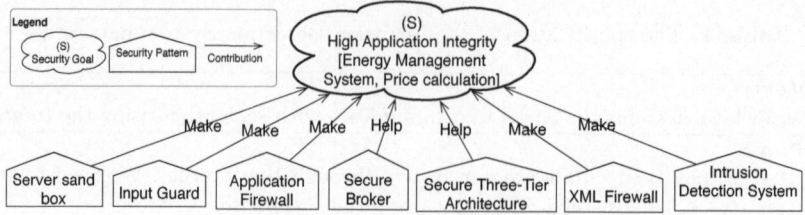

Fig. 2. Security requirements operationalization example

a number of security pattern candidates, among which the analyst must select. For example, as shown in Fig. 2, there are seven security pattern candidates that are identified to tackle the critical security goal *High Application Integrity [Energy Management System, Price calculation]* according to its security property *Application Integrity*. However, the selection among security pattern candidates is a non-trivial task, whose complexity grows with the number of critical security goals. In addition, after choosing a security pattern, the pattern needs to be manually modeled and integrated in the security goal models, which is time-consuming for analysts.

3   An Illustrating Scenario

Our proposed security requirements analysis approach [7] has been applied to a smart grid scenario, which leverages information and communication technologies to enable two-way communications between customers and energy providers. Specifically, the energy provider periodically collects energy consumption data from the customer, based on which they calculate the new price and send back to the customer. Then the customer adjusts his energy usage according to the new price.

We construct a three-layer security requirements goal model for this scenario, consisting of 15 actors, 72 goals, 5 softgoals, 80 tasks, 68 refinement links, 53 operationalization links, and 13 dependency links. Fig. 3 shows part of the requirements goal model within the software application layer. In this paper, our approach will be illustrated using this smart grid scenario.

4   Model Security Patterns as Contextual Goal Models

In this section, we first present a contextual goal modeling language, used to define contextual goal models for security patterns. In addition, we present a detailed process for creating a contextual goal model for a given security pattern. Finally, we summarize some empirical observations derived from modeling 20 security patterns.

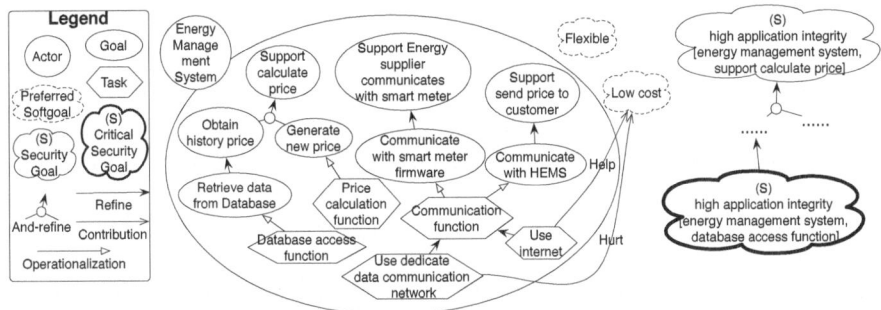

Fig. 3. A part of the security goal model of the smart grid scenario

4.1   A Contextual Goal Modeling Language

We use the goal model concepts of our three-layer requirements analysis [7], including *goal, softgoal, task, domain assumption, refine, and-refine, operationalize, contribution, mandatory, preferred (nice-to-have)*. Specifically, *goals* capture stakeholder desires, while *softgoals* are desires without clear-cut criteria for fulfillment; *tasks* describe behaviors of the system-to-be; and *domain assumptions* are properties of the domain that are assumed to hold. In addition, the *refine* and *and-refine* relations represent the refinement of a requirement into a simpler one; the *operationalize* relation indicates how a goal/softgoal is achieved by the system-to-be; the *contribution* relation captures the influences of *tasks* on *softgoals*; the *mandatory* relation indicates requirements that must be satisfied, while the *preferred* relation indicates "nice-to-have" requirements.

On top of above goal model concepts, we introduce additional concepts to model and analyze contexts within a goal model. In particular, we specify context in terms of *domain properties*. A *domain property* is a fact related to a particular domain, while a *design-time domain property* is a domain property that can be verified at design time by related analysts. For example, "*Computer systems on a local network connected to the Internet*" is a design-time domain property, and analysts can verify this fact during design time according to the designed system infrastructure. For another example, "*The number of users increases significantly*" is not a design-time domain property, as it can only be verified at run-time. Since security pattern analysis is carried out at design-time, we only capture *design-time domain properties* to analyze design-time contexts. A particular context can be arbitrarily complex, consisting of either a single domain property or could be an aggregation of domain properties of any complexity, typically, via *and/or* operators.

As noted in Section 2.2, our goal models are context-dependent. For example, in Fig. 5, the softgoal *Application Security* is required if and only if the context *C1* holds. It is worth noting that the concept *domain assumption* should be distinguished from the concept *design-time domain property*. A *domain assumption* is always assumed to be true during system designs, under which requirements are satisfied, and does not need to be checked. For instance, in Fig. 5, "*other security measures do not cover all possible attacks*" is a domain assumption.

4.2   A Process for Creating Contextual Goal Models from Security Patterns

To build contextual goal models that capture contents of security patterns, we focus on analyzing the five essential predefined sections of security patterns, as illustrated in Table. 1. For each of the five sections of the security patterns, we identify concepts within the contextual goal modeling language to capture the content of the section by considering both of their definitions [3,13]. Our analysis results in a concept mapping, shown in Fig. 4. In the rest of this section, we describe this mapping in detail. Apart from the concept mapping, we further provide detailed guidelines that constitute a systematic process for creating a contextual goal model for a given security pattern. The *Intrusion Detection System* pattern (Table. 1) will be used throughout this section to illustrate the mapping and instructions, with the corresponding contextual goal model shown in Fig. 5.

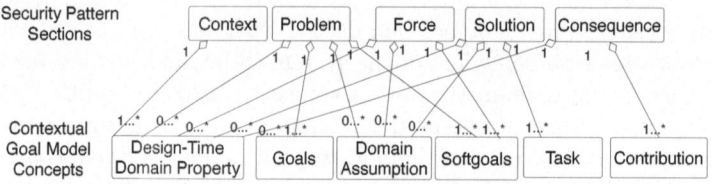

Fig. 4. Concept mappings between contextual goal models and security patterns

Context Section Analysis. This section describes the initial context of the security pattern, in which the security problem occurs and is being solved. We model the context with one or multiple *design-time domain properties*. For example, the context *C1* in Fig. 5 is the initial context, which is represented by one design-time domain property *DTDP1* extracted from the context section. Note that the context *C1*, as the initial context, is attached to the root goal that will be extracted from the *Problem Section*.

Problem Section Analysis. A *problem* is a description of a situation, for which stakeholders do not have a solution. We use one or several *goals* or *softgoals* to capture stakeholder needs concerning such a problem. As the problem is essential to a security pattern, we model the goals/softgoals that capture the problem as *mandatory* requirements, which have to be satisfied by security patterns.

We analyze this section sentence by sentence, each of which usually leads to the inclusion of a goal/softgoal. If there are several goals/softgoals, we need to consider the relations between sentences and determine the refinement structure of these goals/softgoals. It is worth noting that the description of the problem section may also involve domain assumptions, which should be identified and modeled within the refinement structure, such as *"An attacker may infiltrate a system through the internet"* shown in Fig. 5. The root element of a goal model constructed through this process must be mandatory.

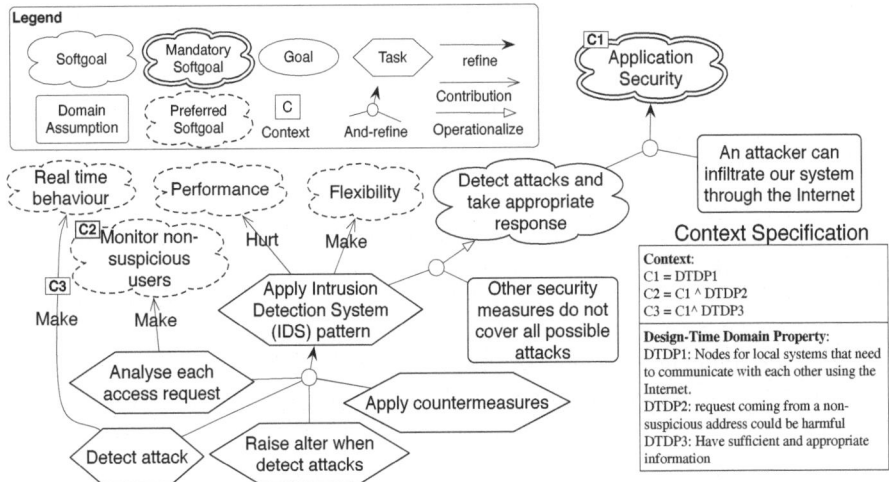

Fig. 5. The contextual goal model of the IDS pattern

To integrate the security patterns with security requirements analysis, we extract not only the specific problems that are solved by the security pattern, but also the high-level security requirements that lead to those detailed problems. If the high-level security requirements are not explicitly specified in this section, we need to do further analysis. In the *IDS* example, the first sentence presents a domain assumption *"Attacker may infiltrate a system through internet"*, which also implicitly presents a high-level security requirement that the security of the software application should be protected. The next sentence *"We need to know when an attack is happening"* specifies a detailed problem, which is a refinement of the high-level security requirement. Thus, we obtain a model fragment as shown in the upper-right corner of Fig. 5.

Force Section Analysis. Forces are considerations, often contradictory, which have to be taken into account to determine the applicability of a pattern. These considerations are often related to non-functional requirements (NFRs), such as performance and cost. We model such forces as *preferred softgoals*, where stakeholders want to satisfy as many of such goals as possible. Other forces may belong to domain assumptions, which are always assumed to be true during the security analysis. For instance, the force *Existing security measures cannot cover all attacks*, shown in Fig. 5, is a domain assumption, under which the *IDS* security pattern operationalizes the security goals.

This section is specified in an itemized manner. Each item starts with a key word, from which we can decide whether the force is a preferred softgoal (e.g. *Flexibility*) or a domain assumption (e.g. *Incomplete Security*). It is worth noting that some preferred softgoals are context-dependent, only needing to be considered in particular context. For example, the softgoal *"Monitor non-suspicious users"* only holds under the context *"requests from non-suspicious address could be harmful"*. If this context does not hold, the force does not need to consider. Therefore, we identify another context *C2* and add it to this softgoal.

Solution Section Analysis. This section describes actions that are carried out by a security pattern. We model them as *tasks*, which specify how the "system-to-be" implements a security pattern. Similar to the analysis in the *Problem* section, the relations between tasks should also be identified and modeled in an appropriate structure. As shown in Fig. 5, we identify four sub-tasks, which are siblings, for applying the IDS pattern. Note that, the granularity of solutions varies from pattern to pattern. If the information provided in this section is too general, we can optionally extract additional information from other non-essential sections, such as the *Structure, Dynamic,* and *Implementation* sections.

Consequence Section Analysis. This section describes the consequences of a security pattern, which indicates both benefits and liabilities of the pattern. We capture these influences using *contribution* links. This section is also documented in an itemized way, and each item should correspond to one force, documented in the *Force* section. However, the correspondence between the *Force* section and the *Consequence* section may not be strict. The *Consequence* section may introduce NFRs in addition to those described in the *Force* section. These NFRs should also be taken into account, via inclusion as preferred softgoals, when choosing a security pattern. For example, the consequence description *"There is some overhead in the addition of IDSs to a system"* (Table. 1) indicates the IDS pattern *hurts* the performance of a system. The NFR (performance), which is not initially specified in the *Force* section, should be added into our model. In other cases, the preferred softgoals from the *Force* section may not be mentioned in the *Consequence* section. Thus, we need to infer the pattern's influences on those softgoals based on our understanding of the pattern, or search for related knowledge from other reliable knowledge bases.

Some influences on preferred softgoals are also context-dependent. As shown in Fig. 5, the task *"Detect attack"* can only *make* the softgoal *"Real time behaviour"* under the context that there are sufficient and appropriate information about attacks. It is worth noting that the influences of a security pattern may also depend on its detailed implementations. For example, as described in the *Authenticator* pattern, the consequence *"The overhead depends on the protocol used"* cannot be directly modeled. We need to first model two alternative tasks *"Apply a simple protocol"* and *"Apply a complex protocol"*, which refines the task *"Apply an appropriate protocol"* and then investigate their influences respectively.

4.3   Pattern Modeling: Empirical Observations

Thus far we have constructed contextual goal models for 20 security patterns[1] described in [3]. During this exercise, we observed several issues, which may affect the quality of resulting models.

1. The specifications of some security patterns are incomplete, such as missing a section.

---

[1] The full list of models can be found at http://goo.gl/u539CV

2. Not all security patterns are specified in a consistent way. For example, some patterns are specified in a threat-oriented manner, while others are in a function-oriented manner.
3. The granularity of descriptions may vary greatly among patterns. For instance, the solution section of some security pattern only describes general idea of the pattern in one sentence, while some other pattern uses several paragraphs to explain related security mechanisms.

These observations disclose that processing and modeling textual security patterns are time-consuming, and additional knowledge related to security patterns is usually required during this process. This fact further explains why security patterns are not widely applied. In the meanwhile, it justifies the value of our work, i.e. constructing *reusable* contextual goal models for 20 security patterns. In addition, the above observations also expose the shortcomings in existing security pattern specifications, which should be tackled by the security pattern community.

5   Integrating Security Patterns with Security Requirements

Once security patterns have been modeled, we follow a systematic process to select and apply them to operationalize critical security goals that are derived from security requirements analysis [7].

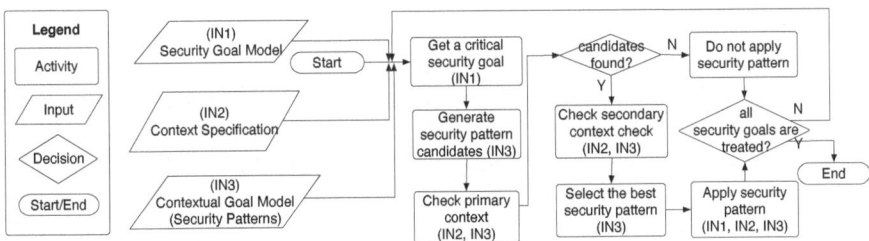

Fig. 6. Security pattern analysis process

As shown in Fig. 6, the process requires three types of information as input: 1) The *security goal model*, which captures requirements and security requirements regarding the domain. In particular, we use our three-layer security goal model (shown in Fig. 3) for this purpose. 2) The *context specification* describes the environments of the domain, which is composed of a list of design-time domain properties. This specification does not need to be complete at the beginning of the analysis, as it can be incrementally enriched during the application of security patterns. 3) A number of *security patterns*, which have been modeled in terms of contextual goal models. Note that, in Fig. 6, each input is assigned a tag, such as

IN1. If the input is required by one activity, the tag of that input will be specified at the end of the description of that activity. The overall analysis process selects the best security pattern for each critical security goal, and applies the selected pattern to the security goal model, as well as updating the context specification. In the rest of this section, we describe each step of the process in detail, and finally illustrate the entire process with the smart grid scenario, described in Sec. 3. In particular, our illustration focuses on the software application layer of the scenario.

5.1 Generating Security Pattern Candidates

The security goal model contains a number of critical security goals, which are analyzed one by one in our analysis process. To apply appropriate security patterns to treat each critical security goal, we first identify security pattern candidates, which can potentially tackle the security goal. Particularly, we match the security property of the security goal with the root goal of the contextual goal model of each security pattern (e.g. *Application Security* in Fig. 5) to determine whether a security pattern can be a candidate solution to the critical security goal. The results of this match will reveal an initial set of security pattern candidates. It is worth noting that the match process takes the hierarchy of security property into account, such as described in [16,2]. For example, the security property *Application Integrity* is a specialization of *Application Security*. Thus, a security pattern that can tackle *Application Security* can also be applied to tackle the *Application Integrity* problem, such as the *IDS* pattern.

5.2 Security Pattern Selection

Once we have the initial set of the security pattern candidates, which typically contains more than one pattern, we carry out context-based selection to choose the most appropriate security pattern. To this end, we need to check each context to determine whether it holds within a particular domain.

As contexts attached to different elements have different effects when they do not hold, we define the context that is attached to root goal of a contextual goal model as a *primary context*, while define the context that is attached to preferred softgoal or contribution links as a *secondary context*. The primary context is essential to the applicability of a security pattern. Such as is shown in the IDS pattern (Fig. 5), here if the primary context *C1* does not hold, the root goal will be deactivated, and the task "*apply IDS pattern*" will be deactivated accordingly, i.e., the pattern becomes inapplicable. In contrast to the primary context, the secondary context mainly affects the quality of the security pattern in terms of its contributions to the preferred softgoals. For instance, in the IDS pattern example, if the context *C2* does not hold, its corresponding preferred softgoal will be deactivated, as well as the contribution links connected to the softgoal.

Having the two types of contexts, we propose two steps for selecting security patterns. As shown in Fig. 6, we first check the primary context of the security pattern candidates to filter inapplicable security patterns. After that, if there is more than one applicable security pattern left, we check the secondary contexts to determine the quality of each security pattern and do further selection. In particular, we quantify contribution links {make, help, hurt, break} as {2, 1, -1, -2} respectively to evaluate the effect a pattern has on the satisfaction of preferred softgoals, aiding in selection. Note that other more complicated goal satisfaction analysis techniques can also be used for this selection, such as those compared and evaluated in [17]

As manual checking whether a context applies is a non-trivial task, especially for complex and large models, we propose an interactive process that semi-automates this task. We first formalize check rules for each context in Datalog and automatically check them against the context specification by using our tool. For example, the context $C1$ (in Fig. 5) can be formalized as below:

R1: $hold(c1) : -Node(N1), Node(N2), communicate(N1, N2, internet)$

R2: $not\_hold(c1) : -Node(N1), Node(N2), dis\_communicate(N1, N2, internet)$

R3: $undecidable(c1) : -not\ hold(c1), not\ not\_hold(c1)$

If neither hold/not-hold can be inferred for a context, i.e. it is undecidable, the system turns to the user and infers the state of a context on the basis of user answers to a list of yes/no system questions.

5.3   Security Pattern Application

Thanks to the reusable goal model we have constructed for security patterns, analysts do not need to manually construct the goal model of a security pattern each time they want to apply it. Thus, after selecting the best security pattern, the analyst can directly insert the goal model of the security pattern to the security requirements goal model, as illustrated in Fig. 7. Note that the red cross indicates the context $C3$ does not hold, and the corresponding contribution link is deactivated. To correctly integrate the goal model of a security pattern into the security goal model, firstly, the analyst needs to merge the softgoals newly introduced by the security pattern with the original softgoals by following the techniques proposed by Niu and Easterbrook [18]. For example, in Fig. 7, the new softgoal *Flexibility* has been merged with the original softgoal *Flexible*. Secondly, the analyst should do a pairwise comparison of all the old elements with all the new elements to find what new contributions should be present. As shown in Fig. 7, two new contributions links are identified with regard to the new softgoal *performance*.

5.4   Case Study Statistics

We apply our approach to the application layer of the three-layer security goal model that is built for the smart grid scenario (Sec. 3) to further exemplify our approach. In this security goal model, we have identified five critical security goals, which need to be treated by specific security patterns. The security properties of these critical security goals, which are essential for initially generating security pattern candidates, are listed in Table. 2.

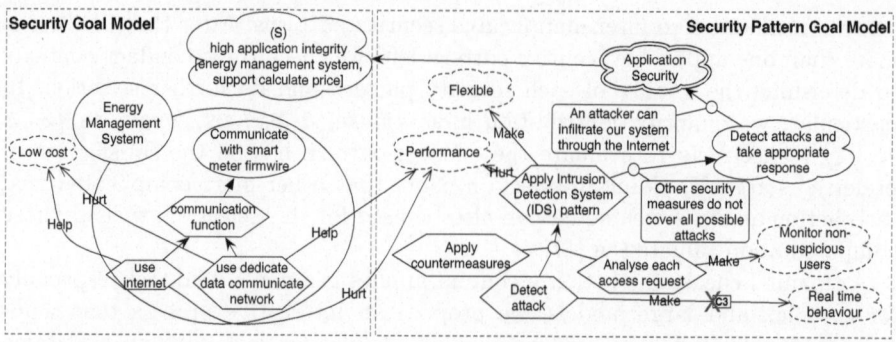

Fig. 7. Applying IDS pattern to the goal model of the smart grid scenario

Table 2. Statistics of applying 20 security patterns to the smart grid scenario

Security Goal	Security Property	All Candidates	Applicable	Applied
SG1	Application Integrity	20	7	5	1
SG2	Application Integrity	20	7	0	0
SG3	Application Integrity	20	7	2	1
SG4	Data Confidentiality	20	6	4	1
SG5	Application Availability	20	8	0	0

In total we have 20 security patterns that have been modeled as contextual goal models. In the first analysis step, we identify 6-8 security pattern candidates for each of these security patterns. Then, we apply the two-step context analysis to select the most appropriate security pattern, the results of which are shown in Table. 2. Note that some security goals may have no suitable security patterns to apply. In such a case, the security goals will be transferred to the next layer of the three-layer model (physical layer), and are further analyzed there. Finally, we apply each selected security pattern by integrating its goal model into the security goal model.

6   Tool Support

We extend our prototype tool MUSER [19], which has been designed to support the three-layer security requirements analysis approach, with a number of features to implement the approach presented in this paper[2]. The enhanced tool allows us to:

- Graphically model contextual goal models for security patterns;
- Automatically check the contexts of security patterns against the domain-specific context, and ask for manual check if necessary;

---

[2] Details of the tool can be found at: http://disi.unitn.it/ li/MUSER/

- Apply selected security pattern by inserting its corresponding contextual goal models into the security goal models.

7   Related Work

There are several approaches that model security patterns as goal models. Mouratidis et al. extend their security analysis approach Secure Tropos by integrating four security patterns [20]. Yu et al. [21] propose to formally specify role-based access control as a security pattern in terms of i* models, and implement a tool to automatically detect contexts and apply security patterns. However, these approaches do not address the pattern selection issues. In addition, only a limited number of security patterns are presented in their work, and no details are provided on how to model security patterns as goal models.

Araujo and Weiss [22] apply the Non-Functional Requirement (NFR) framework as a complementary representation for security patterns, which helps to analyze the tradeoffs between forces. In particular, they define the *force hierarchy* to represent interactions between forces, and model such hierarchy for 14 security patterns. We can extend their results to build the contextual goal models for those security patterns. Asnar et al. [9] propose a method to design organizational patterns from SI* models, which deals with system security and dependability. Their approach proceeds in the opposite way of ours, they aim to extract security patterns from goal models, while we aim to apply security patterns into goal model analysis.

Security patterns have been applied to various models. Shiroma et al. [23] focus on applying security patterns to UML diagrams, and they define transformation rules to automate this application. Sánchez-Cid and Maña [24] provide a language, which describes security solutions to assist software engineers to implement security patterns into software applications.

Several methods have been discussed for classifying security patterns [1], which are essential for navigating and selecting security patterns, such as security properties, logic tiers, security concepts, system viewpoints and so on. Our approach use security properties for pattern classification. We specify the interrelationships among security patterns by using the refinement and contribution relations, with which we can identify relevant patterns that need to apply.

Other work has also been done on systematically analyzing textual patterns. Gross and Yu [25] specify a systematic way to represent, analyze and apply design patterns by using NFR framework. They illustrate their method and experiences regarding to processing textual design pattern in detail, some of which are similar to our systematic guidelines. However, their approach does not analyze the context of a pattern and provide no support for pattern selections. Supaporn et al. [26] focus on generating security grammars, which are specified in extended-BNF formats, by analyzing descriptions of security patterns. Specifically, they build grammar trees to represent the semantics of security patterns, which could help us to better understand and process the textual security patterns as part of our framework.

8   Conclusions and Future Work

In this paper, we propose to integrate security patterns with our previous security requirements analysis technique by modeling security patterns as contextual goal models. Our approach contributes to both the operationalization of security requirements and the adoption of security patterns. In particular, we define concept mappings between security patterns and contextual goal models, and provide a detailed process for modeling security patterns as contextual goal models. Moreover, we propose a systematic process to select and apply security patterns, and illustrate the process with a realistic smart grid scenario. We have implemented a prototype tool, which supports the application of our approach.

Thus far, we have built contextual goal models for 20 security patterns, and we plan to model more patterns in the future. Our current approach is built on our previous work, and we intend to further generalize it to accommodate other goal-based security requirements analysis techniques. Furthermore, when applying a security pattern model, the newly introduced model may influence different parts of the existing model in various ways and make the application process very hard. Thus, we aim to propose new techniques that facilitate this process. Finally, we plan to carry out further, large-scale empirical evaluations of our approach in order to evaluate its validity and usability.

Acknowledgements. This work was supported in part by ERC advanced grant 267856, titled "Lucretius: Foundations for Software Evolution".

References

1. Hafiz, M., Adamczyk, P., Johnson, R.E.: Organizing security patterns. IEEE Software 24(4), 52–60 (2007)
2. Scandariato, R., Yskout, K., Heyman, T., Joosen, W.: Architecting software with security patterns. Technical report, KU Leuven (2008)
3. Fernandez-Buglioni, E.: Security patterns in practice: designing secure architectures using software patterns. John Wiley & Sons (2013)
4. Mouratidis, H., Giorgini, P.: Secure tropos: a security-oriented extension of the tropos methodology. International Journal of Software Engineering and Knowledge Engineering 17(02), 285–309 (2007)
5. Liu, L., Yu, E.S.K., Mylopoulos, J.: Secure-i*: Engineering secure software systems through social analysis. Int. J. Software and Informatics 3(1), 89–120 (2009)
6. Paja, E., Dalpiaz, F., Giorgini, P.: Managing security requirements conflicts in socio-technical systems. In: Conceptual Modeling, pp. 270–283. Springer (2013)
7. Li, T., Horkoff, J.: Dealing with security requirements for socio-technical systems: A holistic approach. In: Jarke, M., Mylopoulos, J., Quix, C., Rolland, C., Manolopoulos, Y., Mouratidis, H., Horkoff, J. (eds.) CAiSE 2014. LNCS, vol. 8484, pp. 285–300. Springer, Heidelberg (2014)
8. Li, T., Mylopoulos, J.: Modeling and applying security patterns using contextual goal models. In: The 7th International i* Workshop, iStar14 (2014)
9. Asnar, Y., Massacci, F., Saidane, A., Riccucci, C., Felici, M., Tedeschi, A., El-Khoury, P., Li, K., Séguran, M., Zannone, N.: Organizational patterns for security and dependability: From design to application. Int. J. Secur. Softw. Eng. 2(3), 1–22 (2011)

10. Fernandez, E.B., Fonoage, M., VanHilst, M., Marta, M.: The secure three-tier architecture pattern. In: CISIS, pp. 555–560 (2008)
11. Schumacher, M., Fernandez-Buglioni, E., Hybertson, D.: Security patterns: Integrating security and systems engineering (2006)
12. Buschmann, F., Henney, K., Schimdt, D.: Pattern-oriented Software Architecture: On Patterns and Pattern Language, vol. 5. John Wiley & Sons (2007)
13. Ali, R., Dalpiaz, F., Giorgini, P.: A goal-based framework for contextual requirements modeling and analysis. Requirements Engineering 15(4), 439–458 (2010)
14. Lapouchnian, A., Mylopoulos, J.: Modeling domain variability in requirements engineering with contexts. In: Conceptual Modeling-ER 2009, pp. 115–130 (2009)
15. Bresciani, P., Perini, A., Giorgini, P., Giunchiglia, F., Mylopoulos, J.: Tropos: An agent-oriented software development methodology. Autonomous Agents and Multi-Agent Systems 8(3), 203–236 (2004)
16. Firesmith, D.: Specifying reusable security requirements. Journal of Object Technology 3(1), 61–75 (2004)
17. Horkoff, J., Yu, E.: Comparison and evaluation of goal-oriented satisfaction analysis techniques. Requirements Engineering 18(3), 199–222 (2013)
18. Niu, N., Easterbrook, S.: So, you think you know others' goals? a repertory grid study. IEEE Software 24(2), 53–61 (2007)
19. Li, T., Horkoff, J., Mylopoulos, J.: A prototype tool for modeling and analyzing security requirements from a holistic viewpoint. In: The CAiSE 2014 Forum at the 26th International Conference on Advanced Information Systems Engineering (2014)
20. Mouratidis, H., Weiss, M., Giorgini, P.: Modeling secure systems using an agent-oriented approach and security patterns. International Journal of Software Engineering and Knowledge Engineering 16(3), 471 (2006)
21. Yu, Y., Kaiya, H., Washizaki, H., Xiong, Y., Hu, Z., Yoshioka, N.: Enforcing a security pattern in stakeholder goal models. In: Proceedings of the 4th ACM Workshop on Quality of Protection, pp. 9–14 (2008)
22. Araujo, I., Weiss, M.: Linking Patterns and non-functional requirements. In: Proceedings of the Ninth Conference on Pattern Language of Programs (PLOP 2002), September 8-12 (2002)
23. Shiroma, Y., Washizaki, H., Fukazawa, Y., Kubo, A., Yoshioka, N.: Model-driven security patterns application based on dependences among patterns. In: International Conference on Availability, Reliability, and Security 2010, pp. 555–559 (February 2010)
24. Sanchez-Cid, F., Mana, A.: Serenity pattern-based software development life-cycle. In: 19th International Workshop on Database and Expert Systems Application, pp. 305–309 (September 2008)
25. Gross, D., Yu, E.: From non-functional requirements to design through patterns. Requirements Engineering 6(1), 18–36 (2001)
26. Supaporn, K., Prompoon, N., Rojkangsadan, T.: An approach: Constructing the grammar from security pattern. In: Proc. 4th International Joint Conference on Computer Science and Software Engineering (2007)

Better Segmentation of Enterprise Modelling Governance through Usage Perspectives

Frank Wolff

DHBW-Mannheim, Information Science, Coblitzallee. 1-9,
68163 Mannheim, Germany
Frank.Wolff@dhbw-mannheim.de

Abstract. Enterprise modelling is an endeavor that involves many different stakeholders in a company and requires a long-term approach to reap major benefits. Due to their differing main tasks the stakeholders frequently pursue deviating goals. Therefore, an appropriate management of the stakeholders is considered a success factor for enterprise modelling. The goals of the stakeholders in respect of an enterprise model and their role in the modelling process are crucial for this distinction. The differentiation can be facilitated by generic goals and a scheme that accounts for influences like variants in the size of companies and the impact of enterprise modelling on business. The application of the outlined procedure is exemplified with an illustrative case of a chemical supplier.

Keywords: Enterprise modelling, Modelling goals, Modelling governance, Participants involvement, Stakeholders.

1 Introduction

Enterprise modelling[1] integrates knowledge from many different domains in a company. Central are information on business processes, organizational relationships and IT-systems. Enterprise models support management with overall information but they also supply specialists with details for their concerns (e.g. [1], [2], [3]). Thereby, an enterprise model serves a considerable number of purposes. The goals that reflect the purposes to create and use an enterprise model in practice vary widely. Some goals are of more operational nature, e.g. to supply IT-service desk employees with an overview on the network infrastructure. Other purposes have strategic impact, e.g., if a company uses its process models to improve the integration of acquired companies or if it applies the models as a blueprint to establish new subsidiaries and production lines faster. The high potential benefits convinced many companies to start enterprise-wide modelling activities.

---

[1] In this paper the term enterprise modelling (EM) is used. This includes enterprise architecture modelling (EAM). EAM is somehow more focused on IT-infrastructures but the similarity with EM is quite substantial as both cover whole organizations and integrate the concerns of management, business operations and IT.

U. Frank et al. (Eds.): PoEM 2014, LNBIP 197, pp. 224–234, 2014.

In the beginning of enterprise modelling, the appropriate modelling methodology and a convenient tool were focused by research (e.g. [3], [4]). Now these concepts and technologies have matured considerably. But the status of enterprise models in many if not most companies is still not regarded as satisfactory [5]. This has been reported for some time and has changed little as the author of this paper noted at a number of recent practitioner conferences.

Many suppose the challenge is rooted in the interaction of the participants of enterprise modelling. Often the organization of the modelling process is very optimistic and does not account for the different perception of the diverse participants e.g. the providers and users of information [6]. Also sometimes organizational constraints hinder the effective usage of enterprise models [7].

Major challenges are 1) that to collect information and reflect them in the enterprise model collaboration of numerous specialists is required, 2) many potential benefits can only be realized over a longer time period and 3) enterprises are not static but transform frequently due to market and technological changes. So a long-term approach is advisable and as different groups of people are involved an active management or governance of enterprise modelling is required [8].

Different schemes have been proposed for a better governance of enterprise modelling (e.g. [9] or [10]). They provide a good outline on the essential elements for general governance activities. But they lack appropriate guidance to support the practitioner or researcher with practical knowledge how to adapt the governance and cope with the individual conditions of a particular company, in particular, its goals for the enterprise model and the different stakeholders involved in the modelling processes.

This paper deals with this shortcoming. It presents a compilation of generic goals for enterprise modelling and takes a closer look on the typical differentiation of enterprise modelling perspectives and other stakeholder models. These elements will be integrated in the dedicated concept of usage perspectives, which assists organizations to segment its management of enterprise modelling activities individually. This is important to create efficient and effective governance structures. Theoretical models tend usually to either simplify this aspect too much or build highly particularized structures [11]. To cater for different enterprise sizes and individual goals an appropriate integration is required.

2   Interests in Enterprise Models

People from distinct departments involved in enterprise modelling processes usually pursue different goals. Those goals are shaped by the individual work context of the participants and to a lesser part the overall goals of the company. The differences in their interests frequently inhibit an ideal creation and usage of an enterprise model, e.g. because it is not completed, updated as necessary or persists in a fragmented state.

To support the involved employees adequately, control the status of models and modelling processes diverse aspects must be accounted for. This topic has been addressed before mainly concentrating on either: a) goals for enterprise modelling, b) perspectives on enterprise models or c) analysis of involved stakeholders.

2.1   Goals for Enterprise Modelling

Theory and publications of providers of enterprise modelling tools stress the advantages and deduce a number of valuable usages of the models. They are often formulated as goals for enterprise modelling. The overview in Fig. 1 depicts a systemized compilation of these goals from literature (e.g. [4], [12], [13], [14]). It is based on an analysis of 18 sources from literature on enterprise modelling directly or specific kinds of modelling which are parts of enterprise models [15]. One important insight of the study was that modelling goals are usually listed without regard to the different extent of their potential effects on the company operations and the business. Some objectives are directly focused on certain actions of participants and others aim at broader effects on the business of a company.

The analysis revealed that goals for enterprise modelling range from strategic issues (e.g. *easing integration* of other companies, *higher flexibility* of a company) to the level of direct support of working activities (e.g. *documentation* or *automation* of work steps). Some goals are positioned at intermediate levels (e.g. *improving coordination*, better *system integration* or the *reuse of concepts*). Last but not least a model can support directly tasks like *communication* e.g. in projects or *provide* required *documentation*

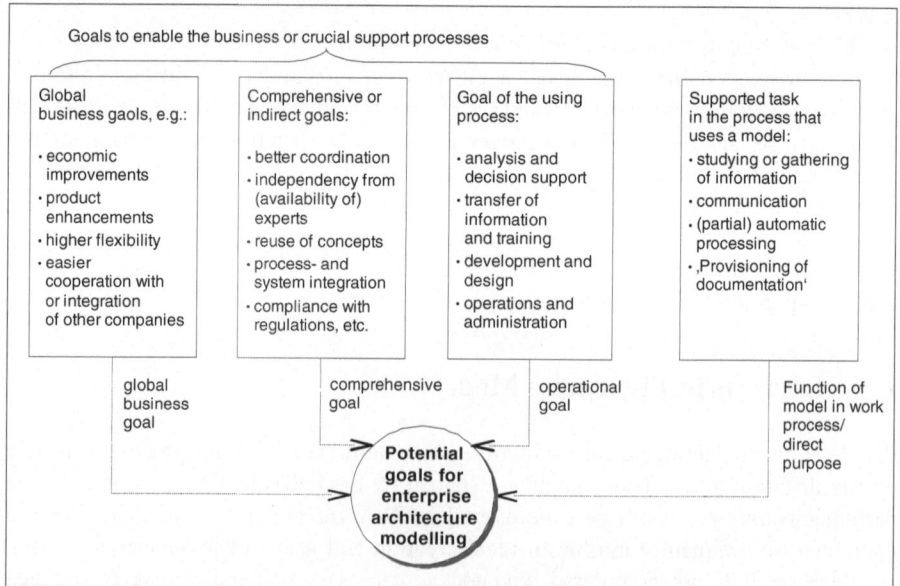

Fig. 1. Goals for enterprise architecture modelling with different levels of organizational effect

The goals in Fig. 1 are generic. In practice they will be connected in various ways. Crucial is the relation to a domain knowledge or model content that is of interest for people in a company, e.g. business processes or IT applications. Then usually the goals have interrelationships e.g. that for the global business goal of *higher flexibility* the realization of a *better coordination* and *process integration* is required. These latter then help employees directly in *development and design* of new processes and systems.

The above presented goals are related to substantial advantages of enterprise architecture models. Considering the typical timeframe and potential pitfalls in enterprise transformation processes it is presumably extremely valuable for a company in such situations to achieve some of the above listed goals by utilizing enterprise models. Nevertheless, even companies that start enterprise modelling initiatives rarely succeed in building and updating all parts of a comprehensive enterprise model [7], [8].

Many obstacles for a smooth modelling process originate from the diverse participants required for a modelling effort of this kind. Some individuals only have very constrained knowledge. So they may have problems to contribute effectively to the overall model. Others could easily produce single parts of the enterprise model but will not reap any benefit from the model as they do not need the information. Another aspect is that for a company it is usually much easier and more economical if the information is documented in the model while the information is well at hand. It is often very dear and costly to reproduce it later when the knowledgeable person has moved to another position or is not available for other reasons.

The above outlined combinations and relationships of multiple goals of involved persons can be analyzed by using goal modelling techniques like KAOS or iStar to identify supporting and contradicting goals [16]. These approaches promise many advantages in critical or perplexing situations. Nevertheless, in this paper a more basic maybe pragmatic approach is chosen, which focuses on the important stakeholder groups for an enterprise modelling endeavor.

2.2   Consideration of Generic Perspectives and Stakeholder Groups in Enterprise Modelling

In most enterprise modelling methods the participants are differentiated by perspectives or views. Very prominent is the distinction into a *management*, a *business* and an *information systems* perspective (e.g. [2], [3]). This focusses on very strikingly different involved groups but will not easily scale up or reflect distinct goals stemming e.g. from particular crucial customer groups.

This issue has been taken up by the research on stakeholders in enterprise models in recent years [17]. The consideration of the stakeholders in an activity is vital if desired interaction can only be reached by many parties interacting in a common direction [18]. The major objective of enterprise modelling is the provisioning of relevant information in a structured form. Therefore, information needs are one determinant shaping stakeholder groups [19]. An adequate representation of stakeholders is fundamental to cater for the requirements of the group so that essential modelling is done. While the stakeholder analysis supports a very detailed analysis of participating groups, it has been noted that this does not fit for many, especially medium sized enterprises [20]. A more flexible way will be presented in the following section integrating the concepts of goals and stakeholders in usage perspectives.

3   Focusing on Usage Perspectives of Enterprise Models

The problem of sufficient motivation and knowledge to model is quite subtle because the collision of interest usually differs for each of the departments involved in modelling and usage of enterprise models. E.g. the controlling department only has some specialized processes to model but needs some detailed information about numerous resources and processes all over the company. The department of IT is accustomed to work with conceptual models. But regularly it is under high time pressure. So IT-departments often hesitate to invest scarce manpower into a concerted enterprise modelling approach. Other departments like e.g. warehouse are unfamiliar with conceptual models. This also may prevent an easy adoption and inclusion of their procedures, tools and systems into an enterprise model.

The concept of usage perspectives[2] comprises these distinct aspects and helps to establish a balanced structure of groups concerned with enterprise modelling which is adapted to a company's characteristics and can also handle the combination of different partial views. This balancing and integration is necessary to foster shared cognition [21] which is a prerequisite to achieve the overall goals of an enterprise model [8].

3.1   Elements of Usage Perspectives

As it has been argued the interests but also problems to create the parts of an enterprise model vary for the diverse groups involved. To prepare necessary subsistence it is indispensable to identify groups with similar characteristics and interests. Fig. 2 depicts criteria to distribute the groups involved in modelling appropriately into *utilization perspectives*.

The distribution is based on two perspectives a) the overall *business perspective* and b) the *modelling perspective*. The business perspective determines the *goals for using models* and thereby modelling. The modelling perspective is rooted in the depicted domain. It is related to the typical *knowledge* of the people working in the domain. The business and the modelling perspectives are important for the *context of work*. The elements of the context of work may stem initially from the generic characteristics of modelling context and the business goals. But it should be noted that in many cases also other conditions impact the interest and cognition of participants e.g. the kind of education, nature of work, geographical or cultural traits. By

---

[2] Alternatively to the term *usage perspective* it was considered to name the concept *involvement perspective*. But this was rejected as the focus on the benefits was perceived to be decisive.

clustering groups of people along their context of work and their typical modelling knowledge important stakeholders in regard of enterprise models can be identified.

As basis the individual characteristics and goals of the stakeholders are discerned. Then the similarities of goals and stakeholder characteristics are the used to discover common perspectives. This analysis is balanced by considering an appropriate number of usage perspectives for an enterprise. This number depends on the size and the strategic importance of enterprise modelling for the company. Besides *basic utilization perspectives* which cover one subject area of a company, e.g. the production of a major product line, also other perspectives are allowed for. If model information from different perspectives is required for an additional purpose *interrelated usage perspectives* are created.

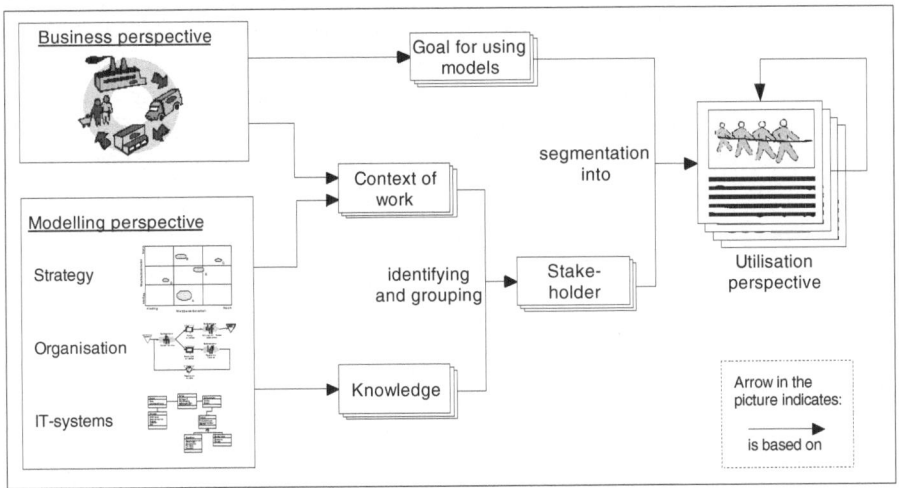

Fig. 2. Criteria to distribute enterprise architecture modelling into utilization perspectives

3.2   Management of the Enterprise Modelling Process

While good enterprise models appear to be simple and intelligible their creation and actualization is quite a perplexing process. The different involved groups are one major challenge. This is due to many cognitive, political and organizational issues [22]. Another aspect is the distribution of changes in time but also in related entities of an enterprise. Also effort for data collection can be very high and data quality is often rather low [11].

All these characteristics call for an active management or governance of enterprise modelling processes ([10], [15]). One main duty of this governance would be to ensure that pending updates for models activate relevant triggers. Besides organizational arrangements also technical coupling is an important force for up-to-date and correct enterprise models [11]. This applies very much for automatic conversion of systems data into models and vice versa. But also connection between different spheres of modelling is of high interest in practice (e.g. business processes and IT-Infrastructure).

The utilization perspectives help an organization to a) discover conflicts of interest between participants and/or company goals, and subsequently to resolve them, b) control the current required update of an enterprise architecture model and c) make up a more realistic assessment of options to model its enterprise ([15], [23]). An appropriately adopted organization has been identified to have high influence on the prospects to reap the benefits from an enterprise model [5].

3.3   Example Distribution of Usage Perspectives

In this section an illustrative example of a chemical supplier company is presented. Outline of the example: The chemical company has two major divisions. One is working for the medical industry and the other is distributing a wide range of basic chemical substances to other non-regulated industries. Some subsidiaries have been founded abroad for doing better business in other countries. The subsidiaries often also profit from lower wages or material prices. Due to their success, more foreign affiliations are planned.

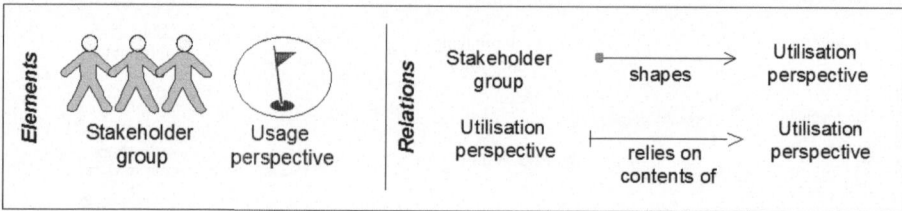

Fig. 3. Elements (left side) and relations (right side) of the usage perspectives structure diagram

The example will be depicted in a diagram which may be connected to other models for control of enterprise modelling endeavors (e.g. in [24]). The model is composed of two main element types – 1) usage perspectives and 2) stakeholder groups (see Fig. 3). The elements are connected through 2 types of relations.[3] The first relation serves to reflect which stakeholder groups are involved in a utilization perspective. The second relation represents the dependency of certain usage perspectives on contents of models created and updated by stakeholders from other usage perspectives.[4]

---

[3] An integration relation for one or more comprehensive perspectives is possible but not in the scope of this paper.

[4] A tool to model Usage Perspectives can be downloaded from the website of the Open Models Initiative - www.openmodels.at. The modelling tool is contained in the package for Evaluation Chains (EC) and includes dedicated reference models for the assessment of enterprise modelling activities.

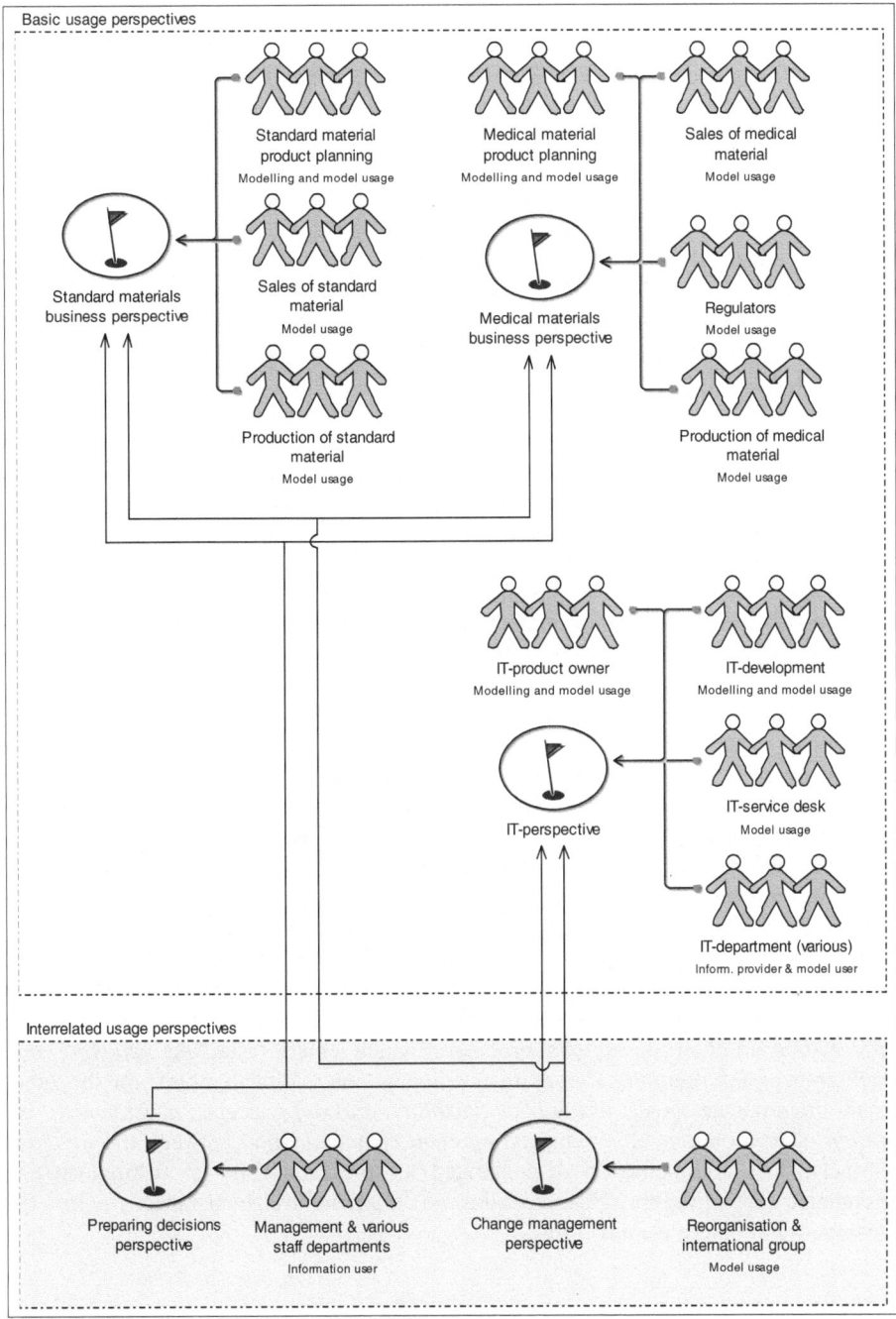

Fig. 4. Illustrative example for Usage Perspectives of a supplier for chemical base materials

While *basic usage perspectives* can be analyzed and managed on their own the depending usage perspectives require a more comprehensive consideration. However, it should be noted that likewise basic usage perspectives may be composed of different groups of stakeholders. These groups are either differentiated by their role in the modelling process (e.g. knowledge provider, modeler or model user) or by their goals for using the models. In the presented diagram goals are only stored in the background. However, to some extent they are reflected in the label of the stakeholder group. The underlying intention was to create a distinct overview on the groups without too many details.

The separation of usage perspectives for the example chemical company is presented in Fig. 4. It differentiates five main usage perspectives, a) *Standard materials business perspective*, b) *Medical materials business perspective*, c) *IT-perspective*, d) *Preparing decisions perspective* and e) *Change management perspective*. The foundational perspectives for the enterprise model that directly create business models are depicted on top of the diagram (a&b). The IT-perspective (c) is in the center and the two perspectives which do not create models but are using information or models from the others are positioned at the bottom (d& e).

The two business perspectives are structurally very similar and only differentiated by the additional stakeholder group of *regulators*. This may seem to be only a small variance. But due to the risks to human life the obligations in medical production lines are very strict and have severe impact on the organization and related procedures in the domain. Therefore, it is reasonable to manage the two business lines in separate perspectives.

In the IT-perspective four main stakeholder groups cooperate. On the top the active modelling groups of IT-product owners and IT-development are positioned. The models of the IT are used by all stakeholders of the IT-perspective. Especially the *IT-service desk* considerably relies in his work on the models provided by the modelling stakeholder groups. As technical details are known only by some specialists it is often essential that some of the other members of the *IT-department (various)* must supply additional information.

The goal analysis of the stakeholders is not represented in the diagram directly but is underlying the example case. As explained in chapter 2.1. the goals regularly are compounds of more than one generic goal. E.g. the IT-service desk requires information *independent from the availability of certain specialists*. They use the information in their *operations processes* which entail tasks like *studying and gathering of information*. The reorganization & international group, on the other hand, often pursues goals, like *higher flexibility*, *reuse of concepts*, *development and design* of new entities all relying on *efficient communication* between the involved partners. This argumentation demonstrated the principles how to distinguish and recombine the different characteristics to segment usage perspective for the governance of enterprise modelling.[5]

---

[5] The model in the diagram had been restricted by the available space. In a bigger company typically more distinctions could be advisable in regard of the difference between production and administration in the business perspectives. Similarly in the IT domain, the operations and the development groups in many cases focus on different areas and contents of the enterprise model.

4   Conclusion and Further Research

Enterprise modelling in companies is frequently faced with problems due to difficulties in the interaction of involved stakeholders. The problems often surface only late because the social implications of these large-scale complex endeavors are not directly visible [8]. The segmentation proposed in this paper serves to organize and control the various activities of enterprise modelling by embracing many of these impeding factors. The proposed procedure adapts to small enterprises with only a handful of usage perspectives up to very large enterprises with perhaps 40 or more usage perspectives. It is fundamental for enterprise modelling that the organizational setting secures that the actors and participants for their part can be fully involved in their modelling, and are not hindered by other interests.

Further research in usage perspectives is planned to be twofold: a) direct examination of the segmentation in more companies to analyze the effects of segmentation in governance on the abilities of an organization to control its achievements with enterprise models and b) further development of a modelling methodology to support the analysis of the relationships between goals, rationales, decisions and organizational contexts in enterprise modelling (comp. [25]).

References

1. Braun, C., Winter, R.: A Comprehensive Enterprise Architecture Metamodel. In: Desel, J., Frank, U. (eds.) Proceedings of the Workshop in Klagenfurt 2005 Enterprise Modelling and Information Systems Architectures, pp. 64–79. GI LNI P- 75, Bonn (2005)
2. Lankhorst, M., et al.: Enterprise Architecture at Work - Modelling, Communication and Analysis, 3rd edn. Springer, Berlin (2013)
3. Frank, U.: Multi-Perspective Enterprise Modeling (MEMO): Conceptual Framework and Modeling Languages. In: 35th (HICSS), Big Island, pp. 1–10. IEEE Computer (2002)
4. Davis, R.: Business Process Modelling with ARIS. Springer, London (2001)
5. Foorthuis, R.M., van Steenbergen, M., Mushkudiani, N., Bruls, W., Brinkkemper, S., Bos, R.: On Course, But Not There Yet: Enterprise Architecture Conformance and Benefits in Systems Development. In: Proceedings of 31st ICIS 2010 (2010)
6. Barjis, J.: Collaborative, Participative and Interactive Enterprise Modeling. In: Filipe, J., Cordeiro, J. (eds.) Enterprise Information Systems. LNBIP, vol. 24, pp. 651–662. Springer, Heidelberg (2009)
7. Ylimäki, T.: Potential Critical Success Factors for Enterprise Architecture. Journal of Enterprise Architecture 2(4), 29–40 (2006)
8. Lucke, C., Krell, S., Lechner, U.: Critical Issues in Enterprise Architecting - A Literature Review. In: Proceedings of the Americas Conference on Information (2010)
9. Gericke, A., Bayer, F., Kühn, H., Rausch, T., Strobl, R.: Der Lebenszyklus des Prozessmanagements. In: Bayer, F., Kühn, H. (eds.) Prozessmanagement für Experten, Springer, Heidelberg (2013)
10. Franz, P., Kirchmer, M.: Value-driven Business Process Management - The Value Switch for Lasting Competitive Advantage. McGraw-Hill (2012)

11. Roth, S., Hauder, M., Farwick, M., Matthes, F., Breu, R.: Enterprise Architecture Documentation: Current Practices and Future Directions. In: 11th International Conference on Wirtschaftsinformatik (WI), Leipzig, Germany (2013)
12. Jeusfeld, M.A., Jarke, M., Nissen, H.W., Staudt, M.: ConceptBase: Managing Conceptual Models about Information Systems. In: Bernus, P., et al. (eds.) Handbook on Architectures of Information Systems, pp. 273–294. Springer, Berlin (2006)
13. Persson, A., Stirna, J.: Why Enterprise Modelling? An Explorative Study into Current Practice. In: Dittrich, K.R., Geppert, A., Norrie, M. (eds.) CAiSE 2001. LNCS, vol. 2068, pp. 465–468. Springer, Heidelberg (2001)
14. Proper, H., Verrijn-Stuart, A.A., Hoppenbrouwers, S.: On Utility-based Selection of Architecture-Modelling Concepts. In: 2nd AsiaPasific Conference on Conceptual Modelling (APCCM 2005) in New Castle, pp. 1–11. Australian Computer Society (2005)
15. Wolff, F.: Ökonomie multiperspektivischer Unternehmensmodellierung. IT-Controlling für modell-basiertes Wissensmanagement. Gabler, Wiesbaden (2008)
16. Horkoff, J., Yu, E.: Evaluating Goal Achievement in Enterprise Modeling – An Interactive Procedure and Experiences. In: Persson, A., Stirna, J. (eds.) PoEM 2009. LNBIP, vol. 39, pp. 145–160. Springer, Heidelberg (2009)
17. van der Raadt, B., Bonnet, M., Schouten, S., van Vliet, H.: The relation between EA effectiveness and stakeholder satisfaction. Journal of Systems and Software 83, 1954–1969 (2010)
18. Fassin, Y.: The Stakeholder Model Refined. Journal of Business Ethics 84, 113–135 (2009)
19. Lagerström, R., Saat, J., Franke, U., Aier, S., Ekstedt, M.: Enterprise Meta Modeling Methods – Combining a Stakeholder-Oriented and a Causality-Based Approach. In: Halpin, T., Krogstie, J., Nurcan, S., Proper, E., Schmidt, R., Soffer, P., Ukor, R. (eds.) Enterprise, Business-Process and Information Systems Modeling. LNBIP, vol. 29, pp. 381–393. Springer, Heidelberg (2009)
20. Niemi, E.: Enterprise Architecture Stakeholders - a Holistic View. In: Proceedings of AMCIS 2007, p. 41 (2007)
21. Espinosa, J.A., Armour, F., Boh, W.F.: Coordination in Enterprise Architecting: An Interview Study. In: Proceedings HICSS 2010, pp. 1–10 (2010)
22. Seppanen, V., Heikkila, J., Liimatainen, K.: Key Issues in EA-Implementation: Case Study of Two Finnish Government Agencies. In: Proceedings of the 2009 IEEE Conference on Commerce and Enterprise Computing, pp. 114–120. IEEE Computer Society (2009)
23. Morello, F.: Creating Incentive-Driven Tasks to Improve Knowledge Management in Sales Chain Relationships. In: Karagiannis, D., Reimer, U. (eds.) PAKM 2002. LNCS (LNAI), vol. 2569, pp. 87–96. Springer, Heidelberg (2002)
24. Wolff, F.: An Evaluation Framework for Enterprise Architecture Modelling. Enterprise Modelling and Information Systems Architectures 3(1), 48–61 (2008)
25. Bock, A., Kattenstroth, H., Overbeek, S.: Towards a modeling method for supporting the management of organizational decision processes. In: Modellierung 2014, pp. 49–64. Proceedings GI LNI P-225, Bonn (2014)

Towards a Code of Ethics for Gamification at Enterprise

Alimohammad Shahri, Mahmood Hosseini, Keith Phalp, Jacqui Taylor, and Raian Ali

Bournemouth University, UK
{ashahri,mhosseini,kphalp,jtaylor,rali}@bournemouth.ac.uk

Abstract. Gamification is an emerging technique which utilises the "fun theory" mainly to motivate people to change their perception and attitude towards certain subjects. Within enterprises, gamification is used to motivate employees to do their tasks more efficiently and perhaps more enjoyably and sometimes to increase their feeling of being members of the enterprise as a community. While the literature has often emphasised the positive side of gamification, mainly from economic and business perspectives, little emphasis has been paid to the ethical use of gamification within enterprises. In this paper we report an empirical research to explore the ethical aspects of using gamification. We follow a mixed methods approach involving participants who are gamification experts, employees and managers. Our findings show that, for gamification, there is a fine line between being a positive tool to motivate employees and being a source of tension and pressure which could then affect the social and mental well-being within the workplace. This paper will evaluate that dual effect and clarify that fine line.

Keywords: Gamification, Ethical Gamification, Well-Being within Enterprise.

1 Introduction

Gamification is commonly defined as the use of game design elements in a non-game context [1]. Examples include the use of points and leader-boards for staff in a call centre to reflect the number of calls answered, the issues resolved, the time taken, and the customer satisfaction [2]. Huotari and Hamari [3] emphasise the creation of an added value to the enterprise, e.g. increasing staff engagement and the affordability of a gameful experience, as core elements for gamification. Gamification has been applied in a diversity of domains including education [4], e.g. to increase performance and engagement of students [5], enterprise, e.g. to increase staff and customers loyalty [6], and design, e.g. to encourage sustainable living [7].

The literature on gamification has mainly advertised it as a creative way to increase engagement and motivation while its downside has been overlooked. When badly designed and applied, it could be a genuine harm for social and mental well-being within the workplace. Stakeholders' awareness of those issues should be integrated in the development process of gamification and its deployment in an enterprise.

In this paper, we make a start in studying the ethical and professional issues which should be observed when applying gamification within an enterprise. To explore this, we adopt a mixed methods approach [8] consisting of three phases; an exploration phase, a confirmation phase, and a clarification phase. Our results are intended to provide a checklist for system analysts when applying gamification within the workplace and raise awareness of this under-researched side of gamification.

U. Frank et al. (Eds.): PoEM 2014, LNBIP 197, pp. 235–245, 2014.
© IFIP International Federation for Information Processing 2014

2   Study Design

Fig. 1 summarises our research method. The first two stages, the exploration stage and the confirmation and enhancement stage contained a study of further aspects which are not discussed in this paper and relating mainly to the definition of gamification, its stakeholders, fields involved, and good design principles.

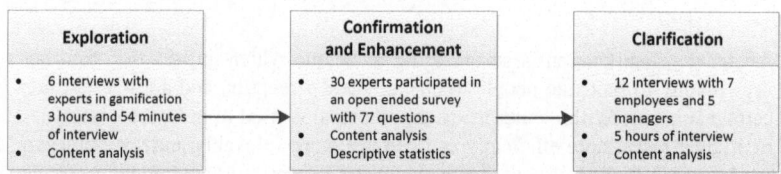

Fig. 1. Research methodology

In the exploration phase, we used interviews, a widely used data gathering tool in qualitative research [9]. Our participants were experts in gamification. In our study, experts were identified based on their constant and influential contribution to the field manifested in peer-reviewed publications. In this phase, we interviewed six experts (four from academia and two from industry). All experts implemented gamification in practice, and three also contributed theoretical frameworks. The experts came from six different countries – UK, South Africa, USA, Portugal, Germany, and Canada. The fields where our experts applied gamification were also diverse and included business, education, human resource development, and creative activities. A content analysis of the answers was conducted by two of the authors and led to 11 main statements.

The confirmation and enhancement phase was survey-based and was designed to confirm and enhance the 11 statements obtained via the first phase. Each statement was converted to a question with a five-point Likert scale reflecting the degree of agreement or disagreement with the statements. A text entry box was also provided for further insights and comments. 42 experts were invited, and 30 of them completed the survey. Our experts worked in various affiliations based in different countries: Germany, Italy, USA, UK, France, Netherlands, Japan, Portugal, China, and Norway. Their fields of expertise included Education, Game Design, Sociology, Modelling and Theory, Economics, Linguistic Annotation, Marketing, Psychology, Enterprise, Ergonomics, HCI, UX, Health, Game Development, Exertion Interfaces, Tourism, Motivational Mechanism, Behavioural Perspective, and Design. The full interview questions and questionnaire can be found on **http://goo.gl/wBZtiR**.

The clarification phase was designed to clarify the findings of the first two phases from the perspective of users. We looked for diversity in users' roles in the enterprise and interviewed 12 people, five who typically had a managerial role and seven who were other employees. We selected participants who were familiar with gamification and who use computers as a main medium for their jobs. Diversity in age, gender and work domain was also ensured, including nine males and three females, and their age ranged from 30 to 58 years old. The full list of interview questions can be found on **http://goo.gl/p15w1j**.

3   Results

By analysing the answers from the eight expert interviewees in the exploration phase, we deduced the below 11 statements on the relation between gamification and ethics. In the confirmation and enhancement phase, these statements were confirmed by 30 experts using a five-point Likert scale. The percentages are shown after each statement (**SA**: Strongly Agree, **A**: Agree, **N**: Neutral, **D**: Disagree, **SD**: Strongly Disagree).

1. Gamification can lead to tense relationship amongst colleagues, e.g. when applying a leader-board (**SA:** 30%, **A:** 43%, **N:** 17%, **D:** 7%, **SD:** 3%)
2. Gamification could lead to rating people and creating classes, i.e. more pressure and impact on the equity principles (**SA:** 17%, **A:** 47%, **N:** 20%, **D:** 17%, **SD:** 0%)
3. Gamification can create tension on the person, e.g. it could be seen as a monitoring system on how well a person is performing (**SA:** 27%, **A:** 50%, **N:** 7%, **D:** 17%, **SD:** 0%)
4. Gamification captures a lot of personal data, e.g. about performance. Privacy policies and data protection need to be augmented by ethical awareness (**SA:** 20%, **A:** 43%, **N:** 27%, **D:** 7%, **SD:** 3%)
5. Gamification can lead to exposure of information users are not necessarily willing to expose, e.g. listing the top 10 performers reveals if someone was never a top performer. (**SA:** 23%, **A:** 47%, **N:** 20%, **D:** 10%, **SD:** 0%)
6. Freedom of Information: Users' ability to see what is stored about them is an ethical issue (**SA:** 43%, **A:** 37%, **N:** 13%, **D:** 7%, **SD:** 0%)
7. Gamification, in certain cases, could mean trying to get from people more than what their job requires, i.e. using gamification as an exploitation-ware (**SA:** 23%, **A:** 40%, **N:** 13%, **D:** 23%, **SD:** 0%)
8. The desire for "wining the reward" could drive some users to overlook how data is gathered and to whom it is exposed. This makes some users, at times, vulnerable (**SA:** 17%, **A:** 47%, **N:** 20%, **D:** 17%, **SD:** 0%)
9. Ethics in gamification could be seen analogous to those in marketing, i.e. gamification could make some tasks attractive to users who would not ethically like to perform without gamification (**SA:** 10%, **A:** 43%, **N:** 40%, **D:** 7%, **SD:** 0%)
10. Ethics should be seen case by case and even at the level of individual users, e.g. the same game mechanic for the same task may be seen differently from ethical perspective according to the user (**SA:** 14%, **A:** 59%, **N:** 24%, **D:** 3%, **SD:** 0%)
11. Gamification ethics are highly dependent on the norms and culture of the organisation (**SA:** 37%, **A:** 50%, **N:** 10%, **D:** 3%, **SD:** 0%)

The experts' comments in these open-ended survey questions were also analysed to obtain further insights which will be reported, together with those obtained from the clarification phase with employees and managers, in the subsequent sections. The analysis in these two phases led to grouping the above statements into five categories:

- Gamification and tension at workplace (1, 2, 3)
- Gamification as a monitoring mechanism (3, 4)
- Gamification and privacy (4, 5, 6)
- Using gamification as "exploitation-ware" (7, 8)
- Gamification and its relation to personal and cultural values (9, 10, 11)

3.1 Gamification and Tension at Workplace

Nature of the Working Environment. The results show that implementing gamification in a collaborative environment will have a negative impact, since it creates an unnatural competition and thus tension, affecting the relationship amongst employees who will be heavily comparing themselves with each other, which is not the best practice for collaborative projects. In environments where competition is natural, e.g. bonuses to the best performers in a call centre, this effect of gamification could be acceptable.

Tasks. A main attribute of a business task, which matters here, is whether it is a collaborative or a competitive task regardless of the nature of the work environment. In addition, gamification seems to suit tasks which are with a measurable outcome, objective and done separately by a group of people. If the tasks can be measured, for example answering clients in a sales environment, then gamifying the task is unlikely to create or increase tension since it will provide employees with a system that showcases their efforts. Applying gamification for subjective tasks may lead to tension since quantifying the actual effort is usually hard. Applying gamification uniformly on different tasks could lead to more tension as "some may have easier tasks than others".

Age. Participants observed that older generation employees might not like to work in environments where gamification is applied, as it may lead to taking them out of their comfort zone and put them under the pressure of learning a new technology and to know in certain cases how to adjust their work style to get the best of it.

Employee's Personality. The achievements may make some employees arrogant or, in contrast, some employees may start to be helpful and try to train others. Some of them might be competitive and like it, while some "might just get stressed by thinking about it". Extroverts typically like showing their achievements, e.g. sharing their badges, while introverts may find it stressful.

The Management Style. In highly hierarchical and centralised management styles, gamification could lead to stressing people by creating the fear of being questioned frequently. Also, managers could use the collected information to compare employees with each other and create competition for promotions, hence creating tension. In different non-hierarchical environments, however, managers may use the data for improving employees' weaknesses, identifying their skills and finding the best role for them.

Employees' Ranks. Ranking employees via gamification could create tension, "If you appear in the leader-board, you are fine, but if you do not, you may feel depressed". Ranking could also have a negative impact on employees' relationships, decreasing the teamwork since "those who are below their peers will feel pressurised". However, ranking could increase teamwork when it is applied to a team instead of the individuals.

Clusters Amongst Employees. Employees who are performing similarly could group together and those who are under-performing might be asked to leave the group since they are deteriorating the team score and profile. However, clustering based on gamification is not necessarily negative as "it may create unity in a team, [since] it can group people [with similar talents] together".

Table 1 summarises our findings about the factors that can introduce tension into the working environment and clarify the fine line between questionable use of gamification and the use which is likely to be acceptable from ethical perspectives.

Table 1. Gamification vs. tension at workplace

	Tension-Problematic	Tension-Acceptable
Working Environment	Collaborative	Competitive
Task	Not measurable	Measurable
	Uniform	Non-uniform
	Subjective	Objective
	Collaborative	Competitive
Age	Older generation	Younger generation
Personality	Non-competitive	Competitive
	Introverts	Extroverts
Management Style	Comparative appraisal	Individual appraisal
	Destructive criticism	Constructive criticism
Rank	Rarely top performing	Regularly top performing
	Individual competition	Group collaboration to win
Clustering	Fear of being isolated	Talent-based grouping

3.2   Gamification as a Monitoring Mechanism

Monitoring performance is a common practice within enterprises even without gamification. The difference is that gamification can do that in a very detailed way. It may also capture sensitive personal data, e.g. the analysis of a webcam to deduce an employee's mood and mental status and reflect it on the avatar representing that employee. Monitoring from the perspective of privacy will be discussed in another section.

The Wide Visibility of Employees' Ranks in Enterprises. Leader-boards can be visible to everyone and can be perceived as a monitoring system. Employees may not like that, given that many will not appear as top performers. On the other hand, top performers embrace this feature as they can showcase their progress to other colleagues and especially managers. Top performers are recognised in traditional monitoring and appraisal systems but with a less frequency and visibility than the case with gamification.

Level of Details. Employees may have various productivity levels during working hours, referred to as highs and lows. Gamification can easily collect such details, giving managers the opportunity to know better the working pattern of a certain staff. Employees typically prefer to have control over how they perform the task and to make only the final results visible to the managers, not their performance during the process to achieve that. However, when detailed information is captured, employees could feel the pressure to have a constant level of performance.

The Nature of Tasks. Monitoring in general, and fine-grained monitoring in particular, puts pressure on employees when the tasks require creativity and one cannot predict how much time they should take. In addition, gamification-based monitoring may not reflect the true nature of the task. In a sales environment, for example, some of the employees may argue that although they have sold less, thus scoring less, but they had to deal with difficult and time demanding customers. Gamification can capture how much work is done, but is often limited in capturing the quality.

The Management Style. Employees tend to accept gamification as a monitoring system, as long as they are certain that managers would use it to help them improve, without comparing them to others and using it to make them put extra effort with the same pay. Furthermore, gamification can spot a performance problem but cannot interpret it and its context. When managers rely purely on gamification, it may lead to a misinterpretation of what is really happening. Managers should keep a direct contact with the employee to give meaning to the data monitored by gamification.

The Employees' Personality. Gamification could be used as a self-monitoring mechanism for employees who are interested in knowing how well they are performing and who use it to self-motivate themselves. However, personality traits could also play a key role here, as employees who are not genuinely interested in the job and who are "looking for promotions and just want to do the job" will rarely perceive monitoring in such a positive way.

Table 2 summarises our findings about factors related to gamification as a monitoring mechanism and how likely they are to raise issues in the working environment.

Table 2. Monitoring mechanism factors vs. their perception

	Likely to Raise Issues	Likely to be Accepted
Rank Visibility	Not in the top list	In the top list
	Frequently shown to all	Occasionally shown to all
Level of Details	Fine-grained details	Overall performance
Nature of Task	Creative	Classical
	Quality-based	Quantity-based
Management Style	No direct contact	Direct contact
	Pressurising for more profit	Improving self-productivity
Personality	Doing the task as any job	Genuinely interested in the task
	Moderately ambitious	Ambitious and self-motivated

3.3 Gamification and Privacy

As a counterpart of monitoring, privacy is seen as a main concern when using gamification. The concerns were centred on the following categories:

What is Being Stored? The use of gamification to capture work-related information, e.g. how many issues an employee has solved, seems to be acceptable. However, it raises issues when gamification captures personal information, or information which can lead to personal information, e.g. analysing the calls to know the mood of an employee and change the avatar accordingly. Also, the stored information should be objective facts, e.g. storing the time taken to solve an issue, rather than judgements which are subject to different interpretation and deduction methods, e.g. storing that an employee is tired or lazy because of the long time taken.

Who Can See the Information? Employees would not accept that gamification data is widely visible even for data reflecting their unique areas of expertise. This privacy concern is lighter when the data is available to managers who are legally entitled to monitor employees performance. Similarly, privacy concerns are less when data is available to relevant colleagues, especially when working as a team. This needs to be still based on clear organisational rules. Anonymity is also another aspect. Through the use of an anonymised or translucent leader-board, employees will know how well they are doing in comparison to the top performers, still without revealing anyone's identity.

The Employees' Personality. Typically, hard-working, competitive and ambitious employees will be less worried about privacy issues when gamification captures data related to their performance. They may see it an advantage, e.g. when applying for promotions or bonuses. Some others may not like competition and this may not be due to their low performance. They typically tend to be introverts and happy with their positions.

The Right to View Information. Participants agreed that employees should have the right to see what gamification reports capture about them. In essence, under the Freedom of Information Act in some countries, people are legally given this right. However, it stays in the grey area whether employees can also view how exactly the data was processed to infer a judgement which might not be straightforward or even algorithmic in certain cases.

Table 3 summarises our findings about factors related to privacy issues in gamification and how likely they are to raise issues in the working environment.

3.4 Gamification as "Exploitation-Ware"

The term "exploitation-ware" refers to the use of gamification to motivate staff to do more than what their job requires [10].

Table 3. Privacy vs. employees perception at workplace

	Likely to Raise Issues	Likely to Be Accepted
Stored Information	Personal, or likely to lead to infer personal information	Work-related information
	Subjective judgement	Objective facts
Information Accessibility	Public/non-relevant peers	Managers/relevant peers
	Real names	Anonymised or translucent
Personality	Introvert	Extrovert
	Non-competitive	Competitive
	Ambitious	Happy where they are
Right to View Information	Actual collected data and their interpretation are hidden	Both are available

The Strategy of Rewarding. The tendency to consider gamification as an "exploitation-ware" increases when the reward strategy depends on the relative performance of an employee with respect to others rather than being dependent on the individuals' performance progress. An example of this is when the top-ten performers get a higher salary while the rest, who still tried their best, are not rewarded. The design of a tempting reward mechanism which attracts many but can be ultimately achieved only by very few employees is likely to raise exploitation-related issues.

The Nature of Reward. Intangible rewards, such as being in the leader-board, have no "real" costs and could still drive employees to work harder. Intangible rewards could be viewed as an exploitation of the social environment and peer-pressure at an enterprise in order to get more work done without a significant tangible investment.

The Transparency of Rewarding Policy. If managers explain how points will be translated to promotions on an objective basis, this makes gamification more professional. Such translation is sometimes not easy to make and managers tend to do their evaluation of performance on a case by case basis by using their tacit knowledge. Thus, the problem is not solely about transparency but also about the ability to concretise and quantify the rewarding strategy.

The Perception of the Traditional Version of the Rewarding Mechanism. When the underlying reward strategy is ethically accepted, then its automated or gamified version is unlikely to be seen differently. For example, if in certain enterprises a draw conducted to choose one of the top performers to receive a gift is a well-accepted practice in the enterprise, gamifying it will not raise ethical issues. If such a procedure is seen as bringing lottery and gambling to the work environment, then gamifying it would raise similar ethical and professional issues.

Employees' Personality. Gamification could be seen as an "exploitation-ware" when applied to people who like intangible rewards and value them in an exaggerated way. Those who are obsessed in developing their online reputation would value a nicer avatar more than a salary increase. A similar observation could be made for those who are socially isolated in the traditional world and who try to compensate in the gamification world. Enterprise management should make sure that such exaggerated appreciation of virtual rewards is handled beforehand.

Table 4 summarises our findings regarding the factors related to the perception of gamification as an exploitation-ware.

Table 4. Gamification as exploitation-ware

	Likely to Raise Exploitation Issues	**Likely to Reduce Them**
Rewarding Strategy	Comparing to others progress	Comparing to self-progress
Nature of the Reward	Intangible costs	Tangible costs
Policy	Non-transparent, unexplained	Transparent, explained
Tasks	Non-concrete/ subjective	Concrete/ objective
Underlying Mechanism	Seen negative	Seen acceptable
Personality Type	Online "ultras"	Balanced
	Looking to compensate online	Balanced

3.5 Gamification vs. Personal and Cultural Values

Gamification and the desire to win, as an underlying concept, could lead to employees acting against their personal and cultural values. For example, in a call centre, an agent would tolerate the language of an angry customer to get the points of solving the issue.

Value-Sensitive Design. Gamification per se is not a reason for people to behave in a certain manner. It is just a facilitator. However, this should not mean that gamification developers and enterprise managers are exempted from any responsibility when applying it. Gamification, especially for the "digital-native" generation, could be a very attractive medium which facilitates acting against their personal and cultural values just to win the virtual reward. On the other hand, employees should have the freedom of rejecting mechanisms they see against their values. This shows the importance of value-sensitive design [11] of gamification as a kind of information systems.

Sacrificing Quality Standards. Gamification could drive people to do things in a cursory manner. The fear of losing their community recognition, when techniques like ranks and status and leader boards are applied, could be a main reason for that.

Cheating to Win/Survive. The desire to win, and also the fear of the failure, could drive people to cheat and do the tasks in a way which would contradict with their own values. This was observed in [5] through a case study in the education sector.

The Culture of the Place. The culture of the enterprise and the country where it resides is a key factor. In certain cultures, showing off is seen as a violation of the norms and conventions of acceptable public behaviour. This means the leader-boards might be incompatible with the norms, thus causing stress in the work environment.

Table 5 summarises our findings regarding the personal and cultural values related to gamification and how it links to ethical issues.

Table 5. Gamification vs. personal and cultural values

	Raise Ethical Issues	Likely to Reduce
Value Sensitive Design	Not-aligned with personal values	Aligned with personal values
	Forced to participate	Participation is an option
Quality Standards	Drive people to be fast	Quality first
	Create clear competition	Soft competition
Honesty	Difficult to win	Everyone can get something
	Consequences on losing	No serious consequences
Culture of the Place	Incompatible	Compatible

4   Conclusions and Future Work

We have investigated the debate regarding the ethical issues that gamification could cause within enterprises. Gamification could be seen as an unfair mechanism to increase productivity with no real costs, i.e. via playfulness. In addition, it could increase pressure on employees to achieve more or avoid being in the bottom of the list. Gamification might contradict with some personality types and cultural norms. In our future work, we will explore these issues related to the ethical use of gamification, including its inter-relation with culture, personality traits, and managerial styles. As a social and moral responsibility, we will also try to standardise a code of ethics for software developers and enterprises who design, build and implement gamification.

Acknowledgements. The research was supported by an FP7 Marie Curie CIG grant (the SOCIAD Project) and by Bournemouth University through the Fusion Investment Fund and the Graduate School Santander Grant for PGR Development.

References

1. Deterding, S., Dixon, D., Khaled, R., Nacke, L.: From game design elements to gamefulness: defining gamification. In: International Academic MindTrek Conference: Envisioning Future Media Environments, pp. 9–15 (2011)
2. Webb, E.N., Cantú, A.: Building internal enthusiasm for gamification in your organization. In: Kurosu, M. (ed.) HCII/HCI 2013, Part II. LNCS, vol. 8005, pp. 316–322. Springer, Heidelberg (2013)
3. Huotari, K., Hamari, J.: Defining gamification: a service marketing perspective. In: Proceeding of the 16th International Academic MindTrek Conference, pp. 17–22 (2012)
4. Simoes, J., Redondo, R.D., Vilas, A.F.: A social gamification framework for a K-6 learning platform. Comput. Human Behav. 29, 345–353 (2013)

5. O'Donovan, S., Gain, J., Marais, P.: A case study in the gamification of a university-level games development course. In: Proceedings of the South African Institute for Computer Scientists and Information Technologists Conference on - SAICSIT 2013, p. 242. ACM Press, New York (2013)
6. Herzig, P., Ameling, M., Schill, A.: A Generic Platform for Enterprise Gamification. In: 2012 Joint Working IEEE/IFIP Conference on Software Architecture and European Conference on Software Architecture, pp. 219–223. IEEE (2012)
7. Volkswagon: Piano Staircase | The Fun Theory, http://www.thefuntheory.com/piano-staircase
8. Creswell, J.W., Plano Clark, V.L.: Designing and conducting mixed methods research. SAGE Publications, Inc. (2011)
9. Myers, M.D., Newman, M.: The qualitative interview in IS research: Examining the craft. Inf. Organ. 17, 2–26 (2007)
10. Nicholson, S.: A User-Centered Theoretical Framework for Meaningful Gamification A Brief. Games+ Learning+ Society 8 (2012)
11. Friedman, B., et al.: Value sensitive design and information systems. In: Early Engagement and New technologies: Opening up the laboratory, pp. 55–95. Springer, Netherlands (2013)

Towards Actionable Business Intelligence: Can System Dynamics Help?

Soroosh Nalchigar, Eric Yu, and Steve Easterbrook

Department of Computer Science, University of Toronto
soroosh,eric,sme@cs.toronto.edu

Abstract. Business intelligence (BI) and data analytics provide modern enterprises with insights about internal operations, performance, as well as environmental trends, and enable them to make data-driven decisions. Insights resulting from these systems often suggest several alternative changes or corrective actions within the enterprise. In this context, to trade-off and find the most proper action(s) is a non-trivial task due to existing dynamics and complexities of the enterprise. This paper proposes a model-based approach to support the analysis and selection of best alternative actions in adaptive enterprise contexts. The proposed approach links and synthesizes two existing modeling frameworks, the Business Intelligence Model (BIM) and System Dynamics, in a systematic step-by-step way to assist decision makers in finding best response action(s) from a given set of alternatives, and hence to make BI more actionable and understandable. The applicability of this approach in illustrated in a scenario adapted from literature.

Keywords: Business Intelligence, Analytics, Goal-oriented Requirements Engineering, System Dynamics, Enterprise Modeling, Simulation.

1 Introduction

Goal-oriented modeling frameworks, such as i^* [25,27], have been introduced for modeling and analyzing the socio-technical contexts of enterprise. These frameworks can be used to model and analyze existing actors in the enterprise, their goals, dependencies, as well as internal operations. Moreover, such frameworks can capture alternative course of actions for achieving goals, express their impact on the strategic goals, and can support assessing whether the goals are met. Recently, the Business Intelligence Model (BIM) [4,14,7] extends goal modeling to incorporate business intelligence (BI) and analytics related concepts such as indicators in order to assist business users to utilize the vast amounts of data about the enterprise and its external environment. Although these frameworks represent various aspects of enterprise, they do not capture the temporal features and notions of time. In other words, these frameworks do not model the behaviour and changes of the enterprise over time.

Consider a global restaurant chain that, by using BI tools, realizes there is a declining trend in total sales in some of their market segments. In such a context, BIM modeling can help enterprises make sense of their data and gain a

U. Frank et al. (Eds.): PoEM 2014, LNBIP 197, pp. 246–260, 2014.

better understanding of business operations and its environment. It conceptualizes strategic goals (e.g., increase market share) as well as performance indicators (e.g., total sales), and provides analysts with an understanding of how well they are doing with respect to their strategic goals. However, the BIM framework does not deal with the actions that the restaurant chain may take in response to improve its situation. Moreover, the changes in indicators over time and the long term and short term impacts of those actions are not addressed. For example, to improve performance, restaurant decision makers may come up with various proposals such as introducing a new product, improving the marketing campaign, or lowering prices. In such a context, the decision makers need to examine how strongly each of the potential actions will improve the desired indicators over time. How much time does it take for each alternative to improve the performance indicators? What are the side effects of the actions on the other strategic goals and metrics of the company?

Today's business environment is characterized by its dynamic nature, increasing uncertainties, and rapid changes. To survive and remain competitive in such a context, modern enterprises need to *sense* the environmental trends and *respond* to them proactively. They need to adjust their internal structures and processes in response to changes in the environment [13,21]. BI and data analytics solutions play a crucial role in realizing the vision of the Sense-and-Respond enterprise [13]. These systems serve as sensing mechanism of the enterprise by assisting business users to identify business situation, monitor the strategic goals, and track performance indicators [26]. A critical challenge in these contexts is to make BI solutions actionable, i.e., to link BI-derived insights to business strategies and organizational processes to take the right action at the right time [17]. Insights resulting from BI and data analytics usually suggest several alternative changes within various parts of the enterprise. Business managers then face the challenge of choosing the best corrective actions.

Analyzing and making trade-offs among enterprise actions is a nontrivial task. This difficulty arises, partially, from the fact that it is very hard to understand how each of the potential actions would influence enterprise strategic goals over time and also how it is influenced by existing contextual factors. Towards overcoming this difficulty, modeling and analysis of dynamic behaviour of alternative actions and their influence on enterprise performance indicators is a major step. This paper proposes a model-based approach that integrates and links the BIM modeling framework with System Dynamics [12,22], to support decision making on alternative enterprise actions. System Dynamics is a method for modeling and analyzing the behaviour of complex systems over time. The proposed approach utilizes the complementary advantages of BIM and System Dynamics framework to conceptualize enterprise actions and their impact on business situation over time, to facilitate decision making over BI-derived insights, and hence to make BI and analytics systems more actionable. The approach includes a set of suggestive heuristics to derive System Dynamics models from BIM models. Also, the proposed approach assists BI analysts to elicit new requirements for adapting the BI systems to the new enterprise context resulting from the change.

In previous work [18], we proposed a model-based methodology for closing the gap between what an enterprises senses from BI insights and the consequent actions and corrective changes. The second and third phases of that methodology includes generating alternative actions and selecting the most appropriate one(s). Although the models and criteria proposed in that methodology help users to analyze the alternatives, the dynamics of the indicators, the notion of time, and complexities of the context are left unconsidered. In this paper we examine how System Dynamics modeling and simulations can be used to analyze the dynamics of the enterprise and to examine how well each of the alternative corrective actions would affect the strategic goals and the situation of the enterprise. The practices that are proposed in this paper would be useful in the second and third phase of our previous methodology whose goal is to make BI system more actionable.

The rest of this paper is organized as follows. Section 2 reviews the baseline of the paper, including BIM modeling language and System Dynamics approach. Section 3 presents a case scenario to motivate the research problem. Section 4 presents the proposed approach and shows its applicability in the motivating scenario. Section 5 presents a set of suggestive heuristics for deriving System Dynamics models from BIM models. Section 6 reviews related work to this study. Section 7 concludes the paper and presents directions for future work.

2   Baseline

The baseline of this work includes the BIM modeling language and System Dynamics modeling. Our goal is to present a systematic approach that links and synthesizes these two to facilitate decision making on the BI and analytics-driven insights, and hence to achieve actionable BI and analytics.

2.1   Business Intelligence Model (BIM)

BIM is a modeling language for representing the strategic goals of the enterprise. Aiming to bridge the gap between business-level understanding of the enterprise with its representation in databases and data warehouses for BI purposes, BIM makes use of well established business concepts to support decision making during strategic business analysis [15,14]. The primitive BIM concepts are goals, tasks/processes, indicators, situations, and influences. This modeling language facilitates understanding of the enterprise and provides a business-friendly way to use huge amounts of enterprise data [7]. It assists enterprise users to keep track of enterprise performance and sense how well they are doing with regard to their strategic goals. References [6,5] provide real world case studies of this modeling language.

2.2   System Dynamics

System Dynamics, initially proposed by Forrester [12] and later extended by Sterman [22] and others, is an approach for understanding and modeling the dynamics and behaviour of complex systems over time. The main concepts in this modeling approach are causality and feedback loop, stock or level (the accumulation of resources in the system), and flow or rate (dispersal of those resources). Two major modeling and representation types in System Dynamics are Causal Loop Diagrams and Stock and Flow Diagrams. While Causal Loop Diagrams allow qualitative modeling of the system variables and their causal effects, the Stock and Flow Diagrams use differential equations for quantitative modeling and simulation of the system. In this study, we illustrate how System Dynamics could be used to facilitate the connection between what an enterprise senses from BI insights to the consequent actions and corrective changes.

3   Motivating Example

In order to motivate the research problem and to show applicability of our approach, we adapt a running example from previous research [14,7]. Using real-world reports, they created a business scenario and applied the BIM modeling and reasoning techniques on that. The example presents BestTech Inc., a generic company that manufactures and sells consumer electronics. Figure 1 is part of the BIM model for this company, representing structure of the strategic goals and their refinements along with corresponding indicators (red on top, yellow on middle, green on bottom) and current business situation. It indicates that the root strategic goal of the BestTech company is *To increase shareholder value*. This goal is AND-decomposed into two subgoals *To maintain revenue growth, To reduce costs* and the task *Acquire a competitor*. Similarly, the *To maintain competitive advantage* goal is OR-decomposed into two alternative sub-goals, namely *To invest in new technologies* and *To establish strategic partnership*. To trace the business situation and monitor the performance, the company has defied some indicators, e.g., *Marketing costs* for the goal *To reduce marketing costs* and *Sales volume* for the goal *To increase sales volume*. Moreover, the BIM model shows how the strategic goals would influence each other. For example, the goals *To offer promotions* has negative influences on the goal *To maintain gross margin*. The model also shows that there is a domain assumption of *High demand*, which must be true in order for the goal *To increase sales* to be achieved. In addition, this model indicates how external situations are influencing the company's strategic goals, e.g., *World-wide increase in fuel price* negatively affects the goal *To reduce distribution costs*.

Currently, using the BIM model in Figure 1, the company finds that it has an average performance (yellow indicator) with respect to its top goal. Moreover. the marketing department finds that the *Sales volume* indicator is below the defined threshold, i.e., deficient performance with regarding to the goal *To increase sales volume*. In addition, the BIM model indicates that the levels of *Gross margin* and *Marketing costs* are not satisfactory. On the other hand, the *Total costs* indicator is green which means that the total level of costs is below the defined threshold. Having these signals about current business situation, BestTech executives decide to initiate some changes within the company in order to improves the sales and revenues while keeping total costs at the satisfactory level (as it is now).

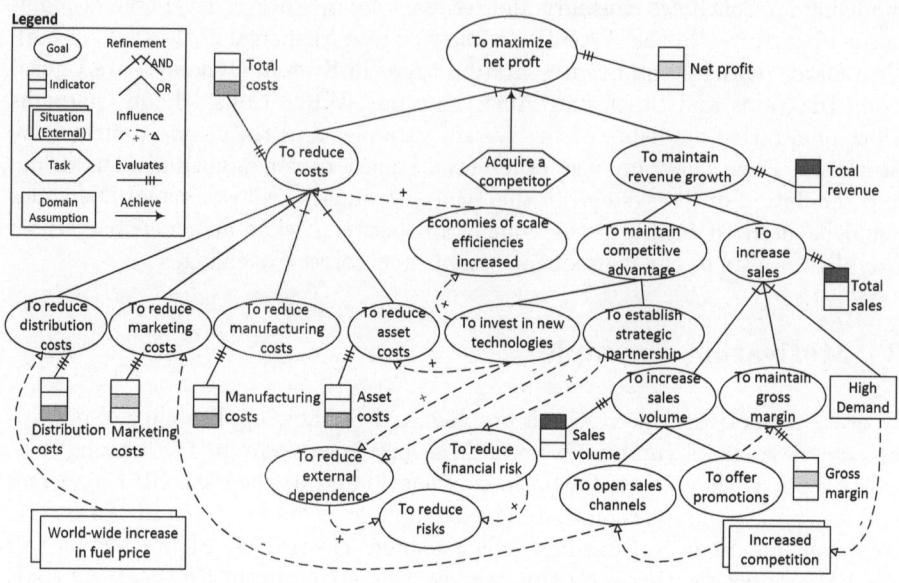

Fig. 1. BIM schema for the BestTech Inc

They want to make the red and yellow indicators green while keeping the green indicators as they are. Towards these ends, the executives initiate brainstorming sessions and motivate the members to find a best actions that the company should take. As a result, they come up with two alternative solutions as follows: (1) Lower the price of products to increase sales and revenues, and (2) Improve product quality levels by training the production lines personnel. Each of these options are possible responses that BestTech could adopt based on what it has sensed from the BI system.

In this situation, to select the best response action(s) is not an easy task due to existing dynamics and rapid changes inside and outside of the company. There are lots of factors to be taken into account and finding the most proper alternative is a great challenge. The decision makers want to know: How and to what extent each alternative would help company to achieve the goals whose indicators are not at the satisfactory level? How fast each alternative would help the company to improve its condition? What are long term effects of each alternative on the strategic goals? How and to what degree each alternative would influence other strategic goals of the company in which they have a good performance at the current time? What are possible influences of existing contextual factors (e.g., *World-wide increase in fuel prices*) to each alternative? The main contribution of this paper is to link and to synthesize System Dynamics modeling with the BIM to use their complementary advantages for making connections between the sensing accomplished through BI and consequent enterprise actions.

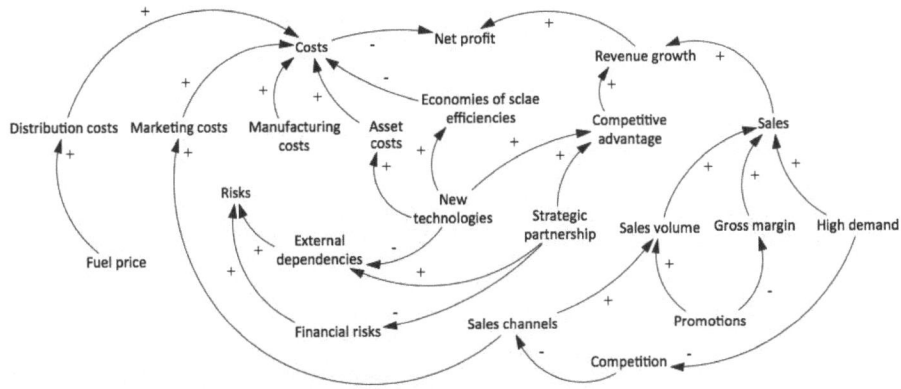

Fig. 2. Initial Causal Loop Diagram derived from the BIM schema

4   Proposed Approach

This section explains the steps and activities of the proposed approach and illustrates its application on the motivation example of previous section. The approach assumes that the enterprise analysts have constructed a BIM schema (to measure the performance indicators) and also have a set of alternative actions from which they want to choose the best one(s).

Step 1: Understanding the Decision Context. The main task in this step is to model the dynamic interactions of elements and factors within the enterprise and to formulate the cognitive model of enterprise decision makers. In other words, the main goal in this step is to represent how various enterprise related concepts and variables are interrelated. For these purposes, we use Causal Loop Diagrams. Section 5 presents a conceptual connection between the BIM framework and Causal Loop Diagrams. Proposed guides could be used in this step for constructing a skeleton of Causal Loop Diagram from the initial BIM model that was an input of the approach. After having the initial Causal Loop Diagram, analysts can add extra variables to enrich that for a better modeling of the context. In this step, the simplicity of Causal Loop diagrams will result in improved communication and comprehensiveness among decision makers.

Figure 2 shows the Causal Loop Diagram derived from the BIM schema of Figure 1. This model shows how different contextual variables and elements would interact and influence each other. For example it shows that a rise in *Competitive advantage* of company will lead to higher *Revenue growth* and consequently will result in an increase to *Net profit*. Moreover, it shows the higher the *Fuel price*, the higher the *Distribution costs* becomes and hence the *Costs* increases. Additionally, it shows changes in *Sales channels* and *Promotions* will reflect in changes in the same direction to *Sales volume*.

The main output of this step is a Causal Loop Diagram, derived from the BIM model, to represent the interactions of enterprise elements and factors within decision context.

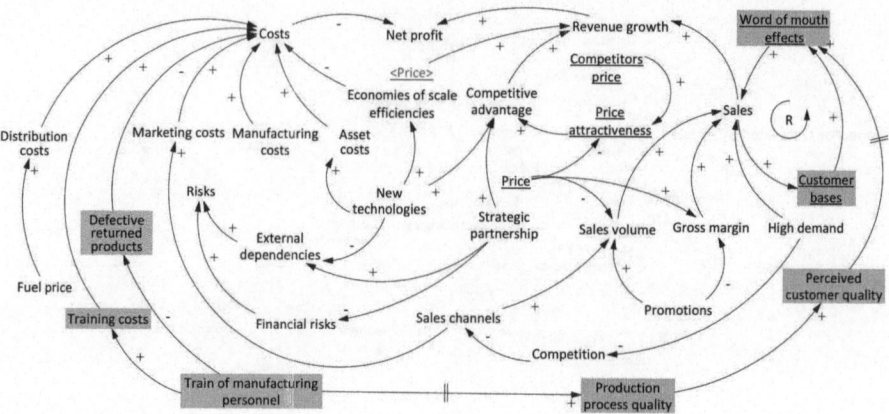

Fig. 3. Causal Loop Diagram with alternatives. Variables with underlined name and their associated links represent the first alternative. Variables with grey background represent the second alternative.

Step 2: Conceptualization of the Alternatives. The next step of our approach is to add the alternative actions as new variables to the Causal Loop Diagram, and to model the causal relationships between each alternative and the existing variables in the model. In this way, the decision makers hypothesize the influences of each alternative to the rest of variables, specially those that are related to strategic goals. In order to achieve a better modeling and understanding of the relationship between each alternative and strategic goals of the enterprise, at this step new intervening variables are added to the model by the analyst. Intervening variables are those that moderate the relationship between each alternative and strategic variables of the enterprise. By adding them, the analyst improves the validity and certainty of these models for later analysis in the approach. It should be noted that as the enterprise adapts to the changing environment, the BI system needs to be adapted accordingly to satisfy new requirements of the users. The new variables that are introduced into the Causal Loop Diagram in this step can be new requirements for the BI and analytics platforms in the enterprise.

Figure 3 shows how the alternative actions of the BestTech company are represented in Causal Loop Diagram in terms of new variables and influence links. Due to lack of space, both alternatives are illustrated in a single diagram. Regarding the first alternative, the variable *Price attractiveness* is affected by the variables *Price* and *Competitors price*. Moreover, as the *Price* of the company's products increases, the *Revenue growth* and *Gross margin* increases, while the *Sales volume* decreases. Regarding the second alternative, *Train of manufacturing personnel* will increase the *Training costs* and causes a reduce in number of *Defective returned products*. This variable, after a delay, will increase *Production process quality* and as a result the *Perceived customer quality* will be increased. An increase in *Perceived customer quality*, after a delay, will positively affect

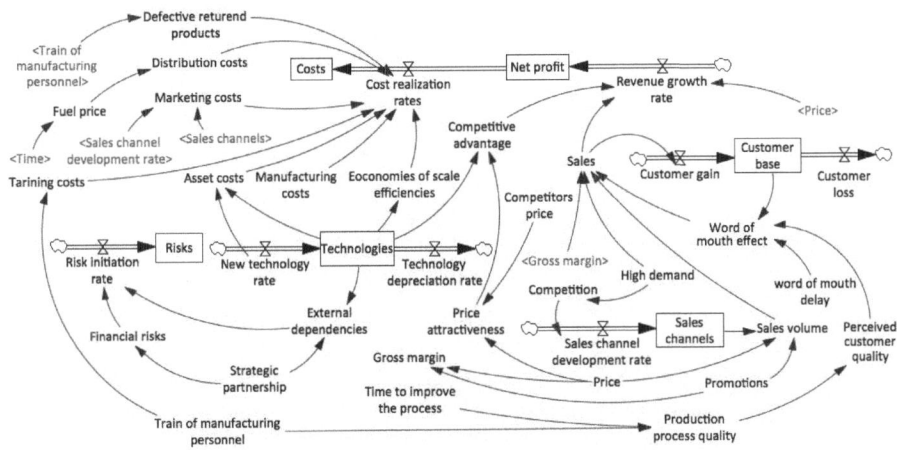

Fig. 4. Stock and Flow Diagram for BestTech Inc

Word of mouth effects, and consequently the *Sales* will increase. Finally, the reinforcing loop *R* shows how existing customers' word of mouth would affect the sales over time. An increase in *Customer base* would increase the *Word of mouth effects*, meaning that current customers would influence and encourage other potential customers to buy electronic products from BestTech and join the customer base. The main output of this step is two-fold. First, a Causal Loop Diagram is created that includes the alternative actions and their influences on the enterprise variables. Second, a set of new variables is identified which represents the new requirements for the BI and analytics systems.

Step 3: Construction of Stock and Flow Diagrams. In this step, the Causal Loop Diagram generated in previous step is transformed into a Stock and Flow Diagram. Stock and Flow Diagrams are more detailed and complex than Causal Loop Diagram and enable quantitative analysis and simulation. In this step, the analyst distinguishes the Causal Loop Diagram variables into stock, flow, and auxiliary variables and also decides about the information or flow links. Moreover, the analyst can add new variables and factors to the Stock and Flow Diagram for a more detailed analysis of the system. Similar to previous step, all these new variables represent new requirements for the BI and analytics systems. Within the literature of System Dynamics, there exist some methods and rules for developing Stock and Flow Diagram from Causal Loop Diagrams. For example, Binder et al. [8] presents a systematic four steps process for transforming Causal Loop Diagrams to Stock and Flow Diagrams. Also, Burns [10] provides a formal description of relationships between Causal Loop Diagram and Stock and Flow Diagrams.

Figure 4 indicates the Stock and Flow Diagram created for the BestTech Inc. case study. Because of space limitations, both alternatives are represented in a single model, while all analyzes and simulations of the alternatives (in the next step) are performed separately. This model shows the *Revenue growth rate* of the company, calculated from *Price*, *Sales*, and *Competitive advantage*, is accumulated in the stock of *Net profit*. As the company spends for various costs with the rate of *Cost realization rate*, those money leaves the stock of *Net profit* and flow into the stock of *Costs*. The model indicates as the company invests on technologies with *New technology rate*, the technologies are accumulated in the stock of *Technologies*. This stock influences the *Economies of scale efficiencies* and its value is reduced at the rate of *Technology depreciation rate*. The *Asset costs*, influenced by *New technology rate* and costs of maintaining current *Technologies*, contributes to *Cost realization rate*. The variables *Time to improve the process* and *Word of mouth delay* are added to the model to quantitatively represent the time delays. Moreover, the *Fuel price* is considered as a function of *Time* and influences the *Distribution costs*. The main output of this step is a Stock and Flow Diagram that could be used for simulation and analysis.

Step 4: Simulation and Analysis. The main activity in this step is to add parameters, initial values, and formulas to the Stock and Flow Diagram. The BI and analytics platforms can contribute to this step by providing many of these information, and hence by assisting the analyst to have a more valid and realistic Stock and Flow Diagram. For example, the initial level of stock variables such as *Net profit*, could be retrieved from BI dashboards. Moreover, at this step, existing System Dynamics validation methods could be used by the analyst to verify if the model is in line with actual enterprise behaviour. Forrester and Senge [11] present several validation tests of System Dynamics models in three categories, namely model structure, model behaviour, and policy implications. In this step, Matlab or Vensim [23] are used to simulate the business actions with differential equations. These simulations assist business users to examine the impact of the alternative actions on the strategic goals and indicators over time, and hence to facilitate business decision supports.

Figure 5 shows results of simulations of the alternatives with regarding to three strategic performance indicators, namely costs, net profit, and revenue over three months. For the sake of illustration, we have added hypothetical equations and parameters to the Stock and Flow Diagram of the previous step. While Figure 5 (a) shows the alternatives are similar in terms of *Costs*, Figure 5 (b) compares the alternatives with regarding to *Net profit*, and shows the second alternative will outperform other options. This figure indicates that during the first month, the first alternative is better due to the time delays that second alternative needs for changing the *Production process quality* and *customer's word of mouth*. However, the second alternative will outperform starting from the second month. Figure 5 (c) shows that while all the three alternatives have increasing revenue growth, due to high demand in the market (coming from domain assumptions in BIM), the second alternative performs better than others in long term. Based on these simulations, the BestTech Inc. decides to follow the second alternative, i.e. to invest on training of manufacturing personnel to improve the quality of products.

Finally, some of the characteristics of the proposed approach are discussed. The proposed approach aims to make BI and analytics systems more actionable by supporting users to make sense of their enterprise data and to find the best

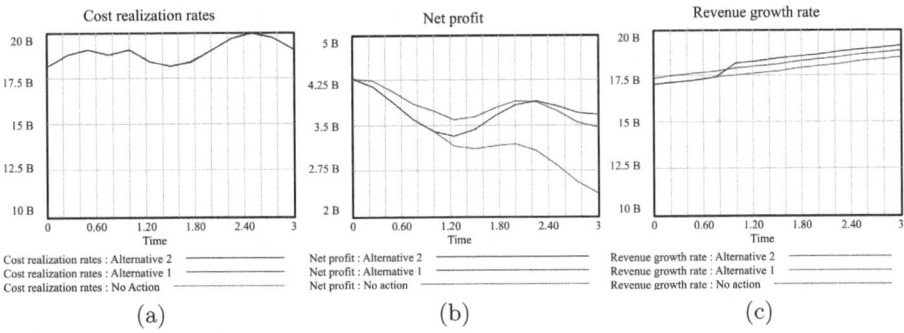

Fig. 5. Comparison of alternatives over three months: (a) Total costs; (b) Net profit; and (c) Revenues

response actions for their situation. This approach utilizes the complementary advantages of the BIM framework and System Dynamics to facilitate decision making on the BI-derived insights, and to find the best corrective action among a given set of alternatives, for improving business situation and achieving strategic goals. This approach comes with a set of guides that assist users to draw a Causal Loop Diagrams from a given BIM model to facilitate faster decision making and hence enterprise adaptiveness. Finally, the approach aids BI analysts in finding new requirements for the BI system to adapt them to the changing enterprise context.

5 From BIM to Causal Loop Diagram

In this section, we propose a set of general guides for developing Causal Loop Diagrams from BIM models. These guides are useful in the first step of the proposed approach (See Section 4) and can assist users to draw a skeleton of a Causal Loop Diagram from a BIM model. It should be emphasized that BIM models and Causal Loop Diagrams express and convey different aspects and elements of the system under consideration and there could not be a mechanistic and automated transformation between them. While the BIM framework represents the intentional aspects of the enterprise, Causal Loop Diagrams represent the enterprise in terms of variables and their interrelated changes over time. Due to inherent differences in purpose and semantics of modeling constructs, we advocate a series of guides and suggestions rather a formalized procedure to convert BIM models to Causal Loop Diagrams. It should be mentioned that developing Causal Loop Diagrams is a context-dependent task which requires understanding and knowledge about the domain. Using the proposed guides would result in an initial skeleton of a Causal Loop Diagram which needs to be further enriched by adding additional variables and links.

Goals: In the BIM framework, goals represent intentional desires towards important contextual concepts in the enterprise. Hence, a goal in the BIM model suggests that there is a corresponding variable in the Causal Loop Diagram. The variable could be extracted from the name of the goal or the indicator connected to it. For example the goal *To increase sales* in the BIM model suggests a variable such as *Sales* in the Causal Loop Diagram. It should be noted that not all goals in the BIM model need to become a variable in the Causal Loop Diagram. Also, there could be variables in the Causal Loop Diagram that are not goals in the BIM.

Decomposition links: Goals can be decomposed into and pursued through sub-goals. When a goal is decomposed into its sub-goals in a BIM model, it is likely that there is a causal link between their corresponding variables in the Causal Loop Diagram. We suggest that the "AND-decomposition" and "OR-decomposition" links between goals in a BIM model can be shown as positive links between corresponding variables in the Causal Loop Diagram. For an example, see the decomposition link between the goals *To maintain revenue growth* and *To increase sales* in Figure 1 and its corresponding causal link in Figure 2.

Influence links: An influence link between two elements in a BIM model represents a relationship between them in a probabilistic or causal sense [4]. This suggests that there is a causal link between corresponding elements in the Causal Loop Diagram. The polarity of the link in the Causal Loop Diagram could be same as the sign of the influence link in BIM model, unless in cases where one side of the influence link in the BIM model is a goal that refers to lowering the value or level of a variable. In such cases the sign should be reversed. For example, in the BIM model of Figure 1, the goal *Economies of scale efficiencies increased* has a positive influence on the goal *To reduce costs*. In the Causal Loop Diagram of Figure 2, that influence link is represented as a negative causal link between variables *Economies of scale efficiencies* and *Costs*.

Situations: The situations are partial state of the world and represent the internal and external factors that influence achievement of strategic goals [14,4]. A situation in BIM model could be represented as a variable in Causal Loop Diagram. For example the situation *Word-wide increase of fuel price* in the BIM model of Figure 1 is represented as the *Fuel price* variable in the Causal Loop Diagram of Figure 2.

Domain Assumptions: In the BIM framework, assumptions are propositions assumed to be true for purposes of achievement of a goal [4]. These assumptions are about concepts related to the domain and can be represented as a variable in the Causal Loop Diagram. This variable will be constant during the simulation analyzes.

These proposed guides were used in Section 4 to arrive at a Causal Loop Diagram from the BIM schema of the motivating example. These guides are, indeed, a series of heuristic connections and correspondences between the BIM schema and Causal Loop Diagram. The enterprise analyst can use them to construct a skeleton of a Causal Loop Diagram from a given BIM model, but it would typically need to be enriched with additional variables, links, and delays. Some of these additional variables and links are indeed new requirements for the BI platform. By making connection between BIM and Causal Loop Diagram, this approach helps BI analysts to elicit new requirements of the BI system and to adapt it to the changing business environment. The suggested guides could be used as a connection between BI systems and System Dynamics models to enable feeding data from a BI platform to the System Dynamics modeling and simulations tools. This will allow BI platforms and System Dynamics modeling to complement each other and assists enterprises to take advantage of this. For the BI side, the System Dynamics models can offer various "what-if" analyses to better serve users' needs. For the System Dynamics side, the BI could offer realistic data to test, validate, and improve the model structures.

6   Related Work

This section reviews related work in three categories.

System Dynamics for Managerial Decision Making. System Dynamics practices have been widely used in managerial decision support. An et al. [1] illustrated how System Dynamics could be used to model and understand the dynamic behaviours of performance indicators in the adaptive enterprise. They introduced optimization elements into the formalism of System Dynamics and embedded it in a technical Sense-and-Respond supply chain architecture. Schoeneborn [20] linked the Balanced Scorecard (BSC) to System Dynamics modeling and showed how it could be used to perform extensive analysis of strategic measures using simulations on a hypothetical example. He argued that BSC considers only simple cause and effect relationships between measures and it leaves the time delays unconsidered. Similarly, Nielsen and Nielsen [19] used System Dynamics modeling to develop time and dynamics dimension into BSC and to examine the effects of skills, customers, and work in process variables on the return on capital employed. Yim et al. [24] used System Dynamics to propose a knowledge-based decision making method for supporting strategic planning and high-level decision making in the enterprise. Our approach is different from these works in that it uses System Dynamics to provide decision support on the BI and analytics driven insights, and hence to facilitate closing the gap between what an enterprise senses from BI insights to its response actions.

Reasoning on BIM Models. The BIM modeling language comes with a set of reasoning techniques to support analysis and answering strategic questions. While the forward/bottom-up reasoning techniques evaluate the impact of different alternative goals on the top goal, the backward/top-down reasoning techniques find a set of goals with minimum costs to be satisfied in order to guarantee achievement of a given top goal [4]. Barone et al. [2] proposed three techniques for deriving values of composite indicators from values of their component using conversion factor, range normalization, and qualitative reasoning. Later, they implemented an Eclipse-based prototype tool supporting these techniques [3]. Horkoff et al. [15] provided a formal semantics of BIM concepts in description logics and used that semantics for supporting "what-if" analyses over BIM models. Reference [14] presents a hybrid reasoning technique which supports reasoning with incomplete indicators. While these techniques facilitate strategic decision making, they do not support decision making on enterprise actions and corrective changes. Moreover, they do not consider the time dimension. Our approach connects the BIM framework to System Dynamics modeling to facilitate decision making on alternative actions resulted from BI insights and to support elicitation of new requirements for the BI system.

Adaptive Enterprise Architecture. In 1995, Stephan Haeckel defined the notion of adaptive enterprise and described a transformation model from a Make-and-Sell enterprise to a Sense-and-Respond enterprise [13]. Motivated by his work, Buckley et al. [9] and Kapoor et al. [16] proposed technical frameworks for implementing Sense-and-Respond business performance management. Yu et al. [26] presented some research challenges and directions for adaptive enterprise architecture and highlighted the need for a systematic framework that supports modeling, analyzing, and designing adaptive enterprise. In another study, Yu et al. [28] examined capabilities of two existing requirements modeling techniques, namely goal-based social modeling (i^*) and process modeling, in capturing the dynamics and changes of application settings, found their inadequacies and modeling challenges, and finally outlined a set of desired features for a new comprehensive modeling framework. This work continues this line of research by integrating two existing modeling frameworks in a systematic way for facilitating decision making on response actions in adaptive enterprise.

7   Conclusion and Future Work

BI and analytics systems play a critical role in modern enterprises by providing insights about business progress towards strategic goals, internal operations, as well as external environment. BI-driven insights often suggest alternative corrective actions and changes within various parts of the enterprise. To trade-off and choose the most proper action(s) is a challenging task due to enterprise dynamics and complexities. This paper linked and synthesized the BIM modeling language with System Dynamics modeling and proposed a systematic approach for decision making on BI-driven insights. The results indicate that System Dynamics modeling offers a range of potential benefits and contribution to making BI systems more actionable that are currently not well catered for by existing tools and platforms. Evidently, the proposed approach needs to be evaluated in real-world case studies. Moreover, using System Dynamics requires the analyst to add new assumptions about the context (e.g., parameters, initial values, formulas) into the analysis. Finding appropriate mathematical equations of quantitative behaviour of the enterprise is not an easy task. BI can alleviate this challenge by providing real data of the variables to make it more realistic and valid.

This paper is part of a broader research agenda whose goal is to propose an enterprise architecture framework for adaptive enterprises. In future, we plan to extend the existing System Dynamic models by adding social modeling elements, such as actors from i^* modeling framework, and to investigate how these frameworks could complement each other for supporting enterprise adaptiveness. Currently, we are investigating conceptual connections and compliances between the goal-oriented frameworks and Stock and Flow Diagrams. Moreover, we are developing a new modeling language to be used for requirements engineering of data mining and business intelligence projects. This modeling language will support organizational use of data mining and analytics tools, connects the insights to enterprise actions, and hence facilitates closing the Sense-and-Respond loops in adaptive enterprise.

References

1. An, L., Jeng, J.J., Ettl, M., Chung, J.-Y.: A system dynamics framework for sense-and-respond systems. In: IEEE International Conference on E-Commerce Technology for Dynamic E-Business, pp. 6–13. IEEE (2004)
2. Barone, D., Jiang, L., Amyot, D., Mylopoulos, J.: Composite indicators for business intelligence. In: Jeusfeld, M., Delcambre, L., Ling, T.-W. (eds.) ER 2011. LNCS, vol. 6998, pp. 448–458. Springer, Heidelberg (2011)
3. Barone, D., Jiang, L., Amyot, D., Mylopoulos, J.: Reasoning with key performance indicators. In: Johannesson, P., Krogstie, J., Opdahl, A.L. (eds.) The Practice of Enterprise Modeling. LNBIP, vol. 92, pp. 82–96. Springer, Heidelberg (2011)
4. Barone, D., Mylopoulos, J., Jiang, L., Amyot, D.: The business intelligence model: Strategic modelling. Technical report, University of Toronto (April 2010)
5. Barone, D., Peyton, L., Rizzolo, F., Amyot, D., Mylopoulos, J.: Towards model-based support for managing organizational transformation. In: Babin, G., Stanoevska-Slabeva, K., Kropf, P. (eds.) E-Technologies: Transformation in a Connected World. LNBIP, vol. 78, pp. 17–31. Springer, Heidelberg (2011)
6. Barone, D., Topaloglou, T., Mylopoulos, J.: Business intelligence modeling in action: A hospital case study. In: Ralyté, J., Franch, X., Brinkkemper, S., Wrycza, S. (eds.) CAiSE 2012. LNCS, vol. 7328, pp. 502–517. Springer, Heidelberg (2012)
7. Barone, D., Yu, E., Won, J., Jiang, L., Mylopoulos, J.: Enterprise modeling for business intelligence. In: Bommel, P., Hoppenbrouwers, S., Overbeek, S., Proper, E., Barjis, J. (eds.) The Practice of Enterprise Modeling. LNBIP, vol. 68, pp. 31–45. Springer, Heidelberg (2010)
8. Binder, T., Vox, A., Belyazid, S., Haraldsson, H., Svensson, M.: Developing system dynamics models from causal loop diagrams. In: Proceedings of the 22nd International Conference of the System Dynamics Society, Oxford, Great Britain, July 25-29 (2004)
9. Buckley, S., Ettl, M., Lin, G., Wang, K.-Y.: Sense and respond business performance management. In: An, C., Fromm, H. (eds.) Supply Chain Management on Demand, pp. 287–311. Springer, Heidelberg (2005)
10. Burns, J.R.: Simplified translation of CLDs into SFDs. In: Proceedings of the 19th International Conference of the System Dynamics Society, Atlanta, GA (July 2001)
11. Forrester, J.W., Senge, P.M.: Tests for building confidence in system dyamics models. TIMS Studies in the Management Sciences 14, 209–228 (1980)
12. Forrester, J.W.: Industrial dynamics, vol. 2. MIT Press, Cambridge (1961)
13. Haeckel, S.H.: Adaptive enterprise design: the sense-and-respond model. Strategy & Leadership 23(3), 6–42 (1995)
14. Horkoff, J., Barone, D., Jiang, L., Yu, E., Amyot, D., Borgida, A., Mylopoulos, J.: Strategic business modeling: representation and reasoning. Software & Systems Modeling, 1–27 (2012)

15. Horkoff, J., Borgida, A., Mylopoulos, J., Barone, D., Jiang, L., Yu, E., Amyot, D.: Making data meaningful: The business intelligence model and its formal semantics in description logics. In: Meersman, R., et al. (eds.) OTM 2012, Part II. LNCS, vol. 7566, pp. 700–717. Springer, Heidelberg (2012)
16. Kapoor, S., Bhattacharya, K., Buckley, S., Chowdhary, P., Ettl, M., Katircioglu, K., Mauch, E., Phillips, L.: A technical framework for sense-and-respond business management. IBM Systems Journal 44(1), 5–24 (2005)
17. LaValle, S., Hopkins, M., Lesser, E., Shockley, R., Kruschwitz, N.: Analytics: The new path to value. How the smartest organizations are embedding analytics to transform insights into action. MIT Sloan Management Review (2010)
18. Nalchigar, S., Yu, E.: From Business Intelligence Insights to Actions: A Methodology for Closing the Sense-and-Respond Loop in the Adaptive Enterprise. In: Grabis, J., Kirikova, M., Zdravkovic, J., Stirna, J. (eds.) PoEM 2013. LNBIP, vol. 165, pp. 114–128. Springer, Heidelberg (2013)
19. Nielsen, S., Nielsen, E.H.: System dynamics modelling for a balanced scorecard: Computing the influence of skills, customers, and work in process on the return on capital employed. Management Research News 31(3), 169–188 (2008)
20. Schoeneborn, F.: Linking balanced scorecard to system dynamics. In: Preceedings of the 21st System Dynamics Conference (2003)
21. Sherehiy, B., Karwowski, W., Layer, J.K.: A Review of Enterprise Agility: Concepts, Frameworks, and Attributes. International Journal of Industrial Ergonomics 37(5), 445–460 (2007)
22. Sterman, J.: Business dynamics. Irwin-McGraw-Hill (2000)
23. Vensim (November 2013), http://www.vensim.com
24. Yim, N.-H., Kim, S.-H., Kim, H.-W., Kwahk, K.-Y.: Knowledge based decision making on higher level strategic concerns: system dynamics approach. Expert Systems with Applications 27(1), 143–158 (2004)
25. Yu, E.: Modelling strategic relationships for process reengineering. PhD thesis, Toronto, Ont., Canada (1995)
26. Yu, E., Deng, S., Sasmal, D.: Enterprise architecture for the adaptive enterprise – A vision paper. In: Aier, S., Ekstedt, M., Matthes, F., Proper, E., Sanz, J.L. (eds.) PRET 2012 and TEAR 2012. LNBIP, vol. 131, pp. 146–161. Springer, Heidelberg (2012)
27. Yu, E., Giorgini, P., Maiden, N., Mylopoulos, J.: Social modeling for requirements engineering. MIT Press (2011)
28. Yu, E., Lapouchnian, A., Deng, S.: Adapting to uncertain and evolving enterprise requirements: The case of business-driven business intelligence. In: 2013 IEEE Seventh International Conference on Research Challenges in Information Science (RCIS), pp. 1–12. IEEE (2013)

Impact Analysis via Reachability and Alias Analysis

Wen Chen, Alan Wassyng, and Tom Maibaum

McMaster Centre for Software Certification,
McMaster University, Hamilton, Ontario, Canada
{chenw36,wassyng}@mcmaster.ca,
tom@maibaum.org

Abstract. This work is concerned with localizing and analyzing the potential impact of changes to large-scale enterprise systems, and, in particular, how to incorporate *reachability* analysis and *aliasing/pointer* analysis to minimise *false-positives* and eliminate *false-negatives*. It is a continuation of our previous work, which included static analysis [1] and dynamic analysis [2] of changes to systems containing hundreds of thousands of classes and millions of methods. This current work adds: reachability analysis that examines the program to see "whether a given path in a program representation corresponds to a possible execution path", such that *infeasible* paths of mis-matched calls and returns can be filtered out from the estimated impact set; and alias analysis to identify paths that are *feasible* but cannot be affected. Using our approach, organizations can focus on a much smaller, relevant subset of the test suite instead of performing their entire suite of tests without any idea as to whether any test is necessary. Also, in the future, we hope to be able to help testers to augment the test suite with new tests that cover the impacted methods/paths not already subjected to testing. We include a case study that illustrates the savings that can be attained.

Keywords: Large-scale Enterprise Systems, Impact Analysis, Reachability Analysis, Alias Analysis, Static Analysis, Dynamic Analysis, Instrumentation, Regression Testing.

1   Introduction

The target system in this study is *large-scale enterprise systems*. Large-scale enterprise systems are commercial software packages that enable organizations to integrate various applications, replacing hard-to-maintain interfaces, eliminating redundant data entries, etc., to accommodate business growth. One of the largest enterprise vendors SAP, had 2012 revenues of 16.22 billion Euros [3]. Enterprise systems are clearly a common phenomenon in the IT marketplace with fast growing needs. However, implementing enterprise systems may lead to high costs for software maintenance and testing, since corrective changes and enhancements are made on a frequent basis. One type of software change, such as vendor

U. Frank et al. (Eds.): PoEM 2014, LNBIP 197, pp. 261–270, 2014.

patches, typically have to be applied as they are required to upgrade the system in order to fix defects, and to introduce new features.

Enterprise systems are complex, critical and costly. For instance, Oracle Corporation's *E-Business Suite* [4] has over 230 thousand classes, and 4.6 million functions. Despite problems due to their inherent complexity, enterprise systems play a critical role in many organizations. They are used to implement actual business processes, information flows, reporting, data analytics, etc. It is estimated that "Large companies can also spend $50 million to $100 million on software upgrades. Full implementation of all modules can take years" [5]. As a consequence of these characteristics, these systems can also often be classified as *legacy systems* and are poorly understood and difficult to maintain.

Impact analysis is the key in analyzing software changes or potential changes and in identifying the software objects the changes might affect [6]. Organizations need a change impact analysis tool to identify the impacts of a change after or even before a making a change. If the impacts can be obtained even before applying the change, it enables the organization to make test plans or to run tests in advance, saving the lag between system deployment and release.

Conventional impact analysis includes static approaches, dynamic approaches or a hybrid of the two. Static approaches identify the impact set – the subset of elements in the program that may be affected by the changes made to the system – by analyzing relevant source code or compiled code. Dynamic approaches collect information about execution data for a specific set of program executions, such as executions in the field, executions based on an operational profile, or executions of test suites.

2   Research Motivation

Our original work in this domain [1] showed that we could obtain a set of static impacts which are safe and more precise than conventional `vanilla` static approaches, while another more recent work [2] combined the static approach with dynamic instrumentation (aspect-based), and is able to identify real impacts at run-time to further improve the precision. However, in spite of the success of this recent approach, the case studies suggested that there still might be a good number of false-positives present in the estimated impact set. That analysis found out that only a tiny portion of the system (0.26% of all top functions/APIs) were affected at run-time. Even though those top functions were executed over 150 thousand times, one could not conclude that the rest of the static impacts were safe to discard. Consequently, testers may still need to rerun many of the regression tests.

While seeking further analysis to remove more false-positives, we realized that *Reachability Analysis* can be used to determine whether, within a graph G, a node s can reach another node t, *i.e.*, whether the path $s \rightsquigarrow t$ is feasible, and so seemed a promising tool in our search for reducing false-positives. We also identified *Alias Analysis* as a potential tool to further remove false-positives by identifying changed and aliased variables and methods that can access them.

3   Related Work

In graph theory, reachability refers to the ability to get from one vertex to another within a graph by traversing edges of the graph. Algorithms for determining reachability fall into two categories: those that require preprocessing and those that do not [7]. Algorithms like *breadth-first search*, in which reachability of one node from another node can be determined directly without the use of complex data structures, are in the first category. While algorithms like *Floyd-Warshall*, *Thorup's algorithm* and *CFL-reachability* fall into the second category, where more sophisticated methods and/or complex data structures are required.

Reps *et al.*[8] showed how a number of program analysis problems can be solved by transforming them to *graph-reachability* problems. The purpose of program analysis is to ascertain information about a program without actually running the program. In his work, program-analysis problems can be transformed to *context-free-language reachability problems* ("CFL-reachability problems").

Many compiler analyses and optimizations require information about the behaviour of pointers in order to be effective. *Pointer analysis* is a technique for statically determining the possible runtime values of a pointer [9]. Aliasing occurs when two distinct names (data access paths) denote the same run-time location. This analysis has been studied extensively over the last decade. Alias information is central to determining what memory locations are modified or referenced. Ondrej introduces a flexible framework SPARK for experimenting with points-to analyses for Java [10]. SPARK is intended to be a universal framework within which different points-to analyses can be easily implemented and compared in a common context. We believe that aliasing analysis is useful in hybrid impact analysis, and that we can use it to identify aliased objects in the static dependency graph to remove false-positives from the impact set.

4   Reachability Analysis

Ordinary (flat) graph reachability analysis does not take into account the fact that, in practice, many apparently reachable paths can be infeasible because of mis-matched calls and returns, and this information can only be obtained by considering control flows and/or data flows of the program. Reps [8] introduced the *Context-Free-Language Reachability Problem* as:

Definition: Let L be a context-free language over alphabet $\sum$, and let G be a graph whose edges are labelled with members of $\sum$. Each path in G defines a word over $\sum$, namely, the word obtained by concatenating, in order, the labels of the edges on the path. A path in G is an *L-path* if its word is a member of L.

Then an ordinary graph reachability problem can be transformed into a CFL-reachability problem by labelling each edge with a symbol e and letting L be the regular language e^*. The reason that we introduce CFL-reachability analysis here is that it can help us answer the *undecidable* question: **"Does a given path in a program representation correspond to a possible execution path?"**. The idea is that we can define a context-free language L to represent feasible

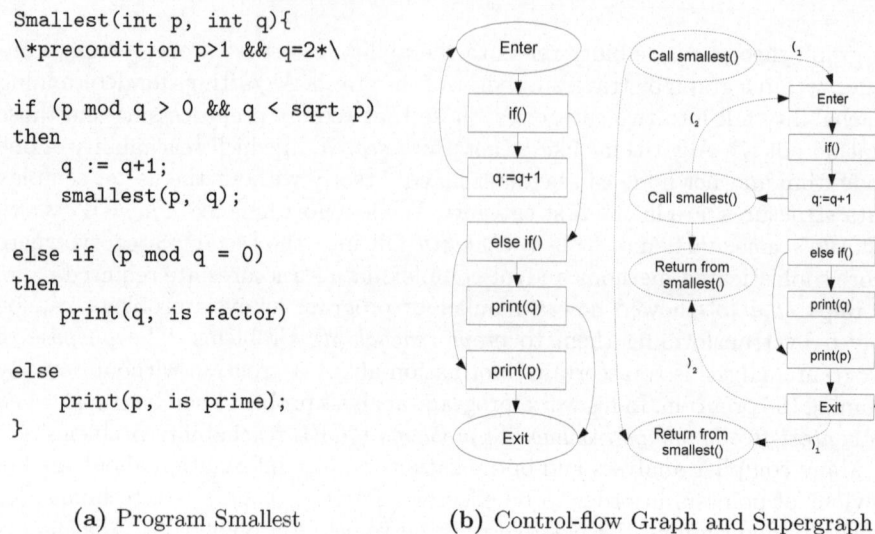

```
Smallest(int p, int q){
\*precondition p>1 && q=2*\

if (p mod q > 0 && q < sqrt p)
then

    q := q+1;
    smallest(p, q);

else if (p mod q = 0)
then

    print(q, is factor)

else
    print(p, is prime);
}
```

(a) Program Smallest   (b) Control-flow Graph and Supergraph

Fig. 1. Program smallest and its graphs. Dashed nodes and arrows correspond to extra nodes and edges while expanding from G to G^*.

paths and then determine if a given string ω is recognizable in L, i.e., is $\omega \in L$? Our assumption is that paths that can possibly be feasible execution paths are those in which "returns" are matched with corresponding "calls". These paths are called *realizable* paths.

A *Supergraph* G^* [8] was defined to deal with *realizable* paths. A supergraph consists of a collection of control-flow graphs – one for each procedure. Each flowgraph has a unique *start* node and a unique *exit* node. The other nodes of the flowgraph represent *statements* and *predicates* of the program in the usual way, except that each procedure call in the program is represented in G^* by two nodes, a *call node* and a *return-site* node. In addition to the ordinary intraprocedural edges that connect the nodes of the individual control-flow graphs, for each procedure call G^* contains three more edges: an intraprocedural *call-to-return-site* edge; an interprocedural *call-to-start* edge; and an interprocedural *exit-to-return-site* edge.

Suppose we have a simple recursive program `smallest` (Figure 1a) to find the smallest prime factor of a positive integer number. In Figure 1b, the graph on the left is the regular control-flow graph of program `smallest`, and the one on the right is the extended supergraph.

In detail, we let each call node in G^* be given a unique index from 1 to N, where N is the total number of calling sites in the program. For each calling site, label the call-to-start edge and the exit-to-return-site edge with the symbols "$(_i$" and "$)_i$", respectively. Label all other edges of G^* with the symbol e. A path in G^* is a matched path *iff* the path's word is in the language $L(matched)$ of balanced-parenthesis strings (interspersed with strings of zero or more es) where $L(matched)$ is generated by the following context-free grammar. Then we can use this grammar to determine if any given path is feasible.

matched →matched matched
     | $(_i$matched $)_i$**for** $1 \leq i \leq N$
     | e
     | ε

From the supergraph, we can identify paths, for example:

– "Call Smallest → Enter → if() → else if() → print(q) → Exit → Return from Smallest", which has word "$(_1eeee)_1$", is a feasible path since the call-to-start edge "$(_1$" is matched by a correct exit-to-return-site edge "$)_1$".
– however, for the same path that exits to the inside return-site node ("$(_1eeee)_2$"), we consider it infeasible – "$(_1$" was mistakenly matched by "$)_2$".

5   Alias Analysis

Alias analysis, *pointer* analysis, *points-to* analysis, *pointer alias* analysis etc., are often used interchangeably to denote an analysis that attempts to analyze pointers and aliases, such as run-time values of a pointer, or an aliased pair of names that point to the same run-time location due to the use of pointers or references. Typically, results of alias analysis are sets of aliased variables, say, $aliased(x)$. If $l \notin aliased(x)$ for abstract location l and variable x in the program P, then x can never alias to variables represented by l in some execution of P.

Suppose we have a program `aliasingTest` to test if the three types of variables in Java can be aliased: *class variable (static field)*, *instance variable* and *local variable*. All the three types of variables (integer arrays in this example) are first initialized (Line[9]-Line[14]) with integer 1 at the first index. Then we create aliased variables to each of the three (Line[16]-Line[18]). Instead of manipulating the original variables, we run functions on the aliased ones (Line[20]-Line[23]).

After the invocations of the first three functions (either static or non-static), the original variables were actually changed (with first element altered to integer 11), even though the functions only manipulated the aliased copies. Our observation is that, if along a path in the access dependency graph of a program one can obtain the aliasing information for each method, dependencies among methods can be identified more precisely. In particular, we follow these steps to achieve more precise dependencies:

1. A *flow-insensitive and context-insensitive alias analysis* to compute a single and valid solution to the whole program.
2. We examine the pairs of aliased variables (static field, instance field, and local variable) throughout the program and obtain a mapping from each method f to variables var_f and aliased variables $aliased(var_f)$ it can access, i.e., $f \rightarrow \{var_f, aliased(var_f)\}$.

3. We examine paths in the estimated impact set, for any other changed function g with mapped variables and aliased variables $\{var_g, aliased(var_g)\}$ that can be reached by f, if and only if there exists any intersection of $\{var_f, aliased(var_f)\}$ and $\{var_g, aliased(var_g)\}$, we say f can be affected by g.

Therefore, in `aliasingTest`, a dependency edge between function *main* and function *alterEmpty* should be removed since there is no aliased variables within *alterEmpty* that was used in *main*.

Listing 1.1. Program aliasingTest

```
1   package aliasingTest;
2   public class aliasingTest {
3       static int[] staticArray;
4       int[] instanceArray;
5       public aliasingTest(){
6           instanceArray = new int
                [6];}
7       public static void main(String
            args[]){
8           //initializations of arrays
9           staticArray = new int[5];
10          int[] localArray = new int
                [3];
11          aliasingTest at = new
                aliasingTest();
12          localArray[0] = 1;
13          staticArray[0] = 1;
14          at.instanceArray[0]= 1;
15          //aliasing to arrays
16          int[] aliasOflocalArray =
                localArray;
17          int[] aliasOfstaticArray =
                staticArray;
18          int[] aliasOfinstanceArray =
                at.instanceArray;
```

Listing 1.2. aliasingTest cont.

```
19
20          //run functions that can be
                invoked within main()
21          alterArrayLocal(aliasOflocalArray
                );
22          alterArrayStatic(
                aliasOfstaticArray);
23          at.alterArrayInstance(
                aliasOfinstanceArray);
24          alterEmpty();
25      }
26      static void alterArrayLocal(int[]
            array){
27          array[0] = 11;}
28      static void alterArrayStatic(int[]
            array){
29          array[0] = 11;}
30      void alterArrayInstance(int[] array){
31          array[0]=11;}
32      static void alterEmpty(){
33          System.out.println("No job is
                doing here.");}
34  }
```

6   Impact Analysis Overall

We extended our previous approachs in [1] and [2] by reachability analysis and alias analysis, to form the new process depicted in Figure 2. Note that, the set of potential false-positives was obtained by subtracting the dynamic impact set from the static impact set. The reachability analysis works on this set to find infeasible paths. The alias analysis continues cutting out false-positives from the reduced set by identifying functions that are not able to access the aliased variables of a changed function, if they are not themselves directly changed.

7   Case Study

In the study, our goal was to investigate whether this new, extended approach can meet our goal, which is to safely remove false-positives from the change impact set. We followed the same order, variables, measures, experiment setup etc., as we did in the experiments in [1] and [2].

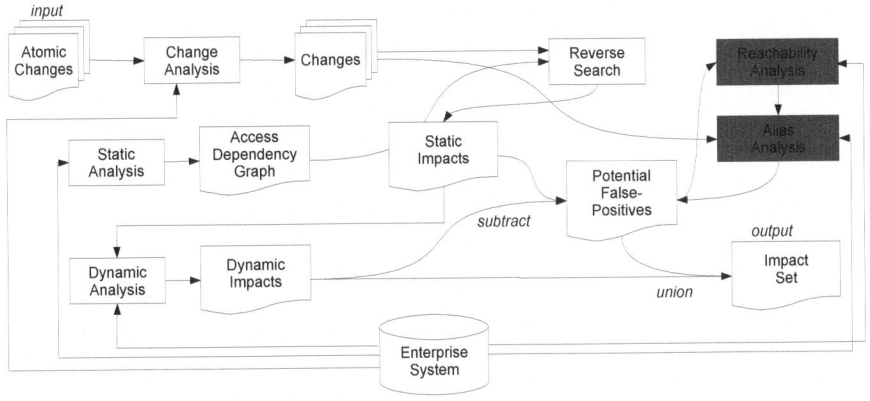

Fig. 2. System Flow of the Complete Approach

Table 1. Oracle E-Business Suite Release 11i and Some Facts

Application	Database	Classes	Entities	LOC
11.5.10.2 (11i)	10.2.0.2.0 (10g)	195,999	3,157,947	8.7 Million

There is only one independent variable in this case study: the extended impact analysis tool. Dependent variables in this study include *precision* and *time overhead*. For the measurement of precision, we used the one in Equation 1, where I represents the number of estimated impacts (functions and fields), and M represents the total number of entities in the program.

$$Precision = \frac{|I|}{|M|} \tag{1}$$

7.1   Experimental Setup

The experiment was set up on a desktop server with a Quad core 3.2GHz CPU, 32G RAM and operating system Red Hat Enterprise Linux Server release 5.10 (Tikanga) 64 bit. We used one release of Oracle E-Business Suite (Table 1) as the object of the analysis, and for the source of atomic changes we used one vendor patch (patch # 5565583, 212MB) that can be obtained either from Oracle E-Business Suite *Patch Wizard* or manually download from Oracle Metalink.

7.2   Experiment Design

We had already collected results from static analysis and dynamic analysis in the impact analysis process from [1] and [2]. Thus, for this experiment we focused only on the improvements made through reachability analysis and alias analysis.

Table 2. Instrumentation Result on Patch # 5565583

Function	Top Function	Static Impacts	Dynamic Impacts	Potential FPs
3,157,947	1,673,132	699,534	4,806	694,728

Table 3. Final Impacts of Patch # 5565583

Static	Dynamic	Rmd By Reachability	Rmd By Alias	Final Impacts
699,534	4,806	61,125	86,374	547,229

Then CFL-reachability analysis was implemented via Wala [11] to cut down false-positives. We ran the Tabulation algorithm [12] implemented by Wala on the set of "potential false-positives". The alias analysis takes the processed "potential false-positives" from the above reachability analysis as the input, and calculates aliasing information, such that methods that have no accesses to those aliased and changed variables in the system are not considered as affected. Another input is the set of changes resulting from the patch analysis. What we need is to find the methods on a particular path that access those changed variables and also variables that are aliased with them. For the sake of safety, we assume here that, if a function is changed, then potentially all of its accessible variables can be changed.

7.3   Results and Analysis

The system used in our case study contains 195,999 classes. We determined that there are 3,157,947 entities (both functions and fields) in the system. The process of building the access dependency graph added over 18.4 million dependencies and took over 9.5 hours to complete. By patch analysis, we found 16,787 direct database changes, and 25,613 direct library changes (classes) for patch #5565583. The static analysis identified 8,154 direct changed functions for this patch, which led to 699,534 affected functions (22% of the total functions), and 160,800 affected top functions (9.6% of the total top functions) in the system. The computed impacts for the patch after static analysis and dynamic analysis are shown in Table 2.

Thus we had 694,728 "potential false-positives" to work on in the reachability and alias analysis. Both CFL-reachability analysis and alias analysis were implemented via Wala. We ran Wala on the enclosing classes of each function in those "potential false-positives", and then mapped identified feasible statements to functions in the system. Then those functions with the direct changes (42,400) were given to Wala's alias analysis framework to find aliased variables for each changed function. In the end, we found many of the functions within the "potential false-positives" were not present in feasible paths (611,253) or able to access any aliased variables (863,374) of changed functions. We therefore removed 6,865,697 (37.3 %) dependencies from the original dependency graph. We summarized the results in Table 3.

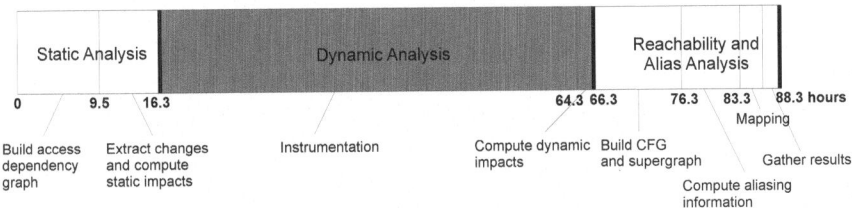

Fig. 3. Execution Time for Patch #5565583

As we can see from Table 3, we achieved a precision of 3.8% at the end of the static analysis and then improved it to 2.98% at the end of the complete approach. The dynamic analysis identified that only 4,806 functions to be executed, which left a large portion (99%) of the static impacts as potential false-positives. The reachability analysis and alias analysis reduced the false positives by 21.8% . At the current stage, our case study does not include a user's application built on Oracle's E-Business Suite, so the impacted entities are confined to E-Business Suite. That explains why, even with a reasonably large number of real executions, the dynamic impacts are associated with just a tiny part of the system.

The entire process requires considerable time to complete (see Figure 3). Considering the sizes of the system and patch, it is still more manageable than rerunning everything in the regression suite. More crucially, it provides testers more confidence as to which parts in the system are affected. The most time-consuming task is the instrumentation, which occupies around 56.8% of the total execution time. As with the static dependency graph, the instrumentation forms a substantial corporate asset for future analysis, and can be easily and quickly updated as needed.

8   Conclusion and Future Work

In this work, we have incorporated CFL-reachability analysis and alias analysis in identifying software impacts. As far as we can ascertain, these two techniques have not been used in this way to cut down on the false-positives in preceding analyses. It has been demonstrated that CFL-reachability with a parenthesis context-free grammar can be used to filter out infeasible paths (mis-matched calls and returns), that may become false-positives in the impact set. An alias analysis was conducted to identify functions that are able to access the aliased and changed variables. We consider those that are not able to access any of the aliased and changed variables to be false-positives, if they themselves are not directly changed. Also, we have demonstrated the practical applicability of the improved approach on a very large enterprise system, involving hundreds of thousands of classes. Such systems may be perhaps two orders of magnitude larger than the systems analyzed by other approaches, so our technique seems to be uniquely powerful.

Initally, considering the running time and effort expended, we were a little disappointed in the percentage of false-positives removed by this technique. However, after examining the results more carefully, we realized that: (1) the actual number of false-positives removed was significant; and (2) as we discussed earlier, because there is no user's application in our case study, the impact analysis is restricted to functions within the system, and in particular, many of the identified impacted functions are system APIs. Further study will be needed to determine whether results are better for a user application built on E-Business Suite. Also, the alias analysis we used is flow-insensitive and context-insensitive. It assumes statements in the program can be executed in any order and any number of times. In practice this is not a precise approach. The imprecision can also come from the context-insensitivity: method calls were treated conservatively, without computing the precise target addresses of the return statements. Hence, in the future, it is worth investigating whether a more precise approach can be derived for large-scale enterprise systems.

References

1. Chen, W., Iqbal, A., Abdrakhmanov, A., Parlar, J., George, C., Lawford, M., Maibaum, T., Wassyng, A.: Large-scale enterprise systems: Changes and impacts. In: Enterprise Information Systems, pp. 274–290. Springer, Heidelberg (2013)
2. Chen, W., Wassyng, A., Maibaum, T.: Combining static and dynamic impact analysis for large-scale enterprise systems (2014) (manuscript submitted for publication)
3. Ag, S.: Annual report 2012, financial highlights (2012)
4. Oracle: Oracle e-business suite integrated soa gateway implementation guide release 12.1 (June 2010)
5. Monk, E.F., Wagner, B.J.: Concepts in enterprise resource planning. CengageBrain. com (2008)
6. Bohner, S.A.: Software Change Impact Analysis. In: Proceedings of the 27th Annual NASA Goddard/IEEE Software Engineering Workshop, SEW-27'02 (1996)
7. Gersting, J.L.: Mathematical structures for computer science. Macmillan (2007)
8. Reps, T.: Program analysis via graph reachability. Information and Software Technology 40(11-12), 701 (1998)
9. Hind, M.: Pointer analysis: haven't we solved this problem yet? In: Proceedings of the 2001 ACM SIGPLAN-SIGSOFT workshop on Program analysis for software tools and engineering, pp. 54–61. ACM (2001)
10. Lhoták, O.: Spark: A flexible points-to analysis framework for java (2002)
11. IBM T.J. Watson Research Center: T. J. Watson Libraries for Analysis Main Page (Julu (2013)
12. Reps, T., Horwitz, S., Sagiv, M.: Precise interprocedural dataflow analysis via graph reachability. In: Proceedings of the 22Nd ACM SIGPLAN-SIGACT Symposium on Principles of Programming Languages, POPL 1995, pp. 49–61. ACM, New York (1995)

Model-Driven Alignment: An Empirical Study

Constantinos Giannoulis and Jelena Zdravkovic

Department of Computer and Systems Sciences,
Stockholm University
Forum-16440, Kista, Sweden
{constantinos,jelenaz}@dsv.su.se

Abstract. Current advancements in the business arena necessitate more than ever before the alignment of *The Business* and *IT* in organizations, which has been acknowledged as a complex issue to address. Our research is aimed at systematically addressing the linkage between *business strategy* and *information systems* (IS). We propose a model-driven approach for alignment, by leveraging the influence of established business strategy formulations from Strategic Management, and model-driven principles used within IS. The objective of this paper is to present the results of an empirical investigation carried out in Sweden on the linkage seeking to obtain insights from practitioners about the relevance of the problem, as well as of our model-driven proposal to address it.

Keywords: Business Strategy, Alignment, IS, Models, UBSMM.

1 Introduction

Information technology (IT) is a fundamental factor for business strategy enactment [1], because it pervades all sectors of organizations regardless of the organization's business, and hence influences the strategy itself. IT comprises the essential information needed to build executable information systems (IS) to support and facilitate business operations for delivering offerings to customers.

Business strategy should be understood and communicated in an organization to define the means required for its successful execution, also making clear for IT what business stakeholders need. This is expressed through business strategy formulations such as the Value Chain [2], Strategy Maps and Balanced Scorecards (SMBSC) [3]). Organizations aligning their business strategy to IT tend to outperform those that do not [4] and increase their performance and profits [5]. While there exist proposals addressing alignment [6–8], it is still acknowledged as an open issue for top-management [9], as well as for IT executives [10].

Despite this acknowledged importance of aligning strategic initiatives and plans with IS, this linkage suffers from shortcomings of existing approaches. Established business strategy formulations are typically overlooked and business strategy is abstractly linked to IS models when it comes to IS requirements and other Enterprise Models (EM) [11,12]. While Enterprise Architecture (EA)

U. Frank et al. (Eds.): PoEM 2014, LNBIP 197, pp. 271–281, 2014.

proposals such as TOGAF [13] and the Zachman Framework [14], as well as Business Architecture proposals [15] include business elements or layers that affect IS, they lack on linking them to business strategy formulations [11, 12].

These shortcomings are indicative of the ambiguity of business strategy for this alignment linkage, which makes even more difficult to grasp strategic initiatives and facilitate the development of IT solutions. Our model-driven proposal for alignment is based on the Unified Business Strategy Meta-model (UBSMM), which is an integration of the conceptualizations of established business strategy formulations from Strategic Management [11, 12]. More specifically, UBSMM integrates business strategy formulations covering three complementary types of strategy-shaping logic; the resource-based type with Strategy Maps and Balanced Scorecards [3], the competition type with the Value Chain [2], the Value Shop and the Value Network [16], and the innovation type with Blue Ocean Strategy [17], which altogether constitute adequate coverage of strategic notions [11, 12]. Leveraging properties of meta-modeling and model-driven development, UBSMM links business strategy with IS models used for IS requirements, with EM and with EA [11, 12].

The objectives of this paper are: to empirically validate that the linkage between business strategy and IS is an issue of concern, and collect insights from the industry about the appropriateness of our model-driven approach, and highlight the benefits offered by UBSMM with respect to the linkage. For the the first, an empirical study is conducted, and for the second, an illustrative case using strategic notions from UBSMM is presented.

The section following includes related work motivating the need for our study. Thereafter, the background and design of the study is presented in section three; section four presents the results of the study and section five discusses our findings. The paper concludes with section six on future research steps.

2   Related Work

Despite the acknowledged importance of business-IT alignment, during the past decade a strong empirical motivation for business-IT alignment has been put forward focusing primarily on: (i) the relation between alignment and business performance or (ii) the relation between types of business strategies (such as conservative or innovative) and (iii) the degree of alignment [18].

However, minimal empirical basis seems to exist specifically for the linkage between business strategy and IS. Such empirical work would investigate the need for, and the existence of a formal business strategy formulation and its potential for the use of models for reinforcing alignment. A common type of empirical work found in the business-IT alignment literature is Luftmans highly cited work, with the annually published CIO survey results [10]. However, the focus is mostly on alignment maturity. Moreover, the linkage between business strategy and IS is not only relevant to CIOs but also to all those affecting it, or being affected both from *the Business* or *IT*.

The works of [19, 20] also follow a modeling approach, however without employing established business strategy formulations. On the other hand, the work of [21] shares our motivation of natural language-based ambiguity of business strategy formulations, and they strive for a conceptualization of Balanced Scorecards (BSC), which aims at reducing practice variability due to interpretations of publications and reports. The purpose of this conceptualization is to become becoming a basis for building tools that are capable of capturing, analyzing and explaining strategic initiatives and intend.

Another effort also aimed at decreasing the ambiguity of business strategy is the Strategy Markup Language (StratML) solely for document management i.e. focused on providing XML-based specifications for strategic and performance plans and reports [22]. This initiative is not concerned directly with business strategy formulations.

3   Empirical Study Design

Designing, conducting and reporting an empirical study constitutes a complex operation involving several steps. For our study, we have adopted Oppenheim's 14-stage framework [23].

Stages one through four refer to going through literature, reflecting upon it, and choosing an appropriate form for the study. Our study aims at empirically validating the relevance of addressing the linkage between business strategy and IS in today's enterprise terrain and collecting insights about using models as an appropriate way of addressing it. Due to the need for reach to practitioners, the design of study selected has been a self-administered online questionnaire. The assumption to be investigated (stage five) is expressed through the three questions formulated in the Introduction.

For the design (stage six) guidelines include establishing objectives, measures and scales, as well as types of questions, layout, wording, flow of questions, and validity concerns. The following objectives have been set for the questionnaire:

Obj. 1: Identify to whom and why is the linkage between business strategy and IS a concern for the Business and IT actors within a company.

Obj. 2: Identify gaps between strategy and systems development hindering the alignment linkage.

Obj. 3: Confirm the use of models as a relevant solution to address such gaps.

The questionnaire has been built with the free online tool *Survey Gizmo* (*http://www.surveygizmo.com*), and consists of 29 questions spreading across six sections. Sections have been derived from the aforementioned objectives; section one focuses on the first objective by capturing whether the linkage between business strategy and IS is a concern and whether this concern is being currently addressed, how, etc. Sections two and three focus on the second objective by capturing respondents' familiarity with strategic formulations, how they are used in their company, and they are used in relation to information systems requirements. Sections four and five focus on the third objective by capturing respondents' familiarity with models and how they are used in their company, as well as their views on the utility of a model-driven proposal for alignment. Section six captures demographic information.

All sections include explanations and examples of core concepts and terms used (i.e. *information system, requirements, strategy, model*), together with information motivating some questions. Types of questions used, include open-ended, multiple choice, checkboxes, and *Likert* scale questions. Options offered cover possible alternatives relevant to the questions without overlapping, while units and scales have been consistently used, and double-barreled questions have been avoided [23]. Questions have been neutrally formulated to avoid bias, and questions for consistency checking across answers have been used.

A pilot study has been conducted (stage seven) to assess the questionnaire's validity and understandability [24]. This included a group of four academic experts on business-IT alignment for conformance to the hypothesis defined (construct validity), and sufficient domain coverage (content validity). Additionally, a convenience sample of 52 professionals from around the world has also been used to simulate the realistic setting of the study allowing to test the questionnaire by providing input on all functional aspects (language, structure, layout, etc.). Apart from language, structure and layout improvements, the pilot study resulted a refined set of questions, from 41 down to 29. The questionnaire can be tested at: *http://www.surveygizmo.com/s3/1305947/Strategy-IT-Alignment* and questions are available at: *http://goo.gl/8rfgf0*.

The sample has been designed (stage eight) following quota sampling, where mutually exclusive sub-groups have been identified. The selection of companies has been stratified across medium and large profit-driven companies registered in Kista, Sweden, based on information provided by the Swedish Agencies Registration Office (http://www.bolagsverket.se). Medium and large companies (more than 50 but less than 250, and more than 251 respectively) have been selected because small and micro companies (less than 50) are typically considered agile and due to size the issue of alignment is not relevant. Also, profit-driven companies have been selected over charity organizations and state-owned companies because the vast majority of business strategy formulations has been defined based on profit-driven companies. Invitation for participation (stage nine) took place via email, stating the objectives of the study, the form and the ethical considerations of handling the data.

The data collection process lasted four weeks (stage eleven) during the late spring and early summer of 2013. Processing the data and statistically analyzing them has been done with the assistance of the aforementioned survey tool (stages twelve and thirteen). This paper constitutes reporting on the questionnaire results and testing of the hypothesis (stage fourteen).

4   Empirical Study Results

The results of the study include the responses of 45 participants coming from seven large and medium profit-driven companies: two active in manufacturing (8 and 6 participants), one active in software development (5 participants), one active in media and publishing (3 participants), and three active in telecommunications (7, 11, and 5 participants), which includes a global leader in networking and a Nordic leader in mobile and internet services. All the objectives of the questionnaire have been met in that the results provide answers along with insights from respondents. Results are presented for each of the objectives accompanied with discussions.

4.1   Objective 1

Results come from the first section of the questionnaire are summarized in Table 1. They indicate that the linkage between business strategy and IS is an issue of concern for the vast majority of respondents. Apart from the overall results, it is interesting to examine responses from different perspectives due to function served (*Business, IT, Both*), and size of the company (*Medium, Large*).

While those who have one distinct function share 100% the view that the linkage between business strategy and IS is an issue of concern, those serving both functions do no share the same absolute. This could be due to the fact that those serving both functions are expected to have a better understanding of both the Business and IT and thus do not consider the linkage between business and IS to be an issue of concern.

Table 1. Results answering: *"Is the linkage between business strategy and IS an issue of concern for your company?"*

Population	Yes	No
All	92.5%	7.5%
Business	100%	-
IT	100%	-
Both	89%	11%
Medium	90%	10%
Large	100%	-

Table 2. Responses on model types used

Model types used	Percentage
Business Models	69.2%
Requirements Models	61.5%
Process Models	61.5%
Use Case Models	42,3%
Goal Models	23.1%
Enterprise Models	15.4%
Conceptual Models	15.4%
Simulation Models	15.4%
No Models	7.7%
I do not know	3.9%

Another grouping presented in Table 1 focuses on the size of the company and shows that the linkage between business strategy and IS is of concern for all large-sized companies (employing > 250 people) whereas it is for most medium-sized companies (employing between 50 and 250 people). This is anticipated and coincides with our assumption to focus on medium and large companies in this study. The larger the company, the more cumbersome it becomes to align all functions, especially when they are as pervasive across an organization as IT is.

Motivation for being an issue of concern (i.e. the why?) has been acknowledged by respondents due to strategy not being clear enough and due to lack of understanding how IS can enhance and support strategy.

In the same section, those that have acknowledged this linkage as a concern for their company, have also been asked to indicate methods and techniques practiced to address it; 30% answered that no method or technique is practiced, 15% answered that their company does not strive for alignment between business strategy and IS and 55% answered they do not know.

4.2   Objective 2

Results from sections two and three of the questionnaire focus on business strategy and how it relates to systems development within their company, particularly system requirements.

First of all, participants were asked in terms of strategy awareness within their company (Table 3). Those fully and partially aware were asked to identify all forms of communication used for business strategy dissemination (Table: 4).

Table 3. Strategy awareness levels

Awareness	Percent
Fully aware	71%
Partially aware	14%
Not aware	6%
No strategy	9%

Table 4. Ways of disseminating strategy within companies

Strategy Dissemination	Percent
Verbally	78%
In text (i.e. reports)	75%
Graphical (i.e. charts)	44%

When asked whether business strategy dissemination was timely understood and whether the business intent of the company was clearly expressed; 58% were positive, 9% negative, and 33% neutral.

When asked about alignment between business strategy and IS; whether IS requirements were utilized with respect to business strategy, whether there exists synchronicity and traceability between IS and business changes, as well as whether strategic objectives are utilized in IS development (directly or indirectly); 33% were positive, 31% negative, and 36% neutral.

Overall, 59% of respondents claim strategy is aligned with IT in their companies, and 41% claim it is not. Those who responded *no* identified reasons hindering the linkage between business strategy and IS in their companies:

For 73% not enough communication exists between *The Business* and *IT*,
For 37% strategy is not communicated at all,
For 37% IS is not related to strategy,
For 27% strategy is not understood at all,
For 27% strategy is not expressing the company's real strategic intent.

A significant conclusive observation from this section is that 85% answered they are fully and partially aware of their company's strategy suggesting that business strategy is disseminated. However, 41% claim strategy is not aligned with IS and the most significant reason for this gap seems to be the fact that there exists not enough communication between the Business and IT (73%).

4.3   Objective 3

Results come from sections four and five of the questionnaire, which focus on models and their utilization for alignment within respondents' companies.

Table 2 presents the types of models most widely used, as indicated by respondents: business , requirements, process, and use case are dominating.

While 81% of respondents have indicated they are familiar with models, for Objective 3 we have selected only those that have indicated a certain level of competency regarding models. The reason behind this selection is that a certain level of knowledge and familiarity with models is needed to assess the use of models for model-driven alignment. The scale of familiarity included novice, experienced beginner, practitioner, knowledgeable practitioner and expert. We have selected the answers from those that have indicated they are practitioners on at least one of the model types shown in table 2. This filtering resulted into 19 respondents and results from their answers are presented along with results from answers coming from the total sample (Table 5).

Table 5. Positive responses on the use of models

Statements	IT	Total
Our company has the know-how to use models for model-driven alignment	44%	32%
Modeling our strategy would improve alignment of strategies across units	72%	68%
Modeling our strategy would improve alignment towards partners	56%	52%
Modeling our strategy would bring value to our company	72%	50%
Modeling our strategy could improve the linkage between strategy and IS for our company	89%	84%

Table 6. Correlation between familiarity with models and the use of models improving the alignment linkage

Familiarity with Models	ρ	R^2	$p < 0.05$
Enterprise Models	0.5474	29.96%	0.0001
Process Models	0.6518	42.48%	< 0.00001
Business Models	0.7112	50.58%	< 0.00001
Requirements Models	0.4157	17.28%	0.004513
Conceptual Models	0.3704	13.72%	0.012259
Information Models	0.5306	28.16%	0.000177
Simulation Models	0.3899	15.20%	0.000195
Goal Models	0.5278	27.86%	0.008106
Use Case Models	0.5817	33.83%	2.8E-05

Respondents have also provided motivation over their positive assertion on the improvement of the alignment linkage between business strategy and IS due to the use of models. The motivations mostly refer to benefits that models bring, such as structure, less ambiguity, understandability, automation, experimentation for possible alternatives and hypothesis testing.

Furthermore, results have shown that there exists a moderate positive correlation between respondents' familiarity with models and agreement that the use of models would lead to improvement of alignment between business strategy and IS. Correlation indicates the strength of the statistical relationship between questions (using Likert scales in this case) but cannot determine cause and effect as in which one is influencing the other.

Scatterplots of two such moderate positive correlations are presented in figure 1 for familiarity with Enterprise models (left) and Business models (right). The vertical axes is scaled 0-5 capturing familiarity with models: 0 for not familiar at all, 1 for novice, 2 for experienced beginner, 3 for practitioner, 4 for knowledgeable practitioner, and 5 for expert. The horizontal axes is scaled 1-5 capturing confidence for improvement of alignment through the use of such models: 1 for strongly disagree, 2 somewhat disagree, 3 I do not know, 4 somewhat agree, 5 strongly agree. This means there is a tendency among those with high familiarity with enterprise models and business models (practitioners and experts) to express higher levels of agreement with the use of models improving alignment.

Table 6 presents the correlation coefficient ρ (second column), the coefficient determination R^2 (third column) and the statistical significance p (fourth column) between familiarity with models and agreement with the use of models improving alignment. For enterprise models, business models, process models, information models, goal models and use case models the correlation is moderate positive as ρ is around +0.5 and moderate percentages of data close to the regression line (27%-51%). For requirements models, conceptual models and simulation models the correlation is weak positive as ρ is closer to 0 and low percentages of data close to the regression line (13%-18%). For all correlations reported there is a 5% likelihood they are a result of chance due to the probability threshold is set: $p < 0.05$.

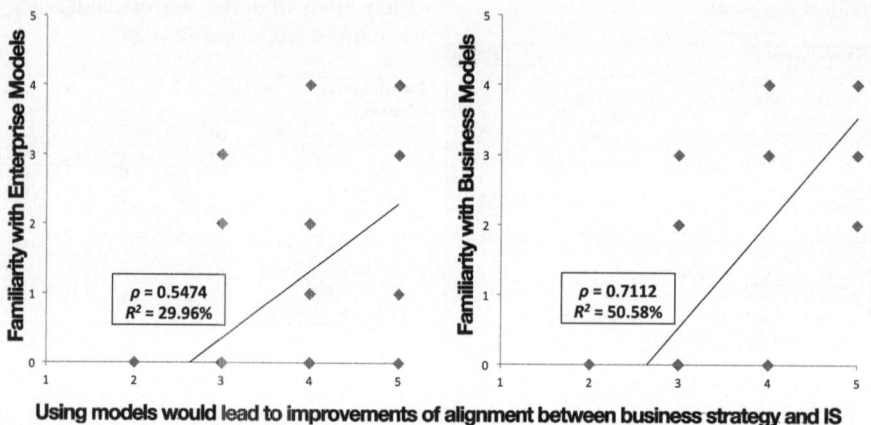

Fig. 1. Familiarity with Enterprise models (left) and Business models (right)

5   Discussion

Business strategy formulations are typically natural language-based, usually accompanied by schematic representations. The ambiguity of such formulations risks their dissemination to be subject of interpretation. The study's results have indicated the most significant hindering factor is insufficient communication between the Business and IT (objective 2 of the study). This difficulty can be overcome by conceptualizing notions of business strategy formulations and thereafter mapping them onto notions of techniques and methods used for IS requirements. Clear semantics are set for strategy notions which facilitate unambiguous understanding and dissemination of business strategy to IS. This does not leave space for interpretation and makes changes less prone to creating problems. Traceability makes the impact of changes in strategy traceable to IS (i.e. requirements, features, etc.)

The use of models has been acknowledged by respondents as a solution to improve the linkage between business strategy and IS (objective 3 of the study). Results have allowed the identification of correlations between familiarity with models and anticipation that the use of models for the linkage between business strategy and IS improves alignment. Particular types of models showed stronger correlations than others (e.g. business and process) suggesting that proposals like ours should focus on these model types for mapping business strategy to IS.

In a broader scope, conceptualizing business strategy promotes meaningful transparency of strategic initiatives across an organization, by making such information available. This enhances internal coordination within an organization as it establishes a shared vocabulary about customers, products, processes and activities, which creates a common base for understanding addressing the problem of business strategy and strategic initiatives being open to interpretation. Decreased ambiguity leads to improvements in automation of mappings towards IT solutions, and thus can ideally increase efficiency of business strategy implementation. Business strategy modeling can be the basis for building patterns when linking different strategy initiatives to IT solutions, which increases organizational agility to shift from one initiative to another.

Finally, with respect to the aforementioned benefits of business strategy modeling and the use of UBSMM, certain limitations should also be mentioned. An obvious limitation is the lack of the techniques and the tools to support development of UBSMM to facilitate mappings towards IS (i.e. process models, enterprise models, requirements models, etc. as well as EM and EA as it is the case with system development tools. Another limitation concerns the scope and extent of evaluation for UBSMM due to the fact that a full scale case study requires a long period of handling business sensitive information, thus being limited to small real-world case studies, published cases and reports [11] such as the one of Southwest Airlines.

6   Concluding Remarks and Future Work

In this paper, we have argued for the need to enrich the current body of knowledge on the alignment linkage by empirically validating that the linkage between business strategy and IS is still an issue of concern. In that line, we have conducted a social study in the form of an online self-administered questionnaire. We have presented the design steps taken and we have also reported on the results of the study by addressing each one of the three objectives set for the questionnaire.

The objectives of this paper has been met in that our findings, within their limitations, constitute a current empirical contribution that justifies the theoretical basis of our proposal for model-driven alignment. Results have validated that linkage between business strategy and IS remains an open issue of concern and addressing it methodically is still suffering. Moreover, results have also indicated business strategy is not utilized in IS development with insufficient communication being the major hindering factor. Finally, results regarding the use of models for the linkage between business strategy and IS are positively received by respondents.

Based on the findings of our study, succeeding steps of our future research have two main directions. One path includes conducting further empirical studies to gain more insights and examine larger populations. Another line of work is driven towards conducting case studies using UBSMM to further assess the utility and applicability of our proposal for model-driven alignment.

References

1. Burns, T., Stalker, G.M.: The Management of Innovation. University of Illinois at Urbana-Champaign's Academy for Entrepreneurial Leadership Historical Research Reference in Entrepreneurship. Tavistock, London, UK (1961)
2. Porter, M.E.: Competitive advantage: Creating and sustaining superior performance. Free Press (1985)
3. Kaplan, R., Norton, D.: Strategy maps: Converting intangible assets into tangible outcomes. Harvard Business Press (2004)
4. Leede, J.D., Looise, J.C., Alders, B.C.: Innovation, improvement and operations: an exploration of the management of alignment. International Journal of Technology Management 23(4), 353–368 (2002)
5. Ross, J.W., Weill, P., Robertson, D.C.: Enterprise architecture as strategy: Creating a foundation for business execution. Harvard Business Press (2006)
6. Henderson, J.C., Venkatraman, N.: Strategic alignment: a framework for strategic information technology management (1989)
7. Luftman, J.N., Bullen, C.V., Liao, D., Nash, E., Neumann, C.: Managing the information technology resource: Leadership in the information age. Pearson Education Upper Saddle River (2004)
8. Chan, Y.E., Reich, B.H.: It alignment: what have we learned? Journal of Information technology 22(4), 297–315 (2007)
9. Luftman, J., Kempaiah, R., Nash, E.: Key issues for it executives 2004. MIS Quarterly Executive 4(2), 269–285 (2005)
10. Luftman, J., Derksen, B.: Key issues for it executives 2012: Doing more with less. MIS Quarterly Executive 11(4), 207–218 (2012)
11. Giannoulis, C.: Model-driven Alignment: Linking Business Strategy with Information Systems. PhD thesis, Stockholm University (May 2014)
12. Giannoulis, C., Zdravkovic, J., Petit, M.: Model-driven strategic awareness: From a unified business strategy meta-model (UBSMM) to enterprise architecture. In: Bider, I., Halpin, T., Krogstie, J., Nurcan, S., Proper, E., Schmidt, R., Soffer, P., Wrycza, S. (eds.) EMMSAD 2012 and BPMDS 2012. LNBIP, vol. 113, pp. 255–269. Springer, Heidelberg (2012)
13. Forum: The open group architectural framework (togaf) version 9.1. Technical report, The Open Group (2013)
14. Zachman, J.A.: A framework for information systems architecture. IBM Systems Journal 26(3), 276–292 (1987)
15. Versteeg, G., Bouwman, H.: Business architecture: A new paradigm to relate business strategy to ict. Information Systems Frontiers 8(2), 91–102 (2006)
16. Stabell, C.B., Fjeldstad, Ø.D.: Configuring value for competitive advantage: on chains, shops, and networks. Strategic Management Journal 19(5), 413–437 (1998)
17. Kim, W.C., Mauborgne, R.: Blue Ocean Strategy. Harvard Business Review Press (2004)
18. Chan, Y.E., Sabherwal, R., Thatcher, J.B.: Antecedents and outcomes of strategic is alignment: an empirical investigation. IEEE Transactions Engineering Management 53(1), 27–47 (2006)

19. Champion, R., Moores, T.T.: Exploiting an enterprise model during systems' requirements capture and analysis. In: Proceedings of the Second International Conference on Requirements Engineering, pp. 208–215. IEEE (1996)
20. Opdahl, A.L.: Model-supported alignment of information systems architecture. Business strategies for information technology management 28 (2003)
21. Business Architecture Working Group: Balanced scorecard metamodel. Technical report, The Object Mangement Group, OMG (2010)
22. ANSI/AIIM: Standard recommended practice - strategy markup language - part 1: Stratml core. Technical Report 21:2009, American National Standards Institute, ANSI (2009)
23. Oppenheim, A.N.: Questionnaire design, interviewing and attitude measurement. Continuum International Publishing Group (2000)
24. Giannoulis, C., Zdravkovic, J., Petit, M.: Model-centric strategy-IT alignment: An empirical study in progress. In: Franch, X., Soffer, P. (eds.) CAiSE Workshops 2013. LNBIP, vol. 148, pp. 146–155. Springer, Heidelberg (2013)

Author Index